Clio's Warriors

STUDIES IN CANADIAN MILITARY HISTORY

The Canadian War Museum, Canada's national museum of military history, has a threefold mandate: to remember, to preserve, and to educate. It does so through an interlocking and mutually supporting combination of exhibitions, public programs, and electronic outreach. Military history, military historical scholarship, and the ways in which Canadians see and understand themselves have always been closely intertwined. Studies in Canadian Military History builds on a record of success in forging those links by regular and innovative contributions based on the best modern scholarship. Published by UBC Press in association with the Museum, the series especially encourages the work of new generations of scholars and the investigation of important gaps in the existing historiography, pursuits not always well served by traditional sources of academic support. The results produced feed immediately into future exhibitions, programs, and outreach efforts by the Canadian War Museum. It is a modest goal that they feed into a deeper understanding of our nation's common past as well.

1 John Griffith Armstrong, *The Halifax Explosion and the Royal Canadian Navy: Inquiry and Intrigue*
2 Andrew Richter, *Avoiding Armageddon: Canadian Military Strategy and Nuclear Weapons, 1950-63*
3 William Johnston, *A War of Patrols: Canadian Army Operations in Korea*
4 Julian Gwyn, *Frigates and Foremasts: The North American Squadron in Nova Scotia Waters, 1745-1815*
5 Jeffrey A. Keshen, *Saints, Sinners, and Soldiers: Canada's Second World War*
6 Desmond Morton, *Fight or Pay: Soldiers' Families in the Great War*
7 Douglas E. Delaney, *The Soldiers' General: Bert Hoffmeister at War*
8 Michael Whitby, ed., *Commanding Canadians: The Second World War Diaries of A.F.C. Layard*
9 Martin Auger, *Prisoners of the Home Front: German POWs and "Enemy Aliens" in Southern Quebec, 1940-46*
10 Tim Cook, *Clio's Warriors: Canadian Historians and the Writing of the World Wars*
11 Serge Marc Durflinger, *Fighting from Home: The Second World War in Verdun, Quebec*

Clio's Warriors
Canadian Historians and the Writing of the World Wars

Tim Cook

© UBC Press 2006

All rights reserved. No part of this publication may be reproduced, stored in a retrieval system, or transmitted, in any form or by any means, without prior written permission of the publisher, or, in Canada, in the case of photocopying or other reprographic copying, a licence from Access Copyright (Canadian Copyright Licensing Agency), www.accesscopyright.ca.

16 15 14 13 12 11 10 09 08 07 06   5 4 3 2 1

Printed in Canada on ancient-forest-free paper (100% post-consumer recycled) that is processed chlorine- and acid-free, with vegetable-based inks.

Library and Archives Canada Cataloguing in Publication

Cook, Tim, 1971-
　Clio's warriors : Canadian historians and the writing of the world wars / Tim Cook.

(Studies in Canadian military history, ISSN 1499-6251)
Includes bibliographical references and index.
ISBN-13: 978-0-7748-1256-6 (bound); 978-0-7748-1257-3 (pbk)
ISBN-10: 0-7748-1256-7 (bound); 0-7748-1257-5 (pbk)

　1. World War, 1914-1918 – Canada – Historiography. 2. World War, 1939-1945 – Canada – Historiography. I. Title. II. Series.

FC149.C68 2006   940.4'127107271   C2005-906961-9

Canada

UBC Press gratefully acknowledges the financial support for our publishing program of the Government of Canada through the Book Publishing Industry Development Program (BPIDP), and of the Canada Council for the Arts, and the British Columbia Arts Council.

This book has been published with the help of a grant from the Canadian Federation for the Humanities and Social Sciences, through the Aid to Scholarly Publications Programme, using funds provided by the Social Sciences and Humanities Research Council of Canada.

Publication of this book has been financially supported by the Canadian War Museum.

Printed and bound in Canada by Friesens
Set in Minion and Helvetica Condensed by Artegraphica Design Co. Ltd.
Copy editor: Rob Giannetto
Proofreader: Gail Copeland
Indexer: Noeline Bridge

UBC Press
The University of British Columbia
2029 West Mall
Vancouver, BC V6T 1Z2
604-822-5959 / Fax: 604-822-6083
www.ubcpress.ca

Contents

Illustrations / vi

Acknowledgments / vii

Introduction: Writing the World Wars / 3

1 Documenting War and Forging Reputations, 1914-18 / 10

2 The War of Reputations, 1918-39 / 41

3 Clio in the Service of Mars, 1939-45 / 93

4 History Wars and War History, 1945-48 / 130

5 Official History, Contested Memory, 1948-60 / 162

6 Forging the Canon of Canadian World War History, 1960-2000 / 200

Conclusion: An Ongoing Dialogue / 253

Notes / 259

Select Bibliography of Official and Semi-Official Canadian Histories / 305

Index / 307

Illustrations

FOLLOWING P. 182

Sir Max Aitken, Lord Beaverbrook, *LAC, PA6477*
Lord Beaverbrook and a companion, *LAC, PA22966*
Canadians assaulting part of the Canal du Nord during the Hundred Days campaign, *LAC, PA3377*
Canadian soldiers, *CWM, George Metcalf Archival Collection, 19930013-789*
"The Canadian in Peace and War," *Canada in Khaki: A Tribute to the Officers and Men Now Serving in the Canadian Expeditionary Force*, Vol. 1 (Ottawa: Canadian War Records Office, 1917), 10
A tank at the Battle of Courcelette, September 1916. *Canada in Khaki: A Tribute to the Officers and Men Now Serving in the Canadian Expeditionary Force*, Vol. 1 (Ottawa: Canadian War Records Office, 1917).
Colonel A.F. Duguid, official historian from 1921 to 1947, *LAC, PA167233*
Sir Arthur Doughty, Dominion archivist from 1904 to 1935, *CWM, George Metcalf Archival Collection, 19790631-024*
Sir Arthur Currie, *LAC, PA1370*
Page from G.A. Drew, *The Truth about the War, Maclean's*, 1928
Colonel C.P. Stacey, *LAC, PA-115818*
Dr. Gilbert Tucker, naval historian, on board HMCS *Assiniboine, LAC, PA-166776*
Captain W.E.C. Harrison, head of the field Historical Section, *CWM, George Metcalf Archival Collection, 20020099-004*
Colonel G.W.L. Nicholson, Canada's most prolific historian of the Great War, *LAC, PA114438*
The Historical Section in Italy, near Campobasso, October 1943, *CWM, George Metcalf Archival Collection, 19760583-048*
Action on a convoy, Battle of the Atlantic, *LAC, PA134342*
Dieppe raid, *LAC, C-014160*
Canadian soldiers involved in fierce urban fighting in Ortona, *LAC, PA114482*
Aircraft assembly work, *LAC, PA-184469*
RCAF historical officer Kenneth Conn and war artist A.Y. Jackson, *CWM, George Metcalf Archival Collection, 19840128-011*
Canadian troops landing at Juno Beach on D-Day, *LAC, PA122765*
Second World War bomber campaign, *DND, PL-32846*

Acknowledgments

Sir Winston Churchill described the act of writing a book as similar to that of surviving a long and debilitating illness. As with all illnesses, the afflicted are forced to rely heavily on many to see them through their suffering.

Thanks must go to my joint PhD supervisors, Dr. Jeffrey Grey and Dr. Stephen J. Harris. Jeffrey Grey of the Australian Defence Force Academy agreed to supervise the thesis, having met me only once at a conference. He allowed me to carve out the thesis topic and conduct research with few constraints, and he offered key advice and editing skills when needed. Closer to home, Steve Harris has provided significant support to me over several years, going back to my first book. He has offered similar support to a host of historians over the last two decades. His expertise at balancing the trials of writing official history and managing ongoing operations at the Directorate of History and Heritage (DHH) is a model for other historians in public institutions, and he took this dissertation on as one more burden. He is the finest public historian working in Canada, and I am a far better historian for knowing Steve.

As I am a ground pounder at heart, and with most of my previous academic writing relating to Canada and the Great War, I turned to two friends and colleagues for insight into Canada's naval history. At the National Archives of Canada, Robert Fisher, a former naval historian at DHH, allowed me to pick his brain on matters of official history and the Royal Canadian Navy. It was also my pleasure to work with Dr. Roger Sarty at the Canadian War Museum (CWM). Despite holding together the CWM new building project for the two years we worked together, he always had time for me and shared freely his love of history as he puffed on his pipe. I peppered him mercilessly on questions of official history, the Second World War, and all manner of salacious gossip. He obliged.

At one stage when writing this book, I thought I would list all of the historians who have influenced my work over the years. That proved impossible, but there is a convivial relationship among most military historians in the country, perhaps due to a perceived siege mentality, brought on by assaults or snide comments from other non-military academics. The sharing of ideas at conferences has remained an important staple for my own development as an historian. The most important annual conference is at Wilfrid Laurier, hosted by Mike Bechthold and Terry Copp, both of whom have done so much for military history in their ongoing editorship of *Canadian Military History*. The profession would not be the same today without their journal.

At the Canadian War Museum, I have been lucky to work with gifted colleagues and brilliant historians. Since my arrival in early 2002, Dr. Cameron Pulsifer and Dr. Peter MacLeod have been good friends and colleagues; they have read almost everything that I've published, including this book. Their knowledge is imposing and I have profited from their generosity. It should be pointed out that this book was written while I was engaged in the satisfying work of developing the new permanent galleries for the CWM. This was a once-in-a-lifetime opportunity, and the thrill of building this museum for all Canadians was never diminished despite a sometimes crushing workload. My colleagues in the Historical Section at the CWM have provided support and friendship, and while most knew only vaguely that I was working on "something," they were an important emotional crutch throughout this project. I have learned much from Dr. Dean Oliver, Dr. Serge Durflinger, Glenn Ogden, Martin Auger, Patricia Grimshaw, Dr. Cameron Pulsifer, Dr. Peter MacLeod, Dr. Laura Brandon, Dr. Amber Lloydlangsten, Andrew Burtch, and Ryan Touhey. I would also like to thank Catherine Woodcock of the CWM library for tracking down countless inter-library loans.

I wish to thank the University of British Columbia Press. My editors, Emily Andrew and Camilla Blakeley, expertly guided this project to publication. Their growing reputations as first-class editors of military history have vaulted UBC into becoming the finest publisher of academic military history in Canada.

As I researched this project, interviewed historians, and presented conference papers, there were many in the profession who claimed it was about time that someone tackled the topic. I benefited from this interest. Most of Canada's leading military historians read through draft chapters of the manuscript and offered keen insight into the writing of the world wars. I profited from the generosity and editorial skills of Dr. J.L. Granatstein, Dr. Desmond Morton, Brereton Greenhous, Dr. Stephen Harris, Dr. Jeffrey Grey, Owen Cooke, Professor Terry Copp, Dr. Roger Sarty, Dr. W.A.B. Douglas, Dr. Marc Milner, Dr. Jonathan Vance, Dr. David Zimmerman, Dr. A.M.J. Hyatt, and Dr. Patrick Brennan. Formal and informal interviews with many of the above, including Dr. David Bercuson, Dr. Serge Bernier, Dr. Geoff Hayes, Dr. Scott Robertston, Dr. Norman Hillmer, and Professor Bob Spencer, improved many sections of the manuscript. While not all the advice proffered was put to use, their suggestions and intellectual prodding strengthened the final work.

My parents instilled in me a love for history. It took a little while for it to catch fire, but it has been burning ever since. While both are accomplished historians in their own right, and I have benefited specifically from my father's patient and expert editing skills over the years, particularly on this book, it is their generosity and love that have had the greatest impact on me. As a father now, too, I better understand the challenge of balancing a professional career and a young family. My parents did so with a loving generosity that my brother, Graham, and I still find amazing. As with so much in this life, this book is partly dedicated to them.

But none of this would be possible without Sarah. She has been my best friend, my confidante, and fellow traveller on this path. Sarah, too, was completing her own dissertation while working a full-time job. But through all of this, she was there at every stage, sharing my excitement and urging me forward, even with only a wry smile and a hug. This work is dedicated to her and to our daughter, Chloe, who puts this all into perspective and has brought much joy to our lives.

Clio's Warriors

Introduction: Writing the World Wars

> *Canada is an unmilitary community: Warlike her people have often been forced to be; military they have never been.*
> – C.P. STACEY

> *Governments and their officials fear historians.*
> – KEITH WILSON

> *Anybody can make history. Only a great man can write it.*
> – OSCAR WILDE

The two world wars of 1914-18 and 1939-45 weave through Canada's history like threads through a tapestry, stitching together myriad experiences to form our identity and culture. There are few aspects of Canadian society that have not been shaped by these wars, from politics to family, from the role of government to the formation of social policy, from the status of women to French-English relations. The loss of more than 102,000 Canadians in these two conflicts caused incalculable grief. Yet Canada emerged a nation transformed in their aftermath.

Unfortunately, the momentous events of the two world wars are slipping from lived experience, from memory to history, as participants die in increasing numbers. Yet it remains the stories, accounts, and narratives of war historians that act as a testimony to Canada's world war experiences. However, this book is less concerned with Canada's military involvement in the two world wars than with how historians have interpreted those events. An analysis of key historians and their works reveals how historical themes underpinning memory and narrative of the two world wars have been constructed within historical writing. The emphasis is on examining the enduring contributions that formed, fashioned, or challenged the canon of Canadian world war writing and constructed memory. Due to the deep scars of conscription in Quebec, the wars are viewed and taught differently in that province. In fact, Canada's twentieth-century military history is largely ignored there, and almost all the academic world war studies are by English-speaking historians.

It has been the official historians of the Department of National Defence who, for much of the twentieth century, have controlled the academic writing on the two world wars, and that history usually has been narrowly defined as the history of military operations. Training, administration, and operational combat have been the focus. Only recently have academic military historians pushed their discipline to explore the impact of the world wars on individuals and society. Nonetheless, the publications of A.F. Duguid, C.P. Stacey, Gilbert Tucker, Fred Hitchins, and more recent official historians provide the central narrative when analyzing the writing on Canada's world wars. While this book is not an institutional history of the Department of National Defence's historical sections, the prominent role of official history in influencing the canon of world war writing requires that significant space be devoted to exploring these historians, their accomplishments, and their historical works.

Official histories can be defined as those authorized by an institution, group, or person, where that same agent agrees to support the project financially. As well, it generally means that full access is often given to otherwise restricted records. However, these unique histories do not automatically equate into hagiography, although that can sometimes be the case. "Official but not history," was Sir Basil Liddell Hart's famous assessment of the British Great War official histories.[1] Liddell Hart's flippant remark was too clever by half, but most academic historians would agree in principle about the flawed nature of official histories. "Beset by PR, puffery, and self-promotion," wrote historian Christopher Moore, "we distrust all official statements and wonder almost instinctively about the real story concealed beneath any authorized version of events."[2] Official history has the added burden of being closely associated with military history, which, as we shall see, has always had an uneasy relationship with academic history.

In Canada the official histories prompted the study of the two world wars, and for this reason they must be analyzed beyond the simple derision of Liddell Hart's glib statements. As the chroniclers of the nation's wartime sacrifices, the official historians were indeed petitioned and pressured, but they fought against writing "court history" that would simply please their political and military masters. While the official histories have their flaws, they are also exceptionally important foundational studies that deserve considerable attention and analysis in their own right. However, the battles of interpretation that raged behind the final published product – pieced together from the archival records of the historians themselves – forms the core analysis of this book.

The official historians were confronted with the monumental tasks of reading and processing millions of pages of documentation. The results they produced met with varied success in Canada, but their influence always went far beyond that of historian and chronicler. Clio, the muse of history who is often portrayed with her books and documents, had her champions, and the official historians saw their role as guardians of memory and keepers of the past. However, following the two world wars, there were reputations at stake, and the official historians were forced to navigate carefully through the contested issues. Yet they retained the power to influence how the wars would be portrayed, and their works were, for the most part, important studies based on the war records. Laying an interpretive framework, the official historians forged an historical legacy through their writings and their lesser-known role as archivists for their respective services. During the two world wars, for instance, the official historians sought out the war records, ensured their survival, and in some cases even influenced the drafting of various types of records. Without the official historians, subsequent generations of scholars would be far less able to reappraise the wars.

Official histories were a test of endurance. All of them required years, sometimes decades, to complete. Putting aside the sheer difficulty of the projects, many official historians suffered from writing contemporary history and this, rather than the "official" designation, presented the greatest difficulty. The first generation of official historians was denied the luxury of waiting for time to dull recent events, and they were expected to produce scholarly, contemporary history for soldiers and civilians very soon after the end of each war. Later generations of official historians had time to reflect on these complex events, but they too faced their own wars of reputations: the burden of contributing to the social memory surrounding the sacrifice of millions, and the pressure exerted on them by politicians and the high command, as well as veterans' organizations, required a nuanced approach. And although censorship rarely came in the form of a red pen, the official historians, both the first and second generation, faced more subtle pressures. "The State needs no heavy-handed censorship," wrote historian Herbert Butterfield, "for it binds the historian with soft charms and with subtle, comfortable chains."[3] How the official historians fought against overt censorship as well as the more covert constraints and responsibilities of their position are important considerations for assessing their work and their role within the larger historical profession.

The official historians were not anxious to embarrass their governments or war heroes. The cautious writing of the official historians has sometimes been criticized for minimizing the culpability of nations or individuals. Yet writing at the coal face of history can provide an immediacy with unfolding events and at the same time a loss of perspective. The official historians were therefore careful about making sweeping judgments and condemnations, especially since, despite their unique positions, they were aware that they could not see or process all the war records. There were simply too many, and some series were too disorganized or scattered to use or, in other cases, were withheld from the historians for years. Official historians also made careful judgments because they understood the consequences of careless writing: they offered the first official conclusions, and having spent years studying documents, their findings had far more weight than other historical works or private memoirs. If contemporary official historians were tempered in their assessments, it is also true that all official works contained damning conclusions of individuals or the role of military units or operations, and sometimes these had a lasting impact on the subsequent historiography. While official historians worked within an "official" structure, the barriers were not nearly as confining as some academic historians subsequently suggested or still believe. No history is without bias, and the work of Canada's official historians must be examined to understand both its defects and its value.

The official historians had a strong effect on the historical profession as they provided the first foundational studies based on official research. Moreover, they did not toil in solitude from their academic counterparts. Official historians like Charles Stacey, George Stanley, and S.F. Wise were leaders in the historical profession, and their command of Canadian history earned them a significant reputation among their academic contemporaries. The Canadian public, too, greeted the official histories as important contributions, with each publication eagerly awaited and extensively reviewed in newspapers. Far from being perceived as publicity exercises by the government of the day or as obscure academic works, the official histories were widely regarded as accurate and authentic accounts based on the official war records.

This unique access to war records also caused some anger and resentment among academics, who could neither utilize the same essential documents nor confirm the findings of the official historians. But as the British naval official historian S.W. Roskill noted, what was the alternative? Should "the archives of all departments be thrown open to all and sundry" as soon as the "guns stopped firing?" Or did historians "prefer that no history should be written until the day comes when the documents are lodged in the Public Records Office?"[4] The former was clearly impossible for modern nations still recovering from the exertions of war, to say nothing of protecting sensitive negotiations or frank comments about continuing allies or former enemies whom were now considered allies. But to close the archives to all would leave the first draft of history to journalists or memorialists thirty or fifty years hence. Official history written while influential participants are still alive is likely to be flawed, but are historians to abdicate their role to popular writers who are first out of the gate, driven by the desire to present "their" version of history before the records become available? With Canadian governments refusing to open the records for at least several decades after the wars, the task of first assessing these conflicts fell to the official historians. They did not always achieve the nuanced interpretations of later historiography, but they understood well their important role in influencing that historiography.

The official historians also shaped the war archives of the nation. If cautious writing failed to reveal the full extent of certain events, crises, or personality flaws, in most cases evidence remained in the war archives – there to be uncovered by future generations of historians. Had the official military historians been producing parochial histories to prop up corrupt regimes, there can be no doubt that controversial or revealing records would have been expurgated.⁵ They were not. The official historians also shaped the archival record by setting guidelines for their creation through involvement at military headquarters, authoring their own reports, and collecting records in the field.

While some military historians have undertaken broad panoramic analyses of the Canadian experience, others have offered micro studies of various aspects in order to piece together complex, disparate events of the past. In effect, some are looking at the forest and some at the trees. Very few, however, have examined the roots. These are the records that underpin both the broad and the narrow analyses, and without them the trees and forest, to continue the analogy, cannot grow. Yet the notion of the archives and their creation being somehow neutral must be challenged. This work, therefore, also analyzes how the war records were created, and what pressures and influences were exerted on them before they were ever transferred to form the defence archives of the nation.⁶

The process of inscription (capturing history in records creation) must be considered as important as the process of decoding (the reading of the text and the compilation of research and writing). Archives are not neutral. There is always a reason to create them, and there is always an author inscribing and interpreting events within a power-shaped context. The act of record creation must be deconstructed, the layers of meaning pulled back and analyzed to better understand the process that influenced the war histories. Archival records are more than simply passive sources of study: their creation, form, and content must also be the subject of historical inquiry.

Less important, but having a significant impact on the writing of history, is an analysis of access to the war records of the nation. As memory fades and events move from shared memory to history, those who control the records control the past. In the historical profession, one must have access to records, or there can be no academic history. Journalists and memorialists can write without war records, but that is a far different type of history. And with the archives closed to academics until decades after the wars, it was the official historians who controlled the records and use of them.

Archives remain sites of contested power and interpretation. The official historians guarded them and in some cases lorded over them, allowing access only to a select few. As such, the writing of the world wars by academic historians remained stifled until late in the twentieth century. This new generation of historians, unencumbered by the trials of contemporary history but still forced to deal with decades of interpretation (including much of what the official historians laid down), were able to employ the war archives to reappraise the past. There remains much to be learned from the archives, but there is also much that can be misconstrued. It is the historian's duty to understand events within the context of the time rather than by reading history backwards with the benefit of hindsight. The latter approach, as we shall see, continues to make Canadian military history highly contested by a number of constituents.

History, in the sense of what occurred in the past, is frozen, inert, and finished. Yet the writing of history is forever engaged: the world wars are constructed, deconstructed, and reconstructed by each generation of historians. The interpretation of the past changes with the ever-evolving social and cultural contexts of the present, and new evidence and methodologies also provide additional areas of inquiry. Yet each new generation is shaped by the ongoing historical work of its predecessors. Official histories drive this story, but significant memoirs, journalistic accounts, and academic histories in the last half of the twentieth century complete the canon of world war writing. And while there have been important historiographical essays over the last eight decades, this book will delve deeper into the writing of Canadian military history through an analysis and exploration of surviving discourse.[7] While correspondence, semi-official memoranda, and even book reviews offer many insights, these sources are not without their pitfalls. Many of these historical disputes are by no means settled; they continue to provoke spirited debate among historians. Monograph analyses or interpretative theories that appear important in 2006 may soon be superseded or discredited. But a principal aim of this book is to assess the historical works in question against the context of their own times.

In short, this is military intellectual history: the history of ideas, individuals, actions, and events that underpin the Canadian documentation and writing of the world wars.[8] To examine the history behind the official history, particularly the items that were never published, is in many ways more telling than those that made their way into print. And this hidden history helps to reveal the major themes weaving through the official histories, archival records, and military reputations.

Historians distill the past, repackage it to find meaning, and draw relevant lessons. Historians are further forced to compress events, arranging them to make sense, while recognizing that their sources are inherently flawed. Some recent historians, in this case lumped loosely under the very large rubric of postmodernism, have claimed that history is little more than fiction, that everything is relative, and that no historian can possibly attain the objective truth.[9] Historians have been influenced by postmodernist theory to the betterment of the profession, becoming more critical of their own biases and blind spots. But while historians have long discarded notions of historical writing containing the truth or being written from an objective point of view, most would argue that the past can be reconstructed through a faithful reading of the surviving archival record. Many historians, after intensely studying the archival records in their many forms, know their ability to reveal the acts, deeds, and events in illuminating detail. History based on a rigorous interrogation of those archival records, and a willingness to understand them within the context of their creation, will allow the past to be rediscovered, recast, and reinterpreted. Historians are not simply writing fiction. Perhaps it is best to turn to one of the great historians and history makers of the twentieth century, Sir Winston Churchill. Speaking of democracy, he said it was the worst form of governance, except for all the others. The same may be said for history. While history is flawed and biased and can never be captured and presented in its entirety, in giving society its vital roots for intellectual growth in the present, it just may be the worst method of inquiry, except for all the others.

There are truths to be uncovered; there are important lessons to be learned; there are sacrifices that need to be remembered. As a profession with a long and rich legacy, it is time for historians to better understand the corpus of records and writings that form the canon of Canadian world war history and the construction of our national memory.

1
Documenting War and Forging Reputations, 1914-18

> *The First World War remains by all odds the greatest event in Canada's history.*
> – C.P. STACEY

> *The world cannot be allowed to forget. Records are necessary to knowledge. There can be no history without them.*
> – SIR MAX AITKEN, LORD BEAVERBROOK

The Canadian Corps was one of the finest fighting formations in the Great War, regarded by both allies and enemies as shock troops that were thrown into the bloodiest campaigns to deliver victory. With an almost nonexistent professional army before the war, Canada raised 600,000 men, of whom 424,000 served overseas from 1914 to 1919. As with other national armies fighting on the Western Front, the casualties were appalling; by the armistice, more than 60,000 Canadians were dead, and another 138,000 had been wounded in combat. Despite this bloodletting, or perhaps as a result of it, the Canadians earned a reputation as determined and efficient soldiers.

Both isolated and idealized, Canada was on the frontier of the Empire. With seemingly free land and a country without deep class divisions, Canada must have appeared carved out of a perfect wilderness by a "hardy and industrious people" to those in England's congested cities.[1] Much of the writing by imperial "mythmakers, enthusiasts and fictionalists" envisioned Canada as a country of hunters and sportsmen, with an unspoiled land that was as rich in adventure and resources as it was as deficient in culture and history.[2] The attributes of those who had settled this harsh land were strength, vigour, and purity. "We are the Northmen of the New World," proclaimed R.G. Haliburton, a Canadian novelist, whose words suggested that it was not only the British who were interested in constructing a hardy image for the new nation.[3] It is not surprising that many of the Canadian soldiers arriving in England were thought to have emerged recently from the frozen tundra. This was a strong race with all the qualities of which any Social Darwinist could approve. Despite this perceived sense of otherness, more than 70 percent of the First Contingent was British born, although many had been living in Canada for decades. By the end of the war, only a little more than 50 percent of the force was Canadian born.[4]

Despite frequent allusions to the country being populated by a race of sportsmen and hunters, the Canadians were not immediately viewed as an elite force. Drawn from the harsh dominion of the North, Canadians were seen as undisciplined, unruly troops who had proved their unconventional but adept fighting skills during the South African War; however, they were deemed more brawlers than soldiers.[5] Moreover, the difficult learning curve on the Western Front was cruel to all inexperienced troops, and the Canadians were no exception. They went through several difficult and costly battles in the first two years of the war that left them viewed as suspect by their British commanders. This changed by the end of the Battle of the Somme in 1916. Like their Australian counterparts, who were also seen as an elite force by the end of the war, as the Canadians gained fighting confidence and skills, they began to develop an independent identity. In the process, the Dominion armies demanded recognition from the British who fought next to them. This sense of distinction helped to foster esprit de corps within Canadian units, but the creation of an identity did not happen by chance. The Canadian Corps had an active propaganda campaign that publicized Canadian uniqueness throughout the war.

The organization behind this promotion was the Canadian War Records Office, headed by Sir Max Aitken, later Lord Beaverbrook, an expatriate Canadian millionaire with close ties to military and political leaders in both Canada and the United Kingdom. With characteristic passion, Aitken employed his considerable skills as a press baron, member of parliament, and influential peer to advance a relentless campaign to extol the heroic deeds of Canadians in battle. Journalistic features accentuating Canadian exploits, the commissioning of artists, photographers, and cinematographers to craft Canadian-content works, the creation of commemorative journals, and even the publication of the first popular war histories, all helped to shape a distinctive Canadian identity. Largely at his own discretion, but also supported by Prime Minister Sir Robert Borden, Minister of Militia and Defence Sir Sam Hughes, and the Ministers of Overseas Military Forces, Sir George Perley and Sir A.E. Kemp, Aitken's active campaign, when combined with the very real accomplishments of the Canadian Corps on the battlefield, enshrined the Canadians' reputation within the British Expeditionary Force (BEF). With an eye on the future, Aitken would provide a steady barrage of media products to manufacture a sense of distinctiveness and identity for the Canadian soldier, while at the same time gathering, writing, and preserving a legacy of war records that would be employed by future historians to understand the Great War.

MANY CANADIANS followed the deteriorating situation in Europe in the summer of 1914, and the government turned to a number of experts for advice. One of the most prominent, Sir Max Aitken, advised his acquaintances Robert Borden and

Sam Hughes that it was unlikely that Britain would ever go to war over an issue in the Balkans. Yet as brinkmanship spiralled into war ultimata, Aitken changed his appreciation, supplying the now scrambling Canadian government with inside information gleaned from British social circles, which included friends such as Winston Churchill, Andrew Bonar Law, and Rudyard Kipling. And when Great Britain declared war on 4 August, Canada too, as a dominion in the British Empire, was at war. The Cabinet needed someone to keep it abreast of the ever-changing situation on the Western Front and in the backrooms of London. Notwithstanding a somewhat darkened reputation, Aitken was well suited for the job.

Max Aitken was born in 1879 and raised in New Brunswick. While excelling at neither his studies nor sports, he exhibited a command of business, running several profitable schemes at an early age. He began to acquire small companies in his twenties, sell shares in them, and purchase new companies with the profits. An exuberant and energetic figure, short in stature and with an enormous grin, Aitken revelled in deal making. He earned grand profits while others floundered in his wake. After making millions from buying up, amalgamating, and creating monopolistic conglomerates, and then selling out at the right time, Aitken left Canada for England in 1910 under a cloud of suspicion.[6] Viewed by some as a market exploiter, perhaps he had simply made too much money too quickly. He had certainly not spread enough of it around to the powerful men who effectively controlled the burgeoning Canadian economy.

Aitken wasted little time in establishing himself in English society. He won a parliamentary seat in 1911, was knighted for his support of the Tory party, and began to buy up newspaper companies shortly thereafter. Nonetheless, Aitken was mistrusted for his dealings in Canada and possibly for his "new money" wealth. Socially active in some of the best London clubs – certainly more so than he was in the House of Commons – he also contributed journalistic pieces to Canadian newspapers. He kept in touch in other ways too, providing support and money to the Canadian Conservative Party, especially Borden and Hughes, to whom he gave campaign money for the 1911 election. When war was declared, Aitken was thus not only seen as the Canadian expert in Britain, but also as a political ally. Yet Sir Max expected to be asked to assist the Herbert Asquith government in prosecuting the war effort, and he was bitterly disappointed when the appointment failed to materialize. After some soul searching, he appealed to his Canadian friends for a fitting position to serve his country of birth.

But Aitken was not without his faults. Borden was unsure if Aitken, who still had powerful enemies among the Canadian business elite, was more of a handicap than an advantage. Undeterred by Borden's lukewarm responses to his initial offer of assistance, Aitken appealed to Sam Hughes at the end of 1914, claiming that the "most important section of London Press agrees to give me opportunity to describe Canadian mobilization in series of illustrated articles." His fervent desire to assist was evident, and he was confident that he could be of "service in the whole Canadian situation."[7] However, this service did not extend to enlisting in the Canadian Expeditionary Force (CEF); he was far too rich and plagued by asthma to serve in the front lines.

On Hughes's urging, the Canadian Cabinet appointed Aitken to the position of Eye Witness, in which he would supply Canadians with wartime information.[8] When Hughes's desire to command the Canadian Division had been politely turned down by the British in favour of selecting an experienced imperial general – E.A.H. Alderson – the minister attempted to influence operations from Canada. Max Aitken would be his eyes in London. Moreover, with an honorary appointment of lieutenant colonel and his own immense funds, Aitken took it upon himself to expand his role within the confused Canadian military hierarchy. Due to an ingrained belief in patronage politics and a desire to keep power in his own hands, Hughes had appointed several commanders in England to administer the Canadian forces, most of whom disliked each other, had overlapping duties, and were in direct conflict with one another.[9] With the British warily standing back and observing this colonial administrative chaos, Aitken, ever successful at exploiting situations, ensured that his role as Eye Witness would include liaising with the British at General Headquarters.

As Hughes's confidant, Aitken's authorization to sit in on British General Headquarters meetings as the Canadian representative at the front gave the minister unparalleled access to information. Aitken's duties, as he reported them to the prime minister, were to keep Hughes informed of British decisions and to act as a rallying point where difficulties between the British and Canadians could be worked out.[10] For much of 1915 Aitken was, in most cases, the primary contact for the British when they were forced to deal with the unstable Hughes. The mercurial minister of Militia and Defence frequently displayed poor judgment in sending off missives from Canada that were both insulting and antagonistic to imperial generals and politicians. As a result, Aitken earned the trust of senior British officers for his ability to defuse military-civilian conflicts between the two countries.[11] Hughes "makes demands on me almost daily," noted Aitken, and the minister's reliance on him strengthened Aitken's role in the Canadian overseas hierarchy.[12] By early 1916, however, Aitken had been reined in: his unofficial role as a liaison with the British was handed to a friend, Lieutenant Colonel R.F. Manly Sims.

The liaison role had been far beyond Aitken's mandate, but it had placed him in an ideal position to expand on his Eye Witness project, and even afterwards, Sims continued to supply Aitken with important military information. Aitken described his goals this way: "to follow the fortunes of the First Division in France, to share its experiences, and to give the public of Canada an account of the performances of its regiments, and finally to enshrine in a contemporary history those exploits which will make the First Division immortal."[13] He would be the self-appointed historian and publicist for the Canadian overseas forces.

To document the war work of the Canadian Division, Aitken travelled behind the front in his Rolls-Royce and interviewed scores of Canadian soldiers and officers in the field. He became a recognized figure and was adept at drawing stories out of tired men, even when the staff officers at the rear disliked his involvement.[14] Aitken's role was nearly unique as there were few war correspondents at the front.[15] Moreover, when he encountered problems with British staff officers bent on enforcing rules to quash all unauthorized information, Aitken utilized his status as special envoy for the Canadian government, as well as his influential position in the Conservative Party, to ensure that he was not impeded. An opponent of censorship throughout the war, Aitken was able to force the military's hand and to relax its strict rules regarding the dissemination of information to the public. "The trouble about the Eye Witness business is that the Eye Witness is ipso facto more or less official," wrote one army censor. "I could not undertake to vet the writings of the correspondent with regard to the truth."[16] His information-gathering skills, money, and official status placed him in a better position to comprehend the events of war than any other person in the CEF. And while General Alderson neither trusted nor liked him, the more junior Canadian brigadier generals and battalion commanders were generally enthusiastic in supporting Aitken, the man who was to chronicle and publicize their actions.[17] In addition to sending back weekly communiqués to Borden and the Canadian government, Aitken's journalistic accounts were published widely in Canadian newspapers. His very readable narratives must have been reassuring for many Canadian families. That was all to change in less than a month, however, as the Canadian Division would be shattered at the Battle of Second Ypres.

As part of an allied British and French force, the inexperienced Canadian Division was ordered to hold a portion of the Ypres salient, a rounded position several miles across that jutted into the German lines and was surrounded on three sides by high ground, which was used to full effect by the German artillery. Although there had been ample warnings of a forthcoming offensive, the Allied armies were caught unprepared for the overwhelming assault that was launched behind the first lethal chlorine gas attack of the war. The gas cloud rolled over the two French territorial and colonial divisions to the left of the Canadians, causing a panicked rout. However, the Canadians held their ground, shifted to cover the now gaping hole in the line, launched counterattacks, and repulsed the Germans in a resolute defence. Two days later, the Canadians were the victims of a second chlorine gas cloud. Those soldiers caught in its path were suffocated outright or left to defend their trenches, gasping and wheezing through ravaged lungs. The Canadians were pushed back into their own lines over the front, but they did not break, ensuring that the two British divisions to the south were not enveloped. In a week of fighting, the division's grim stand had cost 6,000 casualties. And it was Max Aitken who reported on the action.

Canada's Eye Witness made his name – as well as that of the Canadian Division – significantly more prominent with his vivid account of the heroic Canadian stand at Ypres. Aitken's piece was published on 1 May 1915, and through his friendships with other press barons, his own newspapers, and his position as Eye Witness, his account of the brave Dominion soldiers was read widely throughout the Empire.

It appeared that the untried Canadian Division had stopped the Germans alone. The idea that Canadian troops were holding out against impossible odds and the nefarious release of chlorine gas resulted in a stirring narrative for readers in the super-charged patriotic atmosphere in England and in Canada. "The battle ... was bloody, even as men appraise battles in this callous and life-engulfing war." The Canadians were, according to Aitken, "enormously outnumbered" and their performance was "amazing" as the division consisted of "men who ... at the outbreak of the war were neither disciplined nor trained."[18] Further accounts stressed that the division was formed by the "Canadian people," who had joined partly for the "glory of adventure but more of the spirit of self-sacrifice."[19] Aitken turned the battle into an epic story, in line with the rousing accounts of the British Army's last stands against legions of natives in one of their many nineteenth-century colonial battles. This time, though, it was the Canadian boys who held off overwhelming odds, falling in droves, but keeping chins up, and eventually stopping the hordes of Huns advancing behind their death clouds. Aitken's success in carving out a distinguished record for the Canadians as an almost separate fighting force, rather than as Dominion troops fighting within a much larger British Expeditionary Force (BEF) structure, left some British politicians and officers complaining that it appeared to be only the Canadians fighting the Germans, with a little support from the British.[20] They were not, of course, but Aitken's publicity machine was far more effective than that supporting British troops. With the focused nature of his writing, Aitken's account of the Canadians, along with their obvious bravery in battle, began to forge their reputation.

With his journalistic success, Aitken realized that the Canadians needed more than one man to disseminate information about their deeds. He began to build a small office to both protect the Canadian war records and to fashion propaganda on Canadian military exploits. As early as January 1915, Aitken had reported to Hughes that the Canadian records kept by the British at the War Office were "in a state of chaos."[21] This did not sit well with the minister who was already smarting from being denied the opportunity to command and who felt that the British were consistently displaying a haughty attitude towards him and his soldiers. With the full support of Hughes and Borden, and in the wake of his celebrated Ypres account, Aitken acquired a new role for himself as the official Canadian Records Officer in May 1915.[22]

With this title, he began to negotiate with the British Historical Section of the Committee of Imperial Defence to gain possession of the original Canadian War Diaries and operational war records. In one of the most prescient moves related to documenting the war, Aitken – once again at his own behest – pushed for and succeeded in controlling the records and thus the future history of the CEF. The nation that oversees its own archives is able to shape and manufacture its own history and eventually guard its own memory while creating its own identity. Aitken realized this from the start and believed in leaving a legacy of war records that would "lay down the bedrock of history."[23]

The success of the Second Ypres story propelled Aitken towards a full-length monograph on the subject in order to "keep popular interest in the army alive, and above all to stimulate that local pride in local regiments which is the foundation of the Canadian Corps."[24] From June 1915 onward, Aitken pored over the War Diaries, interviewed surviving officers, and crafted his battle narrative.[25]

AITKEN PUBLISHED *Canada in Flanders* in January 1916 to considerable public acclaim, with the book going through four printings in the first month, and twelve printings by March.[26] *The Evening Standard* reported, "The heroic deeds of the Canadians at Ypres make me tingle with pride to be a kinsman to such soldiers. Fruit farmers, editors and ranchers all showed themselves to be of the finest fighting stuff of the world." *The Daily Express* also picked up on the notion of the volunteer contingent: the author "points out, over and over again, that the Canadian Army is almost entirely an army of amateurs ... This fact is of immense significance, particularly as it is equally true of the greater part of the British forces." Aitken was lauded for his evocative prose and the fact that his work, unlike that of so much of the war writing to date, was based on, as one reviewer noted, "a large number of military diaries and official documentation."[27] Subtitled the "official story of the CEF," here, finally, was history based on trusted sources, created by the soldiers themselves, and dutifully reported by their Eye Witness.

Supremely patriotic, sanitized, and uncritical, *Canada in Flanders* must be viewed as a product of its time. Ever the newspaperman and deeply aware of what the public wanted, Aitken focused on telling the story of all men, not just the officers, in order to reach out to the millions of family members and friends left behind in Canada and England. Following the precedent of his first Ypres communiqué, he included regimental names and even personal accounts of bravery and sacrifice in his "heroic" history. These revelations resulted in tensions with the British censors, who were dogmatic in refusing to allow the release of information that they believed would hurt the war effort. Refusing to be cowed, however, Aitken fought against these "intolerable delays" with all the support of his political allies. He eventually convinced Hughes to appeal personally to the War Office to have the censors cease and desist.[28] Aitken believed in the importance of uniting the nation behind the war effort, and he found it absurd that the inclusion of individual soldiers' names – the very people with whom those at home could identify – would somehow endanger military intelligence. As Aitken wryly noted later in the war while still trying to profile the Canadian actions, "here the spirit was willing but the censorship was by no means weak."[29] But with his considerable influence, Aitken succeeded in passing *Canada in Flanders* through the censors, and his was one of the first popular histories, along with Ian Hay's *The First Hundred Thousand* (1915), to reach the public.

Canada in Flanders was indeed, as the reviewers suggested, an important work for breaking the rigorous censorship rules, emphasizing the importance of individuals, and creating a new pantheon of heroes. While *Canada in Flanders* was written in an heroic style, Aitken had also employed war records to impart a sense of authenticity. Nevertheless, he struggled with his history, acknowledging that the account was necessarily "incomplete and partial." Instead, he aimed to bridge the gap between the firing line and the home front. He purposely stayed clear of the controversies surrounding the battle, such as the poor control exhibited by General Alderson, the mishandling of the 3rd Brigade's battalions by Brigadier General Richard Turner, and even the confusing retirement from the front to gather reinforcements on 24 April by Brigadier General Arthur Currie.[30] "It is in no case a grateful task to write a contemporary history," admitted Aitken, and "nothing can be attempted except a kind of rough justice."[31]

AFTER CHRONICLING the Canadians in action, Aitken did not have the time nor seemingly the inclination to visit the front again after witnessing the grim fighting of Second Ypres. Instead, he gathered a small team of wounded veterans and experienced writers to assist him in carrying out his twin mandates of collecting war records and publicizing the Canadian Corps. The Canadian War Records Office (CWRO) was established in January 1916.

Realizing that his vision of leaving a legacy of records would not have been possible if he waited for financial support from the budget-conscious Canadian government, Aitken paid for the CWRO, including the hiring of staff and the purchase of all supplies, out of his own pocket for six months before the government allocated $25,000 to cover some of the costs. In rooms donated by the Public Record Office, the CWRO staff registered, arranged, and examined the Canadian War Diaries sent to them from the field. Other historical material was also collected to better document the CEF, both units training in England and those serving in France and Belgium. General and routine orders, badges, honours, and awards conferred on officers and men, photographs, soldier-published trench newspapers, and an assortment of other historical ephemera were gathered and catalogued. Later in the war, the CWRO would actively create records to capture the Canadian war experience. Photographers, war artists, cinematographers, and historical officers would go into the field to capture their countrymen's actions for all history. "My office," wrote Aitken, "has a voracious appetite for historical documents."[32]

The CWRO became much more than a simple archives, however. Aitken was one of the principal figures administering the Canadian forces in England. Henry Beckles Willson, who worked briefly in the CWRO, gave a description of the organization: it was almost "a corps headquarters in the field ... It was as if Aitken had clandestinely built up a simulacrum of Sir Sam Hughes's office in Ottawa, where place-hunters, contractors, officials, politicians and pressmen came and went all day ... It was, in effect, the real and immediate source of authority of the Canadian Corps in Europe."[33] Willson's exaggerated prose should not detract from Aitken's importance in England. He was recognized by his friends as a man of importance and feared by his enemies as a force to be reckoned with.

From the start, Aitken began to build his historical empire by making sure that senior officers in both England and France knew that he was now responsible for documenting the war and ensuring a legacy for the Canadian soldier. There were stumbling blocks, however. Alderson was particularly concerned that Aitken, whom he rightly associated with Sam Hughes, the minister who constantly interfered in the command of his Canadian Corps, would uncover and publish secret documents.[34] With his honorary military status, Aitken appeared to be just another political crony. To be clear, this was exactly what Aitken was – yet, at the same time, he took his role as CEF archivist and historian seriously. If the responsibility of guarding documents for future generations did not sway the corps commander, the Eye Witness could reposition himself by promising not to reveal battle secrets irresponsibly but, instead, to "make the deeds of Canada shine brightly in this War. No effort will be spared to attain this end."[35] Aitken needed the war records not only to create a proper historical legacy but also to add legitimacy to his publicity projects. Even though Aitken was willing to present the Canadians in the best possible light in his publications, there is no evidence that the CWRO's staff censored or destroyed damning war records.

As Aitken moved from Eye Witness to official record keeper and unofficial publicist, he was assisted by several gifted individuals in his goals: Lieutenant Colonel (later Brigadier General) R.F. Manly Sims, a former British regular officer and businessman, was his chief liaison officer in France; Captain Theodore G. Roberts, the younger brother of the New Brunswick poet and writer Charles G.D. Roberts, took up much of the day-to-day writing; Henry Beckles Willson, historian and man-of-letters, was in charge of War Diaries until his stormy relationship with

Aitken forced his resignation; and later, Talbot Papineau, a well-known French-Canadian nationalist, collected war records and wrote dispatches before returning to the front where he was killed. The CWRO's self-proclaimed guiding principle was to be the "spokesman for the Canadian Army; it was the official reporter of what was good to report; it was the eyes and the pen of the great inarticulate mass of men who were too busy fighting to tell just how they were fighting."[36] The CWRO officers may have been the spokesmen for the army, but they certainly were not neutral or objective in their approach – they judged what to report, and they defined what was to be emphasized and what would be forgotten.

Alderson remained wary of Aitken, but with his removal from command in May 1916, the CWRO had a better relationship with the new corps commander, Lieutenant General Sir Julian Byng. Attesting to his power, Aitken had orchestrated the dirty business of undermining Alderson's position, ensuring that General Sir Douglas Haig, commander of the BEF, kept the questionably competent Canadian-born Major General Richard Turner, VC, in command of the 2nd Division while at the same time sacrificing Alderson for the sake of good relations between the Canadians and the British.[37] As Hughes's right-hand man in England, Aitken was more than an archivist gathering records for some future official historian: this was the man who had manipulated the command of brigades and battalions, had the Canadian Corps commander removed, and would, in due course, have a hand in bringing down the Asquith government.[38] "Sir Max Aitken is a power in the land – at present – has immense influence in both Canadian and English governments and consequently upon the Army," wrote one observer.[39] Although Byng despised civilian interference from Canada and Britain, he was astute enough to curry favour with the powerful Sir Max whenever he had a chance. And if that meant allowing records to be collected or journalistic pieces to be written, even if they went against his professional and personal instincts, then so be it.[40]

Dominion Archivist Arthur Doughty described the war to Sam Hughes in early 1916 as the "outstanding event in Canadian history for generations to come."[41] Doughty was born in England, attended Oxford, and emigrated to Canada at the age of twenty-six. He worked as a journalist and was a respected literary and cultural figure, specializing in the arts before joining the Public Service in Quebec. In 1904 Doughty was appointed dominion archivist. Under his tenure he built up the Public Archives from an underfunded institution into "a treasure house of Canadian history," which collected and made available documents, maps, photographs, works of art, and even artifacts.[42] As a respected historian, a friend and advisor to senior politicians and even prime ministers such as Wilfrid Laurier, Robert Borden, and later, William Lyon Mackenzie King, Doughty was a part of Ottawa's social elite and no political neophyte.

Aitken, as we have seen, was also well aware of the enormity of the war and the need to document the role played by his countrymen. This put Doughty in a difficult position: while Hughes had appointed Aitken as the CEF's Records Officer, it was Doughty who was responsible to the Canadian people for gathering Canadian records of importance and saving them for posterity in the Public Archives. Here was the most important event of his generation, and probably for several generations, and some mischievous millionaire gnome had taken his job.

In December 1915 Doughty had written to his minister, P.E. Blondin, requesting that he should be sent overseas to collect official and private records relating to the CEF.[43] Doughty was suspicious of Aitken, with his shady background and absolute inexperience in history or archives. He remarked to Sir Edmund Walker, president of the Bank of Commerce, that he was going to save the war records in order that a "true account of Canada in the war could be written ... [and] so that we shall not depend on such men as Sir Max Aitken."[44] Doughty also wanted to ensure that the records were to become the property of the Public Archives after the war and not become stored in some English museum or, worse, find their way into the hands of a private individual.[45]

Wearing his new uniform and sporting an honorary rank of major (later colonel), Doughty strode into the London offices of the CWRO in the summer of 1916, announcing forcefully to Aitken and his assistant, Lieutenant Henry Beckles Willson, "that, as Dominion Archivist, all Canadian records – civil, naval, and military – were by statute under his control." With that he promptly turned around and exited, leaving the stunned staff eyeing one another. "I forgot who burst into laughter first," wrote Willson in his diary.[46] Although Doughty's legendary skills at convincing the richest families of Europe to pass their records to the Public Archives seemed mostly absent in this meeting, perhaps the dominion archivist was understandably nervous in confronting Sir Max.

Yet Aitken, realizing that he had overstepped his narrow mandate and aware of Doughty's prestige, not to mention his expertise, chose not to cross swords. Rather, he placated him. His great manoeuvring in business proved that he could do the same in the field of archives. Aitken was able to convince Doughty to relinquish his hold on this future archives for the duration of the war. As part of the negotiations, however, Aitken reiterated his promise to transfer all records to the Public Archives after the war, and he would indeed welcome all advice that the experienced Doughty could provide relating to record keeping.[47] That was enough for Doughty who later wrote: "Sir Max is indefatigable." At the same time, Doughty thought it "strange to find him engaged in the work of making a record of the war. He is evidently in earnest about it and is determined to make it a success."[48] Indeed, Aitken was. However, it was "strange" to find a man so powerful as Aitken engaged in the historical and record-keeping process of the CWRO. What could explain it?

Aitken was always an enigma, and Doughty was only one of many who were unsure if he was motivated by "politics or pure patriotism."[49] Others were more doubtful and not so easily won over. Although the act of archiving was foreign to Aitken, his actions were incredibly far-sighted and he was carrying out a more active acquisition policy than anything advocated by any Canadian officer or archivist at the time. Of course, the publicity aspect of the CWRO was equally important to him, and that was an area where he, as a newspaper baron, had more experience. As Doughty wrote, "Whatever may be his motive he is doing the work well ... [he] is the right man in the right place."[50] Any analysis of Aitken and his passion for the dual roles of the CWRO must acknowledge that all of this work was carried out under his own initiative. Aitken believed deeply in supporting his countrymen in this terrible conflict; he would not stand for interference from anyone in his quest to elevate the Canadian soldier in the eyes of the world or to leave an historical legacy for others to do so in the future.

WITH BYNG'S CONTINUED SUPPORT, R.F. Manly Sims and Theodore Roberts, who were collecting war records at the front, supplied Aitken with information for the CWRO's newspaper communiqués and for the preparation of a second volume of *Canada in Flanders*.[51] However, this was never easy, and Manly Sims confided to Aitken, who was anxious to receive records of the Canadian fighting at Mount Sorrel in June 1916, that he would need a "seer" to understand the true picture of the battle.[52] The confusion and chaos of attack and counterattack did not lend itself to an easy retelling, primarily since most of the witnesses were dead, maimed, or had seen little and understood less outside of their couple of hundred metres of battlefield. Noting that War Diaries and appendices varied in quality, Aitken appealed to Byng to reiterate to his subordinates the importance of keeping accurate and detailed war records.[53] The corps commander did this through a series of orders – one going so far as to warn that, "units which have not kept full and accurate reports may find that injustice has been done to them in [future] historical works."[54] Despite such threats, it was found that many units still produced weak War Diaries and operational reports that failed to provide adequate information or coverage. The 18th Battalion's War Diary on the Somme was so useless that someone within the regiment added a note: "Not much help to a historian."[55] Understanding the need to gather war records and ensure their creation at the front prompted a small team of CWRO officers to be stationed in France.

There had been no CWRO representative on the Somme battlefield from September to November 1916, and the War Diaries and reports created there were considerably weaker than earlier historical records. With horrific casualties, it was not uncommon to lose most forward officers in an engagement, thereby leaving no one qualified to write up the reports of operations. At other times the strain of battle ensured that "some of the diaries are so illegible that they can scarcely be read."⁵⁶ The CWRO field historians, therefore, played an important role in assisting in the creation of records. This active intervention and actual authoring of war records in some cases was essential for providing documentary evidence of the ebb and flow of the war; as one CWRO report noted, "these records were snatched from the firing line and from men still red hot from the fiery ordeal of action." In the war records lay the "rigid testimony of truth," which must not "be allowed to perish with" the men who created them.⁵⁷ Without the CWRO's intercession, the records available to subsequent generations of Canadians and historians would have been far less comprehensive.⁵⁸

In addition to the collection of war records, the CWRO historical officers assisted the regimental war diarists and officers tasked with writing up operations. Besides being overworked, exhausted, and sometimes without the necessary literary skills, the battalion war diarists often did not have a full picture of a battle. How were they to describe an engagement raging across a broad front when they were stationed at rear headquarters? As a result, they often turned to the historical officers to supply them with information or add overlooked details. Captain Talbot Papineau described his role as an historical officer in the field, emphasizing in a letter home that, "You must understand that I am not a mere newspaper correspondent. Nothing makes me angrier. I write many official staff documents as well. For instance yesterday I made a complete tour of our whole battle front – interviewed almost all the Battalion commanders – personally examined the enemy lines and finally wrote a long report which the General favourably commented upon today."⁵⁹

By the summer of 1917, the CWRO had two officers in France, Lieutenant W. Douglas and Captain I.T. Robertson. Throughout the last half of the year, these two officers visited 263 units in the field to "impress on all concerned the importance which is attached to them for historical point of view ... We found in a large number of cases that the object of a War Diary was not realized; that, in fact, it was generally regarded merely as an official return, to be rendered more or less perfunctorily every month. In other cases we encountered the belief that it was not permissible to include full details of an operation, much of the data being regarded as of a secret and confidential nature." Their work, then, was in winning over the confidence of officers who were sometimes "afraid of saying too much, thinking it might be regarded as 'hot air', a thing all fighting men abhor." Equally important, the records officers were to ensure that documents, be they old operational orders, a scrawled note from a company commander, or a map tracing, were not destroyed in the field by those who might not understand their significance.⁶⁰

The historical records improved dramatically with the appointment of roving CWRO officers in France.⁶¹ "The nature of modern war is the prevalence of confused and protracted struggles where the range of vision is limited to a few yards and each small group or unit is aware of nothing but what is happening in its immediate neighbourhood," opined one CWRO report. "And yet it is precisely the stories of these groups which make up the battle as the fragments make up the mosaic, and which yet so seldom penetrates as far as the War Records Office, and through it to posterity. A Company Report or a really extensive and well-written account of an action composed by a Battalion Commander is, therefore, of priceless value, but such things are more rare than they should be, and every day makes them more irreplaceable as memory fades and the witnesses disperse."[62]

The role of the CWRO was not only to improve the quality of the records, but also to actively seek out participants and shape the content of the war record. In assessing the work of the CWRO, Doughty believed that Aitken and his staff had adequately carried out their mandate of archiving the war records, which "will greatly facilitate the work of historians in the future."[63]

All of this active work in creating and safeguarding records had been the result of the energetic interventions by Sir Max Aitken. However, he would not stop there. As part of his desire to promote Canadian soldiers, Aitken hoped to commemorate their deeds by producing a collection of their own writings. With that in mind and basing the project on the very successful Australian *Anzac Book*, he instructed Manly Sims in July 1916 to write to commanding officers that the CWRO wished to publish stories, poems, cartoons, and personal accounts of battle from frontline soldiers in a commemorative "war book for the masses."[64] Unfortunately, the response by most Canadian soldiers was lukewarm. Even then, Aitken complained that the submissions he did receive were "of very low order."[65] As such, he chose only those works that conformed to his own image of the Canadian soldier.[66] Accounts that emphasized fear and bitterness were excluded in favour of stories emphasizing abilities to stick it out and remain cool under fire. One submission read: "A C.O. detailed two Highlanders to escort four German Prisoners back to the prisoners' pen, about one and half miles in the rear. In less than ten minutes they returned, and being questioned by the C.O., about the four German prisoners, replied; – 'They all dropped dead Sir, and we didna [sic] want to miss this fight, so we returned.'"[67] Titled "Fact," the passage was both a mixture of trench humour and the grim nature of fighting on the Western Front – both considerations that were largely unknown to those on the home front. However, a record of the deliberate execution of German prisoners did not fit into Aitken's vision of a book that would glorify Canadian deeds. "Fact" was never published, and instead readers were treated to a collection of anecdotes of the "stiff-upper lip" variety that spoke to bravery, sacrifice, and nationalistic aspirations.

Although touted as a work by Canadian soldiers for Canadian soldiers, volume 1 of this commemorative work, published in January 1917 and entitled *Canada in Khaki*, consisted of a large number of journalistic and CWRO accounts, not to mention articles by Sir George Perley and other noteworthy Canadians. Nonetheless, there were poems and cartoons from soldiers that gave the journal a sense of authenticity. It was immensely successful, selling 40,000 copies in the first week.[68] Two more volumes followed, each selling tens of thousands of copies, and *Canada in Khaki* helped to create an image of the Canadian soldier that was thoroughly different from that of the British Tommy.

Yet what defined the Canadian soldier? Looking at the First Contingent, it was clear that the Canadian soldier was more likely to be British born than anything else. But with Aitken's products, the line between Canadian and Briton became blurred. *Canada in Khaki* is a useful example for analyzing Aitken's approach to myth making. Perley wrote that the Canadian forces were "native-born, British-born, and young men from all the varied races that in recent years have been carried by the tide of immigration into the Golden West." T.G. Roberts, Aitken's most trusted writer at the CWRO, went one step further, musing that although some of the Canadians may have been born outside of Canada, "He is no less a Canadian, either in his own heart or in the hearts of his friends ... Whatever a man used to be, he is now what his cap badge proclaims him." These Canadian soldiers were, according to A.M. De Beck, editor of *Canadian News*, and another contributor to the journal, "Men from the prairies, from the wheat fields and the lumber-yards of the West; men accustomed to the saddle and to sport of all kinds; men who can wield an axe more deftly than I can hold a pen; men accustomed to face death twenty times a year or more, and who have waged war with Nature or with wild beasts all their lives – what wonder that they sprang to the call of war as surely never men sprang before. The clash of battle was as music in their ears." This "hardy breed of men, the stalwart children of nature" seemed, according to *Canada in Khaki*, bred for war. One final example must suffice: a cartoon by H.M. Bateman, entitled "The Canadian in Peace and War, as Imagined by an English Artist," goes to the heart of the image that Aitken was trying to construct. The drawing showed a young man stalking a bear, lumberjacks sitting on a great log, voyageurs exploring the land, gold prospectors striking it rich, and cowboys shooting bottles off a barrel. This "peacetime" iconography led directly to an image of a Canadian infantryman with bayonet herding three German prisoners through the line. Depicting a devil-may-care grin and stone-hewn features on the Canadian soldier, it was clear that our English artist clearly equated the rugged Canadian land with a rough and determined soldier. From cartoons, photographs, and editorials, a unique image of the Canadian soldier was being constructed in the pages of the CWRO-sponsored works.[69]

Along with these publications, Aitken felt that the public should have a chance to experience the deeds of the Canadian Corps by visualizing their exploits: "We must see our men climbing out of the trenches to the assault before we can realise the patience, the exhaustion, and the courage which are assets and the trials of modern fighting men."⁷⁰ Aitken would ensure that not only did the people of Canada know exactly what their sons, brothers, husbands, and fathers were doing in France and Belgium, but also that the rest of the world was told – over and over again – that it was Canadian soldiers fighting as a distinct unit, rather than as colonial cannon-fodder within the larger BEF, who were contributing to winning this war. Although it is beyond the scope of this work, Aitken also organized a media blitz involving photographs, film, and art. It is most remarkable that once again it was Aitken who, in order to meet his self-declared dual mandate of publicizing and documenting the war, forged ahead and established official photographers, cinematographers, and artists to document the war for future generations.⁷¹ "There is no event of any importance that ever happens up and down that long line in France," boasted the CWRO, "which is not chronicled, photographed or painted for the benefit of the people who sit at home."⁷²

THE "MAD MULLAH" OF CANADA, Sir Sam Hughes, was finally removed from Borden's Cabinet in December 1916 for increasingly erratic behaviour.⁷³ There were few tears for the former minister and one of his veteran Cabinet colleagues, Sir George Foster, aptly summed up the situation: "the nightmare is removed."⁷⁴ Hughes had served his country as best he could: his supporters would note his successful prewar preparation of the Militia and his orchestration of the First Contingent in a timely fashion; his detractors fumed at the disorder he had sown by attempting to maintain control of the overseas forces from Ottawa. However one views Hughes – and historians have not treated him kindly – Aitken's service to, and close friendship with, the minister from 1914 to 1916 had paid historical dividends.⁷⁵ Aitken would no longer liaise with the British military and he would no longer influence the appointment of senior Canadian officers. Nonetheless, Aitken had firmly entrenched his small historical empire in the administrative structure, and no one was willing to take on the aggressive Sir Max, even without his former political backing. At the same time, despite having been heavily involved in British politics and having conspired to bring Lloyd George to power, he had not been asked to join the Cabinet. Once again he was bitterly disappointed. Aitken later claimed to friends that he found solace in building an "historical legacy" for Canada, both in a war archives and in creating a war legend.⁷⁶

In addition to its multimedia productions, the CWRO continued to focus on writing full-length monographs, with volumes 2 and 3 of *Canada in Flanders* published in the spring of 1917 and early 1918. With the success of volume 1, both in sales and in public acclaim, based partially on his access to the war records, Aitken used his CWRO officers in the field to supply him with information and documents relating to the 1916 battles of St. Eloi and Mount Sorrel. As both engagements were particularly costly – St. Eloi was an outright Canadian failure – Sir Max shied away from the controversies and again focused on the heroic nature of the Canadian soldier. With St. Eloi, Aitken struggled to portray the actions of confused Canadian soldiers who had been lost on the battlefield, holding the wrong parts of the front and, as a result, had eventually been pushed back by a German counterattack. Aitken had gathered damning testimony that suggested at least a few of the Canadians had reconnoitred the ground and ascertained which parts of the front they actually held, but that this information had been overlooked by Major General Richard Turner's divisional staff. The diary of Captain D.E. McIntyre, the intelligence officer of the 6th Brigade, noted clearly that he had reported on 6 April 1916 that the Germans held the craters at the front and not the Canadians as battalion, brigade, and divisional headquarters believed. Sir Max Aitken tried to deal with this evidence by writing around the question of what the divisional headquarters knew at the time, but in his fourth draft, he struck out large portions of his account, including: "It is curious that his [McIntyre's] observation did not dissipate the error about the craters in the minds of the High Command."[77] In this case of self-censorship, Aitken felt that it was worth avoiding the issue to protect the reputations of Turner and the Canadians, rather than expose the truth that might have tarnished their collective war record. Despite following a similar style and structure, volume 2 was not nearly as popular as volume 1.

By 1917 the energies of the CWRO were spread thin. The responsibilities included overseeing the collection of war records, the official photographs, film and art programs, as well as liaising with journalists and newspapers. The printed word of semi-official histories had been partly supplanted by a host of other publicity tools. There were, moreover, many other British histories that had been published since the first volume of *Canada in Flanders*. But the series remained authoritative for many Canadians, and if the second and third volumes did not have the same influence as the first groundbreaking effort, they were still important in laying the foundation for subsequent historical interpretations. And it was Sir Max Aitken, rather than the soldiers themselves, who was the progenitor of this Canadian interpretation of the war, which he crafted from access to their war records, firsthand accounts, and his own belief in how the battles should be portrayed.

But Aitken had begun to lose interest in day-to-day operations at CWRO in 1917. He was still making all key decisions and lending his name and title to ensure that the CWRO received adequate support, but most of the work was delegated to junior officers. As part of this devolution, Lord Beaverbrook (he had been elevated to the peerage at the end of 1916) handed the reins over to Charles G.D. Roberts to complete volume 3 of *Canada in Flanders*, which would focus on the 1916 Battle of the Somme. With his sturdy build, strongly lined face, and toothbrush moustache, the fifty-seven-year-old Roberts looked comfortable in his British major's uniform. Roberts was one of Canada's most prominent poets and although he would author the third volume, Beaverbrook remained the chief overseer of the series, insisting every so often on editorial changes or that evidence be collected from the

War Diaries to magnify the "heroic deeds" of the Canadians.[78] Amid the grim fighting of the Somme, where 24,000 Canadians became casualties from September to November 1916, there were indeed many stories of sacrifice and bravery. These were emphasized over the futility of a battle that swallowed materiel and men at an unprecedented rate. The image of senseless slaughter that would later come to the foreground in the late 1920s with the outpourings of the "disillusioned" generation, was, under Beaverbrook's guiding hand, subsumed to this heroic notion of brave Canadian lads winning the war.

The writing of contemporary history is always difficult, especially when one's subjects are alive or recently martyred, and it is all the more trying during the uncertainty of an ongoing war. Despite their overwhelming success among the public, all three volumes of *Canada in Flanders* were subject to criticisms by Canadian soldiers.[79] The innate suspicion of soldiers at the front of all things in the rear (basically anything farther back than company headquarters) was keenly directed towards Beaverbrook's work. For those who already knew about his close ties to Hughes, there was the added misgiving that Beaverbrook was producing political propaganda to prop up his friends. Certainly Generals Sir Richard Turner, Garnet Hughes, and David Watson received aid, with the Eye Witness even going so far as to manipulate the appointment of commanding officers to ensure that his friends received their proper due – for example, saving Turner's job after St. Eloi; ensuring that Hughes (the minister's son) received command of the 1st Brigade and later the 5th Division; and removing competitors to Watson so that he was given the 4th Division.[80] That is not to say that without Beaverbrook's support others did not thrive – as generals such as Louis Lipsett, Archibald Macdonell, and Arthur Currie obviously did – but it was clear to many in the highly political and partisan Canadian military structure that Aitken looked out for his friends. Would he also do so in his histories? Some certainly thought so, and when volume 3 of *Canada in Flanders* was published in early 1918, the Canadian Corps commander, Lieutenant General Sir Arthur Currie, responded with vehement criticism.

With his appointment as corps commander in June 1917, Currie was the first Canadian-born officer to take the position. He had been a Militia officer before the war and what he lacked in military appearance – with his pear-shaped body seemingly ready to topple from his horse – he made up for with a planned, methodical approach to warfare. Although Currie had little charisma with which to inspire his men, he was one of the finest generals in the war, leading the Canadian Corps to a series of victories.

While Currie was fully engaged in perfecting the fighting capabilities of his corps, he was also highly cognizant of how he and his men would be remembered in history. When the general read the most recent volume of *Canada in Flanders* and found that his former division, the 1st, had been nearly left out, he was furious that this self-styled "official history" had slandered the memory of his men and their accomplishments on the Somme. Currie fumed in letters to both Prime Minister Borden and Overseas Minister Kemp that "it is my opinion that no one should have the privilege of publishing to the world a work described as the official story of the Canadian Expeditionary Force which is not a true narrative of the facts." One of the most vicious battles of the campaign, the 26 September attack on Regina Trench received only five lines, and according to Currie, his men had been denigrated by a history that proclaimed at no time "did the attacking troops get within striking distance of this last objective." That was untrue, as the 2nd and 3rd Brigades had reached the enemy trenches, suffering 2,800 casualties and receiving over 100 honours and decorations. But the loss of nearly 3,000 1st Division soldiers for no appreciable gain was not the image that Beaverbrook and the CWRO wished to portray to the public. The work of Currie's division had indeed been overlooked; moreover, what was written was inaccurate. Currie insisted that this slight was intentional and raged that the author, Roberts, never even came to see him while he was researching the narrative, this despite being at his headquarters.[81] Seething that the history had "no value whatever as an historical document," Currie was largely accurate in his criticisms.

Roberts had indeed written an uneven history of the Canadians on the Somme. Despite his reputation as a celebrated writer and poet, no major wished to feel the full wrath of his corps commander, and so Roberts pleaded in a personal letter for "allowances" when one has a "huge mass of undigested material, often conflicting, to deal with in a very limited time." But the focus of volume 3 was on the 2nd Division's attack at Courcelette on 15 September 1916, rather than the less successful and costly battles that followed (by the 1st, 3rd, and 4th Canadian Divisions), because he was writing in a style that mimicked Beaverbrook's own work. The CWRO histories emphasized Canadian success, which was very evident at Courcelette, and downplayed the failures. Although Currie demanded more recognition for his men, and a balanced history would have reflected it, he probably would not have wanted Roberts to reveal the futility of the attack, the uncut barbed wire that funnelled the infantry into killing grounds, and the uneven artillery barrage that left his troops vulnerable while crossing No Man's Land. The objectivity of history had been sacrificed at the altar of shaping public opinion and encouraging support for the war.

Despite Currie's demands for more historical accuracy – or, more likely, for greater coverage that emphasized the bravery and sacrifice of the 1st Division – Beaverbrook was unmoved. Having been appointed to Lloyd George's War Cabinet as minister of Information in March 1918, Beaverbrook did not readily accept Currie's criticisms, writing that with the "fortunes of war ... a history cannot be divided off into spaces equally allotted to each unit." That was true, but units, and especially their powerful commanders, could and did insist on proper recognition.

Aware of the partisan hierarchy of command in the CEF and back in England, Currie worried constantly that Turner or another Canadian general waiting in the wings would supplant him.[82] Beaverbrook had done his best to ensure that his friends would be given the most important command positions, and when Currie had bucked at this influence peddling, most prominently by blocking the appointment of Garnet Hughes to command of the 1st Division, he had suffered a campaign of lies and slander intended to ruin his name.[83] Currie could never pin down his enemies, but he believed that Beaverbrook and the Hughes (father and son) were involved. Furthermore, Currie knew that his operational victories from 1917 onward, although garnering the Canadian Corps a reputation as shock troops, had been won at a heavy cost. The casualty lists continued unabated, and Currie needed the historians and publicists to show the full extent of the victories, which would help justify the terrible losses.

The first histories to come out, therefore, had an enormous impact not only on the public but also on the soldiers. As Currie's correspondence made clear, he was aware that his position was insecure, and he therefore could not accept semi-official histories that ignored his men or their acts. There was more, thought Currie and the rest of the Canadian generals, to Beaverbrook's history than the simple scribblings of a political manipulator: he and the CWRO had the power to shape contemporary perceptions and to lay the foundation for future interpretations of the war.[84] If a man as powerful as Currie took notice, then it is clear that others did too.

Although Currie and the CWRO were able to put aside their differences for the rest of the war, it is perhaps not surprising that Beaverbrook cancelled work on the fourth volume of *Canada in Flanders*. Currie had also learned something from the acrimonious exchange: in late 1918 he established his own historical group, the Canadian War Narrative Section, to write his official account of the fighting rather than turning to the accomplished CWRO chroniclers. Despite having his grievances largely ignored, Currie still remained convinced of the essential work of the CWRO and passed several additional orders to all units in the corps, noting the importance of creating proper war records to document their actions and of sending them later to the CWRO for safe archiving.[85] In the end, despite the general's dislike for Beaverbrook, the two agreed to work together because they were both consumed with seeing the Canadian Corps receive its due credit. Currie prepared for both the war of No Man's Land and the war of reputations that would follow.

In this wartime struggle for recognition, the CWRO continued in its role of writing supportive Canadian accounts. The Eye Witness reports of 1915 had been replaced, by 1917, with a concentrated barrage of journalistic dispatches emanating from the CWRO that emphasized the unique nature of the Canadian soldier and were aimed at the British and Canadian public on the home front. The result was an effective propaganda program that disseminated short sketches of

Canadian courage throughout the Empire.[86] For example, the CWRO ran a series of special articles at the end of 1917 "for the benefit of the British Public" in order to emphasize "what a democratic Army Canada possesses."[87] This was not a far leap from the enduring militia myth forged after the War of 1812, which provided a convenient set of Canadian heroes and did not require the government to invest in a professional military. The CWRO continued its publicity campaign with the British press in 1918 by sending out pre-written stories to all British newspapers. A similar article by Major T.G. Roberts, which was published in a series of British newspapers, underscored how Canadian boys had been fashioned into a great fighting army: "The prize-fighter may make a good soldier, but the mild young man in the corner book-shop makes a better soldier ... The junior clerk who yesterday trembled before the displeasure of his paunchy employer today dies gloriously for England on the field of battle." Although Roberts did not detail how or why the civilian made this transition to soldier, the notion of a democratic army was stressed repeatedly in CWRO-disseminated accounts. The idea of the inherently superior civilian soldier who put down pen and plough for rifle to defeat the professional German soldier was in direct contrast with what most British generals, especially Haig and Currie, saw as the key factors in the Canadian operational success from 1917 onward. Instead, it was continuous training and the maintenance of strong discipline in the ranks that had forged the corps' effectiveness.[88] With their long-standing and multi-faceted publicity campaign, the CWRO could rightly claim that its work "has done more than a little to increase Canadian prestige and correct still prevalent misconceptions as to Canadian affairs."[89] Yet some of the ideas emanating from the CWRO conflicted with reality, while others avoided the real structural and tactical reasons for success in favour of highlighting racial or national characteristics that supposedly animated all Canadian soldiers.

From April 1917 onward, the Canadians won an unbroken series of victories: Vimy Ridge in April, Fresnoy in May, Hill 70 in August, Passchendaele in October-November, and the many battles that made up the last Hundred Days offensives. The Canadians had honed their attack doctrine of close infantry and artillery support and evolved into an elite force within the BEF, and Currie was not shy about claiming that his corps was the "hardest-hitting force" in the "British Empire."[90] Nonetheless, due to censorship restrictions, the imperial war journalists were not always able to distinguish between the initiatives of British troops and those of the Canadians and Australians. Many of the successful Dominion operations (the capture of trenches, villages, or what was left of them) had therefore been attributed to British units or the BEF in general. With the Dominion forces now viewing themselves as national armies, Currie was furious at the thought of being cheated out of recognition, and as a result he wrote, "the people in Canada would like to receive the fullest accounts of the doings of the Corps." That was a diplomatic way of demanding proper recognition for hard-won deeds. To codify the sacrifice,

Canadian Corps intelligence tabulated that during the battles of Amiens and the crashing of the Hindenburg Line in the Hundred Days campaign, a two-month period of fierce fighting, the Corps had captured 21,000 prisoners and 300 guns, and defeated 34 German divisions. During this time the Canadian Corps, with its four over-strength divisions, accounted for more than 25 percent of the prisoners and 40 percent of the guns for the entire BEF. It was necessary for Currie that those at home understood the extent of their corps' contribution in battle. Such figures had to be disseminated in order to strengthen his position against the political intriguers calling for his sacking due to the high casualties suffered in these successful but costly campaigns.[91]

Despite both political and military urging by the Canadians, many of the British journalists and press censors continued to believe that there was no need to distinguish between Dominion and British troops.[92] Against this perceived discrimination, the Canadian Corps was forced to rely heavily on its established publicity machine to propagate its deeds. The CWRO remained the focal point for disseminating information from Canadian war correspondents such as F.A. Mackenzie, J.F.B. Livesay, Rowland Hill, Fred James and its own CWRO staff, whose job it was to "stiffen the war-weary backbone of Canada."[93] A conscious effort was made to have Canadian press stories sent to all British newspapers in the hope of combating what staff officers at Canadian General Headquarters (GHQ) viewed as a bias against them.

At the same time, these perceived slights to the Dominion armies were viewed differently within the rest of the BEF, with many imperial divisional commanders complaining that their units were largely ignored in favour of the more easily identifiable Dominion troops.[94] Despite conflicting and chauvinistic views of the coverage, it is clear that armies fighting in the field were also keenly aware of the battle over shaping and sharpening their own reputations. Without the CWRO, it is likely that the Canadians would not have garnered the same recognition. The notion of the colonial storm trooper, which has since been codified in much of the historical writing over the twentieth century and was based primarily on the success of the Australians and Canadians in the last two years of the war, might very well have been more muted. It was not, with one *Manchester Guardian* reporter noting sarcastically shortly after the Armistice that it was "long open to doubt whether there was anybody but Canadians fighting in France."[95] Such an observation reflected Canadian operational victories no doubt, but it also reflected Beaverbrook's work in record creation and archiving and the effective exploitation of such documentary resources in producing pro-Canadian publicity in many forums and media.

ON 11 NOVEMBER 1918, James E. Hahn, a staff officer at David Watson's 4th Divisional headquarters, recounted in his memoirs a toast at the time of the Armistice: "At this moment there are men who are fortunate to be on the Honours Lists, there are men who are fortunate to be on Lists of Decorations; but at this moment how fortunate are we, who are on the list of survivors."[96] With more than 60,000 Canadian dead in four years of terrible fighting, most citizen-soldiers had a fervent desire to go home and be reunited with loved ones. Yet it would be several months before demobilization could begin, as armies were ordered to occupy Germany, and the transportation of millions of men required enormously complicated plans. During this time, the CWRO worried that unit war records were in danger of being discarded or lost, as military discipline was perceived as being far more lax.[97] As they had throughout the war, historical officers therefore went into the field to ensure that records would be properly sent to the CWRO.

The CWRO got what it wished for, but the thousands of records that passed into its control flooded the small staff. Although some preliminary sorting and arrangement was carried out, it was decided that most of the cataloguing would have to be done in Ottawa. In early 1919 the CWRO began planning the transfer of the war records to Canada, which consisted of more than 10,000 boxes (and this did not include the voluminous administrative records relating to pay and personnel held by other record-keeping units). This was done to avoid the possibility of loss or damage, especially in the event those same guardians should be demobilized before the records were loaded on to the ships.[98] The records would eventually go to the Public Archives as Lord Beaverbrook had promised Doughty, but first they would be used by the army's official historian to craft his historical series.

While the CWRO was caring for the war records, Doughty had always believed in the totality of archival material. In March 1917, he had written Acting Prime Minister Sir George Foster that he should document all the war records being created in Canada and overseas. Such a survey would be in the "historical interest of Canada"; an order-in-council was passed, giving Doughty a salary and a staff of two: William Wood and Gustave Lanctôt.[99] All three went overseas in late 1917 to document the war records so that the Public Archives staff would know which series and types of records they would eventually inherit. Despite high hopes, the archives group met with limited success, and most units had little time for these badgering archivists.[100]

While the small group failed to achieve its laudable goals, it was able to play an important role in gathering war trophies for the Canadian people. On an informal basis, Doughty worked with British officers to ensure that some of the captured war trophies, all of which were automatically sent to the new Imperial War Museum for selection, were reserved for Canada.[101] In December 1918, Doughty was appointed to a Commission on War Records and War Trophies, since he was one of the leading civil servants in the country and an expert on history, heritage, and records. The great collector, just as he had for fifteen years, began to negotiate the release of CEF-captured booty to bring back to Canada, and then to distribute it across the nation. The committee also returned with a strongly worded document suggesting that a "Canadian War Archives" be built to act as a memorial for all the tangible documents – texts, photographs, art, film, and other material – that represented Canada's sacrifice in the Great War.[102] Beaverbrook, who had pushed for a similar building to house his war art, hoped to prod the government along and even commissioned an architect to design a building.[103]

In addition to the gathering and archiving of records for the official historian, Canadian War Memorial, or Public Archives, the CWRO continued to highlight the Canadian Corps. The CWRO published a few regimental histories during the war, which were to augment the story told within the *Canada in Flanders* series; another short account of Canadian Victoria Cross winners was distributed after the war. The CWRO also encouraged and assisted in the publication of two histories of the Canadian military effort in the Hundred Days: Fred James's *Canada's Triumph* (1918) and J.F.B. Livesay's *Canada's Hundred Days* (1919). James and Livesay had been war correspondents. They filed their stories through the CWRO during the war, and they benefited from the assistance of the CWRO.[104] James's history had been published before the end of the war, and a hasty second edition of several thousand copies, which carried the Canadians up to the capture of Mons on 11 November 1918, "sold out before they could be delivered."[105] Livesay's work is the better remembered of the two, but it was written in the same heroic mould of the *Canada in Flanders* series. Despite having had significant contact with the infantry, Livesay felt he could still write that "hot-blooded youth doesn't care how long the war goes on; it is his great adventure; to him it is a 'lovely war.'"[106] If Livesay failed to capture the true spirit of the soldiers, he, like Beaverbrook, had written to bring glory to the Canadian Corps and ensure that the nation's fighting force received full recognition for its deeds. Furthermore, while the Canadians had been elevated to elite soldiers, Sir Arthur Currie, condemned by politicians and even some of his own men, was being derided as a butcher who callously drove the Canadians too hard and sacrificed too many to achieve his goals. *Canada's Hundred Days* was written to ensure that Currie received fair treatment in the first histories while at the same time buttressing the general's reputation against the epidemic of rumours that was spreading through the CEF and the home front.[107] It was clear, then, that the war of reputations, both of the Canadian Corps and its commander, had already started early in Canada's first military histories.

BORDEN AND CURRIE met shortly after the war, and the prime minister informed the general that "certain sections of the American press have adopted the attitude of belittling the importance of operations of the Canadians." Although Currie supplied Borden with a short narrative on recent operations, it was clear that a full history was needed to defend the reputation of the Canadian Corps.[108] With Currie still smarting from the belief that both the British press and GHQ had downplayed the success of his corps, an official account based on authentic documents would offer, he believed, just rewards. Equally important, an official report might help to defend against the rumours that were beginning to spread relating to Currie's command in the last year of the war, which had been enormously successful but equally costly to his men.

One of the CWRO reports noted that it was necessary to "secure for Canada those facts of War, which in the dim future may come to be regarded simply as legend or folk-lore unless they are carefully recovered in black and white at the present time and are carefully preserved for all time."[109] Although Currie agreed with the sentiment, he did not want to leave the task of writing the official report of operations to the CWRO. Having lost more than a few battles to Beaverbrook over the nature of the first semi-official CEF history, Currie set up his own historical section to ensure that he had control over how the Hundred Days would be codified in print and presented to the public.

Although there is no indication that Currie interfered with the writing of the history, the corps commander did order one of his most gifted and respected senior officers, Brigadier General Raymond Brutinel, who had been an innovator of machine-gun tactics during the war, to oversee the historical work. "I am very anxious that this report should be very complete and very accurate," wrote Currie, and under Brutinel the Canadian War Narrative Section (CWNS) was established on 20 December 1918.[110]

Currie ordered all divisional commanders to give full support to the narrators. The cooperation was nearly total, as Currie was clearly anxious to see the work published, but also because any failure to comply might result in units being ignored in the final report.[111] Currie also ordered that documents be loaned to the CWNS, which must have been worrisome to the members of the CWRO, as this was obviously an overlap of responsibilities. However, with Currie's backing the CWNS had priority in the collection, arrangement, and use of operational records to craft this history.

Brutinel set guidelines, in particular that the CWNS historians should strive for "clearness and accuracy ... [but that] no adverse comment need be made respecting the leadership or conduct of formations or Troops acting in conjunction with the Canadian Corps."[112] As we have seen, however, Currie wished to see the Canadian Corps receive its full credit. With a mass of documents at its disposal and even more arriving every day, within three months the CWNS compiled a competent, if dry, history of the Corps in the Hundred Days. The pounding nature of the fighting was highlighted and that helped to explain why almost 20 percent of all Canadian battlefield casualties occurred during these ninety-six days of battle. Having spearheaded the BEF, the four over-strength Canadian divisions met and defeated parts of forty-seven German divisions. While Canadian intelligence officers counted every enemy soldier confronted in battle to reach this astounding figure, Currie still crowed to one friend that "We took care of 25%" of the total German armies on the Western Front, "leaving it to the American Army, the French Army, the Belgian Army and the rest of the British Army to look after the balance."[113]

The final history was an important document for Currie as Sir Sam Hughes had publicly voiced the long-standing undercurrent of rumours against Currie in the House of Commons in early March 1919. Protected by parliamentary immunity, Hughes accused Currie of "needlessly sacrificing the lives of Canadian soldiers" in order to elevate his own status among the British. Currie should be "tried summarily by court martial and punished so far as the law would allow ... You cannot find one Canadian soldier returning from France who will not curse the name of the officer who ordered that attack on Mons," lectured Hughes to his fellow members of parliament.[114] Currie was deeply hurt by the attack, even more so since there were few politicians who were willing to stand up for him and against the fiery ex-minister. Without accurate reports, however, many of Currie's friends in parliament had been hamstrung in their ability to rebut Hughes's wild claims. Although the corps commander was eventually defended by Cy Peck, a newly elected MP, former battalion commander, and Victoria Cross winner, no minister rose in defence.[115] Borden, to whom Currie had offered key advice during the war on how to deal with his British political counterparts, refused to engage Hughes until months later, and even then he never effectively refuted the claim that Currie had needlessly killed Canadian soldiers. The CWNS report, then, was an important first step for Currie in reclaiming his damaged reputation from Hughes, his cabal, and the Canadian soldiers, many of whom both believed and added to the rumours.[116]

The CWNS history was also a concern to Currie's divisional commanders. Major General David Watson of the 4th Division wrote to Currie in early February that he wished to read a draft before it was published to ensure that his division received a fair accounting. "I have no objection whatever to your seeing this narrative," wrote Currie, "in fact I would like you to see it, because I am very anxious that it should not only be complete but accurate; but to intimate that, under the arrangements now pertaining, justice would not be done to your Division, is to insinuate something which I don't like." Currie finished somewhat menacingly by indicating that Watson should have "confidence in my ability to do justice to the operations of the Fourth Division."[117] It appeared that Currie, while demanding full glory for the Canadian Corps, would be the final arbiter for ensuring the accuracy and fullness of those first accounts, which laid the groundwork for conceptualizing the conflict.

Currie also paid close attention to what other historians were writing about his corps. When *The Final Blow of the First Army in 1918* was published that same month, Currie had the unenviable task of complaining to his old Army commander,

General Sir Henry Horne, that the accomplishments of the Canadian Corps had been largely ignored in this history. Just as during the war, when the British press downplayed or referred mistakenly to Canadian battles as British ones, "it seems as if the author was reluctant to refer to the Canadians at any time," wrote Currie. No mention was made of the hard fighting on 30-31 August against the Fresnes-Rouvroy line, and no credit was given to the 1st and 4th Divisions' monumental crashing of the Canal du Nord on 27 September. Currie once again showed his desire to have his corps recognized.[118] Horne wrote back to Currie a week later, downplaying the problems of the monograph by noting that it was not an "official history," but indicating that he regretted the Canadians had been ignored.[119] In an often-quoted and decontextualized remark that was originally made in private, however, Horne complained that, "the Canadian Corps is perhaps rather apt to take all the credit it can for everything, and to consider that the BEF consists of the Canadian Corps and some other troops."[120] To the British, the Canadians again appeared bent on self-promotion; to the Canadians, it confirmed that they would have to be vigilant in securing proper recognition for their deeds.

Having finished the narrative on the Hundred Days, the CWNS was demobilized back to Canada. Along with twelve tons of records, the CWNS historians found, on arrival in Ottawa, that no preparation had been made for their establishment, and they were temporarily stationed in an old garage. Equally troubling was the confusion over who was responsible for the CEF's records. Would it be the CWNS or the CWRO? A third organization was also in competition for the records, since the Department of Militia and Defence had appointed Brigadier General E.A. Cruikshank, a soldier with a distinguished military and historical career, as the war's official historian in mid-1917.[121]

Official historians had been established over a decade earlier in the British army. The British Committee for Imperial Defence had been organized in 1904 to reform the British Army, and as a result it developed a small historical section to educate staff officers and create practical "lessons learned" monographs for future soldiers.[122] The military reforms required after the South African War (1899-1902) proved that an army could only improve and evolve if it understood its past operations. From the start, then, official histories had an operational role. Interestingly, though, while a British official history of the South African War was begun in 1907, the Canadian government had planned as far back as 1899 to have an official history written of the Canadian participation. Those plans ultimately failed, however, when the historian, F.J. Dixon, decided to stay in South Africa instead of returning to Canada.[123] But now, eighteen years later, Canada had its first official historian. Would he simply follow the general staff precedent and craft a history primarily for the military profession to understand the nature of warfare? The decision was put off until the records arrived from overseas in mid-1919.

But who would use the records to write an official account of the war, now that there were three historical sections? General Brutinel had his own opinions, and he informed Currie that he hoped that his CWNS could be kept together to author a full history of the war, as it "would be of very great importance to Canada," and he did not think that Cruikshank could finish such a history due to his advanced age.[124] Brutinel also suggested that Brigadier General J.H. MacBrien might write the official history, but MacBrien would set his sights a little higher, becoming the chief of staff. That MacBrien had no training as an historian seemed not to worry Brutinel, who also had none. As official historian, however, Cruikshank was always an outsider since he had not served overseas during the war. But he did have the backing of the department. The CWRO was disbanded first, especially since Beaverbrook, its powerful patron, remained in London. In 1920 the CWNS was combined with the Army Historical Section, and Major A.F. Duguid, a researcher for the CWNS, became chief assistant to Cruikshank. A year later, Duguid would be elevated to the position of official historian, and tasked with the writing of Canada's Great War effort.

ONE EARLY REVIEWER of *Canada in Flanders* observed that the book "lifts the veil of war and tells us not only what our heroes did, but who they were."[125] Beaverbrook and the CWRO may have revealed an aspect of the war that was previously unavailable to the public, but their unveiling was not a disinterested act: while pulling away the curtain, they had their own agenda to present. Not everyone liked Beaverbrook or his work: one Canadian staff officer categorized his writing as "products of hearsay and collaboration, these spurious masterpieces of an incompetent absentee."[126] Currie was not much kinder, describing the historical series as bearing "no more resemblance to the true story of the period it depicts than a mutton stew does to the sheep itself."[127] Beaverbrook was well aware of the pitfalls of writing contemporary history, warning that his history was based on records "snatched from the firing line, and what they gained in vividness, they may have lost in accuracy. It is for the historian of the future to decide."[128] Future historians would indeed clear up mistakes that were made because of a lack of time to consider or even locate evidence. Until then, though, several generations would rely heavily on the first histories produced or supported by the CWRO, and all historians are in debt to Beaverbrook and his staff for their work in collecting and shaping the war archives of the CEF.

Beaverbrook had his enemies, as all powerful men do, but it was his important role in the initial chaotic Canadian administrative hierarchy and his close friendship with Sir Sam Hughes that allowed him to exert considerable power, as no historian or archivist would have been able to in the same situation. Beaverbrook was also one of the premier propagandists of the war. "This strange attractive gnome with an odour of genius about him," was little liked and much feared; more than a few called him "Beenacrook," but they did so behind his back.[129] And although he was distrusted by all three Canadian Corps commanders in the field, both Byng and Currie came to recognize the important work of the CWRO in not only preserving their legacy through the archiving of war records, but also in publicizing the deeds of the Canadian soldier at the sharp end.

Our understanding of the past is always changing, ever nuanced, and always reinterpreted by subsequent generations. Despite Beaverbrook's impressive work, he was practical enough to realize that his histories were but the first of many to follow. Nevertheless, with the actual sources at his fingertips, Beaverbrook and the CWRO were able to "steal a march" on other chroniclers and present their version of the war and the role of the Canadians in it. Beaverbrook wrote with a purpose in mind – to glorify the deeds of the Canadians. And he did so with a flare and style that made his histories bestsellers. Along with his CWRO officers and their vast output during the war, Beaverbrook constructed an image of the Canadian soldier reflecting his own ideals. Canadians were depicted as a northern race of rugged civilian-soldiers who were separate from their British cousins. This image was embraced because it was consistent with British prewar views of the Canadian frontier and the men who tamed it. Yet there was more to it than that. Beaverbrook's writing built on these myths and the CWRO's primary goal, despite the medium used, was a steady barrage of propaganda to distinguish the Canadians within the wider context of the BEF. Beaverbrook laid the groundwork for collecting the war records, and then he used those same records to fashion the first depictions of the war, to present the Canadian soldier in a superior light, buttressed with seemingly authentic official records.

The archival records, then, remained an essential component in supporting the publicity function of the CWRO, and later underpinned all subsequent interpretations of the Great War. It is also clear, however, that archives are not just the bare bones of history for future generations; they are part of the history-making process. Archives are not neutral, nor are their creation impartial.[130] There is always a mandate to collect something, to privilege some voices while silencing others. Such was the case with the CWRO intent on documenting Canadian actions that glorified the heroics of battle over the futility of trench warfare, and emphasized the success of the democratic citizen in defeating the professional German military machine. These records eventually helped to form the official archives that subsequent generations of historians have used to formulate their views of the Canadian Corps. The notion of an objective archival record, collected in a disinterested fashion, is problematic. It is nearly impossible to gauge the influence of the CWRO officers on the war diarists and other creators of war records, but it is clear from the CWRO officers' reports back to London that their prime mandate was to ensure that records were created to document actions. That alone suggests that it was not simply the soldiers at the front who wrote up their daily accounts. They were influenced by regulations, orders, time constraints, and the inability to know what was happening along the front, not to mention the constant prodding by CWRO staff who visited the battalions to inquire into and influence the record-keeping process. There is no evidence to suggest that Canadian records were fabricated to cover up disasters in the war – as disasters, along with the victories, are plainly evident in the war archives. However, one should be cautioned by the anecdote offered by Sir Basil Liddell Hart, who recounted the story of a French general. During the desperate March Offensive, French reinforcements were ordered to counterattack. It was found, however, that the line had already been lost the day before. Upon being informed of the loss, the general refused to destroy the order, and "with a knowing smile, thereupon remarked: '*C'est pour l'histoire.*'" Much time was spent during the war, warned Liddell Hart, in "preparing the ground for its historians."[131] With the CWRO's involvement and the various factors affecting the creation of Canadian war records, these primary documents are products more of process and influence than accurate and disinterested mirrors of acts and facts.

Whatever the operational successes of the Canadian Corps on the Western Front from 1917 onward – and there was an unbroken run – one must at least acknowledge that a portion of the Canadian reputation as shock troops came from the CWRO's publicity campaign. Beaverbrook's desire to nurture a Canadian image separate from that of his British counterparts, when coupled with the Canadian Corps' operational successes, helped to forge a distinct Canadian identity as elite troops. As the sole agency of publicity in the CEF, the CWRO developed a steady deluge of stories, photos, exhibitions, films, commemorative works, and histories to ensure that Canada received its full credit. It is always difficult to estimate the impact of publicity campaigns, but anecdotal evidence suggests the CWRO made an impression. British war correspondent Philip Gibbs commended Beaverbrook in his 1920 memoirs, writing that the Canadians "organized their publicity" in a "masterful way, and were determined that what Canada did the world should know – and damn all censorship."[132] Attesting to that same publicity campaign, John Buchan, the director of Britain's Department of Information, famous novelist, and future Canadian governor general, certainly saw the results of this "human dynamo's" work. He observed somewhat incredulously that the wide circulation of CWRO books and pamphlets, as well as photographs and film, might lead one to believe "that Canada is running the war."[133]

Beaverbrook wisely noted in the preface to the second volume of the *Canada in Flanders* series that the gathering of the war records allowed for the "framework [to be] erected for an official narrative. This is a prudent measure which will be endorsed by Canadian students of history, since there is a growing tendency to demand a full and intelligent documentary record of our progress." Soldiers were often forced to create records in "the face of grave danger and complete exhaustion, when they might well have been excused from troubling about such trivialities as to what posterity would think of them."[134] But posterity would be very interested in these Great War heroes, and countless historians would study them over the next century. These same historians would rely heavily on the war records. The conscious moulding of memory and laying of an historical foundation by Lord Beaverbrook has had an enduring legacy in Canadian historiography since the guns fell silent on 11 November 1918.

2
The War of Reputations, 1918-39

> *History will be kind on me for I propose to write it.*
> — Sir Winston Churchill
>
> *Soldiers fight battles, but historians make the history of them.*
> — Sir Arthur Currie

One need not fully embrace the belief that Canadians gained their identity on the slopes of Vimy Ridge in order to acknowledge that Canada as a country was never the same after the Great War. The incredible exertions in that four-year bloodletting cost more than 60,000 Canadian lives, and another 138,000 battle casualties. With a population of not yet eight million, the equivalent proportional loss for Canada's 2005 population would be roughly a quarter of a million dead, and half a million more wounded and maimed in body and mind. The strain of war left the country fractured along regional, linguistic, and class lines. At the same time, Canada began to emerge as an industrialized nation, largely through the massive war industry that fed imperial and Dominion armies. The Borden government had enfranchised women to vote in 1917, and Canada had distinguished itself as a war ally, even if a junior one, as the nation took important steps towards full autonomy. The Great War signified Canada's coming of age.

When the war ended on 11 November 1918, the civilian-soldiers were aching to be reunited with their families. Within eight months the Canadian Expeditionary Force (CEF) had been demobilized and virtually disappeared. The veterans who were returned to their families, clutching their kit bags and memories, knew all the same that they had taken part in something unique in the history of the young nation. Most soldiers were all too happy to leave the war behind them, but more than a few were anxious about how the war experience would be captured and codified in popular memory. The first generation of historical writing, unofficial, semi-official, or official, was an attempt to find meaning in the war and document its momentous effects. At the same time, much of the literature ensured that the hard-won reputation of the Canadian Corps, its front-line soldiers and commanders, was carefully nurtured and protected.

Lord Beaverbrook took pride during the Great War in crafting an historical legacy for all Canadians. While the words and deeds of Canadian soldiers were "snatched from the firing line, from men still red hot from the fiery ordeal," Beaverbrook acknowledged that his battlefield accounts, and those produced by his Canadian War Records Office (CWRO) staff, were a first stab at history.[1] When it had been suggested in 1916 that he begin work on an official history, Beaverbrook quite rightly believed it could "only be undertaken after the War. As yet many matters of importance to the narrative cannot be disclosed."[2] Moreover, Beaverbrook had done his duty for Canada and was not interested in devoting years, probably decades, to the writing of an official history. That role fell to Brigadier General Ernest A. Cruikshank, a Militia officer and authority on Canadian military history.[3]

E.A. Cruikshank was born in the Niagara Peninsula, and after an education at Upper Canada College, he took it upon himself to document and popularize the role of the Militia in defending Canada during the American Revolution, the War of 1812, and the Fenian Raids. He believed in both compiling and making available the original records in a series of document histories. Cruikshank was a respected historian who was elected to the Royal Society of Canada in 1906, and after nearly twenty-two years in the Militia, he was appointed to the Permanent Force and given the prestigious command of Military District No. 13 in Alberta in 1909.[4] After a long and distinguished career, his reputation was seriously damaged in 1916 when a number of his soldiers rioted in Calgary. Senior officers at the Department of Militia and Defence felt that Cruikshank, who was close to retirement, had lost his grip, and one suggested that "a change in command ... [was] very necessary."[5] Cruikshank was transferred to Ottawa to finish off his career as the official historian.

Although the Department of Militia and Defence did not formally establish the Historical Section until November 1918, Cruikshank had worked on a number of historical projects since his arrival in Ottawa in early 1917, including the orderly selection and destruction of records not deemed historical, extending as far back as Confederation.[6] The general found it difficult to begin researching or writing the official history since the war records were still held overseas by the other two historical organizations: Lord Beaverbrook's Canadian War Records Office and Sir Arthur Currie's Canadian War Narrative Section (CWNS). Perhaps this isolation from the records encouraged Cruikshank's belief that any official history of the CEF would need to be placed within its Canadian military context, since this was something that could be done immediately. And so he started his first volume of the CEF by examining the history and documentary evidence from the mid-eighteenth century. Publishing three volumes of documents copied from the Public Archives, there seemed to be, at best, only a haphazard selection process.[7] The enormous exertions of Canadians in the Great War would require much more.

Cruikshank's fourth volume, completed in 1920, carried the story of the CEF up to the 1915 Battle of Second Ypres.[8] Unfortunately, what Cruikshank gained in expediency, he lost in quality. Unattractively presented, with no maps or illustrations, and containing only twenty-eight pages of narrative and hundreds of pages of decontextualized reports and orders, the Great War monograph was almost unanimously panned by senior officers who, now freed from fighting, began to take an interest in the history of "their" war. "One feels that it was necessarily written by a man whose absence from the operation deprived him of the power of living the events," wrote Currie. "It lacks fire and imagination and impressiveness."[9] This was not a case of senior generals disagreeing with Cruikshank's interpretation but rather that a work of mere documents was simply unacceptable, especially when compared to wartime writing such as Beaverbrook's semi-official histories or Currie's 1918 report prepared by the CWNS.

Although Cruikshank had completed four volumes of published documents and an admirable summary of the war for the *Canada Year Book* in 1919, his vision of an official history did not correspond with that of the senior officers. However, he had received little instruction on the nature of the series, and since most of his previous historical work had consisted of compiling and writing multi-volume document-histories of the War of 1812 and the Canadian Militia, he clearly saw this method as a suitable approach to the CEF official history.[10] Heeding the criticism of Currie and others, Chief of the General Staff (CGS) J.H. MacBrien forbade the publication of his volume on the CEF and Cruikshank was retired in 1921.[11] His replacement was Colonel A.F. Duguid, a decorated artillery officer with a prewar engineering degree.[12] Duguid had no training as an historian, but senior officers saw his CEF service as more important.

Archer Fortescue Duguid was born in Aberdeenshire, Scotland, on 31 August 1887, but moved to Canada in 1906 after a doctor determined that he needed a drier climate to combat health problems. He studied civil engineering at McGill University and held a temporary commission in the Royal Canadian Horse Artillery.[13] When war broke out in 1914, Duguid had recently finished working as a railway engineer and accepted a commission with a Militia artillery battery. As a member of the First Contingent, he served as an artillery lieutenant at Second Ypres and Festubert before he was invalided back to England, suffering from stress and exhaustion. After he recuperated, however, he was promoted to captain and served with the 23rd Howitzer Battery through the 1916 battles of St. Eloi, Mount Sorrel, and the Somme. He proved to be a reliable officer and was elevated to brigade major of the 2nd Canadian Divisional Artillery before Vimy in April 1917. Duguid was wounded less than two months later, but he continued to serve during the 1917 battles of Hill 70 and Passchendaele. Following those difficult campaigns, Duguid was awarded the Distinguished Service Order in June 1918, two months after he had been made General Staff Officer 2, for the 3rd Canadian Division. Without question Duguid could be proud of his military service record.

The 1921 order-in-council that appointed Duguid as head of the Army Historical Section (AHS) was explicit in noting that one of his duties was to fashion an official history of the Great War.¹⁴ Having observed the rough reception of Cruikshank's hurried work, Duguid must have recognized that a proper, official history would have to be a thoroughly detailed narrative, befitting the achievements of the CEF. Almost immediately, however, he was inundated with a number of requests to participate in additional historical projects. Duguid was forced to attend to every one, as all departmental historical concerns were part of his mandated order-in-council duties. With only a limited staff, the resources of the AHS were spread thinly. Furthermore, Duguid received no orders from senior officers regarding prioritization.¹⁵ Although the work of the Historical Section was not a central issue for senior officers, who were struggling to meet the debt-ridden government's demands for massive postwar cutbacks, a May 1921 letter from Minister of Militia and Defence Hugh Guthrie indicated that he believed the "principal duty of the Historical Section will be the writing of the Official History."¹⁶ It is certain that Duguid recognized the importance of a history series, but accomplishing that goal was another matter. An official history would require at least a decade of work, but Duguid soon found that the constant requests for information or historical expertise steadily wore away at the time to complete this long-term research. Putting together location ledgers (to help establish where units were and therefore accurately assign battle honours) or answering inquiries, of which there were 709 in a six-month period in 1921, were detracting from his ability to lay the groundwork for the official history, but these additional responsibilities were immediate and seemingly unavoidable.¹⁷ The official history would have to wait, and in fact it would not be until 1923 that a tentative outline was even proposed.

While Duguid and his small staff began to examine the war records, there were a number of other official histories being undertaken, all of which the AHS assisted. By 1920 the senior officers in the Canadian Army Medical Corps (CAMC), which during the war had consisted of thousands of doctors and nurses, had decided that their service also needed an official history. While Professor J.C. Adami had been named Medical Historical Recorder in March 1917, and he had published a history of medical activities in the first two years of the war, the role of official historian was offered to celebrated physician and professor, Sir Andrew Macphail, who was appointed medical official historian in 1920. At the same time, Matron-in-Chief Margaret Macdonald began work on the nursing sisters' history. A year later, Colonel William Beattie, former director of the Chaplain Service, also completed a history of the chaplains.¹⁸ A history of Canadians who flew with the British flying services was also being researched, and the engineers attempted to find an historian for their service, eventually settling on Sir Andrew's brother, Colonel Alex Macphail, a decorated veteran and engineering professor at Queen's University. All placed considerable demands on the AHS.¹⁹

One of the many reports written by Duguid for his senior commanders, which were read all the way up the chain of command to the chief of the general staff, noted that Alex Macphail had been "entrusted" with the engineers' official history.[20] The choice of word "entrusted" is illuminating as it connotes the care of precious things, which was certainly how Duguid saw these histories. Unfortunately, the first organizational histories published after the war did not live up to his high standards, and the official historian used his power to ensure that several of them were not published. Both the Canadian Army Veterinary Corps and the chaplains' histories were blocked from publication, as it was better, in Duguid's opinion, to have nothing rather than produce a substandard and possibly erroneous work that failed as history, commemorative piece, or didactic textbook. The nursing sisters' history was cut in 1922, but little work had been made on it, largely because the author, Matron Macdonald, was isolated and received little assistance from the medical services or fellow nurses. Duguid did not seem overly worried about these failed attempts, but he did pursue Macdonald relentlessly to track down her archival records.[21] A "fierce little patriot ... a tiny man with the pride, bearing and mien of a Skye terrier," was how one contemporary described Duguid later in life, and the colonel took his job seriously from the start, feeling that anything published under official or semi-official auspices had to be accurate and impartial.[22]

At the end of 1923, after having sorted through more than fifty tons of records and having written a few draft narratives in addition to time-consuming work on a variety of quasi-historical committees, Duguid proposed a plan for the series. It was to be seven volumes (later raised to eight), with an additional four service volumes for the engineers, medical corps, chaplains, and nurses. The volumes would cover chronologically the battles of the Canadian Corps and relevant Canadian fighting units, but there would be no attempt to document the impact of the war on Canadian society. Nonetheless, it was an ambitious project, and since Duguid, who had never written a book in his life, had just commenced it, he could perhaps be excused for having promised that "they will be produced at the rate of one volume annually."[23] Even then, however, it would be almost a decade before the completion of the series.

A FEW HISTORIES had been published during the war but these lacked access to the war records; instead they were based on journalistic sources or a partial picture of surviving evidence. Additionally, these works were often clouded by wartime fervour, depicting Canadian soldiers who could do no wrong and a German enemy that was nothing less than a malignant force that had to be stopped for the sake of liberty and justice. As Arthur Doughty noted, the best of these, Beaverbrook's *Canada in Flanders* series, served as an "excellent picture ... of the achievements of our troops at the Front, at least as far as the army and the censor would allow the picture to be shown." But other histories written from unofficial sources, without access to the war records, "serve little more than the temporary purpose of tickling the palates of patriotic readers."[24] While Doughty predicted the Canadian people would someday demand an official history based on trusted sources, a number of personal histories emerged as well.

Memoirs and collected letters offer a glimpse into the experience of battle. Private Harold Peat's account, aptly titled, *Private Peat* (1917), was a view into the infantryman's war, but as he recounted in the foreword: "I hope, along with the grimness and the humor, I have been able to say some words of cheer and comfort."[25] This and other personal histories like *A Sunny Subaltern: Billy's Letters from Flanders* (1916) were, of course, one man's war, covering a specific period of battle and usually only for a duration of twelve to eighteen months. Most memoirs had a limited readership, although Canadian air ace Billy Bishop published *Winged Warfare* (1918), which was read avidly by a hero-worshipping public. Bishop's wartime actions and written account helped to shape the emerging myth surrounding the man and Canadian fighter pilots in general.[26] As befitting his hero status, Bishop's memoirs were perhaps the most important to emerge from the war, but all these works contained moving passages. These memoirs continue to be mined by historians attempting to understand the "face of battle," but they bring a limited perspective to the story of Canada's war effort.

One of the most ambitious historical projects was the six-volume series by the Makers of Canada (Morang) Limited, *Canada in the Great War* (1917-23). Due to its size, the series offered the most sweeping coverage of any of the first histories, and it boasted a Military Advisory Board of Major General Sir William Otter and Major General F.L. Lessard, among others, to offer guidance. Largely written by journalists, the six volumes covered a wide range of topics both at the front and at home, but was most valuable for its insight into the latter. One reviewer noted that the description of "military operations is sketchy, uncritical, occasionally inaccurate, and biased by the war-time spirit which found after every battle decidedly too much demoralization of the Germans."[27] In most cases, however, these six volumes would surely have been enough for many veterans and their families.

"Many stories have been written about wars but few of them have given the truth concerning the suffering and hardships that the front line fighting infantryman are called upon to endure ... The result is that stories of this type, usually by correspondents, are passed off with a sour laugh by front line fighting men who knew better," wrote William Breckenridge of the 42nd Battalion in his unpublished memoir.[28] Breckenridge's sentiment was clear: veterans knew that journalists rarely got the history right. While there might be poignant passages, overall these works had no authenticity. One publisher wrote to Brigadier General A.G.L. McNaughton in 1922 that an official history based on trusted sources was needed to set the record straight, especially to offset those histories "of the one-man variety written by men who never saw France." Newspapers provided firm evidence of a demand for such a history as they often received letters "from the mildly protesting to the caustically ironic, but all at one in deploring the lack of Canadian initiative and urging the necessity for a historical record of the part played by Canadians in the greatest war of all time." Quite simply, Canadians were not happy with American and British histories that devoted "little space or attention to the part of the Overseas Dominions."[29] Canadians needed their own, authentic history.

The exception to these superficial first-generation histories was a monograph by Frank Underhill, who was then a professor of history at the University of Saskatchewan and a veteran of the war. Underhill crafted a perceptive but short operational history based on interviews with Sir Arthur Currie and brief access to some of the war records.[30] He rightly noted the Canadian failure at St. Eloi and the difficulties at the Battle of Mount Sorrel before turning to the better-known victory at Vimy and those that were to follow. Despite Underhill's refusal to downplay the difficult aspects of the early Canadian fighting, he confessed to Currie, "Naturally I have not felt myself qualified to pass judgment on individuals."[31] That said, Underhill was not afraid to condemn Sir Sam Hughes, former minister of Militia and Defence, whom he described as having "courage, energy, initiative, abounding vitality, qualities of real value to Canada, especially in the initial stages of the war. But his merits were offset by grave defects. At a time when harmonious cooperation was of prime importance, he was not an element of harmony. He was reckless in statement, impulsive in action, and his exaggerated self-confidence caused friction on all sides."[32] Publicly vilified for a number of years, Hughes died in 1921, and was, presumably, a safe target. Nonetheless, Underhill's caution was understandable with regard to other issues: the difficulties of writing contemporary history, but also, as he claimed in his correspondence with Currie, the realization that only a fraction of the war records available could be processed. Even the best of the first-generation histories could only cover the battles in general terms, since they had no chance to study the war records in detail.

War journalist J.F.B. Livesay's account of the Hundred Days was a best-seller, and surprisingly, British soldier Philip Gibbs's *Now It Can Be Told* (1920) was the most popular war memoir in Canada during the 1920s, rather than one of the many Canadian offerings. But the numerous war memoirs and histories were not any more popular than other middlebrow histories and romance novels of the period.[33] Livesay wrote to Currie in 1922 with some worry that the instant and often inaccurate histories were laying the "groundwork of future history ... Are Canadians going to let history get away with this? I don't think that even when published the official history now preparing [sic] at Ottawa will serve the trick; certainly not with this generation."[34] As a proponent of the Beaverbrook school of history, Livesay felt that Canadian historians needed to craft a robust canon of literature to support or defend hard-earned wartime reputations. Notwithstanding his fear that an official history would do little to change perceptions, there were many who felt that "history" would be served by an official, unbiased account of the CEF.

IN 1926 BRITISH FOREIGN SECRETARY Austen Chamberlain informed the editor of the British Great War document series, G.P. Gooch, that it was the government's duty "to preserve peace now and in the future. I cannot sacrifice *that* even to historical accuracy."[35] The British were no different than the Germans or French, all of whom published selective historical documents during and after the war. German politicians abhorred the blame they had received for the blood of millions, as the contentious War Guilt clause of the Treaty of Versailles stipulated, and they presented to the world a selection of official records in the country's defence that seemed to prove that Germany had been threatened before the war, and was only responding to other nations' aggressive policies. The official records were an important tool in casting doubt on the veracity of the War Guilt clause, and both the British and French were forced to respond with their own records in this paper war. Of course, the British and French presented damning documents relating to German foreign policy decisions and withheld evidence that showed their own secret alliance talks before the war. The Russians, with their communist government, revealed all the secret prewar talks in the hope of embarrassing the democracies. There was an unprecedented release of official documents in the 1920s, yet all were selected and strained through a colander of guilt and blame. In all cases, "official documents" were being used as weapons in the postwar conflict of national reputations.

Although the term "official history" now evokes connotations of compromised works at best or state-sponsored propaganda at worst, there is no indication that that is how it was viewed in Canada during the 1920s. The official history was anticipated as being an accurate and unbiased account of the war, written by an historical expert with military experience, and using impartial war records to craft an accurate narrative in ways that a civilian or a journalist could not hope to do. That was Duguid's goal, too, and he believed that his series was to provide a "memorial for participants, a source for historians, a manual for soldiers, and a guide for the future."[36] An official history would also act as the government's published account of the war, which could dispel some of the inaccurate instant histories or postwar antiwar literature. Quite simply, codifying the memory and deeds of the Canadian Corps would be Duguid's life work.

While not trained as an historian, Duguid had an analytical mind. The official historian was not easily fooled by the evidence he encountered, and as he gained experience, he was better able to evaluate rigorously the documents as they were slowly revealed to him. The truth lay in the records, Duguid believed, and the "object is to find out exactly what happened: conclusions cannot be drawn until all information has been arranged in such a form that it can be grasped readily and the relative importance of events weighed. Otherwise conclusions will be faulty and probably entirely wrong."[37] He had aligned himself with the emerging profession of academic historians who distinguished themselves from amateur historians by "scientifically" studying and interpreting the archival record. One could hope to capture the past "as it was," wrote Duguid, by gathering and analysing the records.[38] While this was an admirable, although not infallible, approach to constructing an historical narrative, it resulted in an enormous amount of work, as Duguid insisted on seeing every document, evaluating it, and putting it into a complicated series of cross-referenced outlines. This method would ultimately fail him as he fell victim to the tyranny of the record: the overwhelming mass of records leads to an ever-spiralling search to reconstruct the past that produces greater ambiguity the longer the research continues.

Duguid saw the war archives as the first place to start in order to understand the Canadian military experience, but he was not naïve about the drawbacks of strictly using official defence records. The friction and fog of war and the many complexities surrounding hundreds or thousands of men involved in life-and-death struggles could not be summed up in a short, after-battle report. It was essential for Duguid to correspond with surviving veterans to better understand the war, to augment the war records with their first-hand accounts or personal papers, and to include the actual experience of combat in his narrative. These interviews, both in person and through detailed correspondence, of which there were hundreds – perhaps thousands – over three decades, were painstakingly conducted and analyzed by the official historian in an attempt to uncover every aspect of the hidden history of Canadians in battle.[39] One cannot but marvel at the breadth and depth of Duguid's research and the evidence that now lies in records he compiled, which eventually formed a component of the official defence archives. As the official historian, he believed he had to get the story right. However, that did not mean that he was at the mercy of veterans who wished to see the history bent to their will or written to settle old scores. There were, of course, countless cases where soldiers corrected the narratives that Duguid sent out for review, but he was always stringent in how he evaluated requests for changes; they were compared to the archival records, and when they did not match, the official historian almost always accepted the war record over postwar testimony.

WHILE DUGUID STRUGGLED with his task of gathering material for the official history, he also saw himself as guardian of the CEF's reputation. In that capacity, Duguid fought a high-profile battle with the British official historian, Brigadier General Sir James Edmonds. The conflict centred on Edmonds's 1924 draft chapters, which denigrated the role of the Canadians during the Battle of Second

Ypres. As one of those British professional officers who did not think the Dominion forces deserved the reputation they had received in the war, Edmonds gave the Canadians and Australians little credit for their very real wartime accomplishments.[40] This battle shed important light on postwar reputations and the essential role played by Duguid within the structure of the Department of National Defence.

Historians have often been accused of vicious fighting with one another over the interpretation of events, where the minutiae are often comical and of interest to almost no one but fellow specialists. Yet as Jane Austen suggested, a tempest in a teapot can still be uncomfortable if one lives in the teapot.[41] But this was no teapot, and Duguid's battle with Edmonds involved events of national importance.

The Canadian operations at Second Ypres had resulted in crippling casualties – more than a third of Canada's first and only division at the time, with nearly half of the infantry strength lost in a week of fighting. Although the Canadians were inexperienced and untried in battle, when French and Algerian divisions on the left fled in the face of the first-ever release of chlorine gas, the Dominion troops had stood their ground, shifted over to cover the gap, and counterattacked the larger German forces. In fierce fighting that also involved a second chlorine cloud, the Canadians were only slowly pushed back on their interior lines by the overwhelming assault. They had fought a recklessly brave rearguard action that provided essential time for the Allies to rush up reinforcements, and it was not hyperbole when the War Office had claimed that the Canadians "saved the situation."[42] The survivors had rightly taken pride in their accomplishments at Ypres, even if it had been a costly trial by fire.

In 1924, however, Duguid's Army Historical Section received the first draft chapters of Edmonds's account of the battle, which included the Canadian actions within the larger Allied context. Duguid distributed them to surviving CEF officers, anxious to receive their reactions. All were shocked.[43] "My perusal of the draft of these four chapters has astonished me," wrote one retired officer. "It is obvious that the actual writer, whoever he may be, starts his work prejudiced against the Canadians and takes every possible opportunity of belittling them and the work that they did."[44] Sir Arthur Currie, now Principal of McGill University, felt that the author's "particular bias, even dislike, is directed against the staff of the 2nd Brigade and myself in particular. His statements, particularly his insinuations, are ungenerous, unjustifiable and untrue, if not contemptibly base. I feel that his evident conclusions are founded on absolutely false premise and his mind must, to some extent, have been poisoned."[45]

Edmonds had deliberately downplayed the role of the Canadians. He left the impression that they were simply another of the British units in the line and not the prime defenders of the front in question, victims of the first and second chlorine gas attacks in the history of warfare, and instrumental in fighting against overwhelming German forces that threatened to envelop more than 50,000 Allied troops. Furthermore, Edmonds had portrayed the Canadians as confused and panicky, suggesting that a British divisional commander was forced to take over the battle. Currie, then a brigadier, was singled out as having performed poorly, fleeing the front to receive counsel from senior British officers. This was untrue. Although Currie had left the front, he did so to obtain desperately needed reinforcements that the British would not release. This version of history was unacceptable to the veterans of the CEF, and they turned to their official historian to protect their collective reputation.

Marshalling his resources, Duguid had compiled by May 1925 the comments from surviving veterans to support his argument for correcting the draft chapters. More important, at least in the eyes of both official historians, he presented thousands of pages of war records that refuted a number of Edmonds's points. These, when combined with fifty-three pages of additional commentary by Duguid, gave some indication of the displeasure felt by the Canadians. Duguid argued that General T. D'O. Snow, the commanding officer of the British 27th Division to whom Edmonds gave much of the credit for directing the battle, had in fact done little to assist the Canadian forces. As Duguid knew from the records and interviews, the Canadians had been left to their own devices, forced to fight the battle at the brigade, battalion, company, and even platoon level. As part of his correspondence with Edmonds, the Canadian historian warned: "You will, of course, appreciate the importance to Canada of having the account in the British official history, of this battle in particular, meticulously accurate."[46] It was an indication that surviving officers would not stand for anything less than major revision.

Raising the intensity of the debate, the chief of the general staff, J.H. MacBrien, who had been a brigadier in the CEF during the war, wrote a letter of protest to the chief of the imperial general staff (CIGS), General Sir George Milne: "It is almost impossible for anyone outside to realise the deep impression made by this battle on the hearts and minds of all Canadians and any inadvertent misrepresentation in the British official history would be correspondingly far reaching in its effects on inter-imperial relations."[47] Lord Byng, then governor general of Canada and former Canadian Corps commander, was willing to go so far as a personal appeal to the King in order to "get satisfaction."[48] The Canadians wanted to see a second draft of the history before anything was published, and Edmonds, despite arguing against it, was forced to send a revised version to Duguid for distribution among Canadian officers.

Having been on the receiving end of this barrage of criticism for some time, Edmonds thought the Canadians were pressuring him unfairly. Like Duguid, Edmonds believed in the importance of the war records in containing the representations of truth.[49] The memories of soldiers were important, of course, but one had to be cautious when the passing of time could dull accuracy or when reputations were involved. Although Duguid had supplied him with hundreds of documents, Edmonds had requested to see the original War Diaries from the battle. After some delay, it was revealed that these important records were unavailable. As an experienced historian with two volumes of the British official history series already published, Edmonds's suspicions seemed confirmed: the Canadians were covering up their collective failures.

The War Diaries for Richard Turner's and Currie's brigades were indeed missing, either because they had never been kept or because they were destroyed during or after the battle. G.S. Tuxford, who had commanded the 5th Battalion at Second Ypres, recounted to Duguid after the war that there were no records for his unit because when it looked like his headquarters was "to be overrun, they buried (not burned, which drew fire) the documents in the ground." That any of Tuxford's men survived at all in the face of this "new and inhuman type of [gas] warfare," when "armed with a rifle that refused to shoot and with practically no artillery support," he believed was of greater importance than a few missing documents.[50] That was true, of course, but when the post-battle forensic scientists attempted to analyze the fighting, they needed every scrap of paper.

When Duguid found that the wartime narratives that replaced the War Diaries were not accurate, having been written after the battle by a staff officer who had never been near the front, he sent out a letter in late 1925 to surviving senior 1st Division veterans inquiring about the missing War Diaries.[51] There were, according to the memory of G.C. Gordon Hall, who had been a senior staff officer with the division, few records created during the battle "except for rough and hurried notes jotted down from hour to hour."[52] Contradicting Hall, a number of correspondents believed a War Diary had been completed, but none knew what had happened to it. Although it appeared that the diaries had been destroyed and then rewritten, Duguid decided not to pass this information on to Edmonds because he believed he could not be trusted with the revelation after their earlier hostile exchanges.

Edmonds was not mollified. A dogged researcher in his own right, the British official historian contacted a number of veterans, including the former divisional (later corps) commander, E.A.H. Alderson, who had been treated shabbily by the Canadians and removed from command in May 1916. Alderson remarked to Edmonds that he was "not surprised that you found the account and maps inaccurate. It was written soon after the battle, on 13 May 1915 by one of my Canadian staff. I did not want to hurt his feelings. I sent it in much as he wrote it. They [the Canadians] were very sensitive and I often had to do that."[53] Although Alderson was probably still smarting from his poor treatment at the hands of Canadian politicians, his revelation on the authorship and context of the official documents is telling. Another Canadian, Brigadier J.S. "Buster" Brown, confirmed Alderson's statement, noting that "in the kindness of his [Alderson's] heart towards certain unsatisfactory things that happened in the Third Brigade, I believe that he ordered all traces of conviction against the Third Brigade to be destroyed, as far as possible, and it is probable that the War Diaries compiled at Divisional Headquarters, together with some correspondence connected with the retirement of the Third Brigade, were burnt at the same time."[54]

It was clear to Edmonds, then, that someone in the division had destroyed war records that reflected badly on the Canadians' conduct, and had replaced them with reports that massaged the grimmer aspects of the fighting and retreat. Duguid did not agree, feeling that the Canadians, while engaged in desperate battle, could not have been expected to act as clerks: while there were problems with some records, the vast majority of surviving documentary evidence confirmed the heroic deeds of the 1st Division.[55] With such confusion, it is not surprising that Duguid would spend the next decade tracking down every bit of correspondence – every message, every map, every report, and compare these to the veterans' memories. Reconstructing a battle as complicated as Second Ypres was indeed a monumental task, and even more so when reputations were involved.

With this mutual mistrust, Edmonds continued to believe that Duguid was covering up Currie's battlefield failure. Moreover, if the official records had been corrupted or culled, how could Edmonds verify the integrity of the remainder? Duguid refused to entertain ideas that the Canadian records were untrustworthy, but he also knew secretly that Canadian senior officers were not without guilt. Richard Turner, commander of the 3rd Brigade and a Canadian hero who had won the Victoria Cross in South Africa, had indeed performed poorly in the battle. Turner had misinterpreted several divisional orders during the chaotic fighting, most seriously pulling back his units to a rear defensive line and leaving Currie's flank in the air during a crucial part of the battle. While Currie had carried out an unorthodox manoeuvre to rectify the situation – he left the front to find desperately needed reinforcements – and this certainly must have looked odd to Edmonds, it is clear that he was in control of his front as far as the chaos of battle would allow. Edmonds remained unconvinced. Even when he wrote agreeably to the Canadian historian in December 1925 that he would "cover up" Currie's visit to Snow's headquarters in the rear, Duguid was not assuaged, feeling that it "was unnecessary to cover anything up," as Currie was acting in the best interest of his troops, told his subordinates and superiors what he was doing, and that he was probably the only person to convince HQ to release reinforcements.[56] Understanding the unfairness of attacking Currie but refusing to offer up Turner, Duguid continued to appeal to Edmonds to change his ungenerous assessment of Currie's actions. A powerful lobby of senior officers like MacBrien and Major General F.O.W. Loomis, a former divisional commander, also impressed upon senior British officers to reign in Edmonds, revealing a powerful Currie faction in the postwar years that would broker no criticism of the former commander.[57]

Duguid fought Edmonds for several years over the interpretation of the Canadian actions at Second Ypres, spending enormous time copying files, condensing correspondence from surviving officers, and drawing dozens of battle maps. Edmonds finally retreated from his more offensive statements due to Duguid's strong case, just as he would do with the Australian official historian, Charles Bean, in the coming years after similar battles of historical interpretations. However, he left a bitter report detailing the pressure exerted on him by the Canadians. In it, he made some wild accusations about the Canadians' duplicitous nature and desire to warp history. Edmonds even claimed nonsensically that Duguid had admitted that he "dare not write until the British account had appeared, for fear of their version not being believed."[58] Duguid would have enough trouble over the coming years in completing his history, and he need not be saddled with additional fabricated issues. But it is worth remembering that one of the primary sources of delays to Duguid's work on the Canadian official history was his steadfast defence of his countrymen's reputations from the perceived British official assault.

Just as they had during the war, the Canadians believed the British were trying to cheat them of their laurels. Currie summed up the thoughts of many of his fellow veterans when he wrote, "there was falsification which I cannot believe was anything but deliberate. The old regular soldier was back at his game and clearly determined that the civilian soldier was not entitled to very much respect."[59] At the same time, Edmonds believed that the Canadians were still fighting Beaverbrook-like publicity battles. "As the history proceeds, many and very serious difficulties with the Canadians will crop up," predicted Edmonds in April 1926, after he had been called out onto the carpet by the CIGS. "There was no limit to their lying as the war went on. It is important to make a stand now."[60]

To Edmonds, though, it must have appeared he was facing the whole surviving Canadian establishment from the Great War, all of whom were channelling their displeasure through their official historian who was to bludgeon him into submission. Senior diplomats, governors general, the CGS, and even his own CIGS were involved: the official history was deadly serious business. However, Edmonds was tasked with writing the whole history of the BEF, and since he was unwilling to be dragged further into a battle he could not win, he acquiesced to most of the Canadian demands.

In the end, Duguid believed that his intense study of the primary documents "caused General Edmonds to change his conception of the battle and to rewrite the whole story ... Unless the Canadian Historical Section had helped, General Edmonds would not have given Canada fair representation in the British Official Volumes."[61] By supplying hundreds of pages of narratives and thousands of documents, Duguid spent an enormous amount of time in protecting the reputation of the Canadian soldiers and in combating Edmonds's "remarkable mistrust, misreading and misinterpretation of documents."[62] Duguid was widely praised by Canadian officers for his spirited defence; but at the same time, the eight-volume Canadian official history remained barely started.

WHILE DUGUID was slow in marshalling evidence for the Canadian official history, he was clearly not incompetent. He was, however, overly cautious because he felt he had to get the story right. He also didn't believe the writing should be done quickly. As he pleaded to one senior general: "the impression seems to have become fixed in the minds of many Canadians that accurate and comprehensive military history can be written and produced at the speed of a newspaper or magazine article." It could not, and if his work was to be of "enduring and national importance," he needed time to complete his intensive research.[63]

Duguid's caution is better understood after the public's reception of the 1925 Canadian Army Medical Corps' official history by the celebrated writer and veteran, Sir Andrew Macphail. While it had been published remarkably quickly, it was uneven in coverage and polemical in tone.[64] Alternating between a narrative of military operations and thematic medical sections, and indiscriminately sliding from a service history to the national war effort, the book made for a poor and confusing read. Macphail even provided his own personal observations, which he cloaked in ambiguous references to unnamed Canadian officers.[65] Having written the history in less than a year and relied on much of the research collected by wartime medical historian Professor J.C. Adami, Macphail had little chance to absorb the lessons of the war.[66] His judgments were in many cases overly harsh: to describe shellshock "as a manifestation of childishness and femininity," was, to say the least, an uneducated view on a complicated subject and certainly not befitting an official history, or any history for that matter.[67]

Most striking was Macphail's blatant assault against the former minister of Militia and Defence, Sir Sam Hughes, whom he accused of meddling behaviour and administrative incompetence. Both Duguid and MacBrien were deeply worried about the polemical tone of the history and although they suggested many changes, with Currie and several prominent CAMC generals reading over and lauding the text, there was little that could be done. While the Cabinet had the option of not supporting the history, MacBrien warned that Macphail owned the intellectual rights and would publish it regardless, and probably in the original, unexpurgated form.[68] Although Macphail toned down some of his most vitriolic attacks against Hughes, one also suspects that the medical official historian, who knew and liked Currie, was settling old scores. Nonetheless, while Hughes was guilty as charged in Macphail's account, he had also played an essential role in leading the Canadian war effort in 1914-15, and to a lesser extent in 1916, which was mostly missing from the story.

Reviewers agreed and savaged the history. The *Canada Lancet* accused it of being "neither impartial nor authentic." Despite having carried a disclaimer from the AHS that "the facts and figures used by [the author] have been verified from official sources, the inferences drawn and the opinions expressed are those of the Author himself," the *Ottawa Journal* remarked that "Under the cloak of the title of historian, Sir Andrew Macphail has washed a lot of unclean linen, trifled with the memory of gallant if mistaken men and given a grossly misleading slant to the character of Canada's war effort." Editors at the *Montreal Star* observed, "It is a misfortune to Canada that it should have been issued by the Government, for it will not enhance the authority with which Government publications are regarded."[69] Quite simply, reviewers felt that an official history was not the place for official censure.

Duguid's ongoing concern for crafting an unbiased history had been confirmed by Macphail's polemical work; the official history of the CEF would have to be unassailable in its fairness, accuracy, and coverage for it not to suffer the same fate. Canadians were anxiously waiting, as were newspaper editors and reviewers, but Duguid would not be rushed. He had also been shaken by his experience with Sir James Edmonds, whom he respected as an historian. The British official historian's gross misreading of the Canadian role in the battle suggested to Duguid "how easily and yet how seriously 'history' may err." Once again Duguid felt it necessary to "spike down every move and phase."[70] And that would take time.

ON 13 JUNE 1927, an editorial in a small newspaper, the *Evening Guide of Port Hope*, attacked Sir Arthur Currie's reputation by reiterating the 1919 claims made by Sir Sam Hughes. Hughes had then thundered to the House of Commons that Currie had issued criminal orders in sending his troops to capture the city of Mons on 11 November 1918 before the Armistice came into effect, causing needless deaths. The newspaper editorial eight years later reiterated the accusation:

> There was much waste of human lives during the war, enormous loss of lives which should not have taken place. But it is doubtful whether in any case there was a more deliberate and useless waste of human life than in the city of Mons. It was the last day; and the last hour, and almost the last minute, when to glorify the Canadian Headquarters staff the commander-in-chief conceived the mad idea that it would be [a] fine thing to say that the Canadians had fired the last shot of the Great War ... Canadian Headquarters sounded the advance upon the retreating Germans, unsuspecting that any mad proposal for further and unnecessary fighting was even contemplated. Headquarters, with conspicuous bravery, brought up the rear.[71]

The editors reminded their small readership that after the war "neither government nor Parliament, gave Sir Arthur Currie any official vote of thanks ... or any special grant for his services. And this is the only case of the kind in connection with any of the high commanding officers of the war. He was allowed to return to Canada unnoticed by officials of the government ... and permitted to sink into comparative obscurity."

Having fought the rumours that he was a butcher for almost a decade, twice as long as the very length of the war, Currie saw here an opportunity at last to strike back against Hughes, even if the former minister had been in his grave for six years. Although there was no name attached to the editorial, Currie suspected it was W.T.R. Preston, a well-known fundraiser for the Liberal party with a reputation as a political muckraker. "If I can fasten the authorship on him," Currie wrote, "I propose to take action."[72] The former corps commander, who had just relied on Duguid to fight for his good name against Edmonds's slanderous charges, now found himself once again relying on the CEF official historian to support him, only this time the allegations were from one of his own countrymen.

Currie's memory had begun to fade after a decade, but he believed that there were very few, if any, casualties on 11 November 1918. He therefore asked Duguid to examine the war records relating to the last forty-eight hours of the war – "I am depending on you to tell me what the official records disclose."[73] Duguid responded with casualty figures that indicated that only one man had been killed and thirteen wounded from the 3rd Division on the last three days of the war.[74] Furthermore, the historian sent along operational reports and orders that he thought would support Currie's case. With this evidence, some hard thinking, and much consultation with friends – many of whom suggested he avoid dredging up the past – Currie launched a libel suit against the newspaper and its editors for defamation of character. "I am getting very tired, Colonel, of listening to these libels about my conduct at Mons," wrote Currie to the minister of National Defence, J.L. Ralston.[75]

With close friends raising money for his defence and contacting old soldiers to testify on his behalf, Currie again turned to Duguid in September 1927 to gather maps, operational orders, casualty reports, and any other official record that would bolster his case. Currie was most anxious that Duguid read through the War Diaries to understand the "temper of the troops. For instance, it is commonly said, and I believe it is true, that units did not wish to be relieved in the line, being actuated by the desire to be in at the finish."[76] Both Ralston, a decorated CEF battalion commander, and Duguid were anxious to support Currie, and the AHS devoted precious resources to locating the records and drawing up narratives. Duguid concluded from his intense study that the writer of the article had no evidence for his slanderous charge, and this was passed on to a grateful Currie.[77]

The court case, held in March and April of 1928, would prove to be one of the most vitriolic of the decade. Hundreds of reporters and veterans flowed into the small Ontario town of Cobourg to watch the proceedings. Before the trial began, there was a period of Examination for Discovery, in which both sides could question witnesses and locate evidence. Desperate to strengthen their case, the defence team, lead by lawyer Frank Regan, appealed to the AHS to supply them with war records. The few histories that were available had proven too general to build a case, and even when the defence lawyer utilized a passage from a history book in his pretrial argument, the judge warned "it is not true because it is in a book."[78] The war records, then, were the key to proving Currie's culpability in sending his men to their death. As Lord Acton had written, "What people conceal is not their best deeds and motives but their worst. What archives reveal is the wickedness of man. It destroys idols and scatters theories."[79] Regan and his defendants hoped that Acton was right.

Ralston had initially denied the defence access to the war records, but after receiving a subpoena from Regan and Preston, he authorized Duguid to bring several trunkfuls of documents to Cobourg.[80] Carting off the records, the historian and his assistant, Logie Armstrong, were joined by the Judge Advocate General, Colonel Reginald Orde. The defence had no opportunity to read the thousands of pages of documents before the trial, and so Duguid and Armstrong spent hours with Regan and the defence team answering their questions. Armstrong had created a list of Canadian casualties from 1 to 11 November: it was a shocking 246 killed and 1,694 wounded.[81] Yet the record keeping for the last three days of the war had been haphazard, and it was difficult to narrow down the casualties for just 11 November. Duguid nonetheless insisted that only one man had been killed on that last day of the war. The defence was amazed to find that the records indeed supported the historian's claim.

But since no one had examined the war records since their creation (and, perhaps more important, because these were accounts created by the soldiers themselves), it was possible, indeed likely, Regan believed, that influential officers were covering up the unnecessary slaughter of Canadians troops. During the pretrial, Regan attacked Duguid and the official records. "If it were not for the unfortunate fact that the records were made up to mislead and not to present the true state of affairs the matter would be simple," claimed the defence. "We say the records have been deliberately falsified, and we propose to bring men here to say so, men from every unit engaged in the Battle of Mons."[82] Regan promised to question between seventy-five and one hundred veterans (there would only be a handful in the end) who would give evidence that scores of Canadians were slaughtered in Mons – direct evidence that would contradict the war records. What was to be believed, argued Regan, the testimonies of men who had been at the front or the war records created to support an incompetent general's reputation? While the accomplishments of the CEF were undeniable, so too were the heavy casualties in the Hundred Days. The reputation as shock troops of the BEF had been dearly bought, and even after a decade, Canadians were questioning the price of victory.

Without adequate witnesses or a full grasp of the battle details, and after having found in the pretrial that the war records contradicted the claims of the article, Regan and the defence team once again attacked Duguid and the Army Historical Section during the trial in early April.[83] With headline-grabbing allegations, Regan accused the Department of National Defence (DND) of perpetrating a cover-up of casualties and went so far as to posit that Currie might have ordered the falsification of records.[84] All casualties on the 11th, he claimed, had been backdated to the 9th or 10th, obfuscating the true consequences of attacking Mons. Regan continued to hammer away at the nature of official records and their reliability as authentic reflections of past events. At one point, the judge queried the relevance of how "War Diaries are kept?" Regan replied: "That is all we have to go on, from our knowledge of Mons, War Diaries and records and reports."[85]

Regan continued to attack Duguid and Orde in an attempt to discredit the official records and therefore leave only his few eyewitnesses as the proper authorities. However, the DND officers were not easily cowed. There was "no foundation" for such an accusation, testified Orde, and any falsification of the records would have involved an "extraordinarily large conspiracy," including hundreds of staff at the records office, numerous battalions, field ambulances, casualty clearing stations, and base hospitals.[86] After revealing that diaries were not kept every day, the judge summarized the witnesses' accounts for the jury: "War Diaries were looked upon as a kind of necessary evil, a nuisance, something that men ... were compelled to write for the use, perhaps[,] of the future historian ... perhaps with some haste, but necessarily ... [with] a good deal of hearsay."[87] Although it was acknowledged that the official documents were flawed, the judge would not accept Regan's accusations that they had been wilfully falsified, at least not without any evidence. Regan did little to advance his case, as he argued throughout the trial that some records were untrustworthy while others should be accepted at face value, especially those that supported his defence.

The defence really had very little chance in the end. They had accused Currie of incompetence and butchery without having understood the complexity of warfare on the Western Front; they had no authoritative history to follow; and the war records had remained closed up to the last minute. Preston's editorial might have been written out of malice, but more likely he was simply parroting the remarks made by Sir Sam Hughes. Having accepted Currie's challenge to go to trial was either a sign of profound hubris or gross miscalculation. Or, it might be viewed, as the defence lawyer declared during the trial, as an attempt to garner some recognition for the soldiers who did the fighting and the dying.[88] After a decade there was an attempt to understand the terrible calamity of the war and perhaps hold someone accountable for the crippling losses. The notion of the noble sacrifice no longer offered a suitable framework for understanding the war; the memory of the Great War had become contested ground.

In the end the jury did not accept Preston's specious defence, and the jurors decided in Currie's favour. But it was not an overwhelming victory, since he received only a $500 judgment, much lower than the $50,000 he had requested. Nonetheless, Currie had won. The third battle of Mons, as reporters characterized it, was not about destroying a small-time newspaperman. For Currie, it was about restoring his reputation; it was about running to ground the rumours that had plagued him for years; it was about shaping the memory of the conflict that had raged from 1914 to 1918, cost 60,000 Canadian lives, and maimed countless more.

Significant to this study is how the war records were used during the trial. The seemingly impartial records had been locked up in the AHS's vaults for almost a decade and were not available to Canadian citizens or scholars until an official history was completed. The defence was at a grave disadvantage throughout the trial because it was hampered in putting an effective case together against the more knowledgeable corps commander, who had lived through events, had his own personal archives upon which to draw, and was supported by a sympathetic official historian. In addition, the war records were so voluminous that no defence team could possibly make their way through them without several months of intense research. They relied on the official historian to be the impartial researcher, which, of course, he was not. But Duguid did not have to bury incriminating war records. As with the British official historian, the records again proved the case for Currie. And so, when the records became problematic for the defence, they accused the government of tampering with the representations of the truth. While these accusations were largely reported as ludicrous, they go to a deeper matter.

Who had access to the war records, and why was it that Canadians could not examine for themselves the seemingly authentic evidence of the CEF's exploits? In the "war to end all wars," where Canada had paid an enormous price, the records of those deeds remained under lock and key. The intense scrutiny of the defence archives during the trial, especially the War Diaries, provided a unique insight into the nature of record keeping in the CEF. These were not impartial records, no mirror of the facts, but rather they were artifacts shaped by a number of battlefield factors and their authors' limited perceptions. This is not to suggest that more Canadians were in fact killed at Mons. However, what the Currie trial did was shed light on the inherent limitations of the war records as faultless representations of truth.

ALTHOUGH DUGUID had never received much guidance from senior officers, in the first days of January 1928 the new CGS, Major General H.C. Thacker, questioned Duguid about the "delay in writing the History."[89] Duguid was quick to point out the important work carried out by the AHS, including the arrangement, selection, and appraisal of millions of pages of documents. Furthermore, Duguid sat on the Imperial War Graves Commission and Battles Nomenclature Committees, which also required enormous resources. Countless inquiries, the writing of short historical monographs, and the design of the Memorial Chamber in the Peace Tower were important and recognizable projects completed by Duguid and his staff. The official historian also reminded the CGS that he and his staff had conducted two high-profile defences of the CEF's historical legacy: successfully battling Sir James Edmonds to ensure that the Canadians were adequately and fairly represented in the British official histories; and devoting enormous energy throughout the 1920s (and into the next decade) in assisting regimental historians in producing a canon of literature relating to the war. And all of these duties, the official historian noted, were part of his stated mandate.

Realizing that there was greater pressure on him now to meet the increasing demand for an official history, Duguid wrote breezily to the CGS in March 1928 that if his other work was curtailed a first volume could be ready by January 1929.[90] This was enough for Thacker, and he expressed his support of Duguid and the AHS in a letter to the deputy minister, writing that it would be a "real misfortune" if an official history were not produced, thereby depriving "not only students of war but all Canadians who are interested in the history of their country."[91] Ralston was not so easily convinced. The minister had assisted Currie during the trial and had noted Duguid's encyclopedic knowledge of the Canadian war effort, but he was also aware that the official historian had been at the project for nearly eight years and must surely be close to publishing something. After a decade, the Great War had again become a topic of interest.

Ralston formed a committee in December 1928 to inquire into the writing of the official history. Chaired by Henry Marshall Tory, president of the National Research Council and former president of the Khaki University of Canada and the University of Alberta, the committee of veterans and historians met for three days and issued a short report in January 1929. It recommended that an official history was essential and work should begin immediately, but the committee believed that the DND was not capable of carrying out the project. Under the auspices of the Public Archives, which had, with Arthur Doughty at the helm, a significant amount of experience in crafting Canadian historical monographs and books, the official history would have a better chance of being rapidly completed. But to complicate further the enormous task of drawing together the war history, the committee suggested it should not "merely [be] a history of the war per se, but a history of the national effort of Canada in the face of a great emergency which demanded the mobilization and organization of the entire resources of our people." The committee also recommended that an "historian should be appointed," who would have "complete editorial freedom."[92] Although this was an important precedent, it must have been disconcerting for Duguid to learn that the committee suggested he be downgraded from official historian to chief researcher for the project.

None of the recommendations were ever implemented. The new CGS, Andrew McNaughton, who had proven himself an adept innovator of artillery tactics during the war, and was a power unto himself in the department, believed strongly in an official history, but worried that a monograph that covered economic, social, or political aspects would dilute the focus on the CEF. Furthermore, McNaughton did not want to lose control of the official history, as it was an important work for veterans and their families, but also because he considered it a pedagogical tool for officers that could explain how to fight in a major land war. A more general history would lose the ability to do that. Having seen Duguid challenge the British and beat them in the history game, perform important operational duties for the department, and ably assist Currie in his trial, McNaughton fully endorsed Duguid as the CEF's official historian.[93]

The notion that an academic historian should take over the writing of the history was unacceptable to McNaughton and many of the veterans, who continued to see service in the CEF as a key qualification for a successful official historian. Moreover, the British had found that their attempts to hire civilian historians to work on official histories had resulted in failure. Civilian historians were more expensive and official historians without military backgrounds had a far more difficult time approaching and receiving support from senior officers, who often viewed the civilians as outsiders.[94] While McNaughton could have hired a university professor and CEF veteran such as Wilfrid Kerr, Frank Underhill, or Harold Innis, he also seemed anxious to keep the work within the DND structure. It is unclear if this was a case of empire building, but surely the writing of an official history series required decades of work, and official historians had to bring an almost evangelical zeal to their enormous projects. Duguid had shown abundant zeal, was strongly committed to the memory and men of the CEF, and could be employed on the task for the necessary time required to bring it to fruition. McNaughton was willing to give Duguid the time, but he was increasingly feeling pressure from concerned interest groups.

HAVING ARRANGED AND EXAMINED almost all the war records by the end of the 1920s, as well as selecting for destruction those not deemed "historical," Duguid's method of approaching the massive task of research was to create a number of detailed indices.[95] These were then broken down into sections and subsections until he reached specific events. It was a logical way to approach the subject but it required a significant amount of planning. Scraps of paper containing important battlefield messages or incomplete War Diaries were harder to piece together in the AHS's offices in Ottawa than it would have been a decade earlier in France. While significant progress was made on the first volume, at one volume a decade, Duguid and most of the veterans would probably be dead before he finished half the project.

While Duguid studied the records, almost all other researchers and academics were denied access. This was partly because of their unorganized state, but also because Duguid understood the power of the archives. For the official historian, making these records available would only result in "dreadful things" happening in the "hands of those who do not understand." The records "should be kept secure as far as possible from such violation."[96] The official historian was guardian of the CEF's reputation, and felt that others could not be trusted to study the war. The regimental historians were the only exception.

Long forgotten except by the most avid of bibliophiles, regimental histories are sometimes viewed as quixotic monographs, more akin to publicity pieces or organizational hagiography than to legitimate historical works. Although the regimental histories were by no means the last word in exploring or explaining the experience of war, they filled an important historiographical gap left by the long overdue official history. From 1919 to 1939 more than sixty regimental histories were published, of which more than two dozen were full-length monographs.[97] They were not brought to fruition in isolation, however. The AHS provided advice, expert knowledge, and editing services for the informal regimental history program. These works were seen as integral publications that would not only supplement the official history, but also give a voice to the soldiers who would be excluded largely from the more sweeping narrative of the official history.

Most regiments were anxious to have a history, but they were not easy to create. The 19th Battalion, for example, had served with the 2nd Division during the war, and they appointed former subaltern R.O. Spreckley to craft a unit history in 1935, which was rather late in the game. He appears to have had no experience as an historian, but he was certainly dedicated to the task.

After commanding officers attested that Spreckley was the "accredited regimental historian," AHS staff suggested that he go through the War Diary, put together an outline, and then canvas surviving veterans for personal reminiscences.[98] Spreckley's first questionnaire, which he sent out in early 1936, revealed that "it had been prepared with the idea of getting the gallant, but extremely inarticulate ex-members" to put some thoughts down on paper in order to supplement the "business-like" War Diary.[99] Veteran Charlie Lind recounted, "I don't envy the author of our Battalion History his job ... My impression was that the 19th's diary was the skimpiest and least interestingly written of them all! The thought occurred to me then that our battalion would get relatively little mention when the history of the war came to be written; but in my humble position it was difficult for me to convey this thought forcibly to the Battalion C.O. I ... understood from him that compilation of the diary was looked upon as a bit of a nuisance."[100]

Still, the regimental historian pushed on, and while the AHS suggested he only send the draft narratives or questionnaires to officers, Spreckley ensured that it went out to men who had been from the ranks too. Spreckley hoped that veterans could get together, talk about the old times, and have one among them act as a "scribe." An "intimate" regimental history could not be written, warned Spreckley, without knowing what the "boys did, thought, felt, smelt and endured" during the war.[101]

Despite an enormous amount of work, there were disappointingly few returns from the surviving veterans. A second questionnaire went out that same year, with instructions that if veterans "recaptured some of the facility they displayed ... when they wrangled a green envelope, we would have no difficulty in getting satisfactory results." Even employing the language of the trenches (the green envelope refers to a letter that would not be opened by officers for censorship), Spreckley received even fewer returns, and he had little he could use to enrich the narrative. He refured to give up, however, and another six questionnaires were sent out until, finally, a number of written accounts were sent to Spreckley.

These soldiers' memoirs generally ran a couple of pages in length, although V.E. Thompson penned a forty-two-page account, which he had prefaced: "to go back nineteen years and write my experiences in the year 1918 is a tall order. Memory is a weak thing and is prone to forget many things and concoct many other things ... Names and places and persons and things done and thought have faded with the years and the record which I kept has been little better than something to place these memories in a more logical order."[102]

For those veterans without an illegally kept diary to follow (diaries were against military regulations, but few officers seemed eager to prosecute), they must have had an even more difficult time remembering the specifics of the war. As Ernie Knott wrote to "dear old Spreck," he would try to draw on something from the past for the regimental historian's "gallant and continuing struggle to erect a monument (literary) to the Beloved 19th."[103] Despite these honourable intentions the project was abandoned in late 1937 due to a lack of replies from surviving veterans and the inability to raise sufficient resources. Other Canadian regimental associations, such as those for the 38th and 58th Battalions, experienced the same fate by failing to find historians to carry out the work or lacking necessary funds to bring manuscripts to publication.[104]

One regimental historian noted that his text was "written by a soldier for soldiers and their kin." Veterans with historical training were in short supply, but entrusting the project to a non-serving civilian historian was not a comfortable prospect. In some cases, though, the veterans' desire for a history overrode their reluctance to allow an outsider to codify their memories.[105] Unable to locate an historian within their ranks, the 13th Battalion turned to a McGill University registrar. Under the direction of a committee of ex-officers and commanding officers, Robert C. Fetherstonhaugh was commissioned to write the regimental history. The battalion chose its historian well, and *The 13th Battalion Royal Highlanders of Canada* won the 1926 English History prize for best book in Canadian history. Fetherstonhaugh would go on to write another four regimental histories.[106]

Fetherstonhaugh and his fellow regimental historians benefited from the AHS's guidance. Duguid met with them to discuss methodologies and sources before they commenced their task. Still acting in his position as guardian of the CEF's reputation and memory, Duguid told one historian, "My job is to do everything possible to put the true story of the CEF on paper" and to avoid the "spread of erroneous information."[107] Duguid instructed regimental historians not to embarrass their comrades or their nation. The official historian himself worked under similar constraints. One general even suggested to Duguid that "on contentious subjects no sides should be taken, no opinion or judgment expressed nor bias shown." He should avoid making pronouncements, as one would avoid "the deadliest poison."[108] Duguid was not so easily muzzled, however, and, as we shall see, he passed condemnation when it was warranted and refused to be bullied over his handling of the failed Ross rifle, which jammed in battle, and the difficulties at Ypres. But generally he proceeded with restraint, as have most official historians before and after him.

The regimental histories were similar in structure, followed chronological events, and focused primarily on the larger conflicts such as Ypres, the Somme, Vimy, Passchendaele, and the Hundred Days. The structural uniformity of the histories came from Duguid, who, while not doctrinaire, suggested that "any great departure from the general form is apt to be like stepping off the duckboards to walk on the parapet – all right if you don't get hit or land in a sump hole."[109] Lieutenant Colonel C. Beresford Topp, historian for the 42nd Battalion, noted Duguid's influence, asserting that the official historian had "outlined the general structure of the book with chapter headings, [and] read the proofs as well as the manuscript."[110] Another veteran suggested that Duguid should be recognized as the "Patron Saint of all Regimental Histories."[111] Despite the uniformity that came from Duguid's instructions, each history was distinguished by its battalion's unique experiences, its own maps, official and unofficial photographs, the insertion of poems or trench songs, first-hand accounts, and even drawings.

The regimental historians had the burden of crafting an accurate history for their fellow veterans and the dead. With 5,000 to 6,000 men passing through a battalion over three or four years, however, there was obviously no way that all could be mentioned by name. The officers were therefore privileged in the narrative. Of course, it was the officers who organized a board to supervise the history, and they also chose the historian. And so the thousands of privates who served in the battalion generally remained nameless and indistinguishable in the text. The job of the regimental historian was a difficult one, as it is for anyone who writes with committee oversight, but it is unfortunate that so many histories seem to have left out the enlisted men, who formed the vast majority of the battalion. Will Bird, a ranker of the 42nd Battalion and a widely read Nova Scotian journalist, wrote acidly that regimental histories were essential reading because of the delayed official history, but some, like his own battalion's history, needed "a slight insertion at the beginning 'For Officers Only.'"[112]

While serving as vehicles for explaining the unfolding of events, the regimental histories were also tools used to shape postwar beliefs. They provided senior officers with a forum for how the war would be remembered. Messages of sacrifice and valour were interwoven through a text that highlighted the accomplishments of the battalion. Former Lieutenant Colonel R.L. Ewing of the 42nd Battalion informed his fellow veterans that their regimental history would serve to counter the claims of those who were damaging the reputation of all soldiers. "It seems such a pity to me that some writers with a warped outlook, should prostitute their talents in an attempt to besmirch their comrades and unfortunately give the impression to a newer generation that the War, terrible as it was, with its bitter experiences, physical exhaustion, filth, pain and suffering, brought out as it did the best and the worst, consisted, between battles, in a series of carousals, interspersed with brutal treatment from Officers and Non-Commissioned Officers."[113]

With the antiwar poets and novelists achieving greater influence by the late 1920s, the memory of the war was becoming increasingly contested and fragmented. The regimental histories allowed the soldiers, and specifically, the officers, to present their views on how the social memory of the war would be influenced or constructed. That did not mean a whitewashing of the war, but it did challenge wilder accusations that the infantry consisted of rampaging lunatics or that the generals were butchering incompetents.[114]

Although Duguid had an enormous influence on the regimental historians, he could not force them to accept changes. He did, however, have a trump card. As early as 1923, Hamilton Gault, the millionaire veteran who had privately raised Princess Patricia's Canadian Light Infantry in 1914, had wanted its regimental history to contain a "seal of approval" from the AHS. Chief of the General Staff J.H. MacBrien denied the request on Duguid's advice, but he did allow the regiment to print a note informing readers that the staff of the AHS had read over the manuscript and checked it for errors. Duguid subsequently dangled this official stamp of approval before all other regimental historians, as long as they allowed his staff to read and presumably alter sections they found unacceptable.[115] This saved embarrassment, as overzealous writers would occasionally make claims that, for example, their battalion had never retreated. And while Duguid was not always able to ensure that his staff's editorial suggestions were heeded, the AHS played an important part in ensuring that at least some standards of historical quality were achieved.

By working with regimental historians, the editing process also allowed the AHS to influence the interpretation of problematic events. Duguid's earlier advice to regimental historians laid a foundation for cautious writing, and his correspondence and critiques of draft work are equally instructive. As Duguid suggested to one regimental historian after reading his work, "if there was internal dissension, you should find out all about it, not necessarily for publication, but without that knowledge you cannot reflect the true spirit of the battalion."[116] The truth had to be discovered, but that did not always mean that it should be published. "I would urge you to make sure now, as far as possible, that what you write is made reasonably safe from any who may seek to find something amiss," warned Duguid. "Someone is always looking for a sensation."[117] Caution, rather than revelation, was the watchword; he would not allow his fellow Canadian regimental historians to sully the CEF's reputation.

As most regimental historians were veterans themselves and writing in a constrained manner – either because of their own backgrounds, Duguid's influence, or that of their senior officers – they were not inclined to expose the more contentious aspects of the war. At the same time, however, the regimental historians could not simply write patriotic drivel, as the soldiers would never accept that. The regimental historians did not shy away from describing some of the grimmer aspects of the war. R.C. Fetherstonhaugh in his *13th Battalion Royal Highlanders of Canada* (1925), wrote in a fairly staid and unemotional manner, but his description of Passchendaele rings true:

> The mud was appalling and the fighting for every foot of ground was so bitter as quite to defy description. Men died by the score to capture a miserable concrete "pill box," only to have their comrades find that somewhere in the awful mud ahead lay other "pill boxes" which resolutely blocked their way to victory. No praise is too high for the courage of the men, who, at the terrible cost, pounded these miniature fortresses into submission, nor, indeed, for that of the German garrisons, who fought until the last possible moment and, in nine cases out of ten, died fighting rather than yield.[118]

This excerpt was no aberration: there were similarly poignant and unique accounts of the Great War experience to be found in all regimental histories. As one commentator rightly noted in the early 1930s, "one may assess their future value when one considers how greatly our knowledge of the War of 1812 would be enriched had a similar series been written for all the Canadian Militia regiments within ten or twenty years of the termination of hostilities."[119]

Although the regimental histories are problematic works that were influenced heavily by a number of constituents, they still offer unparalleled insight into particular aspects of the Canadian battle experience. Memoirs and official histories are essential to understand the war, but in order to discern the actions of a battalion they are either too narrowly or too widely focused to offer a balanced picture. There is, quite simply, no better way to grasp where a particular battalion was engaged and what its men did, than to study the regimental histories. Regimental histories provide insight into the inner workings of a unit, evidence that, at best, can only be pieced together by sifting through thousands of pages of original records in the archives, or, at worst, was never recorded at all and therefore lost for all time. Everything, from morale to discipline and from the nature of fighting to the impact of weather, is given varying amounts of space in these histories. For example, the reason behind the promotion of non-commissioned officers to the rank of officers is an important revelation that is presented in several of the histories. Other less obvious events are recorded. In describing the movement of soldiers from England to France, Captain Stewart Bennett recounted that although they were equipped with the essentials of warfare, "probably nothing was so significant in all these young soldiers' preparation as receiving their identification discs. Not even the field dressing or the rifle and its bayonet had the same sobering effect or was so indicative of the seriousness of the conflict in which they were about to participate as the reception of these little metal discs."[120] The issue of identification discs meant that the training was over and the fighting was about to commence – fighting so terrible that many might only have their bodies identified by the discs they wore. Further penetrating observations can be gleaned from the letters, diary entries, and interviews that regimental historians used to colour their narratives. In short, the regimental histories provide a valuable window for those attempting to understand and reconstruct the social history of Canadian soldiers and the units that shaped their wartime experiences.

Duguid heavily influenced the regimental history program, and he did so as a firm supporter of his fellow soldier-scholars. Duguid believed that by assisting the regimental historians, a richer picture of the Canadian war experience would be provided. Although many official historians have been roundly abused for ignoring the enlisted men in favour of officers and generals, Duguid always saw the regimental histories as a balance to his forthcoming, overarching work. When responding to charges that his draft chapters overlooked the combat experiences of average infantrymen (both enlisted men and junior officers), Duguid wrote, "It is unfortunate that the scale of the Official History and the ground it covers restricts the possibility of including many such personal acts of great valour and much interest. On the other hand it is fortunate that ... the interested reader can find these recorded in the battalion histories, which both complement and supplement the wider aspects which I am called upon to present in the general history."[121] Duguid was aware of the importance of providing personal stories and first-hand accounts in the official history, but he felt that the place for a more extensive and personal exploration was in the regimental histories. Considering the success of the Australian official history series that focused on the soldiers, this would be an oversight. Like Charles Bean, Duguid would have had ample space to devote to the Canadian Tommy in his eight-volume history in a way that Edmonds, in attempting to cover the whole BEF, could not. Having made the decision not to do that, though, Duguid felt that supporting the regimental history program was an essential component in ultimately providing a more balanced legacy to the men of the CEF.

The regimental histories supplied a coherent narrative for the soldiers and filled the historiographical gap that resulted from Duguid's delays in publishing his official history. They were also mementos of battle. Few overseas veterans served throughout the entire conflict. As the regimental history for the 4th Canadian Mounted Rifles noted, only two officers and thirty-four men of the original contingent of a thousand remained in the unit at the Armistice.[122] Most of those who started at Second Ypres or the Somme did not finish at Amiens or Mons. For such men, therefore, a history could delineate events in the war that they had not experienced or understood. Moreover, a history might, as one journalist suggested, present an opportunity for "recalling the memories of those glorious, tragic days and renewing old friendships."[123] For men who had collectively sacrificed so much and relied on each other for moral and physical support, a regimental history would be another bond to draw them together in the sometimes harsh postwar years. These shared "tender memories," as Currie wrote to one regimental historian after reading his work, were like "old family treasures that we put away and don't expose to curious gazes in company where they would not be understood. We hold fast to these cherished memories which sustain and comfort us when things go wrong."[124]

Yet while the regimental histories were important sources for the living, they also paid homage to the dead. Grief and commemoration pervaded all parts of life in Canada following the Armistice. Although the war was often viewed as a great rift between the Victorian era and the modern age, the survivors employed more traditional means of commemorating the fallen.[125] The war was envisaged as a noble sacrifice rather than a senseless slaughter, and this ideal was captured in memorials, plaques, and stained-glass church windows. The veterans' association for the 44th Battalion described their regimental history as one of the "old Battalion's ... three post-war operations"; the first being the dedication of the battalion colours in St. Matthews Church in 1921, and the second being the re-erection of the 44th monument, initially situated on the Pimple at Vimy Ridge, in St. James Park in Winnipeg.[126] Regimental histories commemorated the dead and imparted meaning to the war.

Most of the histories contain an honour roll of the men who lost their lives while serving with the regiment.[127] These long lists of names were a precursor to the Book of Remembrance and seem wholly undirected from the AHS. "Their names are gratefully enshrined in the pages of this book, as their memory is cherished by all who knew them," intoned one regimental history.[128] The histories used sacred language to commemorate the fallen. While the soldiers' remains were left on or near the battlefields, the act of naming the dead marked a tangible representation of their sacrifice, which was available to their loved ones in Canada.[129] More than a few regimental historians hoped that their history would "be a source of consolation to the proudly sorrowing hearts" of those "whose nearest and dearest fell fighting in the ranks."[130] Although these regimental lists were difficult to compile and drove up costs, there was, as the 16th Battalion Association attested, "never a thought of printing the book without it."[131] One can almost envision grieving loved ones opening a regimental history, anxiously turning the pages, fingers working through the text and memorial list, to settle on a familiar name. These "literary memorials," as Duguid aptly described them, were more than simply words and maps; they were the embodiment of wartime experience and sacrifice.[132]

As stakeholders in guarding and crafting the social memory of the conflict, the regimental historians, while working closely with Duguid and his staff, played a significant role in explaining and memorializing the war. Although Edmonds thought little of regimental historians, going so far as to call them "hacks ... who wanted to earn their fees as quickly as possible, without research or investigation," Duguid saw them as a notable component in providing complete coverage of the Canadian Corps' experience in the Great War.[133] And since the multi-volume Canadian official history was never finished, the regimental histories became, in the end, key texts in laying the foundation for historical inquiry. Moreover, with Duguid refusing to give access to the war records after 1921 to anyone other than regimental historians, without these histories, there would have been little else available for veterans and their families. R.C. Fetherstonaugh wrote to Duguid in 1929 that once the multi-volume official history was completed, it, along with the "unofficials" – the regimental histories – will make "a most interesting shelf of books on Canada's part in the War." In the end, the shelf was long, but it was the regimental histories that filled it.[134]

THERE WERE INCREASING CALLS for an official history in the 1920s. Yet there were few who took up Beaverbrook's mantle in the postwar years to champion the memory of the Canadian soldier in writing. A contesting national narrative by the Americans offered that they – who had only entered the war in April 1917 – had taken over from the wasted Allies and delivered victory. Those claims left a bad taste in the mouth of almost all Canadians.[135]

This national bickering came to a head when an obscure American reserve officer, General Henry J. Reilly, wrote an offensive and chauvinistic piece entitled "Who Won the War?" for *Liberty* magazine in January 1927. Reilly argued that the Americans had saved the British Empire, whose forces had floundered incompetently for three years, and turned the tide against Germany after the entry of the United States into the war.[136] It was a direct assault on the memory of Canadian participation in the war, and a number of high-profile writers such as Will Bird and Stephen Leacock ridiculed the claim.[137] But an unexpected defender rose to the occasion to lead the Canadian counterattack; that man was Major George A. Drew, and he was armed with statistics and figures drawn from the official records.

Employing detailed information supplied by Duguid and the AHS, Drew dissected Reilly's argument in two widely published *Maclean's* articles a year later.[138] He did not aim to denigrate the accomplishments of the American Expeditionary Forces (AEF), but with the aid of "dispassionate official records," he pointed out that the British Empire had done more than the Americans in every aspect of war: in supplying men, building munitions, and fighting on land, in the air, or at sea. In fact, Drew noted that in the last three months of the war the four Canadian divisions captured 31,537 prisoners and 623 guns as compared with 50,691 prisoners and 850 guns captured by the AEF throughout the entire war.[139] Armed with Duguid's research and archival records, Drew scored a decisive victory in the eyes of Canadians. So popular were the articles that *Maclean's* republished them as small pamphlets, and over 100,000 copies were sold.

Drew had struck a nerve in defending the Canadian war effort. The *Ottawa Journal* reported on 14 November 1928, "The war is long over. Its details might well be left to impartial historians. But if jaundiced attempts are made to belittle the part that the British Empire played, it is not well that they should be accepted in silence."[140] Drew was lauded for his printed defence of the Empire and, by implication, the Canadian Corps, with one newspaper noting that "since the publication of his article ... Drew has been one of the most discussed men in Canada."[141] It appeared that Canadians, at least when challenged, wanted recognition for their wartime deeds. Drew parlayed his historical success into political points, winning the mayoralty of Guelph, Ontario, the premiership of Ontario, and eventually rising to lead the federal Conservative party. And in this war of reputations, behind Drew stood the official historian who had quietly but ably supplied this public defender with the damning statistics drawn from the official records.

Following his defence of the Empire and the CEF, Drew turned to crafting a history of Canadian airmen in the British flying services. While Canada was reported to have as many as 22,000 airmen, there had been no independent Canadian air force until the last weeks of the war. Flyers like Billy Bishop, William Barker, Raymond Collishaw, and other high-scoring aces had been feted during the war, and now Drew sought to codify their reputations in print. Much like Beaverbrook's *Canada in Flanders* more than a decade earlier, Drew felt that these deeds had to be disseminated to an "air-minded" Canadian public.[142]

A similar project had been envisioned during the war, with the CWRO gathering information on Canadians who had served in the British flying services. Yet because the British made no attempt to identify separate nationalities within their squadrons, it was extremely time-consuming work to track down Canadians and then try to piece together some sort of narrative relating to their wartime activity.

One Canadian officer had begun to comb through the air force records, but by the Armistice, only 900 Canadians had been identified. In April 1919 another committee was struck and Captain J.N. McAdams of the CWRO and a staff of five clerks again tried to compile a list. McAdams was demobilized in the summer and the CWRO closed shortly thereafter, sending the records back to Canada for perpetuity. Before he left the service, though, McAdams suggested that Canada must do more than simply compile a list of names, the only goal mandated at the time. It should follow the lead of the Imperials and commission a work of "literary and historical nature."[143] But there had been no time for that, and the 12,000 cards containing Canadian names and relevant information were transferred to the AHS by 1920.[144]

Back in Canada, the focus at the AHS was rightly on Canada's land forces. The Corps had transformed Canada's national destiny, and although the small Dominion had been recognized for its impressive contribution to the air war, it was the "shock troops" within the BEF that gave Canada its claim to greater autonomy and national pride. They would be justly privileged in the official histories. Nonetheless, Alan Sullivan, a former flyer, had offered a very good history of aviation training in Canada. Despite its work on the army history, the AHS understood the importance of Canada's flyers in the overseas war, and it negotiated with the fledgling Canadian Air Force to transfer at least one officer to begin work on the air war component of the Great War history.[145]

By September 1921 Captain O. Berry was assigned to the Historical Section, and for nine months he developed biographical sketches and created a "Who's Who" list of Canadian flyers. The final document was found to be very unsatisfactory, largely due to the incompleteness of the records. The AHS was unwilling or unable to develop a narrative without a full appreciation of the number of Canadians involved in the air war, and the Air Ministry was queried to provide assistance in compiling the list of flyers; unfortunately, this task was considered too labour-intensive. When Berry left in 1922 for a posting as a flying instructor at Camp Borden, there was the short-lived hope of having one of Canada's war heroes, Colonel R.H. Mulock, a pioneer in tactical and strategic bombing, work on the history, but that never developed beyond the memo-writing phase.[146] The project withered away in 1924.[147]

Perhaps it was hoped that the Imperials would pen the Canadian contribution in their six volumes of official histories, *The War in the Air* (1922-37). They did nothing of the sort, believing that while the British flying services were multinational in character, all flew as part of the British war effort.[148] There was no attempt to single out the deeds of the Dominion airmen, and when they were mentioned, there was no linking of their names or deeds to nationality.[149] Although as many as one in four flyers in British operational squadrons was Canadian by 1918, the index to the six-volume history contained only six references to Canada.[150]

With the Royal Canadian Air Force (RCAF) fighting for its very survival in the debt-ridden postwar years, an official history was simply not a priority. Furthermore, as one RCAF historical officer later noted, the intensive and time-consuming task of gathering archival material was "frowned upon as 'too historical' in character" and, presumably, less relevant to the tiny RCAF.[151] And so there remained no official history for another six decades.

Drew aimed to fill part of the gap resulting from the abandoned official history, but his *Canada's Fighting Airmen* (1930) was a hagiography that elevated twelve Canadian aces into knights of the sky. Like his earlier *Maclean's* pieces, Drew was fighting another war of reputations. In attempting to explain the "individual dominance of Canadians among the British fighting pilots," he rubbed even Canadian airmen the wrong way, with one reviewer criticizing the "blatant Canadianism," which "may foster a sense of pride among the younger generation, but it does not particularly appeal to pilots of the war whose first hand appreciation of their British and other comrades, and the wholesome respect for their enemies, and their personal experience of war in the air, give them a somewhat different perspective of the flying accomplishments of friends and foes alike."[152] Nonetheless, with its laudatory account creating a pantheon of heroes, it sold well, going through three printings by 1931. It also set a foundation for Great War aviation military history that has focused, for the most part, on the small group of fighter aces at the expense of the vast number involved in equally important acts of artillery observation and intelligence gathering. These unsung heroes would remain relatively unknown for most of the century.

H. NAPIER MOORE, the editor of *Maclean's*, wrote to Sir Arthur Currie in September 1928 to say that Drew's response to American claims had resulted in the magazine being "deluged with telegrams, letters and resolutions thanking us" for printing the response. "The significant part about all the letters," wrote Moore, "is that in almost every case the wish is expressed that the article should be placed in the hands of every school child in Canada."[153] With that in mind, Moore inquired if Currie would consider publishing a series of articles based on his memories and experiences. It would indeed have been interesting to see what Currie thought of the Canadian Corps a decade after the war ended, but the general was forced to turn down the request as he was still recovering from a stroke he'd suffered after the trial. Had Moore's request been successful, however, he would have scored a considerable coup since Currie and his fellow generals had published almost nothing since the war.

Several of the Canadian senior fighting generals had died by the 1920s, and they and their surviving comrades left only "a thin and unsustaining gruel of written documentary evidence of wartime actions and events."[154] Currie had indicated many times that he wished to present a personal account of the war "to the Canadian people ... Yet one hesitates to do so because statements I would have to make would reflect on the conduct of troops, allied and other-wise[,] with whom we fought."[155] And so he never published his memoirs, despite several accomplished writers offering to ghostwrite them with him. Neither did Sir Julian Byng, Currie's predecessor, who once remarked that he was unwilling to "abuse" anyone, as was often the case, he believed, when soldiers recounted their lives for posterity.[156]

Surprisingly, almost none of the other senior commanders wrote his memoirs, except Major General E.W.B. Morrison, who had commanded the Canadian Corps artillery and authored a series of articles in *The Ottawa Citizen* during the 1920s. However, one of the brigadier generals, G.S. Tuxford, had penned a manuscript, *The War as I Saw It*, and sent it to Currie for comments in 1922. As commander of both a battalion and then a brigade, Tuxford had hoped to glorify his fighting men and the deeds of the Canadian Corps in general, but as he informed his old commander: "There are many things I should like to write about, but that is not politic to do so."[157] Currie did not endorse Tuxford's history, though, feeling that the history was weak and inaccurate, and adding, "There is too much of an ego about it."[158] Tuxford never published his memoirs. Another CEF infantry brigadier general, Victor Odlum, had written to Currie in 1930 that he too was preparing his memoirs, but wanted to "investigate" the war records in Ottawa to augment his memories. Some time later, Odlum remarked that he was too busy to travel to Ottawa to do research into the records, and decided to free himself from the burden of writing "professional history" and instead embrace the freedom of writing his wartime memoirs in a "reminiscent vein."[159] Indeed that would have been easier, but it appears that Odlum, like Currie, could find no time to pen his memoirs. It is interesting to note that even in the postwar years there appeared to be an informal chain of command that suggested junior officers felt the need to consult with their former commanders even when writing their own personal histories of the war.

While the generals were never able to codify their own history, Canadian soldiers had been publishing memoirs and collected letters since the first year of the war. Considering there were more than 600,000 men who enlisted, the number of memoirs was fairly small. Perhaps this was due to veterans trying to reintegrate back into society and unwilling to dwell on the past; perhaps there was simply no market for memoirs. Whatever the case, many returning veterans found it difficult to talk about their war experiences. A few wistful jokes or memories might creep out of some veterans, but for the most part "when they cast aside their uniforms, most of them endeavoured to seal up the book of memory."[160] Pierre Van Paassen, a Dutch-born CEF soldier, wrote, that "something had come between us" and those who did not serve overseas. "Friends wanted to hear stories of the battlefield, experiences, heroism, and you felt like vomiting when the subject was mentioned."[161] Most men dealt with their psychological scars in silence or only in the company of other veterans.

Memoirs are a particular form of writing, often cathartic and part of a healing process – an attempt to "write the war out of their systems and banish the nightmares."[162] For some, a memoir may have its genesis in the motivation to attack or set the record straight; other writers may have been seeking recognition or were simply trying to document or make sense of their role within a momentous historical event. As such, memoirs and war novels based on personal experience became the history of the masses, and they did not rely on the archival record. For men who had the experience of war seared into their brains, they could fashion a narrative that might be deficient in accurately pinpointing events, but it could be strong on emotion. These personal histories also offered a different perspective of the war. Like some of the poignant trench-inspired poetry that helped soldiers cope with the suffering in the trenches, or at least provided a more robust language or "grammar" in which to express suppressed feelings, the same was true for the memoir. The best known of these international memoir-novels was Erich Remarque's *All Quiet on the Western Front*, which, while not the first of these disillusionment works, certainly made the greatest impact after its 1930 publication. The voice of the soldiers was being heard in the "war book boom" of the late 1920s, and it was far different than that presented in the semi-academic, popular, or official histories.

In Canada, there was a steady offering of first-person war books, but few became bestsellers. The average Canadian was not interested in delving too deeply into the terrible trials of the war, observed H. Napier Moore, but rather continued to enjoy "stories of romance and adventure."[163] By the late 1920s, however, a number of veterans began to publish more successful literary memoirs and novels, much as they were doing in the United Kingdom and Germany. Most of these memoirs sprang from the pens of men who had been fighting on the Western Front – and they offered poignant stories of the bizarre subterranean and sub-human world of trench warfare. All of these eyewitness accounts provided new ways of capturing the war experience, and even though it was personal history, many veterans wished to augment their accounts with the war records.

Wilfrid Kerr, a veteran and then professor at the University of Buffalo, had hoped to use the archival records to better understand the war in which he fought and to improve the accuracy of his memoirs when he began work on them in the late 1920s. Yet Duguid denied him access to these records. As the official historian noted in one memorandum, "It was impossible to put any faith in his undertaking to publishing nothing 'to the disparagement of an individual,'" and so Kerr was blocked from viewing the war records to supplement his memoirs.[164] Kerr wrote his memoirs, *Shrieks and Crashes* (1929), regardless, describing in his introduction that he was not aiming to "shock readers by descriptions of horrors of a length and intensity disproportionate to the actual place these filled in the minds of soldiers," and instead he hoped to provide a view of life in an artillery battery.[165] But as one reviewer observed, Kerr offered a "sour contempt ... for those in authority."[166] This was not universal hatred of officers, since Kerr had encountered good ones, but many of them, in his opinion, did not deserve the respect they commanded. Neither did many of the postwar histories. When he wrote a critique of Great War published material in the mid-1930s for the *Canadian Historical Review*, the journal for Canadian academics, Kerr condemned most of the available histories, both unofficial and regimental, "as almost entirely descriptive and uncritical." One of the books that Kerr liked, however, was Will Bird's *And We Go On* (1930), which he felt was the "best service memoir" then available.[167]

In the 1920s Will Bird had also wanted access to the war records but was denied by Duguid. Like Kerr, he had gone ahead and penned *And We Go On* anyway, which provided another candid examination of the war from the ranks.[168] Bird was described by at least one reviewer as an author who exchanged "the rifle and bayonet for the pen and it is a refreshing change from the type of war stories, written by writers of other countries which have flooded the literary market in recent years, and which, for the most part, have lacked the better qualities of either truth or fiction." There is "nothing of the romantic in 'And We Go On' ... no glamour of patriotism is drawn but rather the horrid facts of war are exposed with no attempt to either magnify or belittle them."[169] Bird's account depicted the grim details of life in the trenches and the trials of warfare, but it did so without rancour and disillusionment. The war had been awful and costly, but it had not been futile. And that, perhaps, is what appealed to so many soldiers. The same was not true of a novel published that same year.

Charles Yale Harrison, an American who served with the CEF as a machine-gunner in the 14th Battalion, wrote the harshest memoir-novel of the war in *Generals Die In Bed* (1930). His anger, like many of the "disillusionment" generation, was prompted by the terrible losses, and specifically directed against the generals behind the lines, safe from the fighting, and seemingly homicidally ordering the soldiers into one fruitless battle after another. Writing from the limited perspective of the trenches, Harrison depicted the degradation and suffering of the soldiers, the rampaging and looting of a "liberated" town in the Hundred Days, and even the killing of prisoners of war. It was shocking even for an antiwar novel. Reviewers were divided, but it elicited strong response from all.[170]

Sir A.C. Macdonell, the 1st Division's last commanding officer, and Sir Arthur Currie found Harrison's novel – and what it represented – incomprehensible. For Harrison to describe Canadian troops drunkenly executing prisoners was nothing short of blasphemy: "His book is a mass of filth, lies and appeals to everything base and mean and nasty ... He talks about nothing but immorality, lice, and other not only disgusting but untrue things," wrote Currie. Of course, the filth, lice, and constant "wastage" of men were not the only aspects of the Canadian infantryman, but they were for many the defining characteristics of the war experience.

Currie knew of the trials of the trench soldier, and he was not like the chateau generals in Harrison's novel (nor were his contemporaries, as Currie helped to bury two friends, both major generals, killed in battle). However, more than a decade after the war, Currie believed Harrison's account was a dirty depiction with no redeeming value. The distortion of the war experience lacked balance and was a libel against the memory of the fallen.[171] As a contemporary veteran wrote in the early 1930s, Harrison's work and books of that ilk were the mere "whimperings of neurotic sensationalists."[172] Other critics damned it as unrepresentative, a perversion of truth, and the product of a diseased mind.[173] That was certainly the belief of Currie, Macdonell, and presumably other senior generals. At the same time, the novel's literary success meant that it struck a chord. Was it veterans that bought the book or those who had escaped service that were drawn to its sensational claims?

This bitter battle over memory between veterans was not easy to mitigate, as both constituents had served their countries and witnessed many of the same trials and degradation. With Harrison, the war had been a senseless slaughter that had brutalized the common man; for others, they too documented the horror, but believed that any sustained attack on the nature of the war, be it leaders, clumsy tactics, or the banality of discipline, was an assault on their memory of the dead and living comrades. Yet both views of the war were far more evocative than the dull histories that tried to remind the readers of the context of the war and were generally little read or remembered as time marched on. Perhaps a memoir by General Macdonell might have set the record straight; instead, he wished for a simpler solution: to "live long enough to have the opportunity of shoving my fist into that s. of a b— Harrison's tummy until his guts hang out of his mouth!!!"[174] That probably would have been an end to Harrison's writing, but Currie offered perhaps greater insight when he suggested that "when Remarque wrote 'All Quiet on the Western Front' he started something which he at that time I am sure did not anticipate. His was the first book written in plain, blunt language, and dealing with many things of which we do not speak."[175] It was so powerful because historians, whether they were popular or official, for the most part also did not "speak" of such experiences in their works.

Those veterans who survived the Great War had every right to detest and be revolted by the unfettered slaughter conducted in the trenches. When one adds the hyper-patriotic propaganda and the feelings of betrayal by shirkers and profiteers on the home front, there were strong reasons to question the war, perhaps even to forget it. But soldiers never did. They banded together in the postwar years, just as they had done on the battlefield. Even the Canadian disillusionment writers such as Bird, Kerr, James Pedley, and Peregrine Acland had done their duty in the war; they had not run away or mutinied, and most were even self-acclaimed *frontsoldaten* who had killed in battle.[176] Their antiwar writings focused on death and loss, suffering and discomfort, and even the incompetence of particularly stupid officers, but never on whether the war should have been fought in the first place. That, then, went to the heart of a deeper issue. There appeared to be no uniform view of the war even from that of the "poor bloody infantry" in the front lines, but few would stand for a total abrogation of all that the war had stood for.

Furthermore, while many of these memoirs and novels were drawn from the disillusionment generation, veterans who were trying to come to grips with their war experience and postwar disappointments that had not lived up to the ideals formed by the brotherhood of the trenches, they were not representative of the whole literature. For every Siegfried Sassoon or Wilfrid Owen, there were countless other novelists and poets who wrote without rancour and sold their books in far greater numbers. At the middlebrow level, it was much more common to find war books that were patriotic rather than despondent. That did not mean that authors cast the war in glowing terms of honour and glory, but rather the war was viewed as something that had to be won, and despite the grim conditions, had been carried to victory in the end.[177] In this light, therefore, it might not be too surprising that the Canadian generals did not put their pens to paper to protect their reputations from books such as Harrison's, particularly if they saw these works as the marginalized products of diseased minds. Nonetheless, for the generals who had learned their skills so proficiently in the heat of battle and had built up the reputation of the Canadian Corps, they appeared uniformly inept at bolstering their reputations in the postwar battles.

"IF WE ARE NOT WATCHFUL the Corps will receive scant recognition, as it appears to be the spirit of the time to minimize what it did," lamented Currie in 1929.[178] That belief notwithstanding, the sacrifice of Canadian soldiers had been inscribed in the countless memorials that dotted the nation, grim testimony to the high price of the war. In the 1920s, as well, the Peace Tower had risen out of the ashes of the destroyed Parliament buildings, which had burned down in 1916. Furthermore, in the late 1920s a contract had been let for the National War Memorial, although that would not be officially unveiled until 1939, only months before the next world war. However, the plans for a war memorial and museum that would house Beaverbrook's war art collection, the trophies, and war records had fallen victim to the fiscal restraint of successive governments. The war art remained stashed in crates, perilously stored in leaky basements; the war trophies were gathering dust in warehouses in Ottawa or spread across the country as tangible reminders of the exploits of the CEF; and the war records were under lock and key at the AHS. But only the records had a dedicated guardian. And Duguid was more than just a passive archivist waiting for records to come to him. Like the CWRO during the war, he continued to add to the already enormous collection.

Duguid devoted much energy during the early 1920s to contacting CEF veterans and requesting the donation of their military papers, diaries, or letters to the AHS in order to assist in the writing of the history. As the CEF's archivist too, he was anxious to repatriate the official war records that remained unaccounted. With generals often taking their own personal archives into retirement, Duguid was insistent that his superior officers support him in tracking down this material.[179] Some officers were willing to return their records to the official historian; others had a more difficult time parting with these representations of their war experience. Throughout the 1920s and 1930s, Duguid continued to send out appeals to veterans, through contacts at annual meetings, regimental associations, and even newspaper advertisements, for he would later comment, "It is remarkable how much of the most useful historical material is still held in private possession."[180] Duguid was not only laying the groundwork of history but also building the very archives in which subsequent historians would draw their information and inspiration. That took time, unfortunately, and Duguid was quickly running out of that.

Veterans had begun to lose patience by the late 1920s after having waited over a decade for their history. Believing that society had turned its back on them, the veterans were unwilling to let history do the same. The Legion passed a general resolution at the 1929 national convention indicating that the government should ensure an official history is written "forthwith, while those who led our troops therein and those who actually participated in the great struggle are still alive to ensure that such history when published, shall be a true record of the sacrifice, the suffering and the achievements of all who served."[181] Responding to the pressure, the deputy minister of National Defence, G.J. Desbarats, wrote to McNaughton that all detailed inquires to the AHS should be stopped and all work be directed towards the official history. This was done but there still appeared to be little tangible progress on the series.[182]

Another barrage was fired at the DND in February 1932. While reviewing a regimental history, J.F.B. Livesay commented that although official historians had been working on a multi-volume series "worthy of the Canadian Corps" since 1921,

> not a single volume has been issued. It is an extraordinary state of affairs. Most other belligerents are well on the way to the completion of their war histories. The Australians, whose case is parallel to our own, are making a particularly good job of it with volumes in orderly sequence ... In Canada we have not even produced an official account of Second Ypres, 1915. Why? Is it political? "The Medical services," good book though it be, produced a lot of controversy when it came out in 1924 [sic]. It is possible successive Governments at Ottawa have thought it inexpedient to tell the people of Canada the truth of what happened in France and Flanders ... The upgrowing

generation, with its natural curiosity about Canada's part in the Great War, cannot find to its hand any authoritative and balanced accounts of those stirring years. It is an offense to our youth and a wrong to our dead.[183]

Although Livesay attacked the politicians rather than the historian, probably because that would have greater effect, he also confided privately to Currie, "I pretty much despair about the official war history, what with the politicians ... I doubt whether Col. Duguid is the man for the job. It seems to me he cannot see the wood from the trees."[184]

Over the next couple of months, the Legion made public appeals and exerted greater pressure on the government, including letters to Prime Minister R. B. Bennett.[185] Realizing that the veterans could not be fobbed off any longer, on 16 May 1932, Defence Minister Donald Sutherland announced in the House of Commons that Duguid had been appointed as official historian. This was more than a little bizarre since Duguid had been working on the history for over a decade; however, now the government had admitted publicly to its responsibility. Duguid again failed to deliver, despite promising Sutherland and McNaughton that the first volume of the official history would be available within a year.[186] But delays were more serious now, especially since the veterans were up in arms and the minister had announced imminent publication in the House. Powerful groups and individuals began to take a greater interest in the official history.[187]

The ongoing and ever-lengthening delay was debated and commented on by the veterans in the newspapers, in the House of Commons, and in the Senate. This was clearly an important event for Canadians, even though many were undergoing the terrible financial trials of the Great Depression.[188] The veterans were pleased that the official history now appeared to be a priority, but many wondered what Duguid had been doing since 1921.[189] When Sutherland had made an absurd statement in the House of Commons that Canada was ahead of other nations in producing official histories, including Great Britain (which had published more than twenty volumes on the air force, navy, and army to date), the government did not even have the decency to retract its erroneous statement when properly contradicted.[190]

Veterans were not assuaged. The lack of an official history and the inability of veterans to get access to the war records were crimes, accused Will Bird. "We, the men who served, want them NOW, have wanted them for years. Any accredited person should be given access to any records in the military section at Ottawa, and all records ... Within twenty years the veterans will have gone to their last roll call – then they can bury forever, with the spiders and stale tobacco, everything regarding the Great War. It will then be of no interest to the existing generations."[191]

Although McNaughton still had faith in Duguid, it was obvious that despite having fought important battles over reputations in the 1920s, many also expected Duguid to have made significant progress on the important official history.

In 1933 Sir Basil Liddell Hart gave a lecture at Trinity College, Cambridge, where he noted that the study of war required the application of academic skills, but that that would not occur until professors learned to "regard it as a branch of knowledge worthy of exploration."[192] In Canada the war remained studiously ignored by the burgeoning academic historical profession. Here, surely, was one of the most important nation-building or, conversely, nearly nation-destroying events in the country's history, and few academics had even attempted to study the topic. Fetherstonaugh wrote to Duguid in 1934 regarding a review article on Great War books by professor Wilfrid Kerr:

> I was interested too to find a professor of history looking at the Great War as worthy of historical consideration. Most professors of history look on the War, it sometimes seems, merely as 'stale news.' From a historical point of view, they wish it hadn't happened. It interferes with their teaching and they resent the fact that, in so far as it is concerned, they are not the final authority, as they are in regard to events that happened longer ago. But the War is fast becoming history, whether they like it or not, and I was interested to find that Kerr was accepting this fact instead of trying, ostrich-like, to deny it.[193]

But it was difficult for historians to analyze or debunk the myths of the war, if that is indeed what they were inclined to do, when Duguid was sitting on tons of records, neither making them available nor seemingly using them. And so the professional historians went elsewhere. With academics receiving ample assistance at the Public Archives, which, under the guidance of Arthur Doughty, was encouraging the writing of Canadian history from the primary sources, most professors decided to avoid the AHS and leave military history to the soldiers.[194] Moreover, with Duguid only allowing "accredited regimental historians" into the defence archives, the official historian was controlling and curtailing the ability of academic historians to contribute to the writing of Canada's military history.

While the Canadian historical profession was just beginning to emerge in the 1920s, one suspects that there might have been a few brave historians willing to tackle the Great War and what it meant to Canadians. The then-important fields of economic and political history, which were providing a solid foundation of study for understanding the growth of the nation, could very well have embraced the Great War. However, then as now, historians are more comfortable with topics where the participants are long dead and there is no chance of being labelled a political scientist or an historian of contemporary affairs. Furthermore, the scars of the war were still very raw, and many Canadians exhibited a general revulsion to war.[195] Whatever the case, without access to the war records – the very essence of what defined the new historical profession was analysis of archival records – there was even less incentive for academics to study the war. Even the first academic military historians in the 1930s, Charles Stacey and George Stanley, were drawn to eighteenth- and nineteenth-century military history. The twentieth century was far too recent a subject to study and when Stanley visited the AHS in the late 1930s, he found a very "chilly reception" to his requests to see Great War records.[196] Competing, conflicting, or contested views of the war were impossible when the archival record was guarded and parcelled out only to a select few.

By the early 1930s, Duguid was nearing completion of the first volume, with significant planning already underway for the subsequent works in the series. Although Duguid had been pressured by politicians, soldiers, and veterans groups to get something out, he would not be rushed. "Sift[ing] through the great mass of material" and selecting the proper war records that "both give a true picture in accordance with established facts and at the same time be satisfactory to participants" must necessarily take an enormous amount of time.[197] "Hitherto writers of history have usually been handicapped by the lack of authentic information: some have been carried away by the prejudices and passions of the time; others, tempted by dubious or partial authorities, have indulged at length in unfruitful speculation," Duguid mused.[198] Of course, he took no responsibility for refusing access of the records to these writers. His job was even more difficult than that of his British counterpart, Duguid complained, for while Sir James Edmonds had only to "satisfy military students," the Canadian official history had to appeal to

> participants, military students, historians and general readers ... The difference in approach may be laid to the fact that the first British line of defence is the Regular Army, professionals, while ours is the Militia, citizens. Another difference is that I work on the main axis running from Ottawa to the front line, and have attempted to cover as it were a long narrow strip running from the recruiting office in Canada through the camps in England and the Canadian Corps area – another comparatively narrow strip – to a restricted section of the front line. The point of origin to which I always automatically return is somewhere in the O.P. line in touch with Infantry Brigade Headquarters, for that is the point of contact between plan and action, and the point at which I personally often was placed. My focus is the front line, the point of contact with the enemy, towards which all Canadian effort was directed; so I have[,] as it were[,] traversed the forward area and taken the reader into the fight occasionally, and also let him look into the mind of the man who was doing the fighting as well as the mind of the man who was doing the planning.[199]

Duguid aimed to reveal the actions of the men at the sharp end of the fighting; furthermore, these men were essential to his history as Canada's war effort (like Britain's) was made up of civilian soldiers. The Australian official historian, Charles Bean, also believed in the importance of presenting the experience of war through the personalization of history, and he mentioned an astounding 6,550 individuals by name in his multi-volume histories.[200] Duguid did not live up to his idealistic plan in the first volume, in which there could have been far more attention on the fighting man at the front. Nonetheless, this was a shift away from the tradition of general staff histories, which aimed to elucidate lessons of war for didactic training of future officers. In short, the Canadian history was written for soldiers but also for the public, and it was to serve as a "literary memorial" to the fallen.[201]

But the ongoing delay continued to plague him. As a result, Duguid has often been portrayed as a waffling amateur out of his depth, someone who would not commit to his project.[202] Whatever his level of productivity, Duguid was clearly passionate about his work. His contemporaries, who expected the official historian to be much more than simply an historian, recognized his commitment. Duguid's defence of Currie and the Canadians against the mean-spirited and inaccurate judgments of the British official historian had earned him much respect. Without him, the reputation of the Canadian Corps would have been forever tarnished. And if one wonders why men like Currie, MacBrien, and McNaughton stood by him in the late 1920s and early 1930s when many were calling for his ouster, it was simply a result of the regard he earned from clashing with Edmonds. In addition, there were few others who could do the job as well as he. Duguid had built up a wealth of knowledge, and the military was not willing to hand over the project to an academic civilian, even if there had been one available. The official historian had also designed the Book of Remembrance, conceptualized the Memorial Chamber, and assisted in producing an official war film, *Lest We Forget* (1935), which further raised his reputation among many veterans. Despite this important work on behalf of the veterans, it was also clear that Duguid had misread the public's demand for an official history. There is no doubt that Duguid's Historical Section had been understaffed for years, but so too were the British and Australians, and both Edmonds and Bean had produced several volumes each by the early 1930s. As guardian of the CEF's memory, it was time for Duguid to be a progenitor too.

WITH DRAFT CHAPTERS READY and sent out to surviving CEF senior officers in 1934, Duguid hoped that these men would verify his assumptions or provide detailed comments that could be evaluated against the official records. This was not a new methodology for Duguid. He had been corresponding with veterans since his appointment in 1921, trying to draw on their memories to ensure an accurate rendition of the war's events. The hidden history of the war – that which was not documented in the official records – could only be supplied by the fighting men themselves, although it is unfortunate that Duguid did not devote more energy to finding out the views of the lower ranks. The interviews and correspondence with officers, however, often left him susceptible to overt pressure to conform his judgments to an individual's point of view; as a result, Duguid was always forced to judge critically everything that was presented for the possibility of enhancing reputations. "Their recollections, although vivid, are sometimes at variance with their own and other contemporary written evidence," recounted Duguid. However, "I shall need their help in other volumes, and I am anxious to retain their interest and goodwill."[203]

Two Canadian high-ranking officers, Sir Richard Turner, General Officer Commanding (GOC) of the 2nd Division and former chief of staff in England, and Garnet Hughes, Turner's brigade major when he was a brigadier at the Battle of Second Ypres and former GOC of the 5th Division, were among the many to read draft chapters of Duguid's first volume. They were not pleased with the historian's depiction of Second Ypres and demanded that he further highlight the role of their brigade during the fierce and confused fighting. Duguid was now the master of the battle, having interviewed dozens of veterans, studied tens of thousands of pages of documents, and written about it at great length. He tried to accommodate their requests by adding a few palliative phrases, but their urgings for more coverage – and more glory – were simply not supported by the facts.[204]

The generals continued to voice their complaints to the CGS, Andrew McNaughton. Escalating the criticism, Garnet Hughes wrote pointedly to Prime Minister Bennett in April 1934 that he felt the official history was unfair to both the 3rd Brigade and his father's reputation, as the narrative focused too much on the failed Ross rifle that Sir Sam Hughes had championed. Even more dangerous for the official history program was his complaint that "there should be some check upon the expression, either positively or negatively, of personal views."[205] In effect, Hughes suggested that the official history should be little more than a bland recital of facts and dates. The prime minister, who was quite unsure about what to make of this soldierly squabbling, wrote worriedly to McNaughton that it is "very important that the history of the war should be impersonal."[206] Historical controversies had again risen to the highest political circles. Duguid could have folded in the face of this powerful opposition, and truth be told, his position was already a tenuous one with the delays, but he refused to be cowed. And neither did McNaughton, who supported the official historian and his judgments.[207]

Duguid again tried to mollify the two generals by changing some of the wording in the offending chapters, but when that did not meet with their satisfaction, the official historian retaliated with a sharply worded document that laid out his case in great detail. Both Hughes and Turner had in fact performed quite poorly during the battle, committing a series of errors. But none was more dangerous, Duguid reminded them, than their confused decision to pull back the 3rd Brigade's defensive line on 24 April without informing Arthur Currie, then commanding officer of 2nd Brigade, whose own defence was dependent on them to support his flank. Quite simply, Turner and Hughes's tactical failure could have resulted in the annihilation of Currie's brigade of several thousand men. Duguid had already confronted their gross error in the draft history and had covered it up.[208] In wonderfully unclear prose, Duguid explained that "the truth and nothing but the truth has been told, but – out of consideration for General Turner – not the whole truth: his actions and their results are made clear without comment and without stressing what, another veteran called, their 'disastrous consequences.'"[209]

Why Turner and Hughes continued to push for more coverage when they should have been grateful for Duguid's historical sleight of hand remains a mystery, and perhaps neither fully remembered the battle nor believed that the official historian would air their "dirty linen."[210] The answer might lie in Duguid's observation – and that of many others – that the perspective of participants was "unbelievably narrow," and that the generals, despite their advantage of "overseeing" the battle, did not and could not understand what was happening along the whole front.[211] Whatever the case, in the war of reputations, the official historian held the ultimate weapons: the archival records. Tired of their harassment, Duguid warned menacingly in December 1934 that both Turner and Hughes should be "well satisfied – and well advised – to waive all objections," or he might not provide such obtuse prose to cover their failings during the battle.[212] Both Hughes and Turner dropped their objections shortly thereafter. Duguid must have felt like a junior politician in the government of British nineteenth-century prime minister Benjamin Disraeli, who admonished: "Damn your principles! Stick to your party." The Canadian official historian stuck to his "party," but he would not be browbeaten into completely obfuscating the truth. And he had the will – through his command of the historical record – to stick to his "principles."[213] Nonetheless, Duguid would probably have agreed with Lord Beaverbrook, who presciently wrote in 1917, "It is in no case a grateful task to write a contemporary history, for the judgment of all concerned is obsessed by personal experiences and not sufficiently informed for an adequate judgment."[214] It appeared that the 1930s might still be considered too soon for dispassionate judgments about Canada's role in the Great War.

CHARLES BEAN'S TWELVE-VOLUME HISTORY has been described as "one of the most remarkable achievements of Australian historiography."[215] In fact, Bean probably did more: he influenced the way Australians saw themselves.[216] The image of the digger, which Bean had such an important role in shaping, is an essential icon in Australian culture and identity. There is no corresponding equivalent in Canada, even though Lord Beaverbrook and the CWRO had focused on the national characteristics of Canadian soldiers as essential ingredients as to why they were such successful soldiers during the Great War. Duguid certainly saw the Canadian soldier – his companions – as elite soldiers, and some of his early writing had highlighted national characteristics that supposedly gave them a natural affinity for war, but as he studied the war records, it was clear there were other essential characteristics of the Canadian Corps that had propelled it to success. Strong and open-minded commanders, efficient staff officers, and a corps structure that was semi-permanent all provided the administrative framework to allow active learning and the efficient dissemination of battle lessons. Through intense scrutiny and study of the war records, countless interviews with veterans, and nearly two decades of pondering the issue, Duguid was crafting a work that would go far beyond the romantic and heroic Great War histories of the past.

In 1935 the Canadian Historical Association (CHA) recognized Duguid's massive research project, and he was invited to address its members at their annual conference that same year. He had clearly broken the mould of the amateur military historian, and his command of the Great War and mastery of the records had proven that he belonged in the ranks of academic historians. His history, moreover, was an important one that would complement the national historical school of academics such as Harold Innis, Frank Underhill, Chester Martin, and Arthur Lower, who were examining Canada's evolution from colony to nation through economic, political, and mercantile theories and paradigms. Missing from this national school of writing, however, was the essential role of military history in shaping the nature and growth of Canada. Duguid had been slowly embraced by the historical community, and it is likely that his position as an official historian, alone in the country, still made him something of an outsider, albeit one who was carrying out undeniably important work.

A year after Duguid's CHA paper, Charles P. Stacey, a young Canadian teaching at Princeton, published *Canada and the British Army* (1936). This was a groundbreaking work that examined the impact of the British Army on Canada and the country's development from colony to Confederation. Based on research mined from the Public Archives of Canada, Stacey offered Canada its first scholarly military history, and it would become a harbinger of his work during and after the Second World War. That same year George Stanley published *The Birth of Western Canada* (1936), which was not strictly military history, but it provided ample discussion of the clash between westward expansion and native peoples, particularly the two Métis uprisings in 1870 and 1885.[217] While academics were not yet comfortable delving into the Great War, it appeared that they were inching their way towards the twentieth century.

By 1936 Duguid was nearing the end of the first volume. One last delay for Duguid was his attempt to make the official history more inclusive by having a section devoted to the Royal Canadian Navy (RCN). While Canada's effort in the Great War was based largely on its army, and to a much lesser extent those Canadians in the British flying services, there was also a small navy. The RCN had been established in 1910, but it was less a symbol of Canada's desire for greater autonomy than it was an evasive manoeuvre to avoid being drawn into imperial defence commitments that could not be controlled in Ottawa. The navy's wartime role was uninspiring, with its two obsolete cruisers, *Niobe* and *Rainbow*, doing very little except performing repairs to keep them afloat. While members of the RCN were involved in clearing the dead and rebuilding Halifax after a terrible explosion in December 1917, Canada's navy had a more prominent operational role in raising a fleet of 100 vessels to help protect the Eastern seaboard from enemy submarines.[218] But even when U-boats crossed the Atlantic in the summer of 1916 and, by 1918, seriously threatened the East coast by sinking fishing ships, there was little this small navy could do without adequate anti-submarine tactics, doctrine, or weapons. In contrast to the Canadian Corps, the wartime actions of the Royal Canadian Navy went relatively unnoticed by Canadians except as an example of futility. Following the war, the navy was severely cut back and spent much of the 1920s simply trying to survive. There was no thought of producing an official history. Duguid began negotiating with the navy brass in 1933, however, and while Chief of Naval Staff Commodore Walter Hose wanted to see the history of the RCN captured in print and ordered a number of researchers to draw information from the surviving naval central registry files, nothing ever materialized. As late as June 1937, Duguid was still waiting for a short account of *Niobe* and *Rainbow*, as an official history without them would have been "deplorable."[219] In the end, Duguid and his staff wrote the naval section, and it was clear that senior naval officers were not nearly as historically minded as the army, a characteristic that would continue into the Second World War.

After several additional delays, most of which were not Duguid's fault, volume 1 of the *Official History of the Canadian Forces in the Great War, 1914-1919* was published in 1938, along with a companion volume of documents. Reported on in almost every major newspaper across the country, it received an avalanche of positive reviews.[220] "Canada's immortal story," as the *Sudbury Star* noted, would allow veterans to relive the past and provide a "national" history for all Canadians.[221] The *St. Catharines Standard* felt this history would "give Canadians their due place and their due credit in the world struggle."[222] While the AHS had been "scooped (in journalese) time and again by memorialists and other historians," noted one Calgary newspaper review, "the History's merit is in its official" designation, which imparted a sense of authenticity and accuracy.[223] For almost all reviewers, there was a focus on the enormous amount of work carried out by Duguid and his team, employing scientific historical methods, as one reviewer noted, which allowed them to draw forth the history from the long buried war records. As such, "the historian, a participator in many of the events recorded, does not hesitate to apportion praise and blame, to criticize candidly, his opinions being always supported by documentary evidence."[224] Even military historians like C.P. Stacey and Sir James Edmonds praised the work.[225]

Despite reviews to the contrary, the history still avoided, even twenty years after the war, some of controversies of the 1915 Ypres battle. Constrained by both his role as the official historian and in writing contemporary history, Duguid would later reveal after his retirement that he did not feel the official history of the CEF could be written until after Sir Richard Turner's death.[226] Nonetheless, Duguid had followed his initial vision of producing a "source book for historians," a "literary memorial" for the veterans and their families, and a history that could act as a guide for future generations of officers and politicians attempting to process the lessons of the Great War.[227] The coverage was deep; the history was anchored with 850 footnotes, but with more than 2,600 units in the CEF and 424,589 having served overseas, there would inevitably be, Duguid warned, gaps in the history that future generations of historians would have to fill.[228]

Despite this good work, for two decades veterans and their families had waited for an authentic history based on official records. "Criticism on the point of tardiness," observed one reviewer, "has been vigorously articulate, particularly among veterans." Another newspaper editorial pontificated that "it must have been necessary to collect, select, arrange and synthesize the whole before a single line was written. There is room for debate whether it is better to dash off a history as soon as possible after a war, a narrative inevitably incomplete, ill-balanced and to some extent lacking perspective, but full of the spirit of the times and appealing to emotions still wide awake, or to wait, sift, analyze and attempt to achieve cold impartiality and objectiveness. Rightly or wrongly Canada has chosen the latter course."[229]

The first volume probably lived up to the expectations of most. The delay, however, was "nationally inexcusable," claimed one reviewer, and thousands of the participants had died before getting to read even beyond the 1915 battles.[230] It was hoped that the remaining volumes would follow in quick succession. But Canada's Great War veterans would be greatly disappointed. Duguid would never publish another volume in the series.

SINCE THE LAST BULLET was fired on 11 November 1918, Duguid had been fighting for the reputation and memory of his brothers-in-arms. The order-in-council appointing Duguid and laying down the AHS's mandate was very clear that he was to craft an official history. It did not suggest that Duguid was to be guardian of the CEF's memory, but that became his self-appointed role. And, in fact, he had little choice in the matter when his former comrades turned to him to protect their individual and collective reputations. Duguid's active defence against Edmonds resulted in a victory, albeit a time-consuming one, for the men of the CEF and all Canadians. The official historian's support of Currie was particularly evident in that acrimonious historical clash and later in the 1928 trial.

As both official historian and archivist, Duguid had ultimate leverage in how the war would be historically interpreted. The official historian understood the power of the war records, and he refused to allow anyone other than "accredited regimental historians" to use the material. As a result, Duguid almost singlehandedly controlled the historical memory of Canada and the Great War. There were, of course, a number of popular histories and memoirs forged without the war records, but none of them carried the notion of authenticity or impartiality. We know that neither the official history, nor any history for that matter, can be truly described by such heady adjectives. However, there was an expectation by the public and by veterans groups that Canada needed an official history based on authentic war records that would explain truthfully the war and, equally important, give Canadians and the rest of the world a record of the Canadian Corps' accomplishments.

In undertaking his important series, Duguid was forced to deal with not only British pressure in the 1920s, but also Canadian internal schisms in the early 1930s. Yet because Duguid was the undisputed Canadian expert on the war as well as holder of both official and unofficial records, he was able to ensure that the history was not corrupted by personal agendas. That did not mean that Duguid presented the history of the CEF and specifically the Battle of Second Ypres with all its warts and blemishes, as he surely downplayed some of the problems of the Canadians' first battle, but for those critics who have suggested that the official histories were just the mouthpieces of the generals, it is worth remembering that Duguid refused to cave in to their pressure. As Edmonds confessed to one friend: I "could not tell the truth frankly in an official history but hoped that it would be evident to those who could read between the lines."[231] The same was true for Duguid, and a reading of his official history makes it clear that Turner had indeed performed inadequately during the battle and that the Ross rifle had proved a questionable weapon. This notwithstanding, Duguid's greatest trial was in confronting the nature of writing contemporary history. Contemporary rather than the official designation was what caused Duguid the most trouble in crafting an unbiased and uninfluenced history. If the CEF official history has been since relegated to dusty library shelves, it is also useful to highlight that it had, at one time, been eagerly anticipated and feted for its impartial coverage of the war.

That it took so long to be published was a result of the many strains on the tiny AHS staff in the 1920s, but also because of Duguid's fastidious approach to history. It is here where Duguid can be most faulted. Aware of the fallout from Macphail's official history, Duguid felt his work had to be unassailable in fairness and judgment. Yet every historian must confront the mass of documentation, the tyranny of the records, and there is always the danger of continually researching in the hope of finding one more bit of evidence, one more essential document that will explain everything. Perhaps it was his engineering background that propelled Duguid to arrange every document in the hope that the parts would eventually form the total. Indeed, how could one build a bridge without all the parts? Yet engineering is not history, and historians must draw conclusions knowing that they will never see every record and, moreover, that countless records are never created or never survive to find their way to an archives. Duguid searched and searched and did not feel comfortable putting his conclusions down on paper until it was too late. In one draft introduction to the first volume of the history, Duguid noted that "conclusions cannot be drawn until all information has been arranged in such form that it can be grasped readily and the relative importance of events weighed. Otherwise conclusions will be faulty and probably entirely wrong."[232] This inability to find the balance between a careful reading of the records and the fear of drawing conclusions before every record could be processed was his greatest fault.[233]

While one must account for the many pressures put on Duguid and his staff, the historical sections for Australia and Great Britain, which had to document similar wartime experiences and suffered from the same shortages of official historians after the war, had published nearly all of their multi-volume histories by the time Duguid offered volume 1 in 1938. Canada's single volume was obviously an embarrassment for the government and a source of consternation to veterans. Canadians deserved better.

Duguid had assisted the regimental historians throughout the interwar period; had sat on several high profile and time-consuming committees to assign battle honours, which were extremely important to all units and their perpetuating battalions; had handled thousands of reference inquiries; and protected the reputation of individuals and the CEF in fighting essential, high-profile cases. But in the end he had failed to produce an official history. The wretched statistic of seventeen years to produce one volume hangs like an albatross around Duguid's neck; as a result, it has been too easy for critics to dismiss him as an unqualified and lazy officer who wasted away the resources of the nation, while at the same time denying Great War veterans a literary memorial of their war. This is unfair. Nonetheless, with his unsuccessful attempt to produce a history or make the records available, Duguid had stifled much of the writing of the 1920s and '30s and left no historical foundation for other historians to build upon. Duguid should be damned for this proprietary behaviour that ultimately curtailed the ability of Canadians to understand the sacrifice of their fellow veterans and of historians to later shape the historical memory of the conflict.

The polemical British Great War veteran and military commentator, Sir Basil Liddell Hart, claimed the British official historian may have generally got the facts right, but he wrapped them in interpretations that hid the guilt of British generals such as Sir Douglas Haig. Edmonds's official history, he wrote, was not "merely 'patriotic' history but parochial history."[234] Because of his closeness to events and individuals, Edmonds, like Bean and Duguid, was constrained in what he could say about senior officers and soldiers. Edmonds's critics have been particularly hard on him, accusing him of obfuscating the truth, diverting readers away from disasters, and even destroying incriminating evidence to ensure that subsequent generations of historians would not be able to uncover his lies.[235] The subtle chains that encircled the official historian from within the military hierarchy, of having exclusive access to the war records, and in being appointed to capture the war experiences of hundreds of thousands and codify them in print did not lend themselves to flaying senior officers with the nub of the pen. But that, for the most part, was the nature of the first generation of writers. These generals, who were still very much considered great men in the postwar years, were alive and in significant positions of power. When, for example, Macphail lashed out at Sir Sam Hughes, who had been dead for a few years, but when he lived, had clearly exhibited a flawed personality, the medical official historian had been rebuked forcefully. One can only wonder at the reaction of reviewers and the public if war heroes like Sir Richard Turner or Sir David Watson (probably the weakest of the Canadian divisional commanders), or Sir Arthur Currie for that matter, had been criticized harshly in an official history. Since Duguid never got past the first volume, we do not know what the future official histories would have held, but it is likely that, like his earlier writing, they would have been restrained. Yet we must understand the canon of war writing in Canada during the interwar period and its major historians, of which Duguid is by far the most important, as products of their time. To hold up these historians or histories as straw men and apply historical standards from the twenty-first century is to be ahistorical, but to do so also misses the important constraints and pressures that worked against this first generation of postwar authors. It is worth remembering R.B. Bennett's words of caution when caught bewilderingly in the historical squabble between Turner, Hughes, and Duguid, "Few more difficult tasks could be undertaken than the preparation of the history by a young country."[236]

While Duguid may have failed to produce an historical series, he did not fail as guardian of the CEF's memory and reputation. The role of the CEF official historian was much more than simply writing a history, even if he has been remembered only for that. It is not often that historians are on the front line in defending the memory and reputation of hundreds of thousands of veterans, the government, and even the nation. In his own domain, Duguid was the master of memory and history of the Great War. To see him in this contemporary role, rather than in the one assigned to him afterwards by historians who saw only his limited production, provides a different view. One can have sympathy for Duguid, as he fought and won countless historical battles for the CEF only to lose his own in the final war of reputations.

3
Clio in the Service of Mars, 1939-45

> *General Crerar in conversation with me, while never saying a word against Duguid, made no secret of the fact that in hiring me he was trying to provide against another such fiasco in connection with the second war.*
> – C.P. Stacey

> *The record of battle is more or less confused at best.*
> – Alfred Vagts

When war came in September 1939, there was no cheering as in the summer of 1914. There was only grim resignation, as again Canadians would have to fight in defence of liberty, justice, and, despite their political independence, the British Empire. Canadian Prime Minister William Lyon Mackenzie King hoped for a war on the cheap, which might allow him to avoid the kind of slaughter and divisive conscription crisis that occurred during the Great War. But that proved to be impossible, especially after the fall of France in the summer of 1940. Canada was firmly committed to another brutal struggle, and this time it would take place in many theatres of war: on land, in the air, and at sea.

How would the government officially document this new military effort? Without war records there is no evidence of the historical past other than what lies in the living memory of participants. Aware that the official history program in the last war had failed, senior officers in the army, air force, and navy authorized the establishment of service historians to capture and collect war records for a future historical program. These sections worked independently of each other, although their goals were the same: to document the war through the preservation of records and to write historical narratives to provide a foundation for postwar writing of an official history series. The army's historical officer, Colonel Charles P. Stacey, carved out an important overseas section, which was largely independent of Colonel A.F. Duguid's Ottawa historical operation. The air force, on the other hand, had a centralized historical section in Ottawa under the control of Group Captain Kenneth Conn, DFC. Finally, the navy's official historian, Dr. Gilbert Tucker, was almost entirely divorced from the work of his overseas historical officers, who were directed for much of the war by Lieutenant James George. Yet all of these overseas historical officers influenced, authored, and preserved the war records for future generations. They also employed history to assist operational requirements, proving their worth to their respective services. With Clio supporting Mars, the historical sections were strengthened throughout the war, helping to lay the foundation for the postwar official histories.

WITH THE DILAPIDATED STATE of the Canadian military in 1939 and the frantic scramble to mobilize the resources of the nation, one might suspect that very little thought would be given to another historical program at the start of the war. This was not the case, however. In November 1939 Harry D.G. Crerar, Brigadier General Staff at Canadian Military Headquarters (CMHQ) in London, asked Duguid, senior officer at the Army Historical Section (AHS) in Ottawa, to send an officer overseas to "supervise [the] preparation of War Diaries and [the] collecting of other historical data." Anxious not to repeat the disaster of the last war, Crerar wanted a trained historian on staff from the beginning, so he started making additional requests for Charles P. Stacey, a "well known writer on Canadian military history."[1]

C.P. Stacey was indeed a fine candidate for the position, although even he might have been surprised at being described as a well-known writer. He had grown up in Toronto, attended the University of Toronto, won a scholarship to Oxford, and then earned a doctorate at Princeton. Stacey had subsequently published several articles, both scholarly and popular, and a groundbreaking study, *Canada and the British Army, 1846-1871* (1936), which explored the impact of the British military on Canada. He was also author of the short but perceptive *The Military Problems of Canada* (1940), which attracted Crerar's attention.[2] When war was declared, the expatriate Canadian, who was teaching at Princeton, immediately offered his services – despite being on his honeymoon. He was told to wait for an opportunity that befitted his skills, which were obviously identified as that of an historian rather than a junior signals officer, his Militia calling. When newly promoted Major General Crerar, then serving as chief of the general staff (CGS), cleared away the administrative tangle, he offered Stacey a position as an historical officer in October 1940. At the age of thirty-four, Professor Stacey immediately accepted, resigned his academic post, and was promoted to the rank of major.

Stacey arrived at CMHQ in London with his one-page directive supplied by Crerar during the heavy bomber raids of Christmas 1940. The directive dictated that Stacey was to prepare material for the official historian (who had not yet been appointed) and further document the war effort by collecting historical evidence "not otherwise recorded or available."[3] With this broad but necessarily vague mandate, Stacey was introduced to senior officers including Major General Price Montague, the commanding officer at CMHQ, who warmly greeted the young historian but told him he "had expected someone with long white whiskers."[4] Stacey found that this was not the only misperception related to his appointment, as he was viewed with suspicion by a number of Canadian officers.

Unbeknownst to Stacey and doing him no service, Duguid had augmented the overseas historical officer's initial directive and had sent another one to CMHQ with more wide-ranging and intrusive powers. Unfortunately, staff officers at CMHQ did not believe that an officer would be sent overseas simply to work on a history and assumed that Stacey must be some sort of spy for National Defence headquarters in Ottawa. Duguid's brash statement that Stacey be allowed, among other things, to attend strategic meetings would have been useful for the historical officer, but did little to ease the situation. First Canadian Division's highest-ranking staff officer, Colonel G.R. Turner, wrote a scathing objection to his superior, Major General Andrew McNaughton, about the role of the historical officer. Turner believed it was a "dangerous practice" to share information with this low-ranking outsider until "AFTER the operation is over." Moreover, with Stacey tasked to observe and document all operations, Turner feared this pesky chronicler would "practically be at the Commander's elbow."[5] Realizing his position was fragile at best, Stacey, as a Crerar-man, immediately went about drafting compromise regulations. The resulting guidelines were very similar to the earlier ones but less insistent in tone. The focus remained the same, however, with the historical officer still collecting records and documenting the actions and engagements of the Canadians through historical narratives. With these adjustments, General McNaughton accepted Stacey's mandate and even suggested that he be allowed to interview senior officers to record their impressions of events.[6] Stacey was instructed to develop a far-reaching program that would facilitate the writing of wartime narratives and ensure the creation and care of war records.

Although Stacey was formally part of Duguid's Ottawa Historical Section, by establishing new ties in England he did his best to distance himself from the Great War historian. Stacey's first meeting with the dynamic and charismatic Canadian commander Andrew McNaughton set the tone for his historical work. With the briefest of pleasantries, McNaughton took Stacey into his confidence and discussed high-level policy and the need for continual diligence in exerting control over Canadian forces within the British military organization. After using Stacey as a sounding board, to which the historical officer was told, "Nothing I say to you must go beyond this room," McNaughton agreed to the major's request to have access to all headquarters records and even suggested that Stacey could invoke his name should he run into problems interviewing recalcitrant individuals or accessing records.[7] Stacey's subsequent examination of top secret records allowed him to build up his expertise and knowledge. Further meetings with Crerar, who returned to England in early 1942, were equally positive, and the general emphasized "the importance of recording the atmosphere of the moment while living through it." Following McNaughton's lead, Crerar offered Stacey full access to his private war diary, in which he recorded his occasionally caustic impressions of Canadian-British relations.[8]

Neither Crerar nor McNaughton attempted to censor or force Stacey to accept a certain view of history, and both asked for open, honest accounts of the war. Later, Stacey received support from Guy Simonds, one of Canada's best fighting generals, and E.L.M. Burns, who would eventually command a corps in Italy. Both were strong champions of the Historical Section. Canada's generals did not need much convincing to see the value of history. A proud martial past and culture were embedded in their regimental traditions, while the study of old campaigns constituted essential training at staff colleges. In addition, Stacey's superiors had an understanding of their place in the present conflict, which would surely become one of the most important events of the twentieth century – and it was the historical officer's mandate to ensure that evidence of their actions survived.

Despite this encouragement and support, it is also clear that anyone – trained historian or not – would struggle with recording objectively the war's events. How would Stacey deal with controversies, especially those involving his patrons? Could he be objective while relying on the goodwill of others for continued support? These were difficult questions and little evidence remains as to whether they were pondered at the time. Past official histories were narrative in style, unashamedly patriotic, and largely uncritical of high-level decisions. Initially, Stacey was a one-man unit and, eager to win the support of his superiors in order to advance a plan for an official history, he had no intention of embarrassing them or his nation for the sake of historical openness during the war. But he also knew that disclosure would come in varying degrees after the war. As the war receded into memory, he became more willing to pass judgment, both on the generals and the Canadian Army as a whole. From 1940 to 1945, however, Stacey and his team of historians struggled with writing narratives that reflected the reality of war in order not to mislead the future official historian, while at the same time not offending senior army officers.

Initially though, Stacey did not have to worry about the writing of history because his primary task was securing the archival record. Not content to sit passively as the army's archivist waiting for records to eventually arrive from the field after passing through many layers of bureaucracy, Stacey changed the administrative flow of records within weeks of taking over his position so that he could gain access to all closed files. By consulting these operational records, reading through the War Diaries of units, and interviewing officers, Stacey produced a series of detailed reports on Canadian activities in England. These summaries were circulated to senior Canadian officers for their comments. In addition to building up this chronicle, Stacey was able to provide useful accounts of operations that were soon employed in high-level briefing notes. The historical officer was capturing and making available the institutional memory of the army, and McNaughton, after reading several narratives, ordered that Stacey should not "pull punches."[9]

While working alone through 1941 and early 1942, Stacey produced dozens of narratives of Canadian events, everything from the convoy of troops to descriptions of training operations.[10] However, along with his heavy writing load, he was also responsible for gathering records that would eventually be used to underpin the official histories. The historical officer visited units throughout England, providing advice, prodding lazy war diarists, and meeting with commanding officers to remind them of their duty to document their actions, preserve complete records, and ensure historical accuracy. Of all these textual accounts, the War Diary was the essential historical tool for tracking events; it was to supply authentic material for the history of the unit "with regards to operations, training, equipment, and organization"; and in order to "preserve important original documents for posterity," it was "essential not to destroy" anything of historical value.[11] Constant attention was necessary to ensure that detailed and full historical records were created, as many officers saw this as a mundane administrative task and the least of a unit's worries. Realizing that not all diarists knew what to include in their descriptions, Stacey was also instrumental in writing new regulations and historical guidelines. Nonetheless, the Historical Section spent much of the war continually reminding war diarists to provide detailed accounts, to include secret material, and to disregard all worries about censorship. When appeals failed, commanding officers were told that they and their men might be forgotten by future historians if they ignored this task. Most responded with detailed war records. Even early in the war, therefore, Stacey's role within the General Staff was proving more useful than if he were simply an envoy for Duguid's Ottawa Historical Section.

By such instructions, it is also clear that Stacey, and later his historical officers, had an important impact on the type of documentation being created. These were not neutral records that simply reflected deeds and actions; they were influenced by all manner of factors including pride in the regiment, pesky historical officers insisting that various types of information be included or highlighted, and choices that excluded or minimized actions because the chronicler was not present at an event, could not get reliable information, felt constrained to protect the reputation of a unit or individual, or was simply too busy – or too tired – to pursue the matter. The historical officers were aware that they had a significant influence on what was being recorded during the war; at the same time, they seem to have failed to recognize that their intervention might prejudice the final outcome of how events were recorded.[12]

"One officer engaged in the work now," Stacey wrote, "can probably accomplish as much as three approaching it after the coming of peace, when the actual participants are scattered, when the edges of individuals' memories are dulled, and when there will be little to work with except the documents."[13] While Stacey had been able to collect the records of the early Canadian war effort in England, there was an immediate need to write up events into an historical narrative. In regard to Stacey's appeals for an assistant, McNaughton noted, "I am very much in favour of this so that the comprehensive narrative of our operations and development in 1940 may be prepared at an early date for otherwise there is a danger that we may lose the full story of this phase." As he rightly observed, "much of the intimate history of the more important parts remains in the minds of individuals and has never been committed to paper."[14] It was becoming understood that work on a future official history required diligent toil in the present.

Stacey began to send out invitations in March 1942, and George Stanley, the Oxford-trained professor from Mount Allison University known for his groundbreaking work on Louis Riel, was appointed to the section later that year.[15] Arriving with little knowledge of his duties, Stanley was excited to learn that he would be employed as an historian, immediately responsible for research and writing. Because Stacey had neither been appointed as official historian nor given any direction concerning the eventual nature of the histories, he decided that their narratives were to be written in a "businesslike" style, in which the narrator was not to "express opinions, [but should] ... provide the Official Historian with the means to forming opinions."[16] The historical officers aimed at being seemingly detached collectors of information rather than commentators on affairs, but they would do so with full access to the official records. Although writing a preliminary narrative was but one of Stanley's many tasks, by the war's end this "tower of strength," as Stacey called him, had penned eleven chapters consisting of 300,000 words and 2,569 references.[17] This was just part of the Historical Section's wartime production, and this "usable" history impressed the generals enough for them to support an official history program after the surrender of Germany.

While Stanley worked away on the narratives, Stacey continued in his role as senior historical officer by liaising with his British counterparts. The British had devoted more resources to their historical program and had enlisted the historical community to participate in writing both military and civil-military monographs. Stacey realized that developing good relations with them would be profitable. Not only would the overseas Canadian Historical Section have access to records and detailed narratives documenting strategic issues outside of the limited Canadian war effort, but it would also be able to influence how the British depicted the Canadian participation. As Stacey put it to the General Staff, Canada did not want to repeat the acrimonious exchange that had occurred between Duguid and Edmonds in the 1920s.[18] Stacey's involvement with the British also helped to solidify ideas about the postwar Canadian official history. Following the British lead, he felt the final product should be geared to the general public and not simply to military audiences; he also pushed for access to all high-level British documents in order to provide the context for the Canadian actions. Stacey received assurances that he would see this material, but it would have to wait until after the war, since much of it was in use or inaccessible. Although he accessed some of these documents through the papers of McNaughton and later Crerar, there was much that remained outside his purview. Stacey realized that there would be significant work after the war in piecing together the overall strategic narrative that encompassed Canadian Army operations.

Stacey took leave in August 1942 after nearly twenty months of continuous work. He did not know that the 2nd Canadian Division was about to launch the first major Canadian offensive army operation of the war with an amphibious landing on the beaches of Dieppe. Faulty preparation and lack of combined arms support turned the 19 August raid into a frontal assault against a prepared, dug-in enemy. It was a disaster: of the nearly 5,000 Canadians who embarked from England, 3,367 were killed, wounded, or captured.[19] When the bloodied survivors returned, there was a conscious effort to reconstruct events and incorporate some of the hard lessons of the failed mission into future doctrine and operations.

Having been left out of the information loop, Stacey immediately requested and was given authorization to interview survivors in order to piece together the operation into an historical narrative.[20] Moreover, in the absence of a Royal Canadian Navy historical officer (who had not yet been appointed), Stacey also interviewed naval personnel, transcribing their experiences for the record. For Canadian officers attempting to understand what went wrong, such a detailed outline was seen as a useful addition to their own investigation. Over the following months a steady flow of reports, operational orders, and written accounts were passed to the Historical Section. More pressing, however, CMHQ needed to respond to the federal government's request for an account of the raid. They turned to their historian, asking him for a white paper in order to explain the botched mission to Canadians at home.

With little time to research and write, Stacey searched through the records for the rationale behind the attack and the apparent incongruities concerning why the raid had been cancelled and then relaunched. He received little help from Admiral Lord Mountbatten's Combined Operations Headquarters (COHQ), which had planned the operation. Within a month, though, Stacey had produced his white paper. There can be no doubt that he understood that his superiors wanted the raid portrayed not as an absolute failure but as a necessary, if costly, prelude to planning and launching a larger scale amphibious landing to crack the Nazi hold on Western Europe.

Stacey did not write about the wishful thinking of McNaughton and Crerar or the seemingly ill-conceived plan for returning the raiding force to their waiting ships while engaged with the enemy, but he also did not whitewash the raid. First drafts described a lost operational order that was captured during the assault, the frantic attack and withdrawal of units, and the role of senior British and Canadian commanders. When the draft was sent to COHQ, Lord Mountbatten (who would later spend years covering up his instrumental role in the debacle) erupted in anger, claiming that this historical account was so damaging that it would be worth "500,000 pounds to the enemy," presumably as free propaganda.[21] Responding to the outrage, the Canadians agreed to alter significant parts of the text, but Stacey pressured his superiors who reconsidered, eventually changing the work back to the original text before publication.[22]

The final product was well received in Canada, and J.L. Ralston, the minister of National Defence, was so impressed with the paper that he read it in its entirety to the House of Commons.[23] Stacey had once again proved his worth to McNaughton and further validated the usefulness of an historical officer. In fact, one American war journalist, Quentin Reynolds, had published an instant account of the raid that laid the blame for the planning at the feet of Canadian commanders and questioned the fighting capabilities of their troops.[24] Stacey thought it "pure libel," but McNaughton did not want to enter into a "public discussion" with a journalist for fear that it would prejudice future relations with the British. To defend the Canadians' reputation would mean that the British would have to shoulder more of the blame, and McNaughton told Stacey that he did not want to see "this interpreted as seeking to shift responsibility from us to them."[25] As a result, Stacey's short account would stand as the message to the Canadian people and their allies. Equally important to Stacey was the opportunity to draw together a vast amount of material on the operation for the future official historian to later appraise. McNaughton had ensured that all Canadian records were opened to Stacey, and he even pressured the British to provide what was thought to be full access to their operational records; however, some of the key documents, especially those used by Mountbatten and high-level Cabinet office communications, remained hidden from Stacey, while others were never created in the first place.[26]

Although Stacey's work on the white paper was technically outside his mandate, his ability to represent the military in response to the government's request gave him further opportunity to expand the role of the Historical Section. Not having been informed of the operation, Stacey complained, had left him less able to complete his task of chronicling the army. He stressed that the section should be advised of all upcoming operations and that an historical officer should be attached to all command headquarters in order to document forthcoming actions fully. On 1 October 1942, First Canadian Army agreed and ordered that "the historical officer be kept in the picture in regard to projected operations."[27]

While there had been no formal commitment by the government to produce an official history, senior officers encouraged Stacey, now firmly entrenched in the military hierarchy, to prepare for one by writing narratives and gathering war records. Stacey was also entrusted to coordinate the work of war artists, who would document the war visually as the historical officers were capturing it in writing. In a meeting with the CGS on 12 February 1943, a newly promoted Lieutenant

Colonel Stacey recorded that General Kenneth Stuart stressed the need for a quick postwar official history and, with regard to covering the war effort, the proper "co-ordination of the written word, photographs and paintings."[28] With the full support of the General Staff, the Historical Section was encouraged to search out and shape the war records: by influencing commanding officers and war diarists, by crafting narratives for the eventual official history, and by augmenting the written record with war art.[29]

DESPITE THE SHORT-LIVED MOVEMENT of the 1st Division to France in 1940, the Hong Kong expedition, and the 2nd Division raid on Dieppe, the Canadian Army remained largely unproven in battle. With the desert war in North Africa over by the beginning of 1943, the plan of invading Sicily and then marching up through Italy was seen, at least to the British, as preferable to engaging in a cross-channel attack against occupied France. McNaughton objected to splitting his army (which was one of the factors in his eventual relief from command), but Canadian politicians fought hard to have Canadian forces involved in the Mediterranean. Having won concessions from the high command that an historian would be attached to the expeditionary force headquarters to record the campaign, Stacey had planned to send Sam Hughes, grandson of Sir Sam and future judge in the Ontario Supreme Court. Notwithstanding Hughes's good record as both historian and soldier, Colonel George Kitching, GSO 1 of the 1st Division, overruled the Historical Section, inserting one of his own intelligence officers, Captain A.T. Sesia, into the position. Stacey acquiesced, hoping privately that Sesia might ease the intrusion into the field command circles and keep "the divisional staff sweet."[30]

When told of his appointment, Sesia thought it was some absurd joke. He recounted in his diary, "I could not figure out why I was picked for this type of work. I am not a writer, much less an historian." Stacey was no less apprehensive. But as events would prove, Sesia worked with determination in collecting documents – or "bumpf" as the soldiers referred to it – interviewing participants, advising on the maintenance and disposal of records, and even preparing a rough historical narrative of operations. It should be noted that Sesia's ambivalent attitude to his position changed significantly after the divisional commander, Major General Guy Simonds, sat down with him and expressed interest in his work. Sesia recorded that Simonds "stressed accuracy in whatever I may state as fact. He reminded me that I have a great responsibility on my hands because my recordings will have a definite bearing on the history of the Operation when it will be written." With the textual records covered, war artist Lieutenant Will Ogilvie would accompany Sesia in documenting "the fullest possible pictorial record of operations."[31]

After an uncontested landing in Sicily on 10 July 1943, Canadian soldiers moved north under a blazing sun, trekking through fine white dust, fighting occasional skirmishes and a few battles. Feeling their way in this opening phase of the campaign, both Sesia and Ogilvie were constrained in their duties by lack of transport.[32] Being less dependent on others, Ogilvie better handled the logistical problem by hitchhiking from unit to unit, sketching and painting as he went along. Sesia, on the other hand, was compelled to stay at headquarters in order to follow the course of the campaign, thinking it "would be a sheer waste of time to try to get a brigade or battalion commander to tell his story of action as long as his troops are in contact with the enemy."[33]

When able to break away from headquarters to visit units in the field, Sesia was anxious to question officers in order to obtain a view of combat. After interviewing infantrymen from the Royal Canadian Regiment who had just fought at Leonforte on 22 July 1943, however, Sesia realized, "Most of the officers with whom I had spoken seemed dazed[,] a bit groggy from the fighting of the day before ... I am of the opinion that perhaps it is not well to interview officers immediately after a battle, because it is not likely that they will be able to recall instances while still under the effects of a battle."[34]

Sesia eventually fashioned a seventy-page narrative of the campaign after honing his historical skills over several months. Yet his most important task was in establishing a system for the gathering, selecting, and transferring of war records created during the campaign. After the Canadians invaded mainland Italy, Sesia continued to experience logistical shortfalls, but he happily wrote that he "had full support of the GOC and down [the chain of command]."[35]

During the Sicilian campaign, however, some units felt neglected because Sesia was unable to visit them, and a few commanding officers worried that their reputations would suffer from this perceived historical slight. Reacting to this, Simonds sought coverage for all units and additional historical officers were requested from England.[36] Furthermore, Sesia and Ogilvie's success in the field enabled Stacey, now in charge of a section of twelve historical officers and six war artists, to present and display their collected work – documents, history, and art – to his superiors. A meeting with CGS Kenneth Stuart on 31 August 1943 elicited a very positive response to the historical program, and Stacey recorded that Stuart had "agreed that it was desirable to extend the scope of work, if possible, during the next phase."[37] Following his policy of rotating officers, and never entirely happy with having Sesia imposed on him, Stacey sent Captain Sam Hughes and Captain W.E.C. Harrison, a history professor from Queen's University before the war, to take over the historical duties in Italy.

With significantly more challenging fighting in Italy, including the savage battles of Ortona and the storming of the Hitler Line, there was a pressing need to document the actions of the tens of thousands of Canadian soldiers serving in this expanding theatre. In the process, the role of the historical officers changed, as Stacey decided it was too time-consuming for his historians to "produce comprehensive narratives of operations" in the field. They were told to focus on "recording personal evidence" through interviews and ensure that units provided accurate and detailed accounts of their engagements.[38] This would remain an arduous task, as Brigadier George Kitching, then commander of the 11th Infantry Brigade, cynically warned Harrison: the "main problem of the historical officer was to correlate three sets of lies, those of the unit, those of brigade and those of the division."[39] The true experience of war could not always be uncovered by an examination of the War Diary or an interview with a senior officer.

To the historical officers' credit, they readily understood the limitations of the records. Harrison wrote, when attempting to decipher the history of a unit, that it was sometimes as "difficult to read the truth through a magnifying glass as it is through a telescope."[40] However, in contrast to the British historians, who "tend to lean on War Diaries very heavily, and are dubious of any material from the field," Stacey instructed his historical officers to gather broadly all forms of documentation in order to unravel what occurred – or what was perceived to have occurred.[41] These collected records were then forwarded to Stacey's section, with the understanding that the narrative was to be written after the field historical officer was rotated back to London. It proved a successful policy and the final account of the Liri Valley campaign was described by the CGS as "extremely complete and of great historical importance." Not only were the historical officers collecting documents "constitut[ing] a mine of information," but they also were showing impressive skills in actually producing readable texts of the battle.[42]

At I Corps headquarters in Italy, Harrison found that Crerar, who was obviously busy with his first battlefield command of the war, offered the historical officer full access to his records. In a private interview on 15 November 1943, Crerar also emphasized the importance of the historical work and the need to avoid the failures of the last war when work had "only begun 'when the horses had left the stable.'"[43] As the campaign continued, the historical officers had the full cooperation of Canadian generals in the field, who had instructed their subordinates to comply with all requests of the 1st Canadian Field Historical Section (1st CFHS), as Harrison's unit, with him in command, was now designated.

The 1st CFHS continued to transfer War Diaries, reports, and information back to CMHQ, and Stacey, after examining the documentation, surmised that this historical material might be useful for current operations, especially for units training in England.[44] Shortly thereafter, an historical officer selected extracts from the war records to be published in a series of pamphlets, with a focus on personal accounts of battle, enemy tactics, battlefield conditions, and the value of Allied equipment. Extract number 6, for instance, recounted an interview with a soldier who remarked that, despite what commanders in England thought, "No training exercise in which I have taken part has adequately demonstrated the 'fog of war.' It is complete and utter." Another contained an operational order from the medical services of the 1st Canadian Division, which noted that "it had been proved many times" that field units should carry more plasma.⁴⁵ With this form of operational research sent out to senior officers in England, the Historical Section was almost immediately inundated with requests for more of this type of information from British, American, and Canadian units. The War Office went so far as to write to CMHQ that the extracts "are one of their best sources of information, [with] facts reach[ing] us through this channel more rapidly than through any other."⁴⁶ For Allied officers attempting to make training as realistic as possible and to prepare their soldiers for the eventual invasion of France, the historical extracts were quickly elevated to essential reading. Stacey's superiors at CMHQ urged him to exploit the situation and ensure that Canadian officers realized the importance of cooperating with field historical units in order to produce these important training records. This Stacey did by changing the mandate of historical officers to include the dual purpose of "collecting material which has an immediate training value as well as an ultimate historical value."⁴⁷ Documenting the war had again shown its usefulness. Furthermore, the acknowledged value of the extracts helped to ensure that richer, fuller records were created by fighting units, since it was subsequently found that those units – and especially commanding officers – took pride in having their vanguard experiences and their records employed to assist others.⁴⁸

Along with aiding his chroniclers in the field, working with British historians to ensure greater Canadian inclusion in their narratives, and responding to the occasional crisis at CMHQ, Stacey continued to direct the production of narratives, with the ultimate goal of developing a skeletal account for the postwar official historian. Following established protocol, the Historical Section distributed the draft chapters of these narratives to all senior officers down to brigade level, to representatives at National Defence Headquarters in Ottawa, and to a few select politicians. The narratives were fully annotated and overly detailed; indeed, Stacey warned his readers that this was a first draft that "organized the main facts into a comprehensive narrative" and "that it has no literary pretensions. It is the raw material for a history rather than the history itself." Those who were involved intimately with the events were invited to comment on the veracity of the written account. The fear, of course, was that the narratives would either be ignored or that officers might force changes to present themselves in a better manner to posterity. Yet very few of the senior officers demanded a reworking of the text in any significant manner. They were not silent, however. Many supplied clarifications on various points or actions, which, not surprisingly, did not make them look any poorer. Despite these regular self-serving comments, the changes were generally minor in nature.

The most revealing commentary relating to these narratives came from Brigadier R.G. Whitelaw. In reading over Stanley's preliminary draft, he had little to add but questioned the nature of the history, which he thought had a "certain amount of personal bias ... Undoubtedly this history will be published within the lifetime of many of the personnel mentioned therein, and quite possibly while they are still in the public service. I feel that it would be regrettable, to say the least, if an official history gave rise to public controversy which would probably serve no useful purpose except to wash a lot of dirty linen and shake the faith of the general public in their leaders, past or present ... Of course, I do not for a moment advocate that any official history should omit entirely any mention of mistakes made. Otherwise, our successors, if or when there is another war, will probably drop into the same errors."[49] It is likely that more than a few of the soldiers felt conflicted in this way, but none demanded any form of censorship or downplaying of failures.

Although the comments by participants often provided essential "inside" information on events or incidents, these observations did not go unchallenged. As Stacey's guidelines to historical officers on the writing of narratives revealed, "The comments are examined by the narrator who accepts or rejects them, according to his knowledge of the documents."[50] Stacey acquired essential information from the participants and ensured that they became part of the history-making process. This would make it harder for senior officers to subsequently influence the writing of the official histories. Unfortunately, this was something Duguid could not abide. Still Stacey's superior, and undoubtedly mindful of his experience with Generals Hughes and Turner in 1934, Duguid believed that the practice of distributing draft copies, "if not dangerous, certainly is unwise, for nobody then knows where copies will get to, who will see them, or to what bad use they may be put."[51] But Duguid was far removed from the overseas Historical Section and Stacey, having won the support of the generals, could effectively ignore him. When Duguid later pressed his complaint, Stacey had had enough and invited him to CMHQ to make his case, even though he knew that his superiors thought that the extracts were excellent training tools and that they expected to be consulted by their historian in drafting the narratives. Duguid, who was later described as "a simple and direct Scottish gentleman with no taste nor gift for politics or subterfuge," was soundly put in his place, and afterwards Stacey had few problems with the senior historian.[52] Besides, even in passing around draft narratives, the historical officers did not have to bend to the will of the generals because the participants did not see the second draft of the narratives, which may or may not have incorporated their views. There was little chance for conflict over the historical record during the war, and through this method Stacey was able to cement further his strong relationship with senior officers.

The reports were uncontroversial, largely composed of narrative, and restrained in judgment. As well, many of the generals had a hard time arguing with the thorough nature of the work. They repeatedly complimented the careful, detailed, and comprehensive accounts. "As usual, I find that you and your staff have turned out an excellent job of work which possesses, also, the rare quality of readability," Crerar penned on one narrative.[53] On other occasions it is surprising to note that the generals, given their positions, appeared nervous about interfering with the historical account.[54] Stacey recounted how he was "floored" after meeting McNaughton in a hallway at CMHQ and having the general ask him: "Did you think well of my suggestions?"[55] The professional nature of historical officers' work and their reputations as accomplished historians did not present many opportunities for senior officers to bully them into accepting changes that were not supported by the war records.

The concern that the historical chronicles would be ignored was also unfounded. Readers continued to pass material to Stacey throughout the war and some, like Crerar, who had replaced McNaughton as Army commander in March 1944, kept up a steady correspondence, even sending comments to Stacey on 9 June 1944, three days after part of his army was fiercely engaged in the Normandy landings. Even while leading Canadian troops in Italy and Northwest Europe, therefore, commanders continued to show an interest in how their actions and those of their men would be portrayed in the upcoming history of the war. Despite this attention, very few generals tried overtly to influence Stacey in his writing while the fighting raged. That would change after the war: when the firing stopped, the sniping among the generals would begin anew. But during the war, Stacey profited from the comments by participants and continued to demonstrate his competence and that of his staff by producing a steady flow of narratives.

To ensure that the narratives would be written by the most knowledgeable and experienced historical officers, Stacey began to recall them from the field. Since almost all of his historical officers were academic historians who had been given free rein to write instead of fight, they were motivated and produced a startling number of detailed, fully referenced narratives, combining the war record, personal interviews, and their own "first-hand knowledge."[56] They were also driven by Stacey, who was extremely demanding, it has been said, occasionally reducing his staff to tears.[57] Stanley, Harrison, and Hughes have been mentioned; others like Gerald Graham, J.M. Hitsman, J.R. Martin, J.B. Conacher, and Murray Hunter were also essential in crafting narratives. Almost all had graduate degrees at the masters or doctorate level, and most would achieve respected positions in Canadian universities or other institutions after the war. As well, there was a second group who replaced the first generation of historians when they were rotated back to the London Historical Section. John Spurr, Joe Wrinch, Ralph Currelly, and Joe Engler were recruited from their respective divisions.[58] Engler was the only historical officer killed in combat, when on 1 October 1944 he and war artist Orville Fisher rode into an ambush. Although none of these replacements held doctorates, most had backgrounds in intelligence or public relations, keen eyes for detail, and competent pens to record what they saw.

Back in London, historical officers such as J.B. Conacher and Sam Hughes wrote a series of narratives for the Sicily and Italian campaigns. The use of intelligence reports, narratives of events, logs, War Diaries, and the field historical officer reports situated the Canadian forces within the larger operational and strategic picture. Detailed accounts of battles were given, but for the most part the narratives focused on the divisional, brigade, and battalion levels. While the field historical officers had interviewed soldiers, they often did so to understand the unfolding of events rather than to use first-hand accounts to add poignant quotes to the official records. But while the bravery of individual Canadians went unrecorded, it was not unacknowledged:

> In telling the story of so large a group of men as a division, much of the detail has to be taken for granted. This report seeks to give the broad picture of the operations within a reasonable compass. It goes down to battalion level, and in some cases to company level, but in all the actions described it should be remembered that it was what the individual man in each unit and sub-unit did that brought about the result recorded. The narrative may simply record that in the face of stiff opposition a certain feature was taken by the execution of some particular tactical movement. Such a sentence sums up the tactical picture, but the reader must use his imagination and realize that the job was only done by human beings displaying judgment, coolness and courage. Many such small actions resulted in awards for gallantry – one hundred such awards were earned in Sicily – but even the Battalion War Diaries rarely told the individual stories for they were too numerous; bravery becomes almost commonplace ... But for each brave deed recognized by an award there were doubtless several more that passed unnoticed. On the other hand, there were probably some occasions where lack of decision of adequate action lost the day, but that these were much less common is attested by the fact of the Division's speedy advance in the face of continual opposition.[59]

The narrators' primary goal was to stake down the history, understand plans and operations, and determine whether the units in question were able to carry out their orders. Moreover, the war records were often "uneven in quality and frequently incomplete," with "gaps" and, even worse, "inaccuracies and errors," warned Conacher in one of his Sicily narratives.[60] It would take time to study the war records, comparing and analyzing them to understand their limitations. In the meantime, there was little attempt to paint a vivid picture of the atmosphere of warfare, the trials of the common soldier, or questions of morale or discipline, and this would later have an impact on the nature of the official histories.

As this writing process developed, the 1st CFHS continued to supply records and accounts of battle from the field. This unit was firmly established, with officers serving as part of the divisional and corps headquarters. And when Harrison found in June 1944 that the new brigadier general staff at headquarters, I Canadian Corps, had cut him off from all reports that he did not consider of "historical significance," he was eventually able to reverse the decision by showing correspondence indicating that the "higher authorities [were] tremendously pleased" with the output of the section.[61] Work in Italy continued, despite the main British, American, and Canadian theatre of war having moved to Normandy.

Building on the success of the 1st CFHS, Stacey convinced Crerar that an historical officer and war artist should accompany the 3rd Canadian Infantry Division on D-Day. Despite there being few spaces available within the bridgehead, on 6 June 1944 at 20:00 hours, Captain J.R. Martin set foot in France and immediately began to record operations, interview participants, attend senior-level briefings, and gather historical documents. The records that Martin, a former professor of fine arts from the University of Iowa, sent back to Stacey were incorporated into a new series of Northwest Europe extracts, and immediately used to good effect.[62] Reflecting on the writing of history and the amassing of records, Harrison, who would soon join Martin on the continent, remarked quite aptly: "Few histories have had their materials garnered so close [to the] action, perishables scorchingly snatched from the furnace of war."[63]

As the Allies began to push out from their beaches, they found that their plans for open-manoeuvre warfare were frustrated by formidable German defences and armoured formations. Yet with more Allied and Canadian divisions committed to France behind the lead units, which were inching their way forward, historical officers followed in tow. Stacey, too, would finally see the "hard hand" of war. Behind the front lines, after discovering that no staff officer could write his dispatches with the skill and alacrity he demanded, Crerar had Stacey attached temporarily to his headquarters. Despite enjoying the hiatus from the Historical Section, after a short time in France, Stacey passed the writing duties to Harrison, who became the First Canadian Army historian and commander of 2nd Canadian Field Historical Section. A veteran historian of the Italian campaign, Harrison's role was primarily to act as Crerar's in-house writer, who also produced his dispatches; in the process, the general allowed him full access to his own private records and Army headquarters information on all aspects of the First Canadian Army. Crerar ordered, moreover, that Harrison be given the chance to observe the "secret and personal history of the campaign."[64] This Harrison did, sending back detailed reports to Stacey that included the most secret of records, up to but not including Ultra intelligence, the extracts of intercepted German military information.

At lower levels, the historical officers were generally given full support in their divisions. When the posting of an historical officer for the 4th Armoured Division was delayed, Major General George Kitching (now a divisional commander) complained to Stacey that his division was being "discriminated against."[65] There may not have been a Canadian general of the same calibre as the American George Patton, nor one with the same ego and insatiable desire to propagate his deeds as Bernard Montgomery, but senior Canadian officers were certainly aware of the value of publicity – be it for contemporary use or historical legacy. Canadian generals recognized their place in history and that of their men. Few ignored the historical officers despite the enormous demands and strains in leading forces of thousands in a life and death struggle. This attitude also flowed down to more junior regimental officers. Later in the war, the 3rd Division's historical officer, Captain R. Gray, scrawled in one report that he found the Brigade and Battalion headquarters of all units in his division to be exceedingly helpful, as they were all "most conscious of the value of the written record." In contrast to some of the problems encountered earlier in the war, Gray also noted, "War Diaries generally seem to be a matter of unit pride."[66] Commanders at all levels well knew that those who chose to ignore history ran the very real risk that history might ignore them.

Although the historical officers may have had a less strenuous job when compared with the long-suffering infantrymen, these academics-turned-soldiers worked long hours and endured hardship and discomfort as all others while campaigning. The constant wear and tear, inadequate staffing, long-distance travel, writing by lantern, and terrible weather conditions in addition to stray shelling and sniper fire, made concentrating on historical matters very difficult. Working in such circumstances required stamina. Captain Harrison described R.T. Currelly, the historical officer of the 5th Canadian Armoured Division, as "an explorer, researcher and detective"; another historical officer quipped that the proper man for their job must "be almost superman in his efforts to bring into a single picture events that may be happening in a dozen places at once."[67] By the Northwest Europe campaign, however, the historical officers found that they spent most of their time assisting units in preserving their actions in after-battle reports and battle narratives. "Our function has become less that of historians, and more that of 'scavenger' of official documents," wrote one historical officer.[68] The role of archivist was usurping that of chronicler, but both were essential in gathering, preparing, and authoring the records.

Historical officers played an important role in shaping the war record while in the field. Being ordered to write up the unit's official report was not a sought-after task, and it usually fell to those officers with the ability to form a somewhat coherent narrative or those in disfavour with the commanding officer. The best writers used message logs to track the movement of men and units; the worst relied on written orders instead of what actually unfolded on the battlefield. To help augment their meagre evidence, the diarists turned to the historical officers to provide assistance and context to flesh out the content. Forced constantly to remind diarists that they must include the large picture of what was happening within the brigade, division, or corps, Harrison found that without his badgering, many units allowed the "record to deteriorate into a string of insignificant notes as to render it almost useless for historical purposes." After months of hard work with seemingly good results, Harrison was shocked to find that some diarists still could not grasp the necessity for full documentation of the war effort. On 16 June 1944, after examining the Canadian Corps' General and Administrative War Diaries of the Hitler Line battles, he wrote acidly: "There was no attempt at maintaining a narrative ... It was possible to read the entries covering the greatest battle in the history of 1 Cdn Corps, without realizing that there was a battle on."[69] Bringing the inadequacies of the various War Diaries to the attention of General Headquarters helped to enforce better practices, but without the diligence of the historical officers, the war records might have degraded into useless administrative comments rather than a useful narrative of events.

Yet the hounding of diarists was not the only function of the historical officers. In fact, most of the soldier-scholars wrote up a number of narratives. While frontline units were forced to work up their reports for higher formations, they often found the orders nearly impossible to carry out. After some battles it was very difficult to find someone who was even remotely qualified or capable of writing a coherent report of operations. As historical officer R.T. Currelly discovered when visiting the Perth Regiment after hard fighting in August 1944, the unit's intelligence officer and sergeant had been killed at Montecchio, with all their documents destroyed in the process. No one was left to write the narrative and the unit turned to their divisional historical officer to assist them in fending off increasing demands for a report by divisional headquarters. A similar event occurred when Currelly visited the 12th Canadian Armoured Regiment and found that they were "hopelessly disorganized" in putting together a report of operations. The brigade major, Currelly recounted, pleaded with him to "re-write the whole thing and make it accurate and readable."[70] These were not isolated instances. Captain J.R. Martin, the historical officer for the 3rd Canadian Division in Northwest Europe, found that he was forced to spend a good deal of time attempting to unravel "the tangled threads of the narrative" from units that had been decimated in Operation Switchback, a precursor battle for securing the southern flank for the battle of the Scheldt. When Martin finally received the campaign accounts, he massaged, reworked, and rewrote them.[71] One should not assume that the historical officers were the only ones writing reports in the Canadian Army, as surely the mass of records that form the war archives prove that countless hands cranked out thousands of operational reports and message logs, but it is clear that Clio's soldiers actively sought out the war record, influencing and presenting how the Canadian military experience would be captured and ultimately codified in print.[72]

In the process of shaping the war record in form and content, the historical officers chose to favour the larger narrative and the grand movement of units over that of the private soldier. Such neglect must surely be one of the key flaws in the historical process during the war. Very rarely did they mention any soldier below the rank of lieutenant in their dispatches and narratives. With the fog of battle clouding even the most observant infantrymen, it was certainly more profitable to talk to the commanders who either devised the plans or helped to carry them out. As well, with these historians essentially schooled to place value on "great men and great events" rather than in social history from the ground up, it is unfortunate, if understandable, that a valuable opportunity was lost in failing to record the privates' view of war. The Americans employed the same type of focus, but because of access to greater resources allowed some leeway to interview those at the sharp end. One such American chronicler, S.L.A. Marshall, recorded the experiences of men who were doing the fighting through interviews and questionnaires. Despite a meeting between Stacey and Marshall, the Canadian Army historian was not influenced by the American method.[73] Stacey, like most official historians and notwithstanding Marshall's innovative approach, remained focused on the generals rather than the infantrymen, and the strategic or operational picture of war rather than the experience of battle.

THERE WAS NO PROVISION for establishing an historical section for the Royal Canadian Air Force (RCAF) when Canada went to war in September 1939. The first attempt at writing an official history of Canadian flyers in the Great War had ended in failure, with the deeds of most Canadian airmen buried deeply in the British war records. Yet the chief of the air staff, Air Commodore G.M. Croil, took more interest, and so in January 1940 a section was established to gather records and prepare reports for RCAF headquarters.[74] A position was created in the Directorate of Staff Duties, and a Great War decorated ace, Wing Commander Kenneth Conn, DFC, was appointed. Conn was initially unsure why this had been offered to him, admitting later that he would have preferred many other positions.[75]

After distinguishing himself in the Great War with fourteen victories, Conn had continued to fly, but an airplane accident in 1921 ended his aviation career. He went to university, received his BA and by the late 1920s was the Alumni Secretary and editor of the *University of Toronto Monthly*. He operated historical tours in Europe from 1935 to 1939, and had firms in New York, London, and Paris.[76] There is no indication that Conn ever published an historical work, so it is little wonder that he questioned his selection. Of course, the historical aspect of the job was but one of many that he was forced to juggle.

With Conn at the helm, the principal function of the RCAF Historical Section was the "collection of historical material for future use" in an official history. Initially, he was tasked primarily with ensuring that the various commands in Canada, including the British Commonwealth Air Training Plan (BCATP) bases and schools, were "keeping historical records."[77] Conn's work was similar to that of Duguid in the army, who was documenting domestic army operations, but the two worked independently. To men preparing for or engaged in war, however, Conn was simply one more badgering headquarters staff officer demanding that more paperwork be filed.

The government of W.L.M. King had desperately hoped to avoid the damaging consequences of another unfettered war effort. He, like many Canadians, had been scarred by the effects of conscription in 1917, which had split the country along linguistic, class, and regional lines. A master of compromise and balance, King was determined not to allow a recurrence, and he pushed for an overall strategic policy of "limited liability." Of course, Canada would support Great Britain, but the prime minister hoped it would be primarily through war munitions, food, and credit rather than Canadian lives.

With the growing need for flyers to defend Britain and Canada and later to attack Axis forces, King leapt at the chance to be involved in their training (although he was far more wary about paying for it). Instructing pilots, gunners, and navigators from Britain and its dominions and colonies, the BCATP would be a major Canadian military contribution in the Allied war effort. King believed – wrongly as it turned out – that if the present ground war mimicked the Western Front of the Great War, Canada might avoid attritional warfare and "chewing on barbed wire" if its main military effort was geared towards aviation.[78] Canada would become the "Aerodrome of Democracy," but the country's war effort would not, despite King's fond hopes, be confined to training airmen. There would be nothing limited about the Second World War, and Canada, like most nations, was dragged into the conflagration of battle on land, at sea, and in the air.

Nonetheless, the BCATP was a major and vital war-winning effort, and Conn documented the Canadian training units and bases. Not being an historian, he engaged tenderly in the process. Luckily, the British Great War official historian, H.A. Jones, author of the multi-volume *War in the Air*, had fortuitously been posted to Canada as chief civil officer of the United Kingdom Air Liaison Mission. Jones worked with Conn in setting up the structure of the RCAF Historical Section, and in December 1940, to ensure proper record keeping among the ever-increasing BCATP units, an officer was added to the establishment to assist Conn in record-keeping duties.[79]

With only three squadrons in the United Kingdom in early 1940, little attention was given to these overseas units. In June 1941, though, Conn requested approval for an officer to be sent overseas to research the archival holdings of the Royal Air Force. Conn had received informal "ministerial approval" to explore the production of a multi-volume official history, and he had been instructed to complete the first volume, the pre-1939 history, by the end of the war if possible.[80] The new chief of the air staff, Air Marshal L.S. Breadner, supported Conn, writing that he believed it "necessary to facilitate the preparation of an official history" and to ensure that "suitable records are compiled by and collected from all units and formations of the RCAF at Home and Overseas."[81]

Therefore, in October 1941 two historical officers were posted overseas: W.R. Thompson went to RCAF Overseas Headquarters to supervise the creation of squadron diaries, write brief narratives, and collect war trophies – in effect, to ensure proper record keeping and later manage the RCAF Historical Section; and F.H. Hitchins, a prewar professor of history at New York University, was ordered to conduct research into the RAF archives at Aberystwyth, Wales.[82] While the official history of the air force remained an insignificant side event in comparison with the frenzy of activity in Canada and overseas RCAF headquarters for the current conflict, accurate wartime information remained essential to all levels of command. Throughout late 1941 the RCAF Historical Section proved its usefulness in extracting information from operational files and creating easily digestible reports for senior officers. In August 1942 the minister requested weekly progress reports from all squadrons overseas. However, with a system in place that was described as "somewhat slipshod," Conn took the opportunity to suggest that the overseas section should be expanded to allow historical officers to supply proper information to the minister and progress reports to Canadian newspapers in order to raise the profile of the RCAF.[83] He further argued that with more overseas staff, the Historical Section could begin to craft a "fully documented history of the RCAF and the RCAF personnel in the RAF" that would later be disseminated to the Canadian public. Such a history would be "used as insurance against a recurrence of the general apathy, which invariably sets in after a war and which, in the period between 1918 and 1939, had such a disastrous effect upon the RCAF."[84] Overseas expansion would be a public relations boon, and that, it appears, was what convinced senior officers of the need to expand the section.

While Conn was pressing to document history in the present, he was also hoping to reclaim the past. The research section at Aberystwyth, under the command of Flight Lieutenant Hitchins, was both preparing for a postwar official history and attempting to compile information on Canadians who served in the British air services during the Great War. Although Hitchins had initially been tasked with continuing the work of the ad hoc Air Historical Section of the CWRO, which had compiled thousands of biographical files on Canadian flyers in 1919, he believed a full history was necessary since a "purely statistical account of Canada's aerial contribution in 1914-1918 would be comparable to a pie crust without any filling."[85] Conn agreed and, following Hitchins's penchant for analogies, suggested that an account of the early RCAF history would be "a runway from which the [present] history of the RCAF could take off."

As early as May 1942 Hitchins, having completed much of his Great War research, suggested to senior officers that the RCAF should prepare a small popular history on Canadian flyers during the current war. In the previous year the British Ministry of Information had published a thirty-two-page booklet, *The Battle of Britain* (1941), which sold an estimated fifteen million copies.[86] It was an astounding success that helped shape the memory of the Battle of Britain. Hitchins believed that the RCAF might offer a similar publication, with Canadian content of course, that could be sold in Canada and abroad and also "lay the groundwork for a more detailed history."[87] There appears to have been no formal acceptance of the proposal, but since senior RCAF officers were in support of the history program, Hitchins went ahead and began to craft a narrative.

With additional overseas historical officers appointed to document the actions of Canadian squadrons and groups in early 1943, the historical officers also played an essential role in ensuring that proper war records were not just preserved but also created. In May 1943 Flight Lieutenant L.H. Jenkins began to examine the squadron record books, which contained all the essential operational information relating to a squadron or unit. The "sins of commission," wrote Jenkins, were "less serious than those of omission," but from an historical perspective, some of the writers of the operational books clearly did not understand the role of the document. For instance, "No. 401 Squadron saw nothing noteworthy in the first 'rhubarb'[88] [the squadron] went on, in spite of the fact it was the first attack against ground targets by any RCAF squadron. No. 400 saw nothing important in an Army Co-operation squadron going on a rhubarb for the first time, nor in the fact that it produced first 'blood' for the squadron." Another squadron, No. 418, did not even record that it participated in the Dieppe raid. Jenkins concluded that the "lack of appreciation on the part of the diary officer of what the diary should contain, is a primary cause, the cure for which would seem to be a campaign of education by trained historical officers, by personal contact if possible."[89] Historical officers were not only to hound the diarists, but also to fact-check the operational records, examining them for errors, and later to augment them with interviews. "A little extra effort in the present to see that records are properly kept as we go along may save untold effort and expense in the future." The RCAF historical officers were Clio's watchdogs, demanding the creation of detailed and comprehensive records. As one report admonished: "Operations are the purpose for which the squadron exists and are the most important element in its life, but the record should not be restricted to operations. All aspects of its life should receive attention. The aim of the recording officer should be to present a true, rather than an official, account of the squadron's history ... When things go wrong, when mistakes are made, they should be acknowledged frankly, and an effort made to learn the cause."[90] After some work with squadrons and units, one Historical Section report crowed satisfactorily that the submitted records were "rapidly becoming informative documents, rather than matter-of-fact transcriptions."[91]

Hitchins continued to write key narratives for the popular history and the "secret narrative," which would form the basis for the postwar official history. On orders from RCAF Overseas Headquarters, which was increasingly interested in his work, Hitchins visited RCAF squadrons to document "atmosphere and to see the history 'being made' at first hand."[92] At No. 6 Bomber Group Headquarters in January 1943, for instance, he had the full support of the senior officers, and Group

Captain C.R. Slemon, a future chief of the air staff, gave him free access to the Operations Room. Hitchins found the first-hand experience of war so interesting that he stayed awake for twenty-five hours as he furiously took notes on a number of Canadian bombing operations.[93] These opportunities helped to flesh out both the popular and secret narratives.

By August 1943 the RCAF Historical Section had finished the first popular history and was looking for a publisher. It was a real coup for the section because the book-length manuscript was in advance of anything the army or navy had accomplished to date. However, as its primary author, Hitchins remarked: "A full understanding of the work of the RCAF squadrons overseas requires an examination of questions of high policy – over which Canadians have no control [and therefore no records] – of Command and Group instruction; it inevitably leads to consideration of the work of other RAF formations and squadrons. Baldly stated it might be said, therefore, that the problem confronting the RCAF historian is, how can a history be written of the RCAF Overseas which is not at the same time a history of the RAF?" As Hitchins concluded, given this reality, "the RAF historian is primarily concerned with two matters, policy and units; the RCAF historian must focus his attention upon individuals and deeds."[94]

Conn had planned a popular account that would include a history of RCAF operations with a focus on individual Canadian airmen. Having deflected earlier criticisms by senior RCAF officers that historians could not write popular history, Conn had directed that this work appeal to the masses and be highly personalized. Despite pressure to edit his long history, Conn refused to cut the Orders, Decorations, and Medals section or the Roll of Honour that listed all RCAF members reported killed up to 31 August 1943. As with Great War regimental histories, he believed in the necessity of naming and enshrining those who had given their lives for their country. Some grieving loved ones found comfort in the book. Mrs. Julia Martin, who lost her son Julian, described the account of the raid where her boy was killed as very touching, especially since they had received "no information whatsoever from the Squadron." She finished her letter to the Historical Section by writing that even after hearing about the loss of their son, "both my husband and I cling to the hope that a miracle may yet happen."[95] How many thousands of other Canadians found solace – no matter how small – in the history?

The RCAF Overseas (1944) became available in October 1944, just after the Allied armies had severely mauled the Germans at Falaise, the RCN had turned the corner in the desperate Battle of the Atlantic, and the RCAF was deeply engaged in tactical missions and the strategic bombing campaign. Accompanying the distribution of the book, the Historical Section and Oxford University Press had included an advertisement: this was the history of "the boy next door, the lad from Sioux Lookout, the youngster from Churchill or Trois Rivières, from Wetaskiwin or Smithers, from myriad farms, settlements, towns and cities, Canada's sons have journeyed far." In a radio interview to promote the book, it was suggested that "for the first time an official history will appear while the events discussed are still live topics – while the man in the street has a vivid memory of what he reads."[96]

The RCAF Overseas was very much a product of the war. The book's primary contribution was in bringing the experience of aerial combat to life, and there was a graphic frankness to the history: in waiting for the call to go on operations, the observation that fighter crews "lay around with telephones ringing in their bellies" spoke to the nervousness of anticipation. Furthermore, while there was a patriotic, propagandistic tone to the text that focused on acts of bravery or superior Allied aerial tactics, there was no attempt to downplay the reality that the air war was difficult, the enemy skilled, and that Allied losses would continue. While the chapters on convoy patrols and interceptions failed to do justice to the important work of these aircraft in combating the U-boat menace, the section on Bomber Command was surprisingly revealing: "A list of the RCAF targets reads like a page from Baedeker." There were few targets that would be spared from the bombing runs of 6 Group, and Lübeck, an historic German port on the Baltic with little strategic importance, was bombed on 28 March 1942, leaving it "a seething, smoking mass of twisted and burning rubble." These massive bombing raids were "steadily increasing in 'frightfulness' of the kinds which they [the Germans] were only too happy to hand out in the early days of the war but find hard to take now that the initiative is ours." While there was an impression that bombers could accurately hit their military objectives, *The RCAF Overseas* made no attempt to hide the fact that entire cities were targeted, that civilians were being burned out of their homes and, although not expressly noted, killed.[97]

The narrative relied heavily on squadron record books, supplemented with combat reports, newspaper accounts, and interviews. This was especially necessary for certain squadrons because records had been destroyed; for instance, in June 1943, all of No. 417 Squadron's records had been lost in a fiery aircraft accident.[98] Equally important, as Minister C.G. Power revealed, the history was "based only on such records as can now be revealed without endangering security."[99] And, befitting any wartime publication, the censors combed it for damaging information. They did not cut much, but there was one unacceptable paragraph that suggested the Allies' "indiscriminate bombing [was] objected to in many quarters."[100]

Despite these limitations, the newspapers immediately responded with positive reviews. The *Ottawa Citizen* reported, "This was really a progress report up until 1943," and "you will find no high falutin' poetry of the high skies, no heroics, no blah." This was not true, of course, because there were heroic accounts infused throughout the history, but they did not appear to ring falsely, probably because they were based on official, authentic reports. Torchy Anderson, the *Citizen's* reviewer, finished by suggesting, "Perhaps this book has an unwritten moral. Perhaps it will help to teach Canadians that no task is impossible of accomplishment if you have the guts and the want to do it."¹⁰¹ It was Canadians again, the boys and fathers from down the street, who were putting down plough and pens to engage the enemy; the Militia Myth was alive and well in Canada.¹⁰²

The RCAF Overseas sold out in days, and with reviews by the *Owen Sound Sun Times* claiming that the history "reveals the secrets of the aerial war," the public snatched up the second edition, which nearly sold out by the end of 1944.¹⁰³ With this well-received popular account of the present air war, at least one Great War veteran angrily wrote that he and the soldiers of his generation had been cheated out of their history. The Toronto *Globe* reported Sydney Brown's outrage:

> In startling contrast with the pitiful record of our Army History Section, the Historical Section of the RCAF has already produced its first volume for the present war ... The Air Forces has thus accomplished in 12 months what it has taken the Army 26 years so far, and possible many more years yet. If the Army Historical Section is to be entrusted with producing the story of the military side of the present war, after the last war had been disposed of, then at the present snail-like progress the lads who are now fighting may expect the account of their feats to appear no earlier than a century or two hence.¹⁰⁴

That the CEF official historian, A.F. Duguid, had decided to shelve the Great War history for the duration of the current conflict was not known to the public, but had it been, surely more veterans would have been incensed.

Duguid's plan to shelve the Great War history flew in the face of the CGS's wishes, who had ordered the historian to devote himself to this important endeavour. Instead, Duguid directed his section to administer the Second World War historical duties relating to home front forces, including the arranging and selection of war records, coordinating the work of war artists, and answering historical and contemporary inquiries.¹⁰⁵ And while Duguid had a staff of over forty, he made few allowances for the Great War history. Duguid was unmoved despite periodic calls by veterans and members of parliament for the official history. It would be a fatal and bizarre misreading of the situation by a man who had already devoted more than two decades to the project.

In addition to the broad history of the RCAF in the first four years, Conn aimed to publish more personal accounts of battle. At the end of 1943, the RCAF Historical Section had arranged with the Estates Branch to have a first examination of deceased flyers' personal effects in the hope of garnering diaries or letters that might be useful in "amplifying official documents."¹⁰⁶ Through this policy, the diary of Flight Officer W.S. Large, a fighter pilot in the North Africa theatre who had been killed in January 1943, came to attention of the section.

Diary of a Flying Officer was published in October 1944, sold well, and was an innovative approach to delving into and presenting the lives of average Canadians caught up in extraordinary times.[107] Riding the success of its first publication, the Historical Section proposed two smaller monographs of 30,000 words: *The RCAF in the Aleutians* and *A Ten-Day Submarine Hunt in 1943*. Conn appealed to his editors at Oxford University Press, but they felt the market was "terrifically apathetic at the moment. The story of this war is very like the last in that we shall have to wait for several years before there is any great interest in reading about it, apart, of course, from the exceptional books and official histories."[108] Although the statement did not bear out the sales figures for the other two RCAF publications, Conn shelved the short histories, ordering his staff historians to continue preparing the second volume of the *RCAF Overseas*.

In achieving command of the air, Winston Churchill declared in 1940, "The Fighters are our salvation, but the Bombers alone provide the means to Victory."[109] Thousands of bombers were manufactured, tens of thousands of BCATP aircrew were trained, and new target-finding technologies, which, when combined with new tactics involving path-finding aircraft to lead bombers to their targets and 1,000-bomber raids that unleashed incredibly destructive payloads, wielded the bombers into a more effective offensive arm. But the bombers also continued to fall victim to ground defences, night fighters, weather conditions, and mechanical failure. The more airmen flew, the less chance they had for survival. Among one group of fifty navigators who trained together in the early days of BCATP, only five completed their first thirty missions over Germany, ten were shot down and taken prisoners of war, and the rest died in fiery crashes.[110] The weary crews might very well have cast their thoughts back to their fathers' war. As the Old Bill cartoon joked with irony best appreciated by men forced to face death day in and out: "I feel like a fugitive from the law of averages."

All of this had to be documented by the overseas Historical Section. Conn requested and received additional historical officers in early 1944 to be stationed with the American air force, Italy and Far East Commands, and two additional narrators at Aberystwyth and the Overseas headquarters.[111] Even with more historical officers, by March 1944 there were nearly a hundred squadrons into which RCAF aircrew personnel were posted, and it was becoming increasingly difficult to document the squadrons' actions.

The preservation and authoring of the war records was the priority. Squadron Leader W.R. Thompson, who commanded the overseas historical unit, recorded that historical officers were finding that "reports of operational activity by Squadrons based on the continent were so lacking in detail as to be almost useless for record purposes."[112] The historical officers once again had to exert pressure on the overtaxed squadron officers to provide more detailed records.[113] Moreover, to acquire richer records, Thompson appointed one of his most energetic officers, Flight Officer F.H.C. Reinke, to augment the official record by exploring the experience of the flyers and "unit life" in their squadrons. Official records tended to ignore "customs and superstitions which gradually grow into legends and traditions, location and layout of units, messing and recreational facilities." In the summer of 1944, Reinke began to visit RCAF units and live with them for a period of time to record their inner workings.[114] The RCAF overseas section was ensuring the creation of fuller records to document all aspects of the fighting experience. At the same time, by June 1945 historical officers had penned approximately one million words in dozens of narratives to support the writing of the postwar official histories.[115]

WHILE THE HISTORICAL SECTIONS of the army and air force were structured differently, with Stacey completely eclipsing the role of Duguid in Ottawa and Conn keeping strong control from Ottawa over his historical officers, the Royal Canadian Navy presented yet a different organizational structure.

"Naval Officers prefer to make history rather than write it," remarked the American admiral, Ernest J. King.[116] By the start of the Second World War, Canadian naval officers had done very little of either. While Canada is flanked by three oceans and has relied for much of its history on transoceanic trade, its military history has been portrayed through conflicts concerning land armies. Despite having defended the east coast against U-boat attacks during the last year of the Great War, the Royal Canadian Navy (RCN) had garnered more derision than glory. Deep cuts almost destroyed the service after the war, and it was not until the mid-1930s that the navy received additional modern ships for an expected second worldwide conflict. Yet even when Duguid attempted to include an account of the navy in his first official volume, the RCN was so short of staff that it had been unable to assist him. And so the Great War Canadian naval experience was written by army officers.

While the army began to raise its first division of troops in September 1939, the navy was thrust immediately into the war. The essential lifeline to Europe and Great Britain had to be kept open, and that again pitted the men of the RCN and the Merchant Marine against German U-boats. The Battle of the Atlantic would be the longest ongoing struggle of the war, lasting all six years. At the same time, the RCN went from a prewar professional force of 1,800 all ranks to a navy of 100,000 – a fifty-fold expansion.[117] In 1939, though, there was no one to document the war upon the oceans.

It was Duguid, the department's only historical officer at the time and the keeper of Great War memory, who wrote to senior naval officers in February 1940 that the RCN had done a "lamentable" job in creating records in the last war, so much so that he had been almost incapable of piecing together the RCN's actions for the official history. As Clio's champion, Duguid advised that without records it would be impossible "to do proper justice to the RCN for the war 1939- —." Pointing to the multi-volume Royal Navy histories, which were surely the envy of the RCN, Duguid noted that their official historians could never have written them without "extraordinarily complete logs and other contemporary records."[118] The key to good history was good records; and the creation and collection of those same records had to start now. The chief of the naval staff, Admiral Percy Nelles, reacted strongly to Duguid's warning, and within a month Lieutenant John Farrow was appointed as Controller of Naval Information (CNI), responsible for the "history and historical material" of the RCN.[119]

Married to movie actress Maureen O'Sullivan (and father of Mia Farrow), the famous thirty-five-year-old film director had "walked out" on a movie contract to "get into the Empire's war." It was a minor propaganda coup for the navy, and one journalist chirped, "From now on he takes orders from Canadian naval officers, not from Hollywood producers."[120] Farrow was a student of theology and not a bad choice for an historical officer. But it must have been clear to Duguid when he met Farrow on 19 March that he would not be in the job for long, since he had too high a profile to work with war records. Farrow was the press liaison for the RCN, and after meeting with Duguid, he set guidelines for the creation and preservation of records relating to ships, construction, and supply. However, he left the CNI at the end of the year and was not replaced.[121]

A weekly Naval Service report had been started in September 1939 to keep senior officers and political officials appraised of naval activities, and two months later the Prime Minister's Office had requested access. Looking at these reports for the first time, Acting Deputy Minister of Naval Services K.S. Maclachlan complained to Nelles that they were "entirely unsatisfactory" for the prime minister and for future historians.[122] This was reinforced in a letter from the Prime Minister's Office, which stated that the "growth of the Canadian Navy, its work, its adventure, its romance, and its achievement form, probably, one of the most dramatic chapters in our national history" and must be documented accordingly.[123]

The navy needed an historian. Unlike the army and air force, which had several respected historians to pick from to fill their complement, there was only one distinguished Canadian naval historian, Gerald Graham, a professor at Queen's University and later of King's College, London, who had already made his mark with his work on sea power and trade in eighteenth-century North America. The RCN, it appears, did not know of him, even though he was working within the service as a trainer of cadets. Nor did they know of a Queen's University graduate student, J.M. Hitsman, who had completed the first ever thesis on the RCN in 1940.[124] Both Graham and Hitsman would be recruited by Stacey as overseas army historical officers. Instead, the RCN appointed Dr. Gilbert Tucker, a nineteenth-century commercial mercantile expert who proved to be a good choice. Tucker had served three and a half years in the Canadian Expeditionary Force, held a doctorate from Cambridge, and had taught at Yale.[125] While his historical credentials were strong, Tucker seems to have had little knowledge of the RCN. Unlike historical officers such as Conn, Duguid, and Stacey, Tucker was damned by the fact that he remained a civilian, was never commissioned, and was always considered an outsider. Furthermore, the other historical officers continued to prove themselves throughout the war and then push for more authority and more staff, but Tucker was far more reserved; as a result, his naval section would be the smallest of all the services, and he would even be in the unenviable position of not controlling his overseas historical officers.

With his appointment in June 1941, Tucker began to gather records, develop a mandate, and ease his way into the complex organization at Naval Service Headquarters in Ottawa. He toiled alone for a year and a half, and while there is almost no archival trail to explain what he was doing, he appears to have focused on researching the origins of the RCN. This, surely, would have given little incentive to his superiors to change their outlook on the value of naval history. But they, in turn, seem to have paid little if any attention to Tucker, and he continued to be shunted to the periphery: "It would be fair to say that the navy's high command did not share the army's traditional belief in the lessons of the military past," wrote one future official historian.[126]

Tucker went overseas in August 1942 aboard the Canadian destroyer *Assiniboine*, which during the crossing went into action against *U-210*, a German U-boat. This was history in the making. From the bridge, Tucker recounted that the U-boat "suddenly appeared out of the mist, and there she was, some 50 yards away, and about to cross our bow. She was a big boat, black as the night, and was less than the distance of a city block."[127] The *Assiniboine* tried to ram the U-boat, which narrowly evaded the larger destroyer, and for forty minutes the two ships circled one another, the Canadians looking to ram, and the Germans hoping to stay within the inner turning circle of the destroyer to avoid its bigger guns. All the while the two ships fired away at each other. Aboard the bridge of the destroyer, Dr. Tucker did his part by jumping up and down and hurling abuse at the U-boat. Eventually the *Assiniboine* rammed and sunk the U-boat, and Tucker arrived in England, perhaps more aware of the heroics and actions of the navy in the current war. Despite visiting a number of naval commands there and believing that his time "spent in warships at sea was invaluable," he came back to Ottawa with no clearer plan on how to document the war overseas.[128]

"OUR OBJECT IS TO BUILD UP a Canadian naval tradition and prestige which should be valuable to Canada in postwar years, as have been the traditions and prestige of the Canadian Corps, earned by hard fighting in the spearhead of the attack in the last war," exclaimed one senior naval officer in May 1942.[129] How this was to be done, however, must have been a mystery to those interested naval officers overseas, since their only historian seemed to be delving deep into the history of the navy of the Great War while the ongoing death struggle in the Atlantic went largely unrecorded except through the routine records created by the naval service. It was again the charismatic Lieutenant Commander K.S. Maclachlan, now in uniform after resigning from the government, who argued that the navy needed an historical officer overseas. During the Dieppe Raid, for instance, there had been no one to document the navy's actions, so the responsibility had fallen to the army. Maclachlan rightly saw that as unacceptable. This was further pressed by Captain R.I. Agnew, who informed the secretary of the Naval Board that the army had an overseas historical officer who was both assisting in the production of an official history and creating reports that were valuable for the government. Stacey's white paper on Dieppe was singled out as an example of how history could assist the services.[130]

In January 1943 Lieutenant James George was sent overseas to act as an historical officer, but his position was different from that of both Stacey and Hitchins, his respective counterparts in the other services. Stacey, as we have seen, actively distanced himself from Duguid, the chief army historical officer in Ottawa. Hitchins, on the other hand, was guided more closely by Conn, but he too had much leeway in deciding his own work. George was in an even less formal position, and he had almost no direct contact with Tucker.

James George had graduated from the University of Toronto in 1940 with history and philosophy degrees. He was a pacifist and an active member of the Students Christian Movement, where he frequently made speeches against the war. However, the fall of France in June 1940 forced him to re-evaluate his stance on the war, and despite winning a Rhodes Scholarship, he gave it up and enlisted in the navy. For George the navy seemed the best service because, as he recounted years later, he never wanted to be in the situation where he might have to "drive a bayonet into somebody's guts."[131] He served for two years, both at sea and at the intelligence branch of Dover Command, until he was appointed overseas naval historical officer.

In October 1942 he was ordered back to Canada, survived the sinking of his merchant vessel by a U-boat, and arrived in Ottawa to meet with Tucker. The naval historian instructed him to capture "eyewitness accounts and any records that might not be sent back to Ottawa." George was instructed to attend conferences and document the "developments in organization, strategy and tactics resulting from changes in armament and equipment or other causes," but he returned to England with only a vague notion about how he would establish the organizational structure to be present at these meetings or interview ship captains.[132] None of this would be easy for a lowly lieutenant, and he received little assistance from Tucker, who was in a "different world," George later testified, completely absorbed in his Great War research for the official history and seemingly "uninterested" in the historical events unfolding around him.[133]

George was left to his own devices as overseas historical officer. At Naval Intelligence he was mandated to do both intelligence and historical work, functions that complemented one another. And since he was trying to ease his way into the job where he would be expected to delve into the conduct of the war, including its secrets, by proving himself useful to the intelligence officers, he was slowly given access to documents and high-level personnel.[134] Although senior officers at Naval Intelligence allowed him to visit returning ships and even serve in them, they often failed to keep him updated on naval events. In the first months of his historical service, for instance, he frequently missed vessels returning to port. With no direct link to the high command, George had a difficult time navigating through the bureaucracy, and his junior rank did not serve him well in the naval hierarchy. Nonetheless, he had a flair for mixing with senior officers and drawing out their stories: "You must win trust before you can get the history," he noted astutely in one report.[135]

To understand the larger strategic issues of the war, George inquired at Britain's Admiralty Intelligence, where he had some contacts. As well, a few nights spent on fire-watch duty at Saint Paul's cathedral with Professor W.K. Hancock, official historian of the British civil series, opened doors for the young George. Through these channels he attempted to piece together the naval war and Canada's part in it. By August 1943 the lone historian was sharing a small room with two press officers, and while the place was a "continual madhouse, with visits, interviews, dictation and telephone calls," George was compiling an enormous amount of information. He had access to signals intelligence, as well as British Admiralty records, and he busily copied reports on Canadian operations.[136]

George's experience as a sailor also proved a boon in gaining insight into RCN operational matters. He was able to interview officers and pick up signs when there was trouble on ships. In turn, during the equipment crisis of 1943, officers often appealed to him to bring these technological failures to the attention of higher authorities, which he did, although as he noted years after the war, his efforts did little to assist in the situation.[137] Nonetheless, he was gathering much valuable information that would otherwise never have been recorded for posterity. In fact, like Stacey, who found that the British did not believe in the value of sending historical officers into the field, George, too, was surprised to learn that those within the Admiralty Historical Section "still work on the assumption that everything important will find its way onto paper without any primary work on their part and that keeping in close touch with the ships doing the fighting is of no importance in gaining a true perspective of the stages in battle, the problems of the ships and bases, and the development of ideas and equipment." The Royal Navy's Historical Section appeared not to have heeded the insight of one of its Great War army generals, Sir Ian Hamilton: "On the actual day of battle naked truths may be picked up for the asking; by the following morning they have already begun to get into their uniforms."[138]

While George pieced together Canada's part in the naval war overseas, he was troubled continually by Tucker's failure to provide him with any detailed guidance. Tucker had, for instance, sent only one letter to George in eight months; and George recounted that he had encountered "utter silence" from Tucker on a number of historical questions.[139] Without instructions – it was later found that many of letters from both men had never been delivered – George turned to the overseas structure, much as Stacey had done, to increase his small historical team.

Before that, however, Tucker had assisted George by securing a second historical recorder, Freeman Tovell, who held a history degree from Harvard and had served with naval intelligence. He arrived in London at the end of 1943, and he and George divided up the historical work between them: Tovell worked on the Bangors, Tribals, and Escort Groups at Plymouth, while George was responsible for the Portsmouth vessels – primarily the motor torpedo boats and landing craft as well as the administrative burdens of command. With one motorcycle between them, the two historical officers raced along the English coast hoping to meet with ships that were returning from duty in order to interview the officers on board. Years later, Tovell recounted that the ships' captains were supportive, and he rarely encountered any who felt that he was "telling tales behind their backs." In fact, many officers thanked him for his queries, as they now understood the "big picture" of the operation. The only ill feeling he had encountered occurred on board the *Haida*, the day after its sister ship, *Athabaskan*, was sunk by a German destroyer in the early dawn hours of 29 April 1944. Commander Harry Dewolf, captain of the *Haida*, snapped at Tovell when the historian offered to write up the operation: "'Report!? I'm the captain. I'll make the report.'"[140]

Despite the occasional arrest by naval police who mistook the historians for spies, their work was remarkably successful in documenting the war. Although they rarely made it to sea and George was especially worried about missing the RCN work on mid-ocean escorts, the historical officers had written a number of reports for Tucker by the first months of 1944. Anxious to begin work on fuller narratives of RCN operations, George visited the Admiralty's Historical Section in early January 1944 for some guidance. He was bluntly told that with a staff of two it was ludicrous to think that he could do anything worthwhile.[141] The Canadian historical officers had already produced a number of fully referenced reports, but George realized that he needed more staff to fulfil the historical function. He used his now strong contacts with senior naval officers to request and receive the assistance of Betty McGillicuddy, a fellow University of Toronto history graduate and member of the Women's Royal Canadian Naval Service whose husband had been killed earlier in the war.

With McGillicuddy and a few more staff to follow in the coming months, George could afford to send Tovell to the Admiralty's Historical Section to meet Tucker's request for Great War historical research. However, George still remained unsure as to what Tucker wanted for the present war, and in April 1944 he again asked for more guidance. George hoped, for instance, that Tucker might supply him with draft chapters so that he could target his research.[142] There is no indication in the records that Tucker replied, although the official historian did write an impassioned letter to the Senior Canadian Naval Officer in London for more control over his historical officers, whom he believed were serving five masters, "last of whom was the naval historian."[143] He was roundly ignored.

George coordinated the work of his small but growing historical section, and although he remained a lieutenant he was, like Stacey (by now a lieutenant colonel), administering historical officers and war artists to document the war. In March 1944 C.2, a convoy sub-destroyer group, sank German U-boat *U-744* in one of the longest and most demanding hunts of the war. George wrote a report on the action, and it is instructive for tracking the overseas historian's methods. Working from original documents such as captains' reports, operational orders, signal logs, and deck and engine room logs, George aimed to produce a narrative that was useful both to Tucker and to overseas staff officers who were attempting to impart the lessons of sub killing throughout their command. Interviews were essential, noted George, as there are "great advantages of discussing the debatable aspects of an action while it is fresh in the minds of those whose decisions were vital to the outcome and where checking is easy. These are all the more apparent since it is just those points around which the interest in an action centres that are omitted from the usual dry formula of the official reports of proceedings." Additional background information was gathered from the Admiralty's War Room, as this "would be most difficult to obtain from the ship's [crews,] who seldom know the general picture into which their operations fit, and what the Commanding Officers do know they omit from their reports which are made to authorities who are assumed to know it already. This does not help the historian who is relying solely on documents."[144] Forced to confront both historical and operational concerns, George found a suitable compromise.

Most pressing for George's small historical section was the need to document the forthcoming RCN operations in support of the D-Day landings. The Naval Service Headquarters saw the value of "historical coverage," and ship captains were encouraged to respond to the historical officers' questions. While George's request for a place onboard a ship to observe the D-Day landing was denied, he was allowed to enlist paymasters and chaplains to assist in the historical process. The potential value of a postwar history based on accurate and full records was less important to Naval headquarters than the need for "authentic and up-to-date information on what their ships are doing in order to serve them best." The historians, then, would be making frequent visits to ships during the turnaround, gathering records and processing the information for both operational and historical objectives. During these "prolonged and intense" operations, it was understood that the normal Reports of Proceedings would not be completed for days or even weeks after D-Day, but the historical officers' reports would serve as interim documents and brief accounts that could later be expanded upon by ships' captains.[145]

With the heavy involvement of RCN destroyers, frigates, and corvettes in protecting the ongoing and essential logistical supply line, George and his historical officers were lauded for their coverage. Tucker was so impressed that he implored his superiors to promote George to lieutenant commander, since he supervised seven staff, five of whom were officers. "He is one of the ablest men that the Naval Historian has ever known."[146] Tucker's confidence was not misplaced, but unfortunately his ability to influence Naval Services was: George remained a lieutenant and when the Department of External Affairs was looking for experienced, educated servicemen, they raided George and later Tovell from the Naval Historical Section.

The overseas section completed a number of reports on RCN operations and some, such as George's nineteen-page account of landing ships used to carry the soldiers on the D-Day invasion, offered criticisms.[147] In fact, George reported to Tucker in January 1945, just before he was to leave the navy to join the Department of External Affairs, that he had collected a number of contentious records on the RCN "equipment battle in 1943." The failure to equip Canadian ships with suitable radar was extremely damning, but now with the Battle of the Atlantic nearly won, "it is possible to say things more frankly without arousing too much ire. I do hope that this project turns out adequately and receives the balancing comments at a higher level so that the story can be told fairly to meet the most serious criticism that the RCN in years to come will probably face."[148] Unfortunately, Tucker would find after the war that the RCN was not terribly interested in reading damning reports.

With both George and Tovell leaving in early January the overseas section was, as one historical officer noted, "on very shaky foundations."[149] Tucker had been able to replace George with an able historian, Donald Kerr, who held a doctorate in history and had worked in Ottawa preparing narratives, but the overseas naval section remained chronically understaffed. It was no better in Ottawa.

TUCKER HAD GONE OVERSEAS only twice during the war. Like Duguid, he remained in Ottawa and left matters of the overseas Historical Section to the men responsible there, but unlike the army and air force historians in Ottawa, Tucker had little administrative work to distract him. He had been appointed official historian and he devoted himself almost exclusively to that job. And although he was most interested in the early history of the RCN, Tucker did not entirely ignore the present war.

Using his contacts with university professors across the country, Tucker recruited graduate students and young scholars to assist him. Maurice Careless, Donald Kerr, and David Spring all worked for him, and despite being few in number, they were certainly a far more impressive historical team than the staff of the other services' historical sections in Ottawa, which consisted largely of officers with no historical training. Tucker ordered his talented staff to develop naval narratives on Second World War operations, training, and shipbuilding. Maurice Careless had joined Tucker as his assistant in the summer of 1943, but within months the Department of External Affairs had enticed him away after he had written a stellar narrative on the policy and acquisition of armed merchant cruisers. Tucker was desperate to see the historical work continue and David Spring, a graduate of the University of Toronto who was studying for a PhD at Harvard, was brought in as a civilian and eventually wrote many of the Second World War chapters. Despite the problem of keeping his staff, Tucker was ably assisted by these young historians who drafted all of the key Second World War narratives.[150]

So strong were these draft narrative chapters that Tucker had considered publishing some of them during the war to help bring attention to the RCN.[151] This came to nothing, perhaps because the RCN had already commissioned two civilians to write a popular history. In 1944 Stephen Leacock, one of Canada's most accomplished men of letters, and Leslie Roberts, a young journalist, published the government-sponsored *Canada's War at Sea* (1944).[152] It was a two-volume history, and the second book by Roberts provided a surprisingly detailed account of the naval war. While Roberts placed excessive emphasis on the triumphant exertions in building the Canadian navy, he also provided a frank discussion of the 1942 German attacks against merchant shipping in Canadian waters. The panic inspired by German U-boats in the St. Lawrence had resulted in the closing of this essential waterway and in curtailing the flow of goods to Great Britain. Even the terrible sinking of the Newfoundland ferry, the *Caribou*, by *U-69* on 13-14 October 1942, with the heavy loss of civilian life, was reported, partly again to quell rumours and partly, one must think, to incite Canadians against merciless German aggression, much as the sinking of the *Lusitania* in May 1915 had galvanized Canadians into further supporting the war effort. If Roberts failed to understand the successful Canadian naval response during the Battle of the St. Lawrence that drove U-boats out of Canadian waters for easier pickings to the south, he can be excused since these revelations were only presented forty years later by official historians.[153]

Although Tucker was not as dynamic as Stacey or George, he surrounded himself with young graduate students and gave them the support they needed to draft chapters on the Second World War, while he worked on the Great War history. What is perhaps most significant about Tucker's stewardship of the Navy Historical Section in relation to this study is the lack of operational and administrative records concerning its work. Of course, the narratives and chapters are available, but the correspondence between officers is almost entirely missing. Moreover,

Tucker, unlike Stacey, Duguid, and Hitchins, left no personal papers for posterity, nor did he write much about his wartime service: perhaps Tucker's relative obscurity among historians is partly due to his lack of foresight in writing his history with one eye on history.

"IN FIGHTING, the Canadian Army was as good as any, but in setting down thought or deed on paper its inarticulateness was excelled by none," wrote historical officer W.E.C. Harrison after the war.[154] Harrison is right to remind historians that the records used now to construct the history of the war reflect the limitations of those creating them at the time or under the conditions in which they operated. Initially few in number and without influence, the service historians played essential roles in ensuring that records were created and preserved by the "inarticulate" services, a surprisingly difficult concept to drive home to war diarists and other record creators, who were also continually reminded of wartime security and censorship.

Far worse was the perceived mundane nature of record keeping: these were fighting men engaged in a battle for civilization; why were they being plagued by annoying historian-types to produce fuller reports? There was, of course, an operational requirement for senior officers to understand what was occurring within their commands, and useful training implications as well, but that was not always well communicated to those charged with this administrative task. Yet the historians ensured that the war records were fuller and richer in detail, and although it is impossible to ascertain what the records would have been like without the influence of the historical services, evidence suggests that the historians helped to shape the records by establishing guidelines and actively intervening. If it had not been for the service historians, it is likely that more of the war records that historians have been mining now for more than sixty years would have been poor, scattered administrative accounts, or perhaps they never would have been created at all. History is an ongoing dialogue of contested ground, space, and concepts, but its practitioners are far less able to carry out their roles without records that document the deeds and actions of the past. It is clear as well that these were not "neutral" records, and all subsequent researchers using them should keep in mind Sir Basil Liddell Hart's observation that "nothing can deceive like a document."[155] While the war records are still imperfect, there can be no doubt that the intervention and authoring of these records by the historical officers provided far more inclusive and useful accounts of battle, command, and organization.

The key to the historians' influence in allowing them to shape the archival record and to begin work on their wartime narratives was winning the confidence of the senior officers. At first the historians were seen as little more than paper warriors, another useless burden on the already overcrowded command headquarters. Historians were thought to be old, stodgy academics who were far more comfortable in ivory towers than in Martello towers. But the expert influence of men such as Stacey, Hitchins, and George proved quickly that history and archival collecting could support the operational requirements of war. Historical information drawn from the war records helped to keep the commanders apprised. As senior officers saw the value in what the historians were doing, both in supporting operations and in crafting a legacy to the war, the historical programs were encouraged and strengthened. While the historians were constrained in what they could write during the war, it also allowed them to forge strong bonds with senior officers and gather essential and top-secret records.

The historical sections were also the proving ground for a new, professional cadre of historians. Stacey, Stanley, Graham, Careless, Hitsman, Conacher, Kerr, and a host of other young historians had been recruited from academia to serve their country. All learned to work in the military structure; all had nearly unrestricted access to records and officers who were making history; and all honed their historical skills in the crucible of war. Later, most of those historians would leave the service and return to academia. They took with them a firm understanding of war and the value of military history. No longer would military history be the purview of gifted amateurs or regimental loyalists. Academic historians who were trained to decipher and scrutinize the archival record would bring a new rigour to the discipline. Furthermore, Colonel Charles Stacey, Wing Commander Fred Hitchins, and Dr. Gilbert Tucker transformed themselves from wartime recorders of history and gatherers of archives into outstanding leaders of the ambitious postwar official history programs. Clio had prospered in the service of Mars.

4
History Wars and War History, 1945-48

> *The deeper I get into this vast collection the more I feel like a man who finds himself in a goldmine with only a very small pick and shovel!*
> – Major T.M. Hunter

> *There are no bargain rates in this commodity.*
> – Colonel A.F. Duguid

Canada had been at war for more than ten of the first forty-five years of the twentieth century. After more than 60,000 dead in the Great War, the nation traveled a difficult road to autonomy, culminating in the 1931 Statute of Westminster, which gave full national control over foreign policy. Yet less than a decade later, Canadians again responded to Great Britain's call to fight for the same liberal ideals that had driven an earlier generation. This second war was even more devastating than the first, and Canada contributed 42,000 of its young sons to the estimated fifty-five million worldwide.

For a country that had mobilized one of every eleven citizens, a series of histories were needed to explain the enormous sacrifice and accomplishment of the Canadian people during the Second World War. While for reasons of security and obligations to alliances it was unacceptable to open up the archives to the public for several decades, the task of depicting and describing the war to Canadians once again fell to the service official historians. However, these historians would only focus on the overseas war effort and not the prodigious exertions in Canada. An all-encompassing history would have to wait. Yet due to postwar retrenchment and shrinking budgets, two of the three historical series were cut back deeply. Only the army program headed by Colonel C.P. Stacey, who had shown his brilliance and productivity during the war, was saved. Nonetheless, the official historians headed an enormously complicated historical program that would lay the foundation for the study of the Second World War and shape the canon of Canadian history.

WITH THE GERMAN SURRENDER in May 1945, the overseas historical sections were confronted with a mass of historically valuable records that were stored in hundreds of transitory repositories. With the Canadians ordered to Germany as an army of occupation and to the Netherlands in a humanitarian role, and with soldiers awaiting repatriation, it was essential that trained historical staff begin gathering archival records for the writing of future official histories. While there was an administrative process for collecting these records, it was clear to Stacey that unless there was an intercession by his historical officers, valuable records would be lost or compromised during the frequent moves, upheavals, and faltering discipline in the postwar months.

The field historical officers were expected not only to assist units in transferring their records, but also to ensure the survival of records that were often dumped or left unwanted. Lieutenant Colonel Eric Harrison, who still commanded the field historical section, excitedly reported to Stacey in September 1945 that he had found Lieutenant General Charles Foulkes's II Canadian Corps operations trailer in the woods. It had been abandoned and was discovered with the door open and all the general's files still present.[1] Although this was an unusual case, it is clear that once again the historical officers were playing an essential role in preserving records as they had been throughout the war.

Though the shooting war had stopped, the paper war continued in earnest. Units had initially been instructed to "strip" their files of routine orders before sending them on to Canadian Military Headquarters (CMHQ) so that the future historians were not "swamped by useless paper," but that order was rescinded quickly when units complained that they had no method of determining which documents were valuable.[2] The fate of war files thus fell to the historical officers. The mass of records, eventually numbering in the millions of pages, would prove too large for the small teams involved. As a result, all records were eventually sent back to CMHQ, and then to Ottawa, where they were to be examined and then archived or destroyed over a number of years.

Stacey also pressed for access to war records generated by senior officers with whom he had often developed close friendships. These men often had their own personal archives of records accumulated over a number of years. At the highest levels, these archival collections contained strategic documents that Stacey was anxious to see: "I need hardly say that opening these files to Hist Sec does not imply that personal details better left confidential are going to be printed in the Official History or circulated, in a Preliminary Narrative or otherwise. Hist Sec has had access to a great deal of highly confidential material of this sort, and I think it will be admitted that we have used it with discretion; indeed, we have been criticized, as I think you are aware, of showing too much discretion."[3]

The Army commanders, A.G.L. McNaughton and H.D.G. Crerar, had given Stacey full access to their records during the war, and because of the trust he had forged, this continued in the postwar period. But Stacey went beyond the position of chronicler, and balancing his historical and archival functions, he convinced Crerar not to cull personal information when he found this was the general's aim. He was only partially successful, but more records survived because of his intervention.

Stacey eventually gained access to Crerar's personal war diary, but he was under orders that it should not leave his hands and should definitely not be shown to the British.[4] Personal records were not infallible, of course, and Crerar warned Stacey that he should not accept at "face value" the records created by McNaughton, since "these sometimes gave a version which was less the truth than what General McNaughton had convinced himself was the truth."[5] McNaughton probably thought the same of Crerar's view of events. Despite the beginning of a sniping war among the Canadian generals that would continue for decades over how the historical memory of the conflict would be portrayed, there is no doubt that all respected Stacey largely because of his inspired and dependable wartime work.

"History is the last thing we are about during operations and the first thing we want afterwards. Then it is too little, too late and too untrue," an American publication reminded soldiers during the war.[6] Stacey well knew the difficulty in reconstructing army events by relying solely on the war records, and he understood that without immediate historical work it might indeed be "too little, too late" for a future official historian. He instructed his narrators, many of whom had been in the field and witnessed individual battles as divisional historical officers, to continue crafting fully documented historical accounts to give the soon-to-be appointed official historian "everything he will require, so that he will be able to prepare his History with no documents before him other than those which we provide."[7] This was asking a lot from his narrators, but Stacey realized that the work he required would never be completed unless his experienced narrators could be employed after the end of the war. Using the records and their own knowledge of the fighting, the narrators began to work: Captain J.R. Martin, for instance, began to pull together records to write a narrative of the Canadian role in the D-Day landings even as the Germans prepared to surrender in May 1945.

Stacey also wanted to place the Canadian operations within the full context of theatre-wide events, so that Canadian formations did not appear to be "operating in a vacuum."[8] That was a laudable but ambitious request. While his narrators had mostly been situated in divisional or corps headquarters, they had little access to the highest-level documents of the Army Groups, Supreme Headquarters Allied Expeditionary Forces (SHAEF), or Cabinet. Nor were there any dependable histories that could be used even as rough guides. As one narrator informed Stacey, since it was impossible to track high-level strategic decisions, he was simply trying to understand the complicated unfolding of the "individual units on the ground, and to penetrate the obscurity of the units' War Diaries at moments of importance in their history."[9] It would later fall to Stacey to negotiate access to these "strategic" archival records, but in the meantime he interviewed senior commanders or examined their personal archives to piece together how Canadian forces operated within the Allied command.

At the other end of the command spectrum, Stacey and his officers took every opportunity to interview campaign veterans in order to provide a fuller view of battle. Stacey was anxious to have his historical officers question those men who had been captured at Dieppe, in order to elucidate the "unwritten history" that would not be present in the War Diaries or the short after-battle reports, which attempted to portray the experience of several hundred men during periods of absolute chaos and discordance.[10] Despite these inclusive goals, Stacey and his historical officers were mostly interested in the big picture of the war, and they rarely included the experiences of frontline soldiers in their narratives. Much of the hidden history of the war – the experience of men in combat – therefore went unrecorded in the narratives. The exception was a series of remarkable narratives on Dieppe, which relied heavily on poignant first-hand accounts by soldiers.[11] Unfortunately, most of these were not incorporated into the official history series, partly due to a lack of space but also because Stacey believed archival records, rather than first-person accounts, even those captured immediately after a battle, were closer approximations to unfolding events. In his clinical operational history, Stacey thought he did not need to rely on veterans' accounts.

To produce a more complete picture of the war, in June 1945 Stacey used his connections at Canadian Military Headquarters in London to request that intelligence officers interview German senior commanders on "matters of interest" to the Historical Section.[12] Stacey wanted to know what the Germans thought of the Canadian forces, how they reacted to various operations, and any additional insight they could provide into the grim experience of battle. Within a month he received "valuable information" that was immediately incorporated into the narratives, and he continued to insist that all be wrung out of the German officers who both served in Normandy and Italy.[13] These interrogations lasted for more than a year, and the Canadians found that the Germans were anxious to answer their questions, especially since the Canadians and British were apparently gentler in their methods than the Americans who employed more "treat 'em rough" tactics.[14] While these testimonials were important in augmenting the narratives, there was the danger of the Germans providing self-serving statements or deflecting the blame for the savage actions of their soldiers and the repulsive regime they fought for across Europe. Stacey knew he would have to cross-examine them with the German war records, but these had been transferred to Washington and were therefore unavailable to the Canadians until agreements could be established.

STACEY HAD BEEN the army's official historian from the fall of 1945 onwards, but he had nearly turned down the job to return to academia. Unlike Gilbert Tucker, who had remained very isolated during the war, or Kenneth Conn, who was the Royal Canadian Air Force's (RCAF) senior historian but more of an administrator than anything else, Stacey had carved out his role overseas while Duguid continued as senior historian in Ottawa. The two men had clashed occasionally over Stacey's proclivity to expand his duties, but they had agreed on the importance of a postwar history. Duguid had suggested in 1943 a multi-volume series that would document both the military and civilian war effort, which would include a diplomatic series, a civilian series, and a military series, consisting of the three service histories, and a final series to link them all into an overview history. It was an ambitious plan that would have documented the totality of Canada's war effort, and it was intriguingly similar to what the British had instigated, but it made little impact at the Department of National Defence.[15] Duguid was the senior army historian, but all the overseas commanders had faith in Stacey. It was unlikely that they would endorse a plan forwarded by Duguid alone.

Duguid broached the issue again in December 1944, but this time he astutely brought Stacey back from London. The two historians put forth a modest proposal for a four-volume history, with a one-volume summary published within two years of the ceasefire that would give the Canadian public immediate access to an authentic account of the war. The histories would be aimed at explaining the war to the general reader rather than a General Staff study, but they would be detailed enough so that officers and future historians could process the harsh lessons of combat and the requirements of administering a massive war effort.[16] The two official historians concluded optimistically that the series could be completed by 1950, an unlikely early date probably suggested by the continuing scandal of Duguid's Great War series.

No one predicted it would be easy. Stacey insisted that any official historian would have a "heavy responsibility and a difficult and perhaps in some respects unpleasant job." A large and experienced team of narrators would be needed in order to complete this series on time, and the official historian would have to be given full access to all war records, including the Cabinet records, and be placed in an independent position to make opinions and judgments without censorship or pressure.[17] While there could be no guarantees of access to the Cabinet records since these were outside the army's control, the proposal was supported by the overseas generals, although the chief of staff at CMHQ, Lieutenant General P.J. Montague, wrote to Crerar that "Duguid should NOT be involved in any way." Crerar concurred, supporting an official history, while not wanting to repeat the mistakes of the first war.[18] However, Lieutenant General Guy Simonds, who finished the war as one of Canada's corps commanders, was more wary of an official publication. He suggested that any policy history be "written last, when the issues now so hotly contested politically have had a chance to cool." Simonds also thought that a history would have to be "essentially factual and on points of fact ... quite unchallengeable"; at the same time, it should draw out lessons for the army and the nation, especially the "absurd" notion of trying to fight a "major war on a basis of limited liability."[19] Simonds was convinced of the importance of a history after several interviews with Stacey. The project was eventually confirmed on 25 April 1945 by Minister of National Defence A.G.L. McNaughton, who was in the midst of a short and unhappy tenure, which was made worse by having been forced to support conscription a year earlier after he failed to find the necessary voluntary recruits.[20] Although no official historian was yet named, everyone knew that Stacey was the only suitable candidate.

McNaughton ordered that the official historian should have full access to military records, but the army refused to waive its control over an "official" project, demanding final editorial control over anything published. Duguid had warned that without any "censorship" by Department of National Defence (DND) officers – presumably himself – the official historian's work would be "inconsistent and incompatible" with issues of national security. Stacey had no desire to lay forth the secrets of the nation, but he would not compromise his "intellectual honesty."[21] With such oversight and possible interference, the official history would be little more than the "official" story as the army or government saw fit, and this was unacceptable to Stacey with his academic background. He refused the position of official historian as long as it came with any strings attached.

Stacey immediately began to look for an academic post. The army, realizing the importance of an official history and aware that only he could write it, reversed its decision, but only after senior generals appealed to the new chief of the general staff. This, surprisingly, was not Simonds, a man many considered Canada's best battlefield general; instead, Crerar, as army commander in Europe, had ensured that his other corps commander, Lieutenant General Charles Foulkes, was offered the position of CGS, since Crerar neither trusted nor liked Simonds and had even tried to have him labelled insane during the war.[22] There was no love lost between the two men. Although Foulkes had proved a mediocre battlefield general, he had the right demeanour for postwar command. Simonds had been understandably shocked and felt Crerar had done him in, which, of course, he had. This would later have an impact on Stacey as he tried to steer the interpretations in the official history between these two powerful figures. But Foulkes was a strong supporter of military history and almost immediately pushed for Stacey's appointment with the necessary academic freedom. Equally important, Stacey would have direct access to the CGS should he run into trouble. This was a very unusual reporting structure; there were few, if any, colonels who could directly appeal to the CGS. Stacey was appointed head of the Historical Section as a colonel, while Duguid was given a smaller, separate directorate tasked only with completing the Great War official history, which was still a priority for both DND and veterans.[23] Duguid accepted the demotion without protest, and Stacey began to coordinate the work of his narrators overseas and those now in Ottawa. "We must on no account conceal our failures" were the only words of instruction Stacey received from Foulkes.[24]

BACK IN LONDON, Stacey's narrators continued to gather information and write narratives. Yet most of the historical officers had been demobilized and returned to their academic lives. Stacey knew there would be no hope without the narrators, and he implored Eric Harrison and Sam Hughes to stay on and oversee the work in London. A number of gifted narrators were also drawn from the ranks to assist in writing. Major Robert Spencer, who had been tasked by his commanding officer to write his regiment's history after the war, was invited to extend his stay and help prepare the narratives for Stacey, who was then in Ottawa.[25] In an old Ministry of Pensions building in Acton, narrators ground out page after page of battlefield accounts; these were then sent to Spencer who assembled, edited, and rewrote them. The more polished versions were then passed on to Eric Harrison, who also rewrote or edited them and passed the refined reports to an anxious Stacey in Ottawa, who was already writing draft chapters.[26] The narrators were capturing the history from the records – the War Diaries, operational orders, and after-battle reports – and every detail had to be reconstructed without the aid of secondary sources. Furthermore, all work was rushed since the official historian wanted to place something before the public before it began to view the war as "ancient history."[27] A series of monographs would also prove to senior officers that under Stacey's command, the Historical Section would not repeat the earlier fiasco.

Towards the end of the war, Stacey had ordered that three historical monographs be written as the army's first offerings to the public; they would also form a groundwork for the future official histories. Lavishly illustrated with reproductions of war art, the first two of this three-volume series, *The Canadians in Britain* and *From Pachino to Ortona*, were published in November 1945 and January 1946; Stacey wrote the former with George Stanley and the latter with Sam Hughes. But it was the third volume, *Canada's Battle in Normandy*, which revealed the contested history of the war.[28]

Just as he had done during the war, Stacey had circulated the volume to both Crerar and Simonds for their comments in order to ensure that the history contained no glaring errors. Having had little access to strategic records, Stacey was also desperate to understand the context of Canadian operations.[29] Crerar was pleased with the draft, but Simonds complained that the account of the Black Watch Regiment at Verrières on 25 July 1944, where two companies were nearly annihilated, was inaccurate and off-putting. While the casualties were devastating for the Black Watch, Simonds argued, they were far fewer than at either Dieppe or Hong Kong, and Stacey should not have emphasized this failure. Since Stacey had already responded to the minister of National Defence's request for a detailed account of the battle and had interviewed all surviving soldiers and officers, he knew very well that the operation had indeed been a costly failure that could not be downplayed.[30] Perhaps more important, Simonds stressed that the "misfortune of the day" was not due to the plan that he had conceived and issued, but to the "inexperience of the troops involved."[31] In effect, Simonds was pressuring Stacey to lay the blame on regimental officers at the front who had been ordered to carry out the operation, which was ambitious but also complicated, dangerous, and based on a poor reading of available intelligence. Verrières Ridge was to have been Simonds's Vimy Ridge, and would have been, he thought, if not for the men who were tasked to carry out the fighting.[32]

Foulkes waded into battle too. He found it distasteful that Simonds was blaming his men for the operation's failure. The CGS also had little sympathy for Simonds personally, since his former superior and now subordinate officer had also accused him of poorly handling his forces in the battle. Foulkes counterattacked by suggesting that Simonds's claim that the operation had been a holding attack was nonsense, and that if it had been, he had never communicated that to any of his own subordinates.[33] In fact, the confused operation was many things, both an attack and a holding operation, but certainly Simonds's protests and shifting of blame were uncharitable to say the least.

Stacey was caught in the middle, and with the authorization to publish the history deadlocked, the incident was only defused when the two generals agreed to destroy the written reports they had prepared for the Historical Section. This must have been painful for Stacey, though he ensured that a copy of Simonds's account survived in the archives; and while he refused to accede to Simonds's attempt to blame others, he did discreetly reword the small booklet, removing the devastating casualty figures relating to the Black Watch.[34] Years later Stacey recalled that it was not prudent at that time to argue with an ex-corps commander who was still smarting from the perception that the government had mistreated him.[35] But Stacey included the figures when he wrote the final volume of the official history – only 15 of the 300 men got back to their start lines – and later asserted that "I never changed the official history's text for anybody."[36]

Stacey knew that this short Normandy monograph would be "very closely scrutinized," and he hoped to make it as "sound" and accurate as possible.[37] Yet he also realized the need to modify some of his judgments in the hope of winning the trust of senior officers. While Stacey had negotiated autonomy from interference and still had a direct route to the CGS if he needed it, he was wary of alienating those from whom he would require assistance in years to come.

The monograph was published in the summer of 1946, and much to Stacey's disappointment, was little reviewed in the newspapers, although he received a bevy of compliments from senior officers and his contemporaries. "We embarked on this project in the hope that it would be welcomed as an attempt to give authentic historical information to the public," he wrote, "[and] I hoped we could give a lead to the Canadian publishing industry" that further official histories would follow. While the three booklets sold over 35,000 copies by 1947, and close to 100,000 copies by the mid-1950s (an enormous success by Canadian publishing standards), few newspapers paid attention to them.[38] However, one reviewer noted that Stacey pulled no punches and revealed the harsh fighting at Falaise: "Dead soldiers and dead horses by hundreds and thousands lay on the roadways and in the ditches." Attesting to the sentiment of the times, the same reviewer brayed, "It is pleasant and gratifying to read of this just retribution meted out to the foul Hun in return for all the misery and desolation that he had brought to the peoples of Europe." *The Legionary* also reviewed the monographs, thanking Stacey and his historians for "the timeliness of their splendid service." Canada's veterans were informed that the army's historians would now turn their attention to the official histories, completing them by 1950. That, thought the reviewer, was a "reasonable length of time to wait for such a work," but could not resist a swipe at Duguid, noting, "Paradoxically, the complete tomes of the First Great War may not [yet] be off the printing presses."[39]

The three monographs were tangible proof that Stacey and his section would produce results. Stacey intimated several times that Duguid's failure had nearly destroyed the official history program, and although Stacey had won over the fighting generals during the war, he now had to do the same with the politicians and the veterans. These first monographs, then, set precedent for future works. With time, additional opportunities to examine the war records, and a deeper entrenchment of his position, Stacey would be able to delve further into the contested history of the war and present more controversial findings.

WHILE THE ARMY HISTORIAN was struggling to ensure that history had a role in a postwar DND, the RCAF Historical Section was also trying to build on its wartime accomplishments, widely recognized through the popularity of *The RCAF Overseas* series. Despite this success, Kenneth Conn left the RCAF to return to his tourism business at the end of 1945. He had been an effective director, but he knew his limitations and he was not an historian.[40] He recommended that his two most promising researchers, Wing Commander F.H. Hitchins and Flight Lieutenant H.H. Coulson, be appointed as official historians. Hitchins and Coulson had taught at universities in the 1930s, and during the war had written large parts of the RCAF popular history. However, with the expected rush of veterans back into civilian universities, both had already been offered jobs as professors. Conn thought that unless they were given permanent positions in the RCAF, their expertise would be lost, and the official history would be in jeopardy. Senior RCAF officers and the chief of the air staff "strongly recommended" that their work continue, and on 4

December 1945 Hitchins was appointed air historian with Coulson named associate air historian.[41]

With fourteen staff, this was more than double the number of the Royal Canadian Navy (RCN) Historical Section, but the army dwarfed them both with forty-nine personnel.[42] Set up in temporary quarters at Rockcliffe air base in Ottawa, the section was also in the unenviable position of having its records housed in a building more than a mile away.[43] Moreover, because the RCAF could offer few permanent jobs, the Historical Section had, as Conn and Hitchins warned, a difficult time holding on to its experienced narrators in the postwar job boom. For example, W.H. Bilbrough, the historical officer for South East Asia and the Middle East, had been recalled to London to begin work on the narrative, but was repatriated home on compassionate leave and thereafter was demobilized.[44] With him went much knowledge of Canadian air operations in those theatres. It was a sign of things to come, and many other narrators were soon in civilian suits and new jobs.

As early as June 1941 the Historical Section had been working on the assumption that the plans for a RCAF official history had received ministerial approval. Conn had delayed the discussion of appointing an official historian during the war, but research had continued on the official narratives. Hitchins now began to plan for a multi-volume series, but much to his distress he could find no document verifying ministerial approval.[45] After some soul-searching, he decided to continue on the premise that an official history was still wanted by senior air force officers.

Hitchins aimed for an incredible eight-volume series, covering everything since 1909, including the Great War experience, the role of the British Commonwealth Air Training Plan (BCATP) in Canada, and the work of nearly a hundred Second World War squadrons and over 200,000 personnel. In addition, two or three thematic histories were planned to explore air medicine, technology, and research. Hitchins, a relatively unknown RCAF officer, had presented a plan that was almost three times as long as the army series. It was unlikely to meet with success. He also noted that production time could only be guessed at, as the mass of archival records were still overseas, unclassified, and not yet indexed. Like most official historians before and after him, however, he offered a rosy appreciation that two years would be required for the preparation of each volume.[46]

It would be an enormous job, and it was not initially made easier by the British air services. Overseas RCAF narrators found their work encumbered when the Royal Air Force (RAF) blocked access to higher strategic Allied records, partly because there was no policy for viewing this material but largely because the records were in a "state of confusion." Only a year after the war, the RAF was not yet willing to let anyone see the strategic records, with Canadian personnel having little influence on the decision. The Army Historical Section, which was also attempting to pry open similar British-American archives, fared no better; the British refused to assist the official historians and insisted that all requests come through the High Commission. This was a frustrating hurdle, but in the meantime the RCAF had a second volume of the popular history available for the public.[47]

With an uninspiring title, *The RCAF Overseas: The Fifth Year,* the second volume was published in October 1945. The preface hoped that "this book will be accepted as a token payment of the complete story," which would be displayed fully in the forthcoming official history. There were gaps in the narrative, warned the historian, as "fighting units ... are interested in making rather than in writing history." Despite the limitations of contemporary history, "the historians of the RCAF have not waited until the dust of years has accumulated on the records of our men – but they present the story only a few months after heroic deeds themselves were recorded."[48]

The history appeared authentic. A detailed account of target acquisition would have appealed to many readers, and the stress of flying was not concealed: "The boys who took to the air six hours earlier are nowhere to be seen, their place has been taken by old, disillusioned, dirty men with lack-lustre eyes and heavy hands." The morality of strategic bombing was not a concern: first-hand flying reports and the historians' narrative revealed that whole cities and everything in them were targets. With its emphasis on the flying men and with no access to strategic records, however, there was little analysis of the policy behind the air operations. Important lessons were downplayed and innovations like the jettisonable fighter fuel tanks were simply described as "jet," with no attempt to clarify the significance of this key technological development in allowing Allied fighters to fly deeper into Germany in support of the bombers and eventually destroy the German Air Force.[49]

"Every RCAF man and woman who went overseas will want a copy of this book to read at once, to read in part for years to come, to recall friendship and deepest significance, and to be reminded of the noble contribution of Canada's airmen," waxed John Yocom in a *Saturday Night* review.[50] Based on official records and first-hand accounts from the men who flew, the history offered an authentic view of the air war from the cockpit. Yet sales were not as brisk as during the war, perhaps due to "postwar revulsion from books dealing with the war," thought one RCAF officer. By March 1947, though, it had sold 3,444 copies.[51] The relatively poor sales were noted by the chief of the air staff, and despite Hitchins's claims that almost 16,000 copies of the first and second volumes had been sold by October 1947 and that both had made money, there was no hiding that the second volume had not done as well as the section had predicted.[52]

The RCAF official history was in trouble. As historical narrators left the service, Hitchins made increasing pleas for permanent status for his staff. Air Marshal

G.O. Johnson was one ally, and he suggested in June 1946 that the Historical Section could, in addition to working on the official history, begin to create "lessons learned" documents for RCAF officers, thereby making the section immediately useful to the postwar RCAF.[53] While the RCAF high command appreciated an official history, senior officers hoped to find a greater operational role for their service historians.

A month later Hitchins laid out a detailed plan for the official series, pointing out that the RCAF could not leave the writing of its history to the British, a type of wishful thinking that had failed after the Great War, leaving Canada with nothing. Other air forces were engaged in codifying their experiences in the war, and Hitchins claimed, "Interest and pride in its history is a mark of a nation's maturity and a measure of its culture." Within the RCAF, an official history would help solidify esprit de corps and could be used as a staff study. He also suggested, with little supporting evidence, that the official history would "pay profits in intangible terms of national interest and pride, service benefit and prestige." Again he proposed a series of eight volumes, though recognizing the precarious position of the Historical Section, he now suggested that production of the book would proceed at one a year.[54]

Despite Hitchins's urgings and justifications, the Historical Section remained hamstrung by the lack of a formal wartime authorization for a history. Moreover, the wartime success of the Historical Section and the publication of the first two popular history volumes suggested that producing an official history would not be very difficult. The Air Council meeting in September 1946 to decide the fate of the history concluded, "This project is of concern beyond that of the Royal Canadian Air Force," and it would assist in the "promotion of Canada's national interests and international prestige." But the final decision was to be made by the Cabinet Defence Committee.[55] While the Air Council claimed to appreciate its value, Chief of the General Staff Foulkes received a far different view from a trusted advisor: "In our experience the people of Canada have not purchased the history of World War I and I am convinced that unless the history of World War II ... is produced within five years at the very most, they will not buy that either. In fact they might not buy it if we produced it tomorrow."

The report also noted that the estimated cost of producing the official histories would be $300,000, but experience indicated that the "figure should be at least doubled."[56] With the completion of the Great War official history costing another $185,000, the CGS, faced with the difficult task of slashing the department's budget, had to decide if he wished to put precious resources into codifying the history of the services at the expense of operational capabilities. Such arguments had been used in the past to quash official histories. The cost to the British of fighting the Great War was an estimated £11.196 billion, or £3,500 a minute. When cuts were considered to the official history program in the interwar years, one observer noted that the cost of making the lessons of the war available to the next generation was less than the amount spent during four minutes of the war.[57] Nevertheless, Foulkes recommended to the minister that the official histories should be cut, and there was no protest from the other service chiefs.

The minister of National Defence, Brooke Claxton, a Great War veteran and a respected Cabinet member in King's government since 1944, had been ordered to reduce radically the defence budget.[58] On advice from Foulkes he agreed to shut down the official history programs by 31 March 1948. The Great War series was an easy mark, since no one expected Duguid to produce anything more. The Second World War historians were not so easily brushed aside, but Claxton suggested that the popular histories become the focus: the army was to finish the Historical Summary, the air force was to complete its third volume, and the navy was to get out a volume or two of whatever it could complete. As Stacey informed his deputy director, G.W.L. Nicholson, who was then examining Allied records in England, "The axe has now fallen, and in a manner which none of us anticipated ... A programme approved by two Ministers of National Defence has been repudiated and I must confess that both personally and professionally I am extremely angry ... The whole business is disgusting."[59]

Claxton had strong opinions about how the military should be run and how its history should be written. Although the chiefs of staff had recommended the cancellation of the histories, Claxton had agreed because he was notoriously worried about protecting the Liberals' reputation. For him, the war records and a war history could reveal and reopen old wounds; he even told Stacey several times that "nobody would be interested in reading about the Second World War after 1948."[60] Few statements could be so short-sighted, but it sheds light on what many in the Liberal party believed: having governed for over a decade, they had no interest in presenting the story of the war to the Canadian public.

Angry and frustrated, Stacey asked Professor R.G. Trotter if there was a teaching position available at Queen's University. Trotter had nothing, but he talked to the influential University of Toronto professor, George Brown, who was aghast that the official histories had been cut. Brown called Lester Pearson, the undersecretary of state for External Affairs, who had been a junior lecturer in his department before entering public service, and told him it would be a grave disservice to the country should Canada produce no official history. Prodded by an old mentor, Pearson called Claxton, suggesting that Canada's allies and enemies "might be impressed by the fact that Canada apparently was not sufficiently interested in her armed forces to write a history of their achievements." The knock-on effect continued, and Stacey was summoned to the defence minister's office to discuss options; with nothing to lose, Stacey accused the minister of breaking faith with the veterans and with him.[61] That his three historical monographs had sold over 30,000 copies, while the King's Printer had another 19,000 unfilled orders was a clear indication that there was a market in Canada for an authentic and accurate army history based on official records.⁶² Claxton accepted this argument and agreed to restore the army series, which would still consist of four volumes, but the final one was now to be an inter-service policy volume.⁶³

HITCHINS ALSO TRIED to reverse the decision. Although the third popular history was almost ready, the volumes in this series were, he warned, "quite limited in scope and were not intended to be a history of the Force, but only a preliminary report until the official history could be prepared." It was difficult to understand how an official account of the war could not to be written as the Canadian government "properly draws attention to the contribution made by the Dominion in two world wars" when representing itself to the rest of the world. With all the resources already devoted to the project, cutting the program was not, the official historian suggested, the best way to save money.⁶⁴

Claxton was not convinced and, despite being a strong nationalist, offered the surprisingly naïve view that because "the RCAF fought with the British ... it was up to the British to tell the story."⁶⁵ The air marshals should have dissuaded him, but Hitchins believed that the history was also cut because they were "not interested in history." These feelings were understandable by one who felt the cancellation as a "grievous blow," and while the chief of the air staff (CAS) may not have gone to the wall for the history, it is clear that senior air force officers saw its value.⁶⁶ In the end, though, they were not willing to pay the price.

Despite the project's cancellation, Charles Burchill continued to head the RCAF narrative team overseas and mine the British records for Canadian references. Burchill and his staff had completed the fighter, coastal, and bomber command narratives up to May 1944, but Burchill lamented that their work seemed "doomed to dissolution before much of value can be accomplished."⁶⁷ Although Burchill and his small staff were reprieved until August 1947, their main job was to finish the narratives to D-Day and then forward the records back to Ottawa. Burchill secured an academic post at the University of Toronto, but future historians would be hamstrung in their ability to weave the strategic story of the war into the tactical or operational narrative of the RCAF, since few of the policy records would be available in Canada.⁶⁸

Cancelling the official history series was a loss, but the retirement of Hitchins would even be more detrimental to the RCAF's institutional memory, since there remained an operational necessity to care for the squadron diaries and war records and answer ongoing inquiries. The RCAF had 2,500 feet of historical records, and much of the overseas material had not yet arrived from London. Hitchins was also responsible for deciding which records would be retained, generally those of historical, legal, or scientific value – and which would be destroyed – such as the 900,000 pay cards held by the department's Allowance Board that Hitchins ordered incinerated in June 1946, clearing space and saving money.[69] An officer with knowledge of history and an understanding of the war records was needed to facilitate this process.[70] A position would later be found for Hitchins, but his desire to shape the historical memory of the war within the official series was never met as he toiled largely alone in documenting the RCAF's wartime service.

The navy was the least hurt by Claxton's decision to cut the official history series since Gilbert Tucker had never planned a popular history and was well underway in writing his volumes. Tucker's problems remained internal, as he struggled with senior naval brass for adequate funding. Furthermore, he would later find that as he slowly won over the admirals, he lost the faith of the minister of National Defence.

Tucker and his staff had continued to work in Ottawa, largely in isolation and with little support from senior naval officers. W.A.B. Douglas, a naval officer himself before becoming an official historian, observed, "Sailors have not placed the same emphasis on history as soldiers, but they have used history to further naval aims, particularly in competition with their army and air force counterparts."[71] Although the senior naval brass had supported an official history, the RCN was far less willing to devote scarce resources to history than the other services. This was a result of attempts to shape the postwar RCN as a Blue Water navy, distinct from the service's Second World War primary role of escorting merchant ships and defending against U-boats in the Battle of the Atlantic. Tucker's inability to support operational requirements from Ottawa in a way that Stacey had overseas, and his near invisibility within the naval hierarchy (he even seems to have had no contact with Stacey or Hitchins) meant that he had little support to draw on during the tight postwar years.

Like the other historical services, Tucker immediately began to lose his narrators to academic positions. His best narrator, Donald Kerr, was appointed professor of history at Mount Allison University, but he was allowed to remain with the Naval Historical Section for a year to assist with the official history. Kerr produced a number of key chapters; but as Tucker suggested, the records were only arranged haphazardly, and historians were often "consigned to purgatory" as they looked for missing and misfiled records.[72] Unlike the other two senior official historians who had ordered their staff to produce narratives that would later be used as the foundation for chapters, Tucker had instructed his historians to write more complete chapters.[73] His lack of expertise in some areas and clear interest in the origins of the RCN left him more dependent on his small historical team than his counterparts.

By mid-1946 Tucker had planned a three-volume official history series, covering the early history up to the outbreak of war in 1939; non-operational matters in the Second World War, such as administration, ship building, and home defence; and a final volume on naval operations. With the proper staff, he hoped to have the series completed by 1949, but he warned his superiors that "the records of the German Admiralty, now in possession of the [British] Admiralty and in the process of being arranged and indexed by them, will obviously be indispensable to a definitive account."[74] The operational volume of the series could not be written until he examined the enemy's records. His plan still lacked formal approval in November 1946, and he continued to receive ambiguous support from the naval brass that wanted a history, but at the same time was not interested in one that condemned or passed judgment on naval operations.

The use of history to elucidate the lessons of the war was never fully embraced by naval officers. Captain Herbert Rayner commented on one preliminary manuscript on the actions of the Canadian warship *Huron* in battle, indicating that it should be based solely on what the official reports of the senior officers present had said, and then only modified by other senior officers: "In other places the author takes on to himself to criticize ships' actions, without indicating whether naval authorities agree with him ... Presumably this is supposed to be a narrative and not an analysis. Therefore the author's opinions are not required."[75] Some senior naval officers were clearly not interested in the harsh lessons of history, but only in an anodyne, factual retelling of events. Of course, officers who had no historical background may not have been able to grasp the idea that all history is judgmental or critical in some way, even in deciding what is emphasized and what is cast to the shadows. "War," French president Georges Clemenceau asserted, was "too important a matter to be left to the generals."[76] Perhaps the same could be said for the writing of war.

Tucker lacked full access to records, either German or Canadian, as many remained scattered with the units, and he faced senior officers who neither understood nor seemed to want a frank appraisal of the RCN in action. Nevertheless, he tried to convert his superiors. While he placated some by admitting that James George's historical officers' reports were sometimes "overly given to criticism and appraisal," that was an aspect of history. "Respectable historical writing," he penned to one superior, "is based on a consideration of all the relevant material that is available. No historian who valued his own integrity and professional reputation could possibly agree to restrict himself to certain classes of records, no matter how important these might be."[77] Yet his lack of influence made it harder to affect senior decisions.

In the summer of 1946, Tucker petitioned for access to the prime minister's records and strategic prewar Canadian-British discussions, a request firmly quashed by the deputy minister of National Defence.[78] He continued to make headway into the Great War story and the acrimonious naval debates in Canada, but how he was to write a policy volume without access to policy records remained a mystery. The minister remained unconvinced of the importance of an official history and, as we will see in the next chapter, the naval program was to be influenced heavily by Claxton's hostility.

WHEN STACEY WAS APPOINTED official historian in 1945, Duguid was demoted and given the title of Canadian Expeditionary Force (CEF) historian. He was to have no other duties but to write the subsequent volumes in the Great War series. Foulkes had remained committed to the history and informed the minister in late 1945, after several briefings by Duguid, that their historian could and must finish the series before his retirement, which was only a few years off.[79] Although Duguid had taken nearly twenty years to cover eighteen months of the war, it was assumed by all that he had made significant headway into the succeeding volumes, largely because he claimed to have done so. Although one can imagine how hard it must have been to concentrate on the period from 1916 to 1918 in the middle of another world war, there is little excuse for Duguid to have made no progress on the Great War history. After a series of additional delays and waffling statements as to when the subsequent volumes would be published, it became clear that Duguid would not finish the series, or even any further publishable work. An embarrassed and angry Foulkes was forced to report to Claxton in December 1946 that Duguid's claim of finishing the historical series "was entirely out of line with reality."[80]

Realizing that he had lost the confidence of the CGS, Duguid responded vigorously, promising to have the history completed by 1955, or even 1953 if that was not acceptable. Dates plucked from the air were not likely to inspire the CGS. Nor were justifications. Nonetheless, in 1946 Duguid argued that it had taken an average of 2.9 years to complete each official history volume in Australia and the United Kingdom and that he should be allowed at least that much time himself.[81] Although the Canadian histories had clearly not been produced at that rate, Duguid also claimed that he had only been appointed since 1932, and therefore the snide remarks that it had taken seventeen years to produce the first volume were inaccurate.[82] Whatever the case, and it is evident that he was desperately grasping for a lifeline since he had been working on the series since the early 1920s, Duguid was also nowhere near his projected goal of one volume every three years, and even if he had been it must have struck more than a few that the series would not be completed until the mid-1960s. And since Duguid had proven to be incapable of working at that pace in his prime, it was even more starkly true that he would not have been able to do that as he neared the age of eighty. "On account of ill-informed writings in the press," he lamented, "the impression seems to have become fixed in the minds of many Canadians that accurate and comprehensive military history can be written and produced at the speed of a newspaper or magazine article."[83] This was a good point, and it was evident that official histories required a long-term commitment; however, Duguid had no claim to a further extension.

As part of Claxton's across-the-board cuts, the CEF project was disbanded on 31 March 1947 and the records transferred to the Public Archives the next year, where they were to be made available to all citizens and historians. The fifty-year rule of accessing records appeared to be waived by the Canadian government. But the cancellation left Duguid understandably bitter, having devoted his life to a multi-volume literary memorial. "I had foolishly thought that all these [surviving soldiers and politicians] were with me, and that they shared the view that we had a duty to the dead and to generations not yet born," he lamented. "Am I to go to my grave with six volumes in my head?"[84] Indeed he was.

While few came to his defence, the newspapers took notice of the cancellation. The *New Liberty* reported that with the "discarding" of Duguid's "life project," the "dead and their deeds have been junked ... Canada has no official record of World War I, except in sorry stockpiles of unpublished manuscripts and faded diaries."[85] Most press reports were less sympathetic, reminding readers of the decades already devoted to the Great War series and hoping that the Second World War histories would be completed, in shorter order.

Great War veterans now seemed to be forever denied their history, and no alternative comprehensive study of Canada's involvement in the war existed for its sea, air, or land forces.[86] The records were open to researchers, but there was a strong need for an official history in laying the groundwork for subsequent study, and no scholar was willing to make the sacrifice of time and effort to produce one. The mass of documentary evidence was almost impossible to understand without the proper contextual framework, and Duguid noted that the records were stored "like a pile of untreated ore, a meaningless mass until sifted and refined."[87] While historians have proved subsequently to be expert miners into those same records, the fact that Duguid had worked for over twenty-five years on the project and produced only one volume must not have been terribly encouraging. No one was anxious to take up the mantle of Great War historian. With the meaning of the war increasingly contested, there remained a significant gap in Canadian history, and Duguid's failure was a "missed opportunity to explain the nature of the war experience to the national community, and to help foster a sense of national achievement arising from the national effort."[88]

AFTER THE RESURRECTION of the Second World War army series, and now with a significantly altered policy volume that would encompass all three services, Stacey went back to work on the Historical Summary, which was later titled *The Canadian Army, 1939-1945*. This summary was to be a one-volume overview history for the Canadian public, but it proved enormously difficult to write. Most distressing for Stacey was the slow disintegration of his expert team of narrators. In September 1946 Stacey had written forcefully to Foulkes that he and his staff were engaged in the "slowest and most expensive" part of the history as they tried to nail down the preliminary narratives. But the steady departure of narrators prompted Stacey to threaten resignation unless they were replaced by experienced men whom he could select and train, and he would only remain as official historian if it was "in a manner creditable to the Army and the country and not discreditable to the status of my associates and myself as historians." Quite simply, Stacey wanted to know if the "Department was still willing to 'pay the shot.'"[89] It was, and the Historical Section received its full allotment of staffing positions.

Experienced historical officers like Murray Hunter, J.M. Hitsman, and G.W.L. Nicholson were given essential narratives to produce, and without their dedication and expertise the volume would never have been published on time. Equally pressing was the need to access the high-level strategic documents, both Allied and Axis, which were essential in framing the Canadian story. Busy with administration and writing, Stacey relied on a small Historical Section staff that remained in London to locate these records within the British, and later American, archives.

The overseas section was headed by the highly efficient Lieutenant Colonel Sam Hughes, whom Stacey had persuaded to stay for a year after the cessation of hostilities before returning to law school.[90] Hughes had presided over the transfer of hundreds of tons of war documents and artifacts, the latter of which had been gathered by a war museum team headed by the future award-winning author Farley Mowat. "Beginning as a motley crew of adventurers with a slight tendency to piracy," wrote W.E.C. Harrison, "the Team has become a skilled body of experts and enthusiasts."[91] The museum unit had raced across Europe after the German surrender, "liberating" artifacts as diverse as Tiger tanks and one-man submarines to small arms and communications equipment, much of which was to form the core of the Canadian War Museum.

Hughes also worked with the British to ensure that both historical sections had access to draft narratives and all available documentation, noting in December 1945 that the "balance of assistance given was definitely in our favour."[92] But the Canadians would have more narratives and draft chapters to offer the British once Stacey's team was deeply engaged in writing during the late 1940s. While there was no direct collaboration between Canada and its major allies, Britain and the United States, all were anxious to share preliminary work to assist in the difficult process of writing the first histories. The British and Americans also drew on Stacey's assistance to ensure historical accuracy, which he gave freely, profiting from reading other official works but also because he believed it important that Canada was well represented in those same national histories.

While Stacey worked furiously on the summary, he sent a barrage of telegrams and letters to his overseas liaison officers filled with questions that continuously arose during the writing process. For the Italian campaign, for instance, the wartime narratives had ignored all "periods of static operations" and had made no mention of "troop morale" during the difficult holding operations between offensives. In other cases such as Operation Baytown, which was the invasion of the Italian mainland in September 1943, the original diaries, "O" Group notes, and traces for several units had been lost in an aircraft accident.[93] In early 1946, then, Hughes was digging through the British army archives in the hopes of locating Allied documents that might shed light on these and a number of other issues.

This work in the British archives was only possible because of the strong relationship cultivated during the war with both the British and American official historians. Although these cordial relations resulted in the sharing of documents and mutual assistance, Stacey was denied access to the Allied Combined records and General Dwight Eisenhower's SHAEF records. That was not an immediate cause for concern since even the British historians had condemned SHAEF for not making records available, but Stacey had met several times with his British and American counterparts and stressed that he would some day have to see these records.[94] All had agreed, although no policy was established.

Stacey renewed contact with the British official historians in January 1946 to access the records of the War Cabinet and combined chiefs of staff, an Anglo-American organization with no Canadian representatives but whose actions had a direct impact on Canadian Army operations. Hughes had received limited access to these records, but the bulk of them had remained closed. Still struggling with questions about Dieppe and the strategic planning for the D-Day operations, Stacey was troubled to find that the British, who were being "exceptionally difficult," again turned down his request.[95] The British refused to give him access to the Army or Army group-level records, describing these as "above the military level," let alone strategic or political records.[96] They informed Stacey that they would only search through the archives on his behalf after he had first requested and seen all Canadian Cabinet records to ensure there were no copies filed therein. It was another bureaucratic roadblock. Furthermore, if the records were not found in Ottawa, they would then only assist Stacey when he presented them with research topics through the Canadian high commissioner. Stacey rightly noted that no historian, and especially no official historian, could submit to such restraints, where he could not confirm or judge the extent of the search on his behalf, or even the nature of the documents. The Canadian official historian invoked his privilege and went straight to the CGS. The policy was offensive to Foulkes, too, who could scarcely believe the British were denying access to Combined records after Canada had contributed more than a million men and women to the Allied war effort. As Foulkes rightly noted, this was "an important point of principle."[97]

What followed was a bizarre example of bureaucratic foot-dragging by the British, who stalled and stymied Stacey for the next five years. Stacey had initially wished to keep the requests informal, but when he found those blocked he increased pressure, turning to the CGS. A furious Foulkes took the matter up with senior British army officers, but even their combined efforts made little headway against the British mandarins. Foulkes continued to support Stacey and pushed the issue until the ministers of National Defence and External Affairs were involved. It was a long, sordid affair, and it became a point of significant aggravation for the Canadians, who had sacrificed so much in the war, only to find that Great Britain was still treating their archival request as some sort of colonial burden.

But Stacey needed the records for his summary as soon as possible, and he cast his gaze south. By October 1947 the American official historians had generously given Stacey and his researchers access to the captured German records, which they had microfilmed and stored in Washington, and they also agreed to share the SHAEF records by the end of the year. The Canadians were thus in the odd situation of developing a more intimate relationship with Washington than London.[98] This more progressive American policy was probably the result of General Eisenhower's forward-thinking order in 1947: "The history of the Army in World War II now in preparation must, without reservation, tell the complete story of the Army's participation, fully documented with references to the records used." The army official historians were to have access to all records and the directive was, as Eisenhower ordered, to be "interpreted in the most liberal sense without reservation as to whether or not the evidence of history places the Army in a favourable light."[99] Eisenhower, like most Canadian generals, believed that a useful history was one that showed both the success and failure of war. How else were soldiers to learn?

In addition to Eisenhower's directive, however, the Americans may have decided that as an ally in the war, even if a junior one, the Canadians could not be treated with casual disregard. While Stacey found a way around the annoying British blockades, it was obvious that he would also need access to the British records, since Canadian forces had served in a number of British armies in several theatres. He hoped to clear the archives problem at an official historians' conference in Washington.

The Allied official historians from South Africa, Canada, Australia, New Zealand, the United Kingdom, and the United States met in Washington in February 1948 to establish guiding principles. One of the most important decisions was the acknowledgment that for the completion of "comprehensive and reliable" official histories, accredited historians would require "freedom of research" in the archives of the Allies.[100] The records of the enemy, which had been captured and brought to Washington, would eventually be made available to all of the official historians, but the British continued to argue that the Combined records be excluded from the other national historians.

Stacey fought hard to overturn this view after first being advised by Foulkes to "wave as big a stick" as he needed.[101] This he did, clashing with the British representatives in several of the general meetings and arguing that the public would have no confidence in his or any official history unless all the records were made available.[102] "The U.S. historians, for whom I really feel very deep admiration, consider that the main issue is the preparation of honest histories in which the public can feel complete confidence," wrote Stacey to one of his historical officers. "The U.K., on the other hand, seemed to me at times to be approaching the question from a Civil Service rather than an historical point of view; they were acutely worried about the 'dangers' involved in free access to important papers, and in general seemed to be seeking agreement to restrictions rather than to a liberal policy."[103] As a result of his "acid exchanges" with the British, the Americans privately assured Stacey that he and his researchers would continue to have access to the SHAEF papers.[104]

The British could not understand why Stacey was pressing the matter. In subsequent internal memoranda, they suggested that to give Canada access would create a "problem in security," and that it was "quite out of the question that Colonel Stacey should be given a free run over all the high level national documents to which he might find clues in the Combined records."[105] At the conference, however, Stacey had been persuasive and believed that he had broken British obstinacy in this matter. As an example of the ill will that had developed though, after Stacey returned to Ottawa the British met the Americans and made a side deal that excluded all other countries from viewing the records in question, although this did not change the relationship between the historical sections of the United States and Canada.[106]

Upon finding that he had been betrayed, Stacey continued to press through Foulkes to convince the British to modify their position. Two more years of diplomatic exchanges eventually resulted in access being granted, first to the 21 Army Group records in 1949 and then to the Combined records the next year, but even then the British gave very little assistance to the Canadians in sifting through the estimated eight to ten million files. In fact, Murray Hunter, Stacey's overseas historical officer and primary narrator of the Normandy campaign, was so worried about never again receiving access to the strategic records after the British finally relented in early 1950 that he worked continuously for thirty-six hours to transcribe vital portions of the Casablanca conference.[107] Luckily for the Canadian official history program and Hunter's well-being, he was allowed back into the archives in the coming days, and much of what he found was sent directly to Stacey.

The only good thing to come out of the acrimonious process of "calculated procrastination" by the British was that Prime Minister King, in the last years of his life, granted Stacey full access to the Canadian Cabinet records.[108] This unparalleled look at Canadian wartime policy making would later allow Stacey to produce the most comprehensive policy history on the Second World War ever written. In the meantime, though, Stacey struggled to write the summary. Without full access to the records, it was like trying to put together an enormously complicated jigsaw puzzle, with the pieces turned down, scattered about, and when eventually brought together, many of the essential ones missing.

WHEN STACEY HAD PRESENTED HIS PLAN for an official history to the Canadian Historical Association in 1946, he noted that the summary was to be an "interim report" that would be largely operational in nature. As he noted privately to McNaughton, "It cannot really be anything else, as our historical investigations will not be finished for years yet."[109] Nonetheless, Canadians would get a history based on official records while the war still loomed large in the nation's collective memory.

Official military and diplomatic history in the past had been viewed with suspicion by academic historians who well knew that the official diplomatic publications issued by the major powers in the 1920s were aimed at protecting reputations, either by burying culpability for starting the war, as in the case of Germany, or by obscuring the political machinations behind the scenes, as in the cases of Great Britain and France.[110] In the Canadian context, where Duguid had once been recognized for his solid archival work, he was now remembered as little more than a failed amateur. Furthermore, Duguid's refusal to provide full access to the war records, and his inability to produce anything while he hoarded those same records, left official history an insular and seemingly constrained oddity within the now stronger historical profession. Once again it came down to the control of records. Civilian historians could not access those records, and one of the core functions of the professional historian – to discover and interpret archival sources and then to cite them so that others may consult and judge claims – was impossible to fulfill as a result.

Furthermore, since Stacey was writing within the hierarchy of the army and the DND, many must have wondered at the restraints imposed on him. Stacey's earlier demands ensuring full editorial control were essential to protect him from unwanted interference, but they were also intended to win over the historical profession to accept that the official history would be written without coercion. While Stacey had a substantial reputation among the country's historians, he was in an even stronger position in the army after having earned the trust of Canadian generals. Yet, as early as 1946, after a visit to Washington, Stacey warned his superiors that the Americans had a better system that employed civilian historians to write their massive hundred-volume series. With Stacey as a serving officer, he warned: "It is possible that this may result in our history carrying somewhat less weight."[111] But in Canada it was simply unacceptable for any civilian to view the top-secret and international records that an historian would need to complete an account so recently after the conflict. Moreover, the trust that Stacey had forged with the senior generals, not to mention his unparalleled knowledge of the war, meant that there were few others in the country who could match his qualifications. Whatever the drawbacks of official history, "the choice," as Stacey starkly laid out, "so far as the use of official records is concerned, is between histories produced officially and no histories at all."[112]

The writing of the official history would be extraordinarily difficult and involve not only a high degree of professional competence, but also stamina to see it through to the end. Notwithstanding the differences between Stacey and Duguid, both were dedicated to their projects. Stacey wrote passionately in 1946:

> We have to tell, for the Canadians of today and of days to come, the story of a tremendous human enterprise – the part played by Canada in the defence of freedom against the bloodiest tyrannies of modern times. It was the greatest undertaking in our national history ... such an outpouring of courage, skill, and energy, with the whole map of the world and the most shattering political upheaval in human records for its background, would seem to be the material for poetry rather than for the slow pen of the military historian. Some day, perhaps, the poet will arise who can do it justice; in the meantime, the historian can only do his best.[113]

But Stacey did more than just his best; he succeeded in laying the foundation for future Canadians to understand the war, for future historians to forge micro-studies, and for poets to craft their verse.

By 1947 Stacey and his narrators had finished most of the draft chapters for the summary, involving the sifting of records "so huge as to defy adjectival description."[114] There were, for instance, over 100,000 Canadian monthly War Diaries, and countless operational records from all levels of command, an estimated twenty million pages of paper that did not include the records created by other services, departments, or Allied armies.[115] As Stacey rightly admitted, "We shall never be able to read all of these various papers in detail; to do so would take at least fifty years." Unlike Duguid, who wished to spike down every single document on every engagement, this was a professional historian speaking who knew well "that law of diminishing returns."[116] The narrators would nonetheless cover an enormous amount of ground. And while we have seen that Stacey did not have access to the Combined records, and by 1948 only a small portion of the SHAEF records had been made available, he would, like official historians before him, rely on participants to help him depict the "hidden history" of the war.

Stacey used his intimate contact with senior officers, especially Crerar, Simonds, and McNaughton, to draw out the strategic issues of the war that were not yet available to him in the closed records. Stacey had written the government's 1942 white paper on the Dieppe raid and had seen extensive Canadian records as well as interviewed dozens of the survivors, but he was still unclear about the convoluted planning behind the operation. Interviews with Crerar as early as June 1944 seemed to indicate that General Bernard Montgomery and Admiral Louis Mountbatten had been responsible for the plan and that Crerar had little role, devolving the tactical responsibility to the divisional commander, Major General John Hamilton Roberts.[117] Although Stacey had access to additional records in the intervening years and sensed that there was more to the story, he made little headway on the issue. In the summary there was no mention of the desire by Canadian officers to be involved in the operation, and nor did Stacey follow Simonds's urging to censure Crerar for reinstating the raid after it had been cancelled once. Stacey found no evidence in the records to blame Crerar; but that was not enough for Simonds, who later accused Stacey of whitewashing the planning behind the operation.[118]

Simonds was carrying on a vendetta with Crerar, whose mutual wartime animosity had resulted in Simonds being passed over as the postwar CGS. All the while, Stacey tried to produce a balanced history while admitting to Kent Roberts Greenfield, the senior American official historian, that he had been forced to rely on Crerar for much of the "burden of interpretation in this volume ... Of course, he is a prejudiced witness; on the other hand he has a special knowledge of the matter." The remark downplayed the enormous research already conducted by Stacey and his narrators, but Stacey had peeled back the onion skin relating to the planning only to find that there was no core. The records were withheld from Stacey, and he would discover later that many of the key decisions were apparently never committed to paper.

As he had during the war, Stacey advanced the argument that the D-Day planners had profited from the lessons of Dieppe, a belief that Crerar held dearly but which Simonds derided as nonsense.[119] Stacey, it would appear, had little evidence to support his conclusion, but was strongly influenced by his discussions with Crerar.[120] He erred on the side of caution, refusing to write off an operation that had cost so many Canadian lives. Like Simonds, Greenfield also felt that Stacey had pushed the issue too far. To that, Stacey admitted frankly to another Canadian senior officer that he was "engaged in a little missionary work" and hoped to influence the American official series to acknowledge the important part played by Dieppe in the planning of Overlord.[121]

This "missionary work" statement is a rather extraordinary one for Stacey who strove to explain fairly the controversies of the war in a restrained way after the publication of the summary. But this was 1947, the official history had been cancelled and then revived, and Stacey was forced to rely on participants in many cases rather than on the archival record. As he lamented publicly, senior officers and their accounts "sometimes fail, to a somewhat remarkable extent, to agree among themselves; and their disagreement with the written records is frequently even wider."[122] One can only imagine his more unguarded private assessments.

Stacey did not want to rely on the memoirs of soldiers no matter their rank, believing it was the contemporary record that contained a greater approximation to the truth: "One sentence scrawled on a piece of paper on the eve of the battle is worth two or three thousand words written even a week later."[123] For the summary, though, Stacey was at a grave disadvantage as he struggled to process the mass of records available and could only imagine what was being held from him.

In addition to the Dieppe raid, Stacey struggled to reconstruct both the decisions to send two Canadian battalions to Hong Kong and the confused fighting in December 1941 that led to the surrender of the garrison. Stacey found Hong Kong to be the most difficult operation of the war to write about since he had few narratives, many of the records had been destroyed, key figures had been killed, and the years the survivors spent in prisoner of war camps had poisoned the relationship between British and Canadian veterans who blamed each other for the failure in defence.[124] Even when the Historical Section appealed to General Douglas MacArthur and his staff, who were overseeing the occupation and reconstruction of Japan, to get access to Japanese records, they were "stone-walled" by MacArthur, who seemed, in the estimation of a British officer, a "sort of Mikado." In fact, neither the British nor, surprisingly, the other American historical branches received access to these records, as MacArthur was preparing a multi-volume history, "which he intended to publish privately and for profit."[125] None of these records would come available until 1949, which was too late for the summary, but they were available for the first volume of the official history proper.[126] Furthermore, although Stacey had access to some of the Canadian records, especially Cabinet documents that revealed the decisions for sending the two battalions to garrison Hong Kong only months before it was attacked, the Canadian government refused to allow Stacey to cite them without paraphrasing the sources. Stacey, in turn, appealed to the government to relax its rules, since "any tampering with the exact text of documents is highly undesirable," but he was overruled.[127] It was clear that there were few politicians or senior civil servants who supported an unfettered official history in the immediate postwar years.

Despite these hurdles and with only one preliminary narrative, Stacey drafted a reasoned account of the difficult campaign in the late 1940s. Stacey's measured assessment of Hong Kong gave full credit to the Japanese for their innovative and aggressive tactics, and to the Canadian tenacious defence. Company Sergeant Major J.R. Osborn, who captured a Japanese summit position at the end of a bayonet and then held it for three hours against a number of counterattacks, was just one of the infantrymen highlighted. Towards the end of the battle, his position surrounded, Osborn smothered a grenade with his body to protect his comrades. For his sacrifice he was awarded a posthumous Victoria Cross. Others such as Canadian Brigadier J.K. Lawson, upon finding his position overrun, was last heard saying that he was "going outside to fight it out." In his battle history, Stacey alluded to the lack of training for the two Canadian battalions, but claimed that "their casualty lists fully and poignantly show" the nature of their grim defence.[128]

Stacey chronicled the Canadian soldier and, much like Duguid, defended his reputation. In 1946 when General C.M. Maltby, the British commanding officer of the Hong Kong garrison, was preparing his official report for publication, he accused the Canadians of poor training and discipline.[129] Stacey rushed to the defence of the Canadians and produced evidence that it had been Maltby who had a very shaky grasp of command throughout the whole operation. By marshalling war records and personal accounts, Stacey intervened before the report was published (the Canadians had received an advance copy) and many of the derogatory remarks were cut.[130]

Army strategic decisions and the campaign in Northwest Europe were the third of Stacey's most difficult assessments. Canadian divisions had fought from D-Day onwards, and Stacey was forced to reconstruct the decision making, the fighting, the consequences of battle, including the terrible slaughter at Verrières Ridge on 25 July, the reinforcement crisis, and the overall strategy of the campaign. He did this by relying again on the official records and the personal archives of McNaughton and Crerar. For instance, when Stacey wrote a draft about the decision to send Canadian forces to the Mediterranean, a move that McNaughton had vigorously objected to and rankled him still, the general wanted Stacey in June 1947 to strike at his enemies for imposing this strategy on him. While McNaughton felt that Stacey's account was a marvel of "conciseness" and "completeness," he also believed that Stacey should condemn the groups "of unscrupulous office seekers," men such as the CMHQ Chief of Staff Kenneth Stuart and Minister of National Defence J. L. Ralston, whom McNaughton hated for having undermined him as army commander and, he believed, forced the government to invoke conscription.[131] To strengthen his case, McNaughton wrote, "It seems to me quite clear that some of the most important documents concerning this phase of the History of the Canadian Army have not as yet reached the Historical Section." The importance of archival documents, and lack thereof, forced Stacey to place significant weight on McNaughton's advice. While Stacey agreed with McNaughton and was influenced by him on the strategic error of splitting the army in two major theatres of war and thereby diluting Canadian independence and clout, he never fully reckoned with the pressure on the Canadian government and its soldiers to be doing something, anything, after training and then stagnating in England for nearly four years.[132] No doubt, Stacey's interpretation was formed early on and was predisposed to McNaughton. If it seems that McNaughton had an unsettling influence, one must remember that Stacey was still stumbling through the records and trying to understand everything about the war from tactical operations to strategic objectives, both military and political. As he noted to Nicholson after reading through McNaughton's personal archives, "A good many of the points which emerge are new to me." That was to be expected, but it was also true that men such as Crerar, McNaughton, and Simonds held strong sway over how Stacey interpreted and presented the war, at least at this early stage of the writing process. However, Stacey refused to submit to McNaughton's or Simonds's urgings to condemn the government, the allies, or Canadian officers. As he instructed one historian, "An official writer must cultivate extreme precision in matters relating to individuals." He hoped his history would "let the facts speak for themselves," so that critics would have a harder time attacking it.[133] Stacey also realized that he indeed did not know the whole picture of wartime decisions and events, and that knowledge rightly forced him to restrain his judgment in case he found that further evidence would reveal him to be in error.

While it is impossible to recount all the difficulties that confronted Stacey and his narrators between 1945 and 1947, it is clear from the archival records that they were forced to deal with almost every contentious issue with which historians have struggled over the last half-century: from political questions to grand strategy, from the manoeuvring of armies and corps to the tactical engagements of battalions and companies. The work was of staggering proportions. Furthermore, while Stacey was writing the Canadian story he was also forced to understand at least the contextual decisions that had an impact on Canadian operations. For this he was lauded by reviewers who called the summary one of the most comprehensive war histories yet written. Claxton had other concerns and it was the questions relating to Canada that mattered: political decisions relating to the reinforcement crisis, conscription, or the removal of senior officers worried him, and the minister did not want to open old wounds. So, amidst the strain of dealing with the British over access to the records, caught between generals who despised one another, and trying desperately to decipher the strategic context of major decisions with almost no published histories on which to rely and the records hidden from him, Stacey's own minister, who had seen little value in the histories from the start, demanded that the two meet to resolve Canadian controversies.

While the soldiers were rarely afraid to tell Stacey what they thought his history lacked, or even hoped to use him to bludgeon an enemy, they seemed, for the most part, to want an honest recounting. Claxton, however, saw his role as ensuring that Stacey did not embarrass the government. This resulted in a number of wearying interferences in Stacey's manuscript and demands to rewrite particular paragraphs, everything from an account of the Seaforth Highlanders' Christmas dinner in a church at Ortona, which the minister thought would incite Catholics and Protestants, to the use of bulldozers to cover German common graves on the Gothic Line, which he thought "too brutal."[134] The church dinner survived, the bulldozing of the slain did not. Many of Claxton's additional demands were cleared up in a face-to-face meeting on 11 August 1947, but Claxton remained deeply worried about

Stacey's handling of McNaughton's forced resignation in 1943.[135] While the minister was much relieved when Stacey informed him that he had circulated the chapters to McNaughton, Stacey also admitted in the meeting, and even in the historical summary, that he could not properly touch on the controversy since he had not seen all the available records.[136] Furthermore, McNaughton, who was still an active Canadian figure on the international scene as representative to the United Nations, was still too daunting a character for Stacey to portray in print. But Stacey's hand was forced. These issues had to be addressed, if only partially, because the Canadian staff officer and war journalist, Dick Malone, had published an unofficial account, *Missing from the Record* (1946), in which, although he did not have access to the archives, he speculated freely over the controversies of the war, including a gossipy and revealing account of McNaughton's firing.[137] In fact, Malone claimed to have written the book through concern that these embarrassing truths would be cut from the final official history. Stacey rightly believed that the summary would have to delve deeper into the controversies since Malone had completed his history "in a great hurry" and was "quite wrong" about a number of issues.[138] The summary, as reviewers would note, was unique in drawing conclusions from the archival record.

While Claxton's interference was intensely aggravating, it was but one more hurdle after having already run the gauntlet through the generals, the politicians, the DND, and even the British and American services. Stacey and his team had "slaved days, nights and weekends, [and] went without leave" to publish *The Canadian Army, 1939-1945: An Official Historical Summary* by the summer of 1948.[139] Quite clearly, no matter how skilled the historians or how big their teams, official histories took considerable time to complete. Nonetheless, the Historical Section's dedication was well acknowledged by critics, who, in contrast to the earlier army historical monographs, reviewed the official history extensively when it was published.

"A masterful study of care and precision, a monument worthy of the brave men whose deeds it records," lauded *The Legionary*.[140] Others were no less acclamatory and all noted the carefully researched work that was offered to the Canadian public so close to the end of the war. Major General R.H. Keefler wrote in *The Gazette* that Stacey refused to "whitewash" the army's performance: "Mistakes were made; every attack was not a local victory." But "the civilian reader who wants to clear away the fog formed by war-time press releases, will find this Official Historical Summary the most satisfying record yet offered to the public."[141] Many reviewers were staggered by Stacey's ability to condense the complicated nature of the war into one volume. The use of a variety of sources, from War Diaries to generals' comments to the evidence in the German records, provided a balanced view, even if the Dieppe section was privileged in the narrative with more space, while Normandy, which already had the 1946 monograph, was covered more lightly than one might expect. Nonetheless, this was not simply a victors' history or a commemorative script for the grieving; as one British reviewer noted, "This book will certainly add to the reputation of the Canadian war historians ... and it will be surprising if its successors better it."[142]

The quick production of the official history in front of all other nations, and especially with Canada's dismal Great War official history experience, was heavily emphasized, but more than a few reviewers, while still soundly endorsing the history, remarked on the difficulty of writing contemporary history with the senior participants still alive. The following review sheds important light on the issue, even more so since it was written by Eric Harrison, one of Stacey's key historical officers during the war, who had returned to his professorship at Queen's University:

> The writer of contemporary history, especially if it is official, is in an inhibited and ironical position. It may not be in the general interest that he [the official historian] publish all he knows or all he thinks. He may sit on material which, if a hundred years old, would furnish him with a marketable though harmless revelation. Dead men become public property: the living belong to themselves ... Tact as well as restraining must guide the pen of a contemporary who will be widely read through foreign spectacles.[143]

Writing contemporary history was indeed difficult, but at least one historian, Arthur Schlesinger, observed, "The distortions of perspective which come from being too near are outweighed by the distortions of distance."[144] In short, the official historians, while no doubt constrained by having lived through the events they were writing about, also had deep knowledge of the war in which they were involved, and had access to participants and records in order to better understand the myriad of complicated undercurrents that informed every decision made and carried out by soldiers.

If contemporary history required a nuanced approach, dealing with the personalities involved demanded even more delicate consideration. It was not easy for Stacey to criticize his senior commanders – many of whom had strongly supported him in the historical work. *Saturday Night* magazine speculated cheekily that while *The Canadian Army* was a brilliant overview, since Stacey had not delved into McNaughton's firing, some enterprising publisher might "assemble a bevy of uninhibited generals and compile an anthology under some such title as 'Who Fired Me but Not Why' or, since there were some notable survivors, 'Why I was Not Fired.'"[145]

The Canadian Army became a bestseller and winner of the Governor General's 1949 award for non-fiction. Stacey, as an official historian, had carefully and skilfully walked that tightrope between telling the truth, or as much of it as could be elucidated, and ensuring that reputations, both personal and national, were not trampled. As Robert Palmer, an American official historian and professor at Princeton, testified, "I wish we could have such a book on the American army also. But we never will have [because] ... the Canadian Army and operations in the war were of more human size than the U.S., and for that reason it may be possible to write a book about it that is really a book."[146] At the same time, Palmer did not believe the United States had anyone of Stacey's skill – someone who could condense such an enormous event into something readable for the public and soldiers. The praise and awards were gratifying, but it would be a long road ahead, filled with frustration and sacrifice, as Stacey worked to offer Canadians a history worthy of their war effort. In the process, though, he would help legitimize the study of Canadian military history.

THE YEARS FOLLOWING the Second World War were a time of reckoning and cutbacks, and the official historians pushed hard to ensure their series survived. The Great War history was a justifiable target. While the cancellation was a terrible blow to Duguid and to all Great War veterans, it was clear it would never be finished. After considering the years that had been devoted to researching the Great War story with little return for the investment, the Second World War official histories became nearly stillborn, with the services and the minister believing there were better ways to spend money. Tucker was allowed to finish his work, although he too would have personal and professional battles to fight in the future. Most disappointing was the RCAF program, which of all the historical sections had produced the best wartime monographs for Canadians. Hitchins felt betrayed when his history was cut, but he continued to craft the RCAF's wartime historical legacy in the coming years.

The army historical program survived through outside intervention. Nevertheless, it was Stacey's professionalism as an academic historian that brought a rigour to his work. Furthermore, his wartime reputation kept his history from being perverted by the gauntlet of would-be editors. The importance of the war records was also not lost on Stacey, and his influence allowed him to use the private papers of senior generals and to push relentlessly for access to the Combined records held by the British and Americans. Stacey was also able to rely on some excellent wartime and postwar narratives to underpin his history. But an analysis of these works shows that while the narratives helped to guide his hand, the official historian still had an enormous amount of work in drawing together the multiple strands of history and weaving them into a coherent story. In fact, it is clear that Stacey used these narratives as a base but not a crutch. *The Canadian Army* was cautious history, deeply influenced by its contemporary nature, and at the same time it was a bestseller that reached the Canadian public, which further cemented his position within the army hierarchy. In the coming years he would build on these foundations and produce some of the finest works in Canadian history.

Claxton's banal forecast that no one would be interested in the Second World War after 1948 has been shattered time and time again, and Canadians, just like Americans, Britons, Australians, and the citizens of all nations touched by that terrible conflict, continue to consume war histories. If in this modern political climate it has been harder to convince academics of the value of exploring our collective martial past and its impact on shaping the twentieth century, it is worth remembering that in the 1940s and 1950s, Canada's military historians, with Stacey at the forefront, had a formidable reputation. In Stacey the army found both an expert in the English language and a master historian whose command of military history was nearly unrivalled. He would need to draw on his accumulated expertise to surmount the formidable challenges of writing official history in the coming decade.

5
Official History, Contested Memory, 1948-60

> *The small partners in a great coalition war must write their own stories if they wish to be told in reasonable detail. The larger partners ... have no inclination to do this task for them.*
>
> – GAVIN LONG

> *To keep one's archives barred against historians is tantamount to leaving one's history to one's enemies.*
>
> – LORD ACTON

The historical services laid the foundation for future Second World War writing by gathering and arranging war records from 1939 to 1945. Although this archiving of records would continue into the 1950s, the primary postwar responsibility of the official historians was the writing of the service histories. Due to postwar budget cutbacks, the air force and navy historical sections offered reduced series, while the army, which built upon the success of previous publications, crafted three important operational histories. All of these official studies would have an enormous impact on the discipline of Canadian military history, and the interpretations by the official historians would remain largely unchallenged until at least the 1980s.

The official historians also continued to provide important support functions to the Department of National Defence (DND). Far more than simply authors, the official historians remained the defenders of reputations, both of veterans and of the government. They still controlled the war records, and while the restrictions on access were loosened slightly, there remained few opportunities for unofficial historians to write military history based on archival records. While there were a number of important memoirs and popular histories, the official historians continued to construct the scholarly interpretation of Canadian World War history.

The official histories were monumental works of synthesis that offered the first authentic historical accounts. Although the historians struggled with the challenge of writing contemporary history and were forced to run the critical gauntlet of politicians, civil servants, and serving officers, these histories laid the foundation for the canon of war writing in Canada.

WHILE THE ARMY had garnered much recognition for *The Canadian Army* (1948), the air force's and navy's plans for multi-volume official histories of their respective world war endeavours had been quashed a year earlier. Despite the efficient wartime work of the Royal Canadian Air Force (RCAF) Historical Section, Brooke Claxton, the minister of National Defence, and the chiefs of staff, had decided that the historical series would be abolished – "shot down in flames," as C.P. Stacey put it years later, "leaving a disgraceful gap in the national historiography."[1] As Wing Commander Fred Hitchins prepared to depart in 1948, he put the final touches on the third volume of the popular history and organized the aviation war records, which filled forty large steel cabinets.[2] The RCAF senior officers realized that their official historian had played an essential and specialized role in the air force hierarchy, and a secret memo noted that despite the popular monographs, once Hitchins left the service at the end of March 1948, "there will be no proper history of the RCAF." Although Stacey was tasked to complete a volume on overall policy that would include the RCAF, it was observed ruefully that "the Histories will be largely Army with only ⅓ of one volume strictly RCAF."[3] The chief of the air staff (CAS), Air Marshal W.A. Curtis, took notice of the warning and requested that some means be arranged to continue Hitchins's service.

Curtis had always acknowledged the importance of an official history in not only elucidating the war's lessons, but also in publicizing the RCAF's deeds to all Canadians. Yet it is also clear that the CAS was not willing to devote significant resources to the project. Much of the RCAF's history was "buried in the files," lying "scattered through many records, and is slowly being lost as the dust settles," lamented one officer.[4] A permanent service historian would bring this buried heritage and history together in training manuals, lectures, and someday, an official history. Hitchins's job was saved, but the assistant historian, H.H. Coulson, was let go.

Hitchins and his staff had finished the third volume of the popular history by the reprieve of early 1948, and he was anxious to see it published. With a staff of only two, moreover, it was unlikely that the RCAF Historical Section would ever publish much else. The minister had read and approved the text of the third volume by September 1947, but wanted Hitchins to find a private individual to underwrite the costs of publication. While Conn and Hitchins had struggled with Oxford University Press, which had been a troublesome publisher since 1944 – offering little advertising, supplying books consistently late, and proving quarrelsome in other administrative matters – Stacey had had a relatively easy time publishing his three monographs during 1945 to 1946 with the King's Printer, and at the expense of the department.[5] It is unclear if Hitchins found a guarantor for the book, but Claxton's directive delayed the publication by almost two years. Demand was still there, however, and advance news of the publication had alerted the Canadian public. One mother, W.J. Sorel, wrote to the section that she was anxious to see the final volume: "Our son was reported missing on the night of July 28-29th, 1944 and that's the last we heard of him ... reading the book will give us a little comfort."[6]

The RCAF Overseas: The Sixth Year was published in August 1949 and, like the first two volumes, was reviewed widely. At over 530 pages, the third volume was the longest of the popular histories; furthermore, Hitchins and his staff had written the final volume with the full knowledge that the official history would probably never be published. Hitchins looked to guard his reputation by noting that the series had not been "planned as, nor do they profess to be, a [complete] history of the RCAF." There was no account of the British Commonwealth Air Training Plan (BCATP), "the essential foundation for victory in the air," no use of enemy records, nothing on the operational commands in Canada or their assistance in protecting the coasts and convoys, and almost no discussion of the strategy behind the air war.[7] The history remained a story of individuals, a methodology that the other two services had avoided. Almost every Canadian flyer killed was mentioned in the text, and it sometimes degenerated into a litany of names and brief combat biographical entries. Nonetheless, there was an underlying message: the RCAF played an "important and often decisive part in the victories of the Army, and was instrumental in saving the lives of tens of thousands of our soldiers."[8]

Despite the limitations of the history, reviewers were largely supportive, and the *Saskatoon Star-Phoenix* noted that while it was "gripping reading, even the dullest of historians would have an easy task here" with the wealth of material. With censorship relaxed, the review highlighted the impressive role of 6 Group, which "virtually destroyed or heavily damaged" almost every major German city. There was little ambivalence about the morality of the war. While the Nazis had "sown the wind" during the blitz in England, by the last two years of the war they were forced to "reap the whirlwind."[9]

However, several other reviewers criticized the history. "Brave is the man who undertakes to write a war history as close as five years from its end," observed John Yocom in *Saturday Night* magazine.[10] The avoidance of interpreting the controversial "Canadianization" policy (the attempt to create national squadrons, even if it meant breaking up established multi-national aircrews) was an omission caught by several reviewers.[11] George Stanley, former army historical officer and now a university professor, wrote pointedly, "Despite the assurance that the relaxation of war-time controls has made it possible to add to this volume information which had, of necessity, to be omitted from earlier ones, *The Sixth Year* lacks what its predecessors lacked, any real attempt to appraise the general strategy of the Allied air offensive and the role of the RCAF within it."[12] Reviewers hoped that "some day a comprehensive history of Canada's air effort in the last war will be prepared."[13] Now that the war was over, the critics wanted a more inclusive examination of policy, administration, training, and logistics. The Historical Section had been hamstrung by the two-year delay in bringing the manuscript to publication, but it was clear that an official history based on authentic records would be a welcome addition to the historiography. With more than 2,000 copies sold in four months, it also appeared that the public was willing to embrace an air force history even five years after the event.[14]

WHILE GILBERT TUCKER, the Royal Canadian Navy's official historian, had made good progress on the first two volumes of his three-volume series by early 1947, there appeared to be no attempt by senior naval officers to support his continued request for access to the German naval records. Without them, Tucker again warned, there could be no operational history. Despite the limitations of records and general ambivalence by senior officers, Tucker made sail and completed both volumes by the summer of that year, leaving the third operational volume until the records were available. The vice chief of naval staff read the second volume in early 1948, describing it as a "well-written story of our great expansion from the administrative point of view, and as such will be of considerable value if we had to do the same thing again. I don't think the man-in-the-street would find it very interesting – but that of course is not the object."[15] That, unfortunately, was precisely who Claxton hoped would read the history. For him, the publicity that the volume would bring to the navy was more important than the didactic or historical value of the work.

Claxton disliked both of Tucker's volumes. The dry academic prose paled in comparison to both the army and air force popular histories, and in particular, Tucker's devotion of significant space in his first volume to an exploration of German naval policy before the Great War angered the minister. In fact, Claxton had initially "ruled that none of the ... volumes would be published." It was only through the intervention of the former chief of the naval staff, Percy Nelles, that the series was saved and later published.[16]

But Claxton demanded that the two volumes be distributed to "experts in the field of historical writing" to see if they were acceptable as a "permanent historical record of the Royal Canadian Navy."[17] Departmental expert C.P. Stacey was pleased with the naval contribution, especially the Second World War policy material, which he believed would assist him with his volume about the three services. "I am particularly glad to see that the History is going to deal adequately with the creation of the Canadian North-West Atlantic Command," he wrote in October 1948. The "Americans were deliberately censoring the references to this arrangement out of their official histories. This makes it all the more desirable that we should emphasize the matter in our own publications."[18] Professor George Brown of the University of Toronto was harsher in his comments, but he only felt that the Canadian history sections, rather than the naval history sections of the first volume, needed "substantial revisions." One of these amendments centred on Tucker's reference to the "vulnerability of Fort Churchill and Hudson Bay" in the eighteenth and nineteenth centuries, which Brown thought should be removed for modern strategic concerns.[19] It would appear that the official historians were open to all manner of indignities.

While Tucker made a number of changes, by 1948 he was already looking to close down the Naval Historical Section and return to an academic position at the University of British Columbia. Despite a lingering illness, he assumed that he would write the third volume from the west coast. But Claxton had other plans. With an official historian who seemed to be writing unreadable history and refusing to start the third and most anticipated operational volume without the German records, the minister sought a new author.

Claxton first turned to journalist Leslie Roberts, whose *Canada's War at Sea* had won accolades, and offered him use of all naval operational records, chapters, and narratives.[20] The precedent of allowing a civilian to access the naval records seems not to have been discussed, but for reasons unknown the Roberts project fell through. The department went looking for another author, consciously targeting writers and journalists rather than historians. Joseph Schull, a former naval information officer with experience in "public relations" and an "excellent writer of the more serious type," as one scouting report noted, was selected to author the operational history in March 1948. He would have one year to produce a 100,000-word monograph that covered the Battle of the Atlantic, the Mediterranean, naval support of the D-Day invasion, and "other areas where our ships operated."[21] With his limited time for preparation and writing, there would be nothing on the role of the air force in the war against the U-boats, but considering inter-service rivalries, this was not a lesson the navy wished highlighted in the postwar years.

Schull relied almost exclusively on the records and narratives crafted by the Naval Historical Section. True to his profession as a journalist, though, Schull met his difficult deadline and in an admirable manner. His history was vibrant, especially in comparison to Tucker's dry prose, and even Stacey was won over, remarking that it was a "really distinguished piece of writing." Nonetheless, Stacey offered six pages of comments upon receiving draft chapters. And although Schull had no intention of writing the narrative like an "official history," Stacey still suggested "that it will probably be the only officially fostered publication dealing with Canadian naval operations in 1939-45. Inevitably, therefore, it will be used, whether you like it or not, as a book of reference, simply because there is nothing else available." Stacey felt Schull should keep this in mind and control his lively writing style.[22]

Draft chapters were also sent to dozens of senior naval officers. Their comments were almost universally positive. Rear Admiral E.R. Mainguy, the vice chief of the naval staff, wrote that he liked the history "very much, particularly as you do not try to maintain that the Canadian Navy was thoroughly efficient." Commodore V.S. Godfrey echoed Mainguy in his praise and felt that "the absence of technical wording and the simple language in which the story is told will, I know, make the book appeal just as much to the lay public as it did to myself." And Louis C. Audette, a former North Atlantic veteran and commanding officer of a naval reserve division in Ottawa, complimented Schull, writing that his draft was a "thoroughly readable history of what might well have been a rather acrid statistical recitation." At the same time, Audette hoped that Schull might include the story of seaman Clifford E. McNaught, who had been wounded in a U-boat attack on the *Saguenay* on 1 December 1940. Audette, then a junior naval officer, had been ordered to take charge of the after guns because the "bows of the ship had been blown away and the fore was on fire." He asked for volunteers, and in the darkness and chaos McNaught agreed to supply him with the necessary shells. "This he did," wrote Audette, "until the fire forward burst into particularly bright flares and by the light I observed that his hands and face were so horribly burned by the flare of the original explosion that the flesh was hanging in places."[23] These were the men who should be highlighted in the history, thought Audette; Schull evidently agreed and McNaught's heroism was included in the official history.[24]

Far Distant Ships was published in 1950 and garnered positive press reviews, especially for its well-written prose and for its quick completion.[25] It was, nonetheless, a far cry from the multi-volume American and British official history series. Historian David Zimmerman has suggested that "the navy wanted its story told in the fashion of a Hornblower novel: romantic, action filled, and always ending with heroic victories."[26] That was indeed true for some, but it was also acknowledged by many senior officers that they wanted a critical history and that Schull's was a stopgap work. Only two years after the publication of *Far Distant Ships*, one naval memo noted that despite its "popular appeal, attractive style and timely publication," the "official academic history of the RCN's operations at sea, 1939-1945, has not been written."[27] And nor would it, thought Stacey, who believed that because of Claxton's meddling and his desire to have a popular naval history, Canada had missed the window of opportunity, lost its expert narrators, and would never have a scholarly Second World War naval operational history.[28] Stacey would not be disproved until the 1980s.

Tucker's double-volume history was published two years later and largely ignored in the press. It remains the worst example of impenetrable official history. Although the two books contain reams of valuable information, other than dedicated researchers or naval personnel, few would enjoy sitting down with them as anything other than tools for reference. At the same time, though, Tucker broke the mould on the official histories by examining more than just RCN operations. He documented policy changes and the consequences of military issues in Canadian society. The naval debates of 1909 to 1913 had not transformed Canada in the same way as the Great War, but they were an indication that Canada's military history could not be hived off from the rest of society.

Tucker also believed that his official history was not a starting point for future historians, but the destination: "In the case of nearly any other scholar, should the well of truth be muddied because he has done inferior work, the water will probably be cleared again by those who follow. The official service Historians, on the other hand, will almost certainly have the last word."[29] The official historians controlled the field of military history for at least three decades, and Tucker's conceited belief might very well have been true had it not been for a new generation of official and unofficial historians engaging in a new reading of the archival records. Tucker was more correct to note, however, that historians had paid "little attention" to Canada's naval history, and unfortunately his two official works did little to excite the imagination of future historians.[30]

LIKE DUGUID during the interwar years, the roles of the official historians went far beyond simply writing history. As important and perhaps more relevant to the Department of National Defence (DND) were the official historians' responsibilities in determining the scheduling of records, recommending their destruction, or transferring them to the Public Archives of Canada.

The war had resulted in the creation of an avalanche of records, and the 200,000 Canadian Military Headquarters overseas files were but a fraction generated by the other two services, along with every other federal department engaged in the work of winning the war.[31] C.D. Howe's Department of Munitions and Supplies, which manufactured during the war tens of thousands of airplanes and ships in addition to a mind-boggling 800,000 trucks and other vehicles, also produced, as a by-product, tons and tons of records. Who would decide their fate? This was a major concern of the Canadian Historical Association, and Professor George Brown had written in 1944 about the "deplorable" and in "some respects scandalous" record-keeping practice of the government: "Those familiar with the history of this question can give many examples of records dumped into garrets, cellars and other corners without regard to their value, and there left to destruction by light, dust, dampness, rats, mice, and in some cases even rain and snow. This is not much better than shovelling them into furnaces, or sending them for waste paper, and there have been many examples also of that."[32]

Better care of records was not needed just for future historians, wrote Brown, but for a government that might have to defend its actions some day, or at least return to those decisions for clarification. While Sir Arthur Doughty, Canada's long-serving Dominion archivist during the first three decades of the century, had been an influential public servant, his successor, Gustav Lanctôt, had not had the same presence among the mandarins and politicians in Ottawa. Neither, however, had been able to influence legislation that would force departments to preserve or transfer their records to the archives, and until 1944 only a handful of federal departments had "ever sent any records."³³ The Public Archives had to be strengthened to ensure that the historical memory of the country was not lost.

The government had considered the thorny question of war records as early as 1942, when the Prime Minister's Office had ordered departments to prepare plans for the preservation and proper destruction of their records. In June 1944 a public records committee was formed with senior departmental officials to consider the question of government records, and especially war records. A.F. Duguid and Kenneth Conn represented the historical sections and they, along with Gustav Lanctôt, Dr. George Glazebrook from External Affairs, and the secretary, W.E.D. Halliday of the Privy Council, agreed that a permanent committee should be established to pass judgment over the efficient transfer and destruction of records.³⁴ Following the surrender of the Axis powers in 1945, the committee met regularly in the hope of controlling the paper explosion. As one committee recommendation noted, 75 to 85 percent of all government documents could be destroyed "without impairing the records of administrative experience or historical documentation."³⁵ But before destroying the majority of records, the most significant ones first had to be identified for preservation.

With the committee examining the creation of records in the government, it discovered that whole series of documents had been destroyed during the war without any overseeing body to judge their historical value. In the immediate post-war years, civil servants transferred jobs, new staff arrived, and whole departments were cut or reorganized. Record keeping was not a priority, but historians continued to push for preservation of records. By 1945 the committee ensured that all three service official historians were present, and later two representatives from the Canadian Historical Association were invited to the meetings. This was most gratifying for the country's professional historians, but it is also clear from the minutes that it would be the government's historians who carried much more weight in the discussions. This did not always result in the preservation of records. In December 1945, for instance, Tucker recommended that some 2,000 Great War naval files relating to merchant shipping and coastal defence, including casualties, movement of ships, and cargoes, be destroyed since he had "made all the necessary extracts from the files" for an official history.³⁶ It is tragic that no one objected to Tucker's recommendation, and therefore countless valuable records were incinerated. What is significant about Tucker's thinking was the belief that since he would write an official history, the records would no longer be needed. For Tucker, the official history was the product of all the records, the "last word"; for Stacey, it was clear that his histories were a foundation for future works, and as a result the war records had to be carefully guarded for future generations.

As Tucker and Hitchins were engulfed by departmental duties in 1948, it was Stacey or his representative who offered much of the historical advice to the committee, and not only for defence records. It was evident to Canada's professional historians that Stacey was protecting their interests. The archivist's role was dear to Stacey, and in 1950 he would be called upon by the Royal Commission on National Development in the Arts, Letters and Sciences, better known as the Massey Commission, to write a brief on the nation's archives. Despite this support of the larger historical profession, he had great difficulty in establishing a policy on access to the defence records for historians and the public.[37]

Duguid allowed only the accredited regimental historians access to the Great War records. Stacey, however, had been a professional historian before an official one, and he pushed hard to allow limited access to the records for his fellow academics or researchers. Immediately after the war, for instance, Stacey convinced his superiors to allow him to share some of the Army Historical Section's narratives with the BBC's Chester Wilmot, who was writing a book on 21 Army Group, to ensure that the Canadian Army received sufficient coverage.[38] But what was Stacey to do with others who were requesting the declassification of records? The First Canadian Army ordered that units prepare short histories, and by September 1945 more than a hundred units had sent officers to conduct research into the regimental records.[39] Researchers were allowed to see the records in London (although it made for some crowded research rooms), but events became more complicated after the units and records were repatriated to Canada. Stacey intervened with his superiors to ensure that a copy of the War Diary went to the unit should it be requested, and the section continued to offer historical assistance over the coming years. Both Duguid and Stacey recognized the important contribution of the unit histories, since their official histories would never be able to document adequately the role of most regiments or batteries in battle.[40]

For civilian historians, too, Stacey argued for and succeeded in getting a far more liberal policy than in the past. In January 1946 George Stanley had written a briefing document on access to records, which Stacey fully endorsed; it suggested that there be a "provision for civilian Historians preparing serious studies in Canadian military history. I feel strongly that we should do everything we can to encourage the study of military history in Canada, and should not bar the door to any civilian of reputable academic standing who is anxious to do research in the field."

This would be in direct contrast to Duguid's prewar policy, which Stanley described as "very chilly" to academics.[41] While the public was still to be shut out from many of the records that documented decision making at higher levels, the Army Historical Section – now named the Directorate Historical Section (DHS) – was anxious to promote the serious study of military history in Canada. This was no clear-cut issue, however, and it would be questioned in the coming years by the department, which was quite unsure about whether it wished outsiders to employ its records even in limited way, since no legislation required any opening of archives to researchers.

Just months after supporting the liberal access document, Stacey turned down S.R. Rye, a veteran attempting to read the War Diary of 9 Canadian Field Ambulance, because he was not considered a serious student of military history. So, too, did Stacey block access to records a few years later when a soldier attempted to consult his unit's War Diary in support of his pension claim. In a letter that went out under the deputy minister's signature, the DHS noted that there is "no authority under which they [records] can be made available to private persons." Around the same time, though, Stacey was making records available to R.W. Queen-Hughes, a former Canadian Women's Army Corps member, who wanted to write a personal history of her service in the war. For another history student, in May 1949, Stacey was supportive of Robert Rumilly's bid to see the war records relating to Quebec units in the two world wars. And while Stacey would not "open them unrestrictedly for him," he and his staff answered inquiries, provided access to narratives, and even supplied extracts from the War Diaries.[42] Despite a slight easing of restrictions, there appeared to be little justification for deciding who would receive access to the records, although fellow academics were privileged over the public, or even veterans.

Stacey was also forced to deal with the inquiries of senior officers. In 1947 General Guy Simonds, then languishing as an instructor of the Imperial Defence College, had visited Stacey's overseas historical officer, T.M. Hunter, in order to conduct research for his memoirs. Hunter was unsure about the access policy, but rightly suspected that he could not prevent Simonds from seeing the records. Stacey confirmed this, but warned him not to let Simonds see Crerar's or McNaughton's personal papers, which were in Hunter's possession, as he was drafting a narrative on the Normandy campaign.[43] A few years later, in 1950, General E.L.M. Burns wished to review all official records relating to manpower questions during the war, a contentious issue that had led to the conscription crisis. No academic historian would have seen these records, but Burns, as a former corps commander and deputy minister of Veterans' Affairs, had far more clout. Nonetheless, Stacey went all the way to Foulkes to confirm access, and although it was eventually granted, there was a great deal of concern that Burns would reopen old wounds.[44]

Burns's book, *Manpower in the Canadian Army* (1956), was a revealing history that analyzed how the Canadian Army used and allotted its reserve personnel during the war. With access to the defence records and DHS narratives, Burns concluded that tens of thousands of recruits had been squandered in logistical or administrative areas, as opposed to being at the "teeth" end of the army that was doing the fighting and suffering the casualties. This, in turn, had led to the infantry shortages in 1944 that had precipitated the conscription crisis. While Burns did not assign blame, he concluded that there had been severe administrative problems.[45] It was an important history that looked at the fighting capacities of the nation in the early 1950s by analyzing the Second World War, but it was more of a general staff study rather than an academic treatise.

Throughout this period, Stacey was instrumental in opening war records to academics. He endorsed Stanley's first access policy in 1946, and he encouraged Claxton to write to the CHA in 1947, highlighting the "liberal access to documents with a view to encouraging civilian historians to write military history." The following year, when the DND decided to deny regimental historians access to war records, he reminded his superiors of Claxton's letter to the CHA and Eisenhower's well-publicized dictum that demanded openness of records to researchers, which eventually reversed the restrictive policy.[46] Stacey even used his many connections with academics to advise them to push the Massey Commission to "include in the report a good strong 'plug' for a liberal policy in access to documents by historical scholars."[47] While Stacey struggled to reveal the full story in his contemporary history, he knew that his future role as official historian would be easier if there were others working in the field and if some of the more contentious issues had already been addressed in published works. As he wrote in 1949, "Only Canadians will look after Canadian interests. Nobody else can be expected to make it his business to do so; nobody else is likely to know what our interests are, or even realize that we have interests."[48]

AN IMPORTANT ASPECT of Stacey's role as official historian, then, was to encourage the writing of Canadian military history. He did so by advocating the opening of the archives, but he also offered advice to a number of Canadian historians, including official, demi-official, and international historians. Like Duguid, he also acted as watchdog to protect the army's reputation in print.

His most formal supporting role was to Dr. W.R. Feasby, the Royal Canadian Army Medical Corps' (RCAMC) official historian and editor. Research had begun during the Second World War for an official medical series, but postwar cuts and the department's inability to guarantee a permanent position resulted in the wartime historian, Lieutenant Colonel Athol Gordon, eventually returning to his prewar medical practice. Before Gordon left he proposed a six-volume series that Stacey advised him to reduce to four, which he did; however, the coordination of that goal fell to Stacey. With his pressing projects, Stacey was worried that any involvement in the medical history, especially since the RCAMC seemed incapable of finding a suitable replacement historian, would result in delays for the army history.[49] In late 1945 and early 1946, though, Stacey drafted a number of memos for senior officers at the DND that argued for a medical history series.

In the summer of 1946, Feasby, a practising doctor in Toronto, editor of several Canadian medical journals, and a legally blind veteran who had served in a series of senior medical capacities during the war, was given a contract to work part-time on the history. With two researchers in Ottawa, whom he and Stacey would manage, Feasby would rely on these men to examine the mass of files, most of which had not been opened since the war. It was not an ideal research situation, yet Feasby was dedicated and began work immediately. It was almost short-lived because in 1947 Claxton was aiming to cut the medical history and get out a popular volume within the year.[50] Stacey hit back hard for the medical history, suggesting that many other nations were engaged in far more complex histories and any popular history offered within a year would only be a rushed affair that would denigrate the RCAMC's valuable service. It would, he cautioned, be "better to publish no Medical history at all."[51] Feasby also met with the minister, putting on "a very impressive performance," and argued that a medical history would be "perhaps the only useful salvage of the war," presumably in so far as medical lessons were captured for postwar doctors. He also warned that there was "no such thing as a popular medical history."[52] The medical history was saved, but reduced to a two-volume inter-service work: one to cover the operational history of the RCAMC and a second to document specific medical issues and treatments.

Over the next half decade, Feasby worked on the project, and Stacey offered support, advice, and assistance with navigating the history through the choppy waters of the DND headquarters. Feasby was to coordinate the work of a number of medical experts, not all of whom understood their roles or agreed that he should be the historian. Furthermore, since the medical history was multi-service, there were constant problems over how much space would be devoted to subjects and themes, some of which were more important to one service than another. By the summer of 1947, for instance, the RCAF had written a series of letters bemoaning that their aviation medical advances would receive only one-thirteenth of the space in the official history. For the next three years their contributors were obstructionists, as they alternately sulked and railed against the project.[53]

By early 1948 Stacey had received a number of draft chapters. They were unacceptable, and Stacey was forced to intervene immediately and provide guidance about the sensitive nature of writing official history. Perhaps he should not have been surprised at Feasby's infelicitous inclination to make quick and harsh judgments, since his only guide was Macphail's 1925 work. But Stacey advised Feasby to be cautious, for "until you have actually had some experience of it, you cannot conceive the sensitiveness of official people concerning records for publication. We discovered [that in] 1943, when we began circulating our preliminary narratives, that even the most apparently harmless comment can arouse a surprising amount of suspicion and resentment."[54]

As they stood, Feasby's initial draft chapters would "probably cause an explosion," especially his condemnation of officers involved in the early war work of the RCAMC. Having dealt with equally difficult questions, Stacey was right to remind

Feasby that most of the senior officers in the first years of the war, be they medical or army, were forced to "make bricks without straw." They deserved more sympathy, and their trials had to be placed within the context of the time. And because Feasby was an official historian, warned Stacey, his comments "carry more weight than those of a private historian."[55] Here, Stacey was indeed offering key advice that he had learned the hard way. He was not trying to influence Feasby into obfuscating the truth, only that the medical historian must approach his subject with a firm understanding of all the challenges present. His unique position as official historian required that he be wary of hasty accusations in judging the actions of the near past. Stacey also learned that to write an inter-service history where one relied on a number of contributors was "extremely inefficient" – a disheartening lesson considering he, too, was facing an inter-service policy history.[56] The two medical volumes were published in 1956, and while they were insubstantial in many areas of study, they offered a key foundation for further work, even if historians have not yet been drawn to the field.[57] One can only wonder what RCAF veterans, or those from the Great War for that matter, thought of the RCAMC getting their official histories while their series remained unwritten.

As the primary contact at the DND for historical issues, Stacey also acted as the guardian of historical accuracy for other projects outside of the department. He reviewed almost every Canadian publication relating to military history in an official or demi-official capacity, and that included the naval histories and John de Navarre Kennedy's monograph of the Department of Munitions and Supply. Kennedy's history had been one of many commissioned by the government to document the essential wartime work of federal departments, but most of these histories were either disbanded or never published in the immediate postwar years. Kennedy's monograph also nearly failed, as he had no research staff to assist him and, as a result, had relied extensively on the narratives prepared by the various directorates and sections of the department. These were episodic, self-serving, and even worse, had largely been written in 1943, two years before the war ended. Kennedy admitted he had no chance to examine the departmental files, which were voluminous and unorganized, and instead relied on a series of questionnaires with surviving civil servants. Stacey had unfortunately seen the history too late to make more than "minor improvements and eliminate some passages which could have been particularly embarrassing." It was not, Stacey opined, a book that could be "relied on with confidence."[58] At the same time, it was stronger because of Stacey's editorial interventions, and surprisingly still remains one of the seminal works for gauging Canada's wartime production. Historians might best take Stacey's opinions to heart when using it as a source.

As it had with Duguid, the department relied on its official historians to protect the Canadian Army's reputation. Stacey had done so during the war by writing the first white paper on Dieppe; he had done so again by correcting Maltby's dispatches on Hong Kong; and he would continue to monitor how other official and semi-official international histories portrayed the Canadian war effort. Both the Americans and the British sent Stacey all draft copies of their histories, and he corrected errors relating to the Canadian forces and also ensured that the "junior ally" received proper coverage where it was warranted. For example, in November 1949 Stacey received an advance draft of Christopher Buckley's *The Raid on Dieppe*, an official history commissioned by the British from a civilian historian. Stacey was shaken by its amateur nature. *The Canadian Army* had come out the year before and presented Dieppe in thorough detail, more so than anything in print to date. But it appeared that Buckley had failed to read the Canadian account, and it seemed to Stacey that *The Raid on Dieppe* might have been "written a week after the operation." The twelve pages of notes from Stacey were an indication of the serious problems in the text, and he strongly recommended to the British that it not be released for fear of causing an international scandal. Furthermore, Stacey warned it would sully the reputation of the British official historical program and all official histories, as it was thoroughly "mischievous," dull, and inaccurate. "Although Buckley's knowledge of the operation is so limited," remarked an incredulous Stacey, "he engages in the most sweeping strictures against those responsible for it."[59] The British heeded Stacey's outrage and assigned one of their most experienced official historians, Captain Wilfrid Miles, to rewrite the entire text. Although the revised draft elicited another three pages of comments and was still "very weak" according to Stacey, at least the British had changed the most outrageous earlier claims, such as the suggestion that the Canadians had demanded a frontal assault to blood their troops.[60] All of Stacey's work in defending the Canadian soldier was reported to the chief of the general staff (CGS), who kept an interested eye on issues relating to the reputation of the army, but had enough confidence in Stacey to allow his official historian to act independently. By the end of the decade, Stacey was not only Canada's expert on the Second World War, but also acknowledged as such by the Americans and the British.

As DHS staff continued to research and write more detailed narratives for the first and second volumes of the official history series, it was clear that Stacey's goal of finishing the books by 1950 was unrealistic. The CGS and minister were not worried, however, feeling that *The Canadian Army* had placated the public's desire for an immediate history.[61] In a revealing document, Stacey noted that throughout this period and into the 1950s, he had only been able to devote half of his time to work on the official histories, with administrative and operational issues consuming the rest. G.W.L. Nicholson, his deputy director after George Stanley retired in 1947, spent approximately 70 percent of his time writing the Italian campaign official history, but that was only because Stacey had been able to free him from much of the bothersome daily administrative tasks in the section.[62] As with Duguid, the role of the official historian consisted of much more than simply producing an official history – queries of an historical nature or those concerning the country's heritage were often passed along to him because there was no one else with the necessary skills. Even with a full-time staff member answering inquiries, there were constant demands on Stacey's limited resources. Without his highly developed managerial skills and long-term vision, the immediate and constant barrage of heritage issues would have eroded the time available for the official history.

In late 1949 the DND called upon DHS to fulfill another operational mandate. The army had developed a new training program for officers and non-commissioned officers (NCOs), with an important component being the study of military history. The Directorate of Military Training (DMT) found, much to its trainers' collective annoyance, that most of the available histories were British in origin and out of print. The DMT turned to Stacey, and despite the crushing responsibility of writing the official histories, he responded to the request, believing that the study of military history was essential to soldiers and that it could only be fulfilled with his section's assistance – a belief acknowledged by other directorates as well. Stacey had effectively avoided many of the public affairs demands that plagued the navy and air force historical sections, but he knew when it was important to support the operational requirements of the department. Once again, though, Stacey demanded and was given nearly complete freedom to develop the curriculum.[63] He ordered a number of his staff to prepare brief histories that would first be published in the *Canadian Army Journal* and then later brought together in a small publication, *Introduction to Military History for Canadian Students* (1951). It eventually went through more than half a dozen editions, and more serving officers have probably read this book in its many variations than any other history ever published in Canada.

Stacey believed strongly in the value of military history for officers, but it did not, he warned, provide ready-made solutions to strategic or tactical problems; "History is said to repeat itself – but it doesn't repeat itself *that* much," Stacey quipped.[64] History was a guide for soldiers engaged in the deadliest of professions. It has often been remarked that soldiers must train for something they hope never occurs. It would be the same as doctors who study their whole lives for a single operation: a little pointless, perhaps, but unless one has put in the time beforehand, one is liable to lose the patient on the operating table. Soldiering is too dangerous and too important a profession to learn as you go; and even then it is usually too late to learn without unnecessary suffering and casualties. While some servicemen did not see the value in studying wars of the past, many others agreed with Stacey that there were no easy solutions; but perhaps the path ahead would be a little less trying if one knew that men have always struggled in these situations.[65]

So popular was the DHS's booklet that the DMT appealed for additional histories, especially since Militia units continued to write "scathing letters" and were "bloody annoyed" about the unavailability of military history texts.⁶⁶ This became all the more urgent in September 1954 when the CGS reaffirmed that "an essential part of an officer's training is the study of military history."⁶⁷ To fulfill this operational mandate, the DHS published a number of military histories over the next decade, including books on Marlborough's campaigns, the Western Front in 1914, and a study of Marshal Ferdinand Foch by T.M. Hunter, which was hailed internationally as a classic.⁶⁸ Although it must have seemed inconceivable to surviving Great War veterans that the Historical Section was publishing histories on all military topics but the one that really mattered to them, it is also clear that Stacey was forced to balance the operational requirements of the department with the writing of his official series.

With a slow trickle of articles published in the *Canadian Army Journal*, as well as the army's commitment to the study of military history, there was a growing acceptance about the value of understanding Canada's world war history. At the same time, though, academic historians still avoided the subject. Despite Stacey's push for better access to the records, Canada's academic historians continued to be more interested in the nation-building school of history that examined economic and political factors in the development and evolution of Canada. There is a "certain fear in academic circles," postulated Sir Michael Howard, that "military history is liable to be regarded as a handmaid of militarism."⁶⁹ Another military historian writing in the early 1960s believed that "historians have generally avoided it as a subject unworthy of study, if not downright dangerous. It is as if they hoped that by ignoring war they might eliminate it altogether."⁷⁰ The study of our martial past does no more to encourage militarism than the study of medicine propagates disease. Nonetheless, while military history played a key role in shaping the nation, it was quite clearly being left to Canada's official historian to tell that story.

In 1949, however, Richard Preston, a new history professor at the recently reopened Royal Military College of Canada (RMC), published an important article. With the Second World War having resulted in the massive mobilization of entire nations, and the erasure of the distinction between soldiers and civilians as legitimate targets still casting its long shadow over the rest of the decade, Preston articulated that war was "more than a clash of arms." Both world wars had shown that most Canadians had been involved in some type of war work, either, to use the Great War's Canadian Patriotic Fund's slogan, to "fight or pay." A new military history methodology was needed, argued Preston, to reflect the changing nature of warfare, and it had to be based on an "adequate understanding of political, economic, social, diplomatic and technical history."⁷¹ Historians were slowly reckoning that military forces, especially civilian ones, are shaped by their society and shape their society in return, and the discipline must include the study of both.

Within five years of Preston's appeal, George Stanley, one of his fellow history professors at RMC and Stacey's second in command during the war, published the first overview of Canadian military history. *Canada's Soldiers* (1954) was brilliantly subtitled *The Military History of an Unmilitary People*, an expression that has been repeated countless times to describe Canadian military history. The history, which offered little coverage of anything other than warfare on land, was strongest in documenting military events up to the Great War. For the Second World War, Stanley wrote only one chapter, and even his second edition, which came out in 1960, still pointed the reader to the "official history of the Canadian army ... for the details of this story." Nonetheless, Stanley hoped that the history would "provoke or stimulate other Canadian historians." Military history, he added, "has been the Cinderella of Canadian historical studies; perhaps this book will point the way to further investigation of an interesting and profitable, although neglected field."[72]

Stanley's history was an essential text for laying a foundation for how military history has underpinned Canadian society in its many incarnations over several centuries. However, there were few other academic military studies during the 1940s and 1950s besides the official histories, soldiers' memoirs, the occasional biography, and Stacey's output, which offered an astonishing range of publications in academic journals. Even with these new studies into Canada's military history, almost all the historians concentrated on pre-Confederation warfare. Civilian historians faced great challenges in writing about the two world wars if they lacked direct exposure to the hard hand of war overseas, did not have access to military records, or were without the official histories as reliable foundations on which to build. But to ignore military history and its impact on Canada was to turn a blind eye to an important factor in shaping the nation. Canada's history reveals a nation forged in the fire of war and willing to engage in warfare on behalf of our Allies. Native and colonial societies were predicated on fierce competition and warfare; the Seven Years War decided the fate of North America; the defeat of American forces in 1775 and during the War of 1812 kept Canada a British colony and fortified imperial links; even the supposedly undefended border with the United States in the nineteenth century was a myth, something that Stacey revealed in a seminal 1950 article.[73] And, of course, even a cursory understanding of Canada's involvement in the two world wars provides countless examples of how conflict has shaped Canada and how its citizens, while not militaristic, have been willing to embrace military solutions for reasons of loyalty and self-preservation. Perhaps *Canada's Soldiers* should have been subtitled: a military history of a military people.

WITH THE CANADIAN ARMY having won Canadian and international acclaim, Stacey turned his attention to the three-volume army history and, afterwards, the policy volume on the three services. The immense hurdles in getting the summary published proved that a war history series would be contentious and closely studied. Four more volumes were too much for one person. Stacey had therefore passed a volume of the official history, the Italian campaign, to his deputy director, G.W.L. Nicholson, the only historian whom Stacey entrusted with the role.

Nicholson was born in England, but came to Canada in 1919. He graduated in arts from Queen's University and then received a teaching degree from the University of Toronto, which later propelled him towards the position of principal of a Saskatchewan high school. During the Second World War, he served as an officer in the Prince Albert and Battleford Volunteers (Non-Permanent Active Militia or NPAM) until 1943 when he joined the Historical Section as a narrator for Pacific Command. In that role he provided accounts of west coast operations, the 1943 Kiska campaign, and the first narrative on Hong Kong. He had been recruited by and served with Duguid in Canada, and was therefore not a "Stacey man," but after most experienced narrators left the service in 1947, Nicholson played an increasingly important part in the directorate, largely because Stacey felt that he "had a distinct flair for military history."[74] Stacey had hoped for a veteran of the Italian campaign to write the history, but admitted that there were no suitable historians now that Sam Hughes and W.E.C. Harrison had returned to civilian life. By late 1947, Nicholson began work as the primary author on the Italian campaign.

Stacey set the guidelines for the study, pushing Nicholson to ensure that it would be accessible to the general public, and that "it must not be allowed to degenerate into a wooden military textbook." At the same time, Stacey instructed Nicholson to place the Canadian Army within the Allied strategic operations.[75] That did not leave a lot of room to discus the impact of war on individuals. For Stacey, the importance was in the overall campaign rather than in the multitude of narratives that formed it; he saw war history as a top-down affair. But it would have to be accurate: "We must be sure that the tone is just right: dignified and official without being stodgy, always understating rather than overstating, and being most careful to avoid any usage which could possibly draw a smile from an old soldier."[76] A blatant denigration of the enemy or a heroic narrative of the past was unwanted by both the soldiers and their official historians; Stacey wished to avoid anything that reeked of victors' history.

Although Nicholson was remarkably independent in writing his volume and had full control over a small team of narrators, Stacey read over draft chapters and offered advice. Nicholson had been supplied with a number of very strong wartime narratives written by Hughes and Harrison, which he found "tremendously valuable," and even a doctoral dissertation on the Sicilian campaign by J.B. Conacher, a former historical officer. There was "no shortage" of material, remarked Nicholson; the real problem was "one of selection."[77] But despite the writer's proximity to events, the narratives were bland, factual chronicles of the war, "bloodless" in their description of battle and the men who were engaged in it. So Nicholson was forced to return to the War Diaries, operational reports, army-level records, and German material in Washington to reconstruct the story.[78] But this was no easy task for either Nicholson or Stacey, who a year later would begin writing his first volume. "Documents come out of hiding only gradually," remarked Stacey, which was an added burden for any historian writing contemporary history.[79]

Nicholson had finished most of the draft chapters by the summer of 1948, and Stacey authorized him to spend two months in Italy studying the terrain and walking the battlefields. It was a profitable research trip for Nicholson, who came back with a new perspective on "the tremendously difficult terrain" faced by the Canadian infantrymen. His subjects, the dismissively labelled "D-Day dodgers," had fought on some of the most difficult battlefields of the war. Nicholson was also hospitalized with jaundice, perhaps even better first-hand evidence of the constant struggle against the harsh environment that the Canadian soldier faced from 1943 to 1945.[80]

Nicholson had placed the Canadian operations within the larger Allied context, but it was difficult to evaluate the entire campaign. It was assumed that Italy was only a sideshow to the preparation and fighting of the real battle in Northwest Europe. Yet while Nicholson focused on the Canadians, he was right to note that the Allied forces in Italy had held down a large number of German forces and diverted important strategic resources from the Eastern and Western Fronts. Nicholson also struggled to assess individuals, especially the firing of Lieutenant General E.L.M. Burns from command of I Canadian Corps in November 1944. The narratives, for instance, almost completely ignored the issue. When Nicholson sent out his draft chapters to senior officers in late 1951, Brigadier G.A. McCarter, the I Canadian Corps chief of staff under Burns, had queried how he would handle the general's removal. The official historian wrote back, "The question of dealing with senior officers' shortcomings remains one of the most difficult problems which we have to face in the preparation of this history. We have no intention of applying the white wash brush indiscriminately."[81] However, such matters would have to be treated carefully. Later that year, both Stacey and Nicholson interviewed Burns about the campaign. When asked about his removal, "He took a very impersonal and objective attitude," Stacey wrote in his diary; Burns "agreed that the question of his leaving the command of I Canadian Corps required to be discussed in the Official History for the benefit of future commanders and governments."[82] While still an important figure with his work in the Department of Veterans Affairs and, later, on several high-profile peacekeeping missions, Burns's agreement to a frank appraisal of the incident was a telling indication of his professionalism and his respect for historical accuracy.

Nicholson also struggled to write about the Canadian soldier, and he was reprimanded by several senior officers who thought after reading draft chapters that he had given "inadequate credit" to his "fighting qualities."[83] Stacey had instructed Nicholson to ensure that the German forces received full coverage for their expert and determined fighting retreat across the Italian mountain ridges, but he had said very little about the Canadian soldier.[84] While the Germans had indeed fought a tenacious series of battles, it was the Canadians, and other Allied troops, who had been forced to advance up the supposedly "soft underbelly" of the fiercely defended mountains and valleys of Italy, fighting, probing, and continually punching through one German line after another. After a series of rewrites, Nicholson's history was far more sympathetic to the Canadian soldiers, and he was more willing to use their stories and first-hand accounts to depict the nature of combat.

While Nicholson pushed forward with his history, so too did Stacey, although he was plagued with administrative burdens. The first volume of the official history would cover the Canadian Army from its rapid expansion, through its training, to its work in the United Kingdom. It would also analyze the Dieppe raid, Hong Kong battle, and the Aleutian campaign. Stacey had already tackled many of these thorny historical issues in *The Canadian Army*, but he had not had full access to records then; nor had he felt comfortable in assessing some of the more contested issues surrounding battles or individuals.

Stacey kept to "a middle course" with this new volume, especially with controversial operations like Hong Kong and Dieppe.[85] After being granted access to the Cabinet records, he studied them during eight valuable months in 1949.[86] Although it was slow in coming, additional access to the British Combined records after 1950 revealed other pieces of the puzzle. Stacey continued to search through personal archival collections, too, and he used previously withheld papers from McNaughton, who advised Stacey that these records were for his eyes only and not to be opened to anyone "unless it's desirable there should be a controversy."[87] These "desirable controversies" would probably have been for building an historical case to support McNaughton's many grievances, such as the splitting of the Canadian Army in 1943 or as ammunition against one of the many Canadian or British individuals whom he believed had wronged him. Stacey took this all under advisement, judging cautiously the evidence and crafting his chapters with care. Equally useful to Stacey were a handful of international histories published since 1948 that helped to further situate Canadian operations into the larger Allied strategic context of the war. Some unofficial historians such as Robert Sherwood had been given access to the Combined records before Stacey, something that had infuriated the Canadian official historian, while others such as Chester Wilmot, whose *The Struggle for Europe* (1952) had been based on Montgomery's personal archives, revealed information Stacey wasn't able to access while researching his first book.[88]

Stacey continued to receive support from the senior generals, and many provided comments on his draft chapters. Simonds, who became CGS in 1951, showed an ongoing interest in the history of the war, and he was particularly willing to present a detailed commentary on the direction of the Normandy campaign. As Simonds had been a disciple of Field Marshal Sir Bernard Montgomery, it is not surprising that he insisted to Stacey that the British general's single-thrust strategy was far superior to the broad-front strategy of Supreme Commander Dwight Eisenhower, which was, he insisted, really a lack of control and vision.[89] While Simonds's argument failed to account for the logistical restraints on the Allies, the strong personality of its commanders, or the intricacies of managing a multinational force in battle, Stacey was still forced to confront the large questions of strategy without full access to the evidence, as many of the most controversial issues were not recorded in the official records or remained buried in personal papers. At the same time, Stacey struggled to come to grips with even the most basic facts; for example, he was surprised to find in September 1951 that the records were unclear as to the D-Day casualty figures for the 3rd Canadian Division.[90] Responsible for laying the groundwork upon which future generations of historians would build, Stacey confronted all issues, from the tactical to the strategic, from establishing basic facts about casualties and the movement of units to the overall interpretation of contentious events in places such as Dieppe and Hong Kong. The first and second volumes were keenly anticipated, and would be even more closely read by politicians, soldiers, and allies. But before that, Stacey needed government approval to publish the history, which proved far more difficult than could have been imagined.

CLAXTON HAD HELD SERIOUS RESERVATIONS about *The Canadian Army* in 1948, everything from the inclusion of details considered too grisly to the handling of controversial issues surrounding individuals or governments, but that was only three years after the war. When Stacey submitted the first volume in March 1953 to the minister and, within months, the second volume, he hoped to have the official histories available to the public by the end of that same year. It was not to be: Claxton refused to authorize their publication. The questions raised by failures such as Hong Kong and Dieppe, and the reinforcement crisis that led to conscription, were all covered in stark detail. And so the histories sat on Claxton's desk, day after day, month after month, as the minister waffled and worried that these official accounts might somehow have an impact on the Liberal party, which had been in power during the war and was still in power.

With silence from Claxton's office, Stacey began to inquire about the status of the project, even going so far as to make personal appeals to the CGS. Ever a supporter of the history program, Simonds wrote to and even met with the minister to hasten the approval of the histories. It was to no avail. While the historians had worked days and nights to meet almost impossible deadlines, the minister was sitting on these histories, despite claims by his party in the House of Commons that they would be published in 1953. Simonds warned that the government must not repeat the "fiasco of the Official History of the First World War, which occasioned such criticism," but still, unbelievably, Claxton did nothing.[91]

Sir Max Aitken, Lord Beaverbrook, was the driving force in documenting Canada's Great War effort. A shrewd and politically well-connected businessman, he crafted a memorable and profitable legacy of the war. LAC, PA6477

Lord Beaverbrook was renowned for his parties and female companions, yet he always found time to act as self-appointed liaison between the Canadian government and British General Headquarters, and frequently meddled in British politics and the command of the Canadian Expeditionary Force. LAC, PA22966

FACING PAGE, TOP TO BOTTOM

A rare photograph of Canadians assaulting part of the Canal du Nord during the Hundred Days campaign. Historians struggled to document the Canadian experience of battle. LAC, PA3377

Canadian soldiers acquired a reputation as elite troops hardened by the wilds of the Canadian north. This soldier seems to support that assumption. But despite Beaverbrook's best publicity efforts, there was no denying that Canada had tens of thousands of clerks, bankers, and grocers who had rarely been outside of the cities, let alone had a hand in carving out a civilization from the snow and ice. *CWM, George Metcalf Archival Collection, 19930013-789*

This 1917 cartoon, "The Canadian in Peace and War," equates the rugged prewar Canadian voyageur, hunter, and adventurer with a tough and resilient Canadian soldier. Cartoons like this supported Beaverbrook's goal of shaping the image and reputation of the Canadian soldier during the war. *Canada in Khaki: A Tribute to the Officers and Men Now Serving in the Canadian Expeditionary Force*, Vol. 1 (Ottawa: Canadian War Records Office, 1917), 10.

Canadian Official Photograph
A BRITISH "TANK" GOING INTO ACTION

Lord Beaverbrook's Canadian War Records Office acquired the first images of tanks at the Battle of Courcelette in September 1916. *Canada in Khaki: A Tribute to the Officers and Men Now Serving in the Canadian Expeditionary Force,* Vol. 1 (Ottawa: Canadian War Records Office, 1917).

Colonel A.F. Duguid, official historian from 1921 to 1947, fought to safeguard the historical reputations of Canadians. He is remembered mostly for never having completed his multi-volume official history series. LAC, PA167233

Sir Arthur Doughty was Dominion archivist from 1904 to 1935. He collected war trophies for distribution across the country and helped to nurture academic Canadian historical writing. *CWM, George Metcalf Archival Collection, 19790631-024*

Sir Arthur Currie is considered Canada's greatest general. Despite marshalling resources to care for his soldiers' lives, he was later accused of being a "butcher" for having lost so many men in battle. Nevertheless, he won a high profile court case in 1928 to restore his reputation. LAC, PA1370

The Truth About the War

By MAJOR GEORGE A. DREW

An irrefutable answer to the slander, published in certain United States magazines, that in the Great War the British Empire shirked its responsibility

Reprinted at the request of thousands of Canadians from the July 1st, 1928 issue of

MACLEAN'S
CANADA'S NATIONAL MAGAZINE

Canadians were always prickly about American claims to have won the Great War. G.A. Drew, *The Truth about the War*, Maclean's, 1928

Colonel C.P. Stacey served Clio as historical officer, official historian, and finally, professor of History at the University of Toronto. No other writer has had more influence on how Canadians view their nation's military history. LAC, PA-115818

FACING PAGE, BOTTOM, LEFT TO RIGHT

Captain W.E.C. Harrison, professor of History at Queen's University and head of the field Historical Section. He cynically remarked that the "main problem of the historical officer was to correlate three sets of lies, those of the unit, those of brigade and those of the division." *CWM, George Metcalf Archival Collection, 20020099-004*

Colonel G.W.L. Nicholson, Canada's most prolific historian of the Great War. LAC, PA114438

Dr. Gilbert Tucker, naval historian, on board HMCS *Assiniboine*, after having returned from sinking a German U-boat. LAC, PA-166776

The Historical Section in Italy, near Campobasso, October 1943. Historical officers Guy Sesia, left, and Sam Hughes, centre, with war artist Charles Comfort in the right foreground, document the war from the sharp end. *CWM, George Metcalf Archival Collection, 19760583-048*

The historians of the short-staffed overseas Naval Historical Section were not able to sail on convoys, and therefore missed much of the terror of the Battle of the Atlantic. LAC, PA134342

The Second World War was a total war, involving all the fighting arms and the millions at home who "backed the attack." The official historians documented the Canadian forces in battle but were not mandated to capture the war experience on the home front, such as this aircraft assembly work. LAC, PA-184469

FACING PAGE, TOP TO BOTTOM

As the army's historical officer, Colonel C.P. Stacey was furious that he had not been informed of the Dieppe raid. After he became official historian, Stacey spent much of his life trying to unravel the raid's complexities. LAC, C-014160

Canadian soldiers involved in fierce urban fighting in Ortona. The field historical officers tried to capture the face of battle but were often forced to gather their information from the rear headquarters. LAC, PA114482

The historical sections of the three services supported the official war art programs. *Second from left,* RCAF historical officer Kenneth Conn is seated next to war artist A.Y. Jackson, *centre. CWM, George Metcalf Archival Collection, 19840128-011*

Canadian troops landing at Juno Beach on D-Day. Among them, historical officer Captain J.R. Martin recorded his experiences for the future official history. LAC, PA122765

The Second World War bomber campaign still had the power to incite strong feelings among veterans decades after the end of the war. DND, PL-32846

As this unconscionable delay was beginning to verge on the ridiculous, Stacey turned his attention to writing an article on the Permanent Joint Board of Defence (PJBD), the Canadian-American board that had been struck during the war to coordinate hemispheric defence. However, since the board was an ongoing organization that dealt with ongoing security issues, Stacey's work was viewed with real suspicion. In February 1954 Stacey circulated the article to his superiors, but found that all avoided "committing themselves on paper" as to whether it could be published or not. It went all the way to Foulkes, now chairman of the chiefs of staff (a position established in 1951 to oversee all three services), and the Privy Council Office. It was there among this powerful group of mandarins who advised the prime minister that Stacey received the strongest objection, primarily towards his direct references to Cabinet War Committee records and wartime policy decisions. Having already dealt with the overly cautious, almost paranoid public servants on the same issues in his official histories, Stacey had not actually referred to any of the individual members of the PJDB, but he had felt it necessary to refer to the dates that key decisions were made. The Privy Council Office objected and wanted no references other than the "'Canadian Government' had made decisions," with no indication of what decisions were made, who made them, and when.⁹² This was exceedingly frustrating for Stacey, and he used his well-established contacts to break this culture of secrecy. Both his official history and now this article had been delayed, first by politicians and later by civil servants; the latter, to borrow loosely from Churchill, neither civil nor servants. The matter was eventually brought before Secretary of State for External Affairs Lester B. Pearson, who raised the matter in Cabinet in March 1954. As Stacey rightly noted in his personal diary, if the question of references was cleared up at that level, it would set a "helpful precedent for the Official History."⁹³ Further delays and debates among the most senior ministers shed some light on the perceived contentions of the project, and a week later Stacey was told he could publish the article; however, he could make no mention of specific decisions or even of the Canadian War Committee itself, which had been mentioned in the article. This, it must be pointed out, was almost a decade after the War Committee had disbanded after the coming of peace. It was a disappointing decision for Stacey, not because he cared so much about the article, but because it was very clear that it would be a battle to have the official histories passed by Cabinet.⁹⁴ Canadian civil servants, and politicians for that matter, Stacey complained, "believed in secrecy for secrecy's sake."⁹⁵

Matters became more complicated in July 1954 when Claxton resigned from Cabinet to work as an executive in the private sector. He was replaced by his former associate minister, Ralph Campney, also a Great War veteran, but no more anxious to authorize the official history. And so the historians continued to wait, finding that nervous, new politicians were just as bad as the nervous, old ones.

Both Claxton and Campney worried about Stacey's handling of controversial events and hoped, it would appear, that this tiresome issue of an official history would just fade away. That was unlikely with the time and effort already devoted to the project. After further pressure by Stacey in July 1954, senior officers informed him that Campney and Claxton would divide the histories between them and pass judgment. When three months later nothing had occurred, Stacey again went to the CGS and was advised by Simonds to talk directly to Campney's executive assistant. This he did, charging that the histories, of which there were now three with the addition of the medical history, had sat with the minister for over fifteen months, and that the matter was becoming "extremely embarrassing" to him. Stacey made no threats, but he considered quitting and going public with the scandal.[96]

Simonds realized the serious ramifications of losing Stacey and a failure to authorize the history would have brought scorn on the government and the army. In a long meeting with Campney on 20 December 1954, Simonds was able to extract the authorization that the volumes could be typeset, and therefore published when Campney and Stacey had a chance to meet. That did not happen for another five months, however, and Stacey was again forced to convince Simonds, who remained sympathetic, that the delay would be blamed on the official historian and unless something was done very soon he would resign.[97] Simonds was finally able to secure a meeting for Stacey with the minister.

Campney and Stacey talked in April 1955 and again the next month. While the minister thought the history of the war was "excellent," he could not "see how such an account could be published under the name of a serving officer."[98] Campney clearly had no idea what an official history was for, and Stacey rightly noted that for "these fundamental policy questions [to] be raised at such a late date is very disturbing."[99] Desperate to find a way through the impasse, though, Stacey and Campney met again in July, and the historian explained the nature of official histories: "The underlying considerations leading to the production of official histories are the need of governments for a record of experience for future guidance, and the assumed right of the public, after the lapse of a reasonable period of time, to authentic accounts of great national crises as revealed in the official records." Since the records could not be made available to unofficial researchers, and with the task of writing the history of a war so enormous that it could not be undertaken by a single individual, the result was that the government must, suggested the official historian in a memorandum, "undertake the work." Stacey went on:

> The basic problem in planning an official history is that of combining provision for the requirements of security and the general interests of government with that degree of objectivity in presentation which alone can protect such histories against the charges of "dishonesty" which are frequently levelled at them. The usual expedient is to appoint, to take charge of the work, a qualified historian who has the confidence of the

government and whose reputation will at the same time serve in the eyes of the public (and particularly of the country's historians, who are the group most directly interested) as a guarantee that the history will be an honest presentation of the facts.[100]

Stacey persuaded Campney to go to his Cabinet colleagues and get authorization for the histories, since not to publish them – especially after they were already written – would leave the government open to charges of obstruction, which would be far more damaging than any of the harshest judgments in the history.

As part of this struggle to convince the minister, Stacey had also appealed the earlier decision on his PJBD article to not quote government decisions. Simonds again supported Stacey and, on advice from his official historian, reminded Campney that Claxton had allowed the quoting of documents in *The Canadian Army*, and that A.D.P. Heeney, the long-serving clerk of the Privy Council, had published an article on a similar topic in 1946. To be disallowed from providing full citations or even reference to individual decisions would be a monumental step backwards for the first and second volumes of the official history, and would appear to the public that the government was withholding the truth and being unduly secretive.[101] This was undeniable and Campney seemed to accept the argument for he went to the Cabinet on 16 August 1955, and it was decided that the histories would be published containing full citations. Campney argued forcefully in the meeting that Stacey could be trusted, and that official histories should not be tampered with by the government.[102]

After more than two years of delay, the first and second volume and the medical histories went to the printers. For those who question Stacey's method of writing careful history based on a close reading of the records, it is worth remembering that anything else would probably not have been accepted by the government. The civil servants and Liberal politicians with their culture of secrecy and desire to wait out all potential conflicts were looking for almost any justification to block the histories. As Stacey recounted later in his life, the Liberal government of the day felt that an official history was a "menace rather than ... something to be desired."[103]

AS WITH THE CANADIAN ARMY, reviewers heaped praise on the histories, but they were also deeply interested in the controversies of the war: Dieppe and Hong Kong in the first volume and the removal of General Burns in the second volume.

In the *Six Years of War: The Army in Canada, Britain and the Pacific* (1955), Stacey claimed that there was still a grave difficulty in reconstructing the events of Hong Kong due to a lack of records, or records that were created months or years afterwards.[104] The Canadian soldier had not failed in combat, wrote Stacey, and supported by Japanese reports he concluded that the men of C Force had fought with distinction as they slowed and impeded the enemy advance.[105] Privately, however, Stacey noted that "from this international point of view, and with an eye to the political, personal and regimental aspects, it seems out of the question to *publish* an absolutely frank discussion of what took place at Hong Kong." Stacey finished by observing that there was "of course no doubt that the two Canadian battalions sent to Hong Kong were unfit for battle in December 1941."[106] He might have also mentioned that the same was true for every other Canadian or British battalion. Nonetheless, Stacey had resisted classifying the Canadians as untrained, since it did not reflect well on the unit or those senior military officers and politicians who sent them to Hong Kong.

But Stacey's analysis went beyond questioning Canadian operations and effectiveness. While the official historian did not condemn the British commander, General C.M. Maltby, for his control of the battle, he pointed out that he had prepared weak defensive lines and had employed the Canadian battalions poorly, since these were not trained for their role as a counterattacking force.[107] In the end, without blaming any senior officers or politicians for the actual deployment of troops to this theatre of combat, although his mentor, Crerar, was as responsible as any for the government's actions, Stacey rightly noted that the "decision to reinforce Hong Kong was a mistake."[108] It was a mistake that cost 557 Canadian lives and untold horrors for the close to 1,500 more who were starved, beaten, and tortured in Japanese prisoner of war camps. The reputation of nations, generals, and fighting units were all at stake at Hong Kong: Stacey offered only measured judgments when he could have been far more damning of the British and Canadian forces in battle. Constrained by the nature of contemporary history and the war of reputations, it is not surprising that Stacey felt he could not have drawn harsher conclusions, but his volume must be assessed against this contextual backdrop.

Dieppe was an equally contentious matter for Canadian soldiers and civilians, and here, too, Stacey was hampered by a lack of records, especially in determining the convoluted reasons behind the raid. Using German documents to better understand the operation, Stacey declared that the defenders did not have intelligence relating to the Allied landing, one of the many lingering controversies. The failure was instead put on the Allied planners who were hindered by inter-service rivalries and failed to orchestrate enough firepower to suppress German defences. Stacey was undoubtedly right here, but at the same time he still believed that Dieppe had provided valuable lessons for the D-Day landings, and was not willing to conclude, as at least a few Canadian generals had suggested, that Dieppe was a useless waste that had contributed little to the overall war effort. While the lessons of Dieppe – the need for overwhelming firepower, permanent naval assault forces to support the infantry, closer inter-service cooperation, dedicated air support, careful planning and goals, and the desirability of attacking around rather than through areas of resistance – would have been identified and processed through other campaigns over the next two years, especially with American amphibious assault landings in the Pacific, it is also true that painful lessons are always the most sobering and memorable.[109] With nearly twenty years of study devoted to Dieppe, Stacey wisely noted that after sitting in the United Kingdom for three years, no one could have held the Canadians back from the raid, but he also clearly pointed out that the Canadians should never have been asked to carry out the operation.[110]

G.W.L. Nicholson's *The Canadians in Italy, 1943-45* (1956), the official history of the Sicily and Italian campaigns, was eclipsed by Stacey's history, which was generally reviewed at the same time and attracted the attention of those more interested in Hong Kong and Dieppe.[111] An unfortunate review by Bill Bates of the Canadian Press had been picked up by a number of the newspapers nationwide, and while it lauded Nicholson's history, it also played up the difficulties between Burns and his superior British general, Sir Oliver Leese, including the former's firing. Although at least one reviewer for the *Kingston Whig Standard* reminded his readers that an actual examination of the chapter revealed an event not nearly as sensational as Bates suggested, a small fervour erupted over this clash of generals.[112] The intense and brutal fighting of Canadian soldiers attacking over the most difficult of terrain against a desperate and dug-in enemy was lost among a battle of reputations between Leese and Burns. Nonetheless, the history remained a model of its sort. With Hong Kong, Dieppe, and Burns's dismissal presented to the public, the official historians seemed to have laid bare the most controversial aspects of the war, although there was much that still needed to be unearthed from the nation's archives.

Not only were the official histories held up as works of integrity, but they were also seen as significant additions to the very nature of Canadian history in the twentieth century. One editor of a small newspaper opined that the official histories were a "distinct contribution to Canadian nationhood."[113] The editor, it would appear, was caught up in the moment, but even American historian Forrest C. Pogue, while offering a more measured response, noted that with the official histories, Canada's role in the war would no longer be obscured by the exploits of the British and American forces.[114] Across the Atlantic, Michael Howard praised both histories for drawing on German sources "available only to official historians," and he recommended these works, given Stacey and Nicholson's ability to distill complex strategic issues, as essential reading for all Second World War scholars. Furthermore, Stacey's masterful ability to make training, administration, and supply interesting was unique in the annals of military writing: "It is hard to recall any other official history which even attempts so forbidding a task."[115] While it is almost impossible to gauge the impact of the histories on the general public, the sales were astonishing; by 1960 the two volumes had sold over 25,000 copies.[116]

The official histories, it was clear from reviewers, were much anticipated and lauded for their impartial handling of difficult operations. While the writing of contemporary events was trying in all circumstances, the official historians struggled to provide a balanced view of the most difficult issues, and had to fight against their allies and political masters to view records and publish their findings. Even the soldiers tried to influence the historians by presenting one version of history or another. While guarded in some respects, these authentic official histories brought recognition and repute to the army, both within the three services in Canada and among its allies around the world. The army official historians had rescued the deeds of the Canadian soldier from the dustbin of history.

F.H. Hitchins had argued in 1946 that an official history would do the same for the RCAF, and he surely would have grimaced when he read a 1956 letter of congratulation from Air Marshal C.R. Slemon to the chief of the general staff, Lieutenant General H.D. Graham: "I must congratulate the Canadian Army on the excellent way in which it has handled and is producing a worthwhile and interesting history of its Second World War efforts. You people have done exceptionally well in this matter whereas we, the RCAF, in my opinion have failed. For this, I am afraid that I must personally accept a fair share of the blame in that I didn't fight as hard as I should have for adequate support of the RCAF Historical Section. Obviously, your historical people have had the support they deserve for their important task."[117]

Hitchins had indeed received little support from the RCAF, but he had remained busy. Between 1947 and 1949 the RCAF official historian had single-handedly prepared full-length historical narratives (50-150 pages each) on thirteen squadrons and another fifteen briefer squadron sketches (2-10 pages). Air stations, schools, wings, and depots were also written up in narratives and reports. Hitchins published more than a dozen articles in *The Roundel*, the RCAF's service magazine, and remained an important contributor to keeping the historical memory of the air force from fading. To fulfill necessary record-keeping functions, Hitchins coordinated a number of boards to vet records and ensure that "material of historical value was not destroyed."[118] Much of his time was also spent in answering queries from RCAF units, the Army Historical Section, government departments, and individuals. The prolific Hitchins also published *Among the Few* (1948), the story of Canadian participation in the Battle of Britain, and the following year, the *RCAF Logbook*, a short chronological history of the RCAF. Despite these accomplishments, all this work is now forgotten, just like Duguid's extraneous Great War work, and the gap in the nation's air force historiography is noted only when one speaks of the early RCAF official history program.[119]

IN AUGUST 1955, just as the positive reviews of the official histories were hitting newspapers, Stacey read through a draft copy of Farley Mowat's *The Regiment* (1955), a hybrid memoir and regimental history of the Hastings and Prince Edward Regiment. "This book is full of low-level prejudices," remarked Stacey, "but I am sure we cannot take any but unofficial action except on security grounds."[120] The book was deeply emotional and focused on the experience of battle. "The result is not a history in the accepted sense of the word," wrote Mowat, "since I have made no great attempt to evaluate the past through the cold and retrospective eye of the historian. I have chosen instead to concern myself primarily with the living understanding that fighting men had of events that were yet in being; and with the emotions which belonged to those men in the days when war was here – was now."[121] Concentrating on the men in the ranks as much as the officers, Mowat revealed the diseases that ravaged the troops and the ceaseless and sometimes senseless death that claimed the men he knew and loved. He was as forthcoming about the soldiers that displayed uncommon valour as he was about those who feigned sickness or found ways to avoid the mundane tasks of war. "In every battle there comes a moment when the certainty of the commander is shaken, when his doubts become agonizing, and when the weight of responsibility becomes intolerable," wrote Mowat in one revealing passage. And from the soldiers' perspective, he wrote authoritatively, "Those who are constantly under fire can armour themselves with apathy. But those who must come and go, knowing a steady sequence of relief, followed by exposure to new terror, those are the ones who pay the greatest price."[122] This, indeed, was very different history from that of Stacey, Nicholson, Duguid, and Tucker. There were others, too, who refrained from following the unemotional, archives-based narratives of the official historians.

Journalism is said to be history's first draft. Peter Simonds, the brother of General Guy Simonds, along with wartime correspondent Ross Munro wrote easily digestible, journalistic histories in the immediate postwar years. Simonds's *Maple Leaf Up, Maple Leaf Down* (1946) harkened back to the writing of the Great War, and there was much space devoted to the Canadian "shock trooper," men of "rugged individuality" who "wanted to fight." Munro's account, *Gauntlet to Overlord* (1946), is the better remembered of the two and offered equally engaging text as he followed the Canadian Army through its bitter campaigns. Both were excellent examples of war journalists writing gripping history that was supplemented by first-hand observations and interviews but not archival records.[123]

In 1946 Dick Malone, a talented journalist, staff officer, aid to General Montgomery, and editor of the soldier-run newspaper *The Maple Leaf*, published his memoirs. Episodic and impressionistic, his book nonetheless had a wonderful "tell-all" quality about it. Malone claimed to write the memoir to "help fill in a few of the gaps in the official record." And of course he did. More troubling for Stacey, though, was that Malone called into question the impartiality of the forthcoming official histories. Malone revealed that during the war, official draft chapters had circulated and "occasionally" these drafts "might be returned with marginal notes such as, 'suggest this be deleted as it places so-and-so in a rather bad light.'"[124]

Malone did not understand the nature of the narratives circulated to officers to augment the record and whose comments, if overly negative for no other reason than to obfuscate the truth, could be ignored; but the title of his memoir, *Missing from the Record* (1946), was provocative and suggested that the work would describe history too controversial for the official publications.

Malone noted that he "may have been too closely associated with certain events to see them in proper balance," but he nonetheless recounted in his gossipy prose much that was unknown to civilians.[125] He reported the peculiarities of Montgomery through a string of amusing anecdotes, and also revealed the British high command's growing loss of confidence in McNaughton, the disastrous Spartan training exercises in 1943 that had sealed the Canadian general's fate, and his eventual dismissal.[126] Crerar fared no better, and a number of his command errors and character flaws were exposed. All of this was, quite frankly, far more satisfying to read than Stacey's guarded prose, but at the same time no one would confuse it with history, as there were no dates, chronology, or consideration of a balanced account. Malone had his favourites and also those whom, as he observed from the wings, he found lacking proper command qualities. But Malone's book had forced Stacey to confront McNaughton's dismissal in more detail than the official historian had initially planned. It also gave him justification for tackling additional issues, especially the ones that government officials and politicians wished to ignore. Although few of these memoirs had a direct impact on the official histories, they offered a fresh and welcome perspective.

Except for Malone's first-hand account of life at headquarters and the infighting between the generals, there were far fewer memoirs published by the fighting men of the Second World War than had been published after the Great War. The RCAF was the most noticeable in this respect, as it is difficult to find even one full-length memoir until the 1970s.[127] Murray Peden's 1979 classic, *A Thousand Shall Fall*, was the first significant history of the war from a bomber crew member. Peden began to write his memoir in 1970, after an air force reunion impelled him to relive the war. His father had saved every letter he wrote home during his overseas service, and along with his log book and conversations with flying mates, Peden reconstructed the faded past.[128] Yet to wait too long, as many did, was to imperil the chance of ever catching the flights of memory.

The navy fared a little better, and in 1945 William H. Pugsley published *Saints, Devils and Ordinary Seamen*, an insightful book that explored the hardship and bravery of the sailors who were engaged in the desperate, six-year Battle on the Atlantic. Temporarily reverting in rank, he served with the men of the Lower Deck, providing a voice to the voiceless. While Admiral Nelles thought the "project slightly mad," Pugsley provided a glimpse into a world unknown to most Canadians and unrecorded in most of the histories that would be published in the coming decades.[129] Despite this dearth of writing, there were also a number of short memoirs and anecdotes published in the force's service journals after the war: *The Roundel* (RCAF), the *Crow's Nest* (RCN), and the *Canadian Army Journal*.

One can only speculate why there were far fewer memoirs in the initial two decades after the Second World War than in the decades following the Great War. Were the best-remembered antiwar memoirs and novels of the previous war viewed as too negative for the Second World War, which, after the revelations about the Nazi Holocaust, was rightly viewed as a "good war?" Good war or not, the terror and drudgery of battle never changed for the infantry at the sharp end, the bomber crews flying night after night, or the sailors who braved the freezing North Atlantic. If much of memoir writing is cathartic, then perhaps there was less of a desire or need to come to grips with events of the war. That seems an unsatisfactory answer since 42,000 Canadian dead would have still been devastating to communities, families, and individuals across the country. However, there had been less naïveté in 1939, especially since the first war had only been a generation away. Moreover, the postwar disillusion after 1918 had been avoided by the successful Veterans Charter, which had created a "land fit for heroes." Whatever the case, Second World War Canadian veterans did not begin to publish in earnest until the 1980s, about the time when most of them would have retired and had a chance to look back on their lives.

"I hear my generals are selling themselves dearly," quipped Sir Winston Churchill about the flood of memoirs by British generals after the Second World War.[130] That was not true in Canada. The trend from the last war continued, and Canadian generals offered very little for the present or posterity. Crerar had retired after the war and never wrote his memoirs. The other senior generals, McNaughton, Burns, Simonds, Foulkes, and Bert Hoffmeister, were exceedingly busy with new responsibilities and few, it appeared, had the time to capture their memories and experiences on paper. Simonds had begun research for his memoirs in 1947, during a professionally unrewarding period in his life, and he dabbled at the writing over the next two decades. But like so many generals, he was not inclined to long hours at his desk with a pen. Canada's most intelligent, if least charismatic senior commander, Burns, wrote several well-respected histories on the wartime reinforcement crisis and nuclear war, and in 1970 he penned his revealing and honest memoir, *General Mud*.[131] A few others, such as Maurice Pope, George Kitching, and Chris Vokes, published accounts that were useful in providing insight into the history "missing from the record," but these too were only available decades after the war.[132] More important was McNaughton's decision, at the end of a long and illustrious career, to enlist one of Stacey's former historical officers, John Swettenham, an historian at the Canadian War Museum, to write his biography. It was more hagiographical than historical, and perhaps attesting to that, ran to three volumes.[133] McNaughton, it seems, could still inspire men. Despite this, it could be argued that most of the senior commanders must have been content with Stacey and his official history program, or at least they were waiting to see what he would conclude of their wartime experiences.

STACEY EMERGED from the ordeal of the first official volumes with a series that was hailed as among the very best accounts of the Second World War for any country. But he still had one final army history to write, as well as the tri-service policy volume. The third volume had been worked on since the end of the war in one form or another, and dozens of historians had produced useful narratives for Stacey. However, he was still forced to carry out an enormous amount of primary research. Stacey remarked to his old patron Crerar that the "job itself is so complicated because it has to be done right."[134]

The resulting history, *The Victory Campaign: The Operations in Northwest Europe, 1944-1945* (1960), revealed the brilliant and painstaking research by the DHS staff: the movements, from armies down to companies, are tracked almost to the minute.[135] The enemy, too, is pinpointed using their records in order to build up the narrative of operations. At the same time, though, there is a detached nature to the writing as there had been with Stacey's other official histories. While the reader understands the actions involving units and sometimes even the desperate nature of the fighting, passages that attributed the supposedly slow advance off the Normandy beaches to infantry that were "rather too easily satisfied" provide little insight into the experience of battle, the struggle of soldiers dealing with German defences that had largely been untouched by the heavy air and sea bombardment and, strangely, the fact that the Canadian division made the farthest penetration of all Allied divisions on D-Day.[136] While Stacey offered an excellent analysis of senior command decisions with the evidence then available to him, and the operations from divisions to battalions, he was far less capable of portraying the experience of the Canadian soldier in battle.

The Victory Campaign ran into few problems with the politicians, partly because a new Conservative government was in office and the senior wartime generals had all retired from National Defence Headquarters, and partly because time had marched on and potential embarrassments in the early 1950s had seemed to lose their pointedness. However, Stacey still did not feel comfortable revealing the details of McNaughton's removal from command and especially the British loss of confidence in his ability to lead the army. At the last moment, Stacey pulled the material from the history, believing that nothing could be published until McNaughton no longer represented Canada on the international stage.[137]

Like earlier histories, the third volume received positive reviews. One American suggested that Stacey's name alone was "sufficient guarantee of the high standard" of work. Another reviewer applauded the official historian for offering personal observations that went beyond "plodding factual presentations."[138] This, presumably, referred to Stacey's penchant for presenting criticisms rather than soldiers' first-hand accounts, which were scarce throughout the history. Stacey again proved to be a bestselling author, however, and within three months of publication *The Victory Campaign* had sold 6,000 copies.[139]

Former divisional commander Major General Chris Vokes wrote that the book "seems to have caused a bit of a furor, here and there. There will always be people who dislike the truth."[140] The third volume of the Canadian Army trilogy was by far the most critical. Like his earlier works, however, Stacey still felt constrained in what he could write about the senior commanders, almost all of whom were still alive. Crerar, to whom Stacey owed so much, Simonds and Foulkes, both of whom had risen to the post of CGS and fought hard for him in getting the first two volumes published, were all difficult subjects to evaluate. Moreover, Canadians were still willing to embrace the notion of war heroes, and there was no political or societal desire to tear down these distinguished men. Yet all three had occasionally performed poorly during the Northwest Europe campaign. Crerar was never an inspired leader and was probably the weakest Allied Army commander of the war.[141] Foulkes was even less capable than Crerar, and had nearly been fired by Simonds during the Normandy campaign.[142] And Simonds, long regarded as Canada's premier general of the war and the only Canadian who Montgomery believed had an innate understanding of battle, was indeed a gifted and innovative commander, but he could be faulted for operations such as Spring (25 July 1944) and Totalize (8-11 August 1944), which were based on plans that were far too complicated for the combat forces to carry out.[143] As Stacey would later write with regard to more junior officers who had been removed from command during the war, "It seemed undesirable to pillory these officers by reporting these circumstances in public print." And so he tried to include enough insight into all aspects of the operations to meet "the needs of historical honesty without exposing individuals to unnecessary and painful publicity."[144] While he could have condemned Crerar, Simonds, Foulkes, or any other Canadian senior commander for questionable command decisions, he avoided any censure, even the veiled variety. Since Stacey also believed in the pedagogical aspect of his official histories, one can only surmise that he truly thought the high command was not to blame for the occasionally mediocre showing of the Canadian Army. Who was at fault then?

Stacey knew that in several cases the Canadian Army had not achieved its objectives in Normandy, especially in capturing key territory around Caen or closing the Falaise Gap, and he could not gloss over these failures. Following the lead of Simonds, the official historian blamed the junior regimental officers rather than the generals. In an unguarded passage from *The Victory Campaign*, Stacey laid out the final judgment for Normandy: "There still remained ... that proportion of officers who were not fully competent for their appointments, and whose inadequacy appeared in action and sometimes had serious consequences."[145] Stacey had passed draft histories with these conclusions to senior officers before publication, and

Crerar had written to Stacey that he felt this assessment "fairly critical of the leadership of units and formations of the First Canadian Army. However, I believe that the comment is generally fair and in accordance with the evidence provided during that period."[146] One wonders what more junior officers would have thought, but they were not included on the distribution lists.

Yet in the same paragraph in which Stacey condemned some junior officers for their "casual and haphazard" approach to warfare, he also noted that the "vast majority of the rank and file did their unpleasant and perilous jobs with initiative, high courage and steadily increasing skill ... As for their officers, the Canadian regimental officer at his best (and he was very frequently at his best) had no superior."[147] So unlike many historians who have since remarked that Stacey laid the blame at the junior officers' feet, he offered, as he always did, a more nuanced conclusion.

But Stacey did not keep his criticism only to a group of Canadian officers, and he wrote penetrating comments on various units and battles, and even on grand strategy. But in attempting to write cautious history that did not impinge on the allies, Stacey occasionally offered misleading conclusions. At the bloody fighting around Buron and Authie in the days following the D-Day landings, vicious and eventually costly German counterattacks threw back overextended Canadian battle groups. While the Canadians had made the Germans pay for the attack, Stacey noted that they had fought "with courage and spirit but somewhat clumsily."[148] Yet much of the failure of the two Canadian brigades that pushed deep into German lines on D-Day and in the days that followed can be attributed to the open flanks left unguarded by the failure of British divisions, especially the 50th, to keep up. While the Canadian spearhead units were attacked on two open flanks and defeated, Stacey clearly did not feel comfortable enough to criticize the failed British support. It was left to the reader to piece together the details, and many concluded that the Canadians, despite their deep advance, were amateurs who were outfought by German units.

Stacey's writing and personal diaries provide evidence that he was proud of Canada's effort in the two world wars, but he was almost always able to keep those nationalist claims in check. Stacey recognized the danger of official historians sliding into the role of court historians or national hagiographers. He was too good an historian for that, but one wonders if the infamous Balance Sheet assessment in *The Victory Campaign*, in which Canadians were reviewed unfavourably, and other criticisms of the Canadian Army, were a result of Stacey's attempt to straddle that line between his role as official historian and that of academic historian dedicated to finding and presenting the truth as best he could. Stacey knew there were problems with the battlefield performance of the Canadian Army, and quite clearly he seemed incapable of holding the generals to blame. Stacey had served with most of the generals during the war and had been assisted by almost all of them afterwards. Moreover, McNaughton, Crerar, and Simonds were all leaders who exuded strength and charisma, and it was not easy for Stacey to distance himself from the force of their personalities in order to write dispassionately. Stacey was also witness to many of their plans during the war, all of which were professionally prepared. To Stacey, then, perhaps these men were the professionals that the army should aspire to emulate. If there was failure, it seemed not to come from above but below, with the thin ribbon of junior officers responsible for carrying out the battle plans.

There is, of course, nothing wrong in criticizing the Canadians in battle, and all would agree that in the chaos of war mistakes are made. However, a revealing letter that Stacey penned shortly before his death offers some insight into the issue: "Sometimes I almost regret having written the rather severe comment on Canadian regimental officers. Even if it is sound, I did not anticipate the use that UK and US writers would make of it. I may be wrong, but I don't think any of them has examined their own ops [operations] quite as closely as I examined ours; and they use my stuff as a basis for assuming the superiority of their training and work in the field to ours. Perhaps the Second [British] Army was better trained than the First Canadian Army; but I haven't seen it proved."[149]

All armies had severe setbacks in the Normandy campaign. Some of the strongest criticism was directed towards the slow closing of the Falaise Gap by the Canadians, but it is also true that in the same battle the British and American forces also failed to seize the initiative due to nationalistic squabbles. As S.M. Lett, who had been second in command of the Queen's Own Rifles in Normandy, remarked in disgust after reading Stacey's book in 1960, "All I can say is that he wasn't there trying to close that gap."[150] In the end, it was the Canadians who closed the gap, and they did so with pitifully few forces. Other historians, however, understanding Stacey's measured judgment and his monumental reputation, have taken his findings and amplified them to portray the Canadian Army as poor cousins to the Americans and British. It was not what Stacey would have wanted, nor what he believed.

A reading of *The Victory Campaign* reveals Stacey's profound respect and admiration for the Canadian soldier who was forced to struggle through an attritional death-match with a fanatical enemy. At the same time, Stacey's overall evaluation was that the Germans outfought the Canadians. That may have been the case, although recent scholarship is beginning to question that assumption; however, Stacey certainly might have better attempted to assess the combat efficiency of the Germans and their very real advantages of fighting on the defensive.[151] Instead, Stacey believed that the Allies' brute force, with their overwhelming firepower and command of the air, had bludgeoned the Germans into surrender.[152] Yet for the first six weeks of battle, the Allies never had overwhelming numbers of troops on the ground, and they suffered from a series of problems throughout their campaign, including inferior weapons and a lengthy and tenuous logistical supply line.

Even the much-vaunted effect of tactical airpower did not provide an unfettered advantage, as post-battle investigations indicated that far fewer destroyed German vehicles could be attributed to the air assault. Stacey gave too much credit to the Germans, who indeed fought a tenacious series of defensive battles, but at the same time proved again and again that they, too, were usually stopped cold by Canadian defenders when they counterattacked. In fact, while the Germans had fought desperately, it is also clear that in many parts of the Normandy front, and especially opposite the Canadians, the enemy stacked some of their strongest forces and their best panzer divisions."[153] Stacey did not make this clear enough in his history, and he might well have emphasized the German strength in various sectors as being equal to or even greater than the strength of the Canadian attackers, who were forced to engage on narrow fronts. In fact, four years after *The Victory Campaign* was published, Stacey revealed to one correspondent that he felt the Canadians had higher casualty figures during the Normandy campaign because they "faced more hard fighting."[154] However, he also noted that to prove that postulation one would need to conduct a detailed study of various armies, something that was beyond the reach of his staff until scholarly studies of other Allied forces were published.

The Victory Campaign remains one of the finest operational histories of the Second World War. With time dulling the impact of harsher judgments, Stacey went beyond what other international official historians were willing to write. That Stacey saw the failure at the front line of the battle rather than with the generals in the rear is perhaps understandable due to his close relationship to the generals, but it was obviously a failing in the history. "Objectivity is something that historians are supposed to strive for – but rarely attain," wrote Stacey. "Most historians wear blinders of one sort or another."[155] This is true for all historians, both official and otherwise, and it would take another three decades before Canadian historians would offer a new interpretation for assessing the Canadian Army during the war.

"CANADIAN 'OFFICIAL' HISTORY is largely the story of the Canadian Army," A.M.J. Hyatt wrote in 1966.[156] Indeed that is still true today, even though the RCAF and RCN have finally begun to receive their official histories. Although many of the senior officers of the RCAF and RCN were deeply interested in seeing their service histories capture operational lessons and also share their stories with the Canadian public, they were not fully committed to the process. Despite the appearance of RCAF and RCN official and semi-official histories, neither could be fairly compared to the enduring army series, which had far greater resources and time devoted towards it. Wing Commander Fred Hitchins, Dr. Gilbert Tucker, and Joseph Schull had all produced important histories within exceedingly tight deadlines and amid the ever-present challenge of writing contemporary history; however, both services hoped for and realized the need for more complete official histories. Unfortunately, they would have to wait several decades.

Stacey retired from the army in 1959, the year in which he completed the manuscript for *The Victory Campaign;* he published *Quebec, 1759,* a history of the Battle of the Plains of Abraham, which has remained a classic to this day; and, almost unbelievably, another book of records of the Nile Voyageurs.[157] In fact, from 1945 Stacey published over forty academic articles in Canadian and international journals on aspects as varied as the Seven Years War, the War of 1812, officer development, and the nature of military history.[158] While Stacey was replaced by Nicholson as director of the Historical Section, no one would ever match his brilliance and historical tenacity. But Stacey did not sever his relations with the section. When he started a new career as a professor of history at the University of Toronto, he agreed to work on the last history in the series, the inter-service volume, on his own and with only minimal support from DHS.

Stacey had achieved a significant task in bringing the three army official histories to publication through difficult and trying obstructions from soldiers, politicians, and Canada's allies. At the same time, Stacey redefined the nature of official histories and military history in Canada. His measured judgments earned the respect of his superiors, veterans, and the historical profession. Stacey was no court historian, and his election to presidency of the Canadian Historical Association in 1952 was an indication of his work's impact and the respect he garnered as both a scholar and a champion of historians. As president, he attempted to make the profession more inclusive, setting policies, and embracing regional historians, high school history teachers, and French Canadian academics.[159] Furthermore, Stacey's creation and safeguarding of records as part of his official historian duties had resulted in a legacy for future historians. His desire to promote the study of military history resulted in more liberal access to the defence archives, and is evidence of his willingness to engage in tasks that fell outside the narrow mandate of author. These projects, which were ably balanced to provide operational support for his fellow historians and his department, won Stacey accolades from all who prospered from his diligence and historical output. The "Colonel's" generosity to friends was equalled by his sardonic wit, but as one colleague noted, "He was not to everybody's taste."[160] Stacey pushed his narrators hard, and himself harder; his legacy is nearly without parallel. Perhaps foremost, though, he played an essential role in the canon of Canadian history by bringing legitimacy to the study of military history through his stringent scholarship.

But how are we to judge his work? The army official histories were a model of narrative history, built upon a mass of documents that would have overwhelmed most historians. While Stacey relied heavily on his trained narrators, he kept his finger on the pulse of his section, always coordinating, prodding, and pushing his skilled historians. Afterwards, he took their work and pulled it together, writing and rewriting as he went along. He was a methodical master historian who prided himself on getting the story right, and then getting all the details right as well. While Stacey frequently worked without access to the full war records, and he never saw or even knew about the top-secret Ultra intercepts until they were revealed in 1974, his works are still the foundation for any study of the war and an indication of his success and influence.[161] His constrained writing style was the only one possible for an official historian at the time, but he proved to be a technician of the historical profession in a way that has remained nearly unmatched to this day. In relation to this generation of official historians and their works, American military historian Allan Millett wrote, "One sometimes feels that the rest of us are the historical division's country cousins."[162]

True, perhaps, but the official historians were not without their flaws. "Generals and Historians: the makers of history, and the humble little chaps who merely write it," Stacey remarked in 1960.[163] Having lived through and participated in the war, and having seen the terrible pressure and choices confronting the generals, Stacey well understood the burden of command for these history makers. "We pulled a fair number of punches," reflected Stacey at the end of his career; "not because we were told to do so, but because we felt that there were certain things that it was difficult to say in an official publication. I am particularly conscious of this in connection with personalities." There were no guidelines, and the official historians were forced to work with only their own knowledge and conscience. "By the end of the war," wrote Stacey, "I had a wide acquaintance among the senior officers whom I had to write about, and I am prepared to admit that it is not easy to write pontifical comments about one's friends – especially when one is writing in the agreeable safety of an office in London or Ottawa, and when the subject is the performance of men often running horrible risks and always carrying crushing responsibilities which one never carried oneself."[164] That was a fair reflection on the difficulty of writing contemporary history, and had Stacey written without restraint, like Farley Mowat or Dick Malone, it is likely that he would not have had his work passed by the government of the day, which was highly recalcitrant in releasing any information to the public. Could Stacey have offered more pointed condemnations on some aspects of the war, such as the nature of command and control in the Normandy campaign? Certainly, and he would have probably been supported by the generals, for even when they did not agree with him, as in the case of Simonds, they did not interfere or go above his head, as had been Duguid's misfortune in the 1930s. Yet even if Stacey felt he could not accurately represent the army high command, he could still have left hints in his text about their faults. He never did, and that might be Stacey's greatest failing as an historian.

Stacey's empathy for the soldier in the lower echelons must also be questioned. He had remained a headquarters historian throughout the war, had been friends with staff officers and senior commanders, and had only visited the European battlefields a few times. While he had interviewed soldiers, he never seemed to have developed the same sympathy for the common ranker or the junior officer, as he did for the great men such as Crerar, Simonds, McNaughton, Burns, and Foulkes. If the crushing weight of command was to be reckoned with by historians, then so too must the confusion of battle be accounted for when trying to assess soldiers at the front. Some of the indictments in *The Victory Campaign* clearly demonstrated this lack of empathy. Equally important in shaping his judgment was his appreciation of the German soldier, whom he respected, as did almost all from his generation. There is no doubt that the German defenders were fierce and deadly adversaries, but Stacey should have offered a more nuanced appreciation of the trials faced by the Canadian Army in battle, which was often ably supported by massive firepower from aircraft and artillery. However, this did not always tip the balance in favour of the Canadians. More often it fell to the "poor bloody infantry," as it had in wars of the past, to engage the enemy in fierce close-order combat. And in that role the Canadians often bested their enemy.

The official histories are contested sites of memory and interpretation. At first study they appear impartial and authoritative. With hindsight and subsequent generations building upon their findings, some have suggested that they are flawed works. Somewhere in between lies the process of the historian's work, and an analysis of the struggles of Stacey, Nicholson, Tucker, and before them, Duguid, the history behind the history reveals the contested nature of war writing. The writing of official history always involves the balancing of the "official" and the "history." The two are not incompatible, however. And while the politicians would have always wished that no histories be published and that the records remain under lock and key for decades, Stacey attained that difficult balance that appealed to both the politician and the generals, but also to the veterans, the historical community, and the book-buying public. Stacey's important accomplishments laid the foundation for all subsequent studies of Canada's army in the Second World War. His painstaking attention to detail would also influence the methodology of future air force and naval official historians. At the same time, Stacey provided a "scholarly legitimacy and academic respectability" for the study of military history in Canada that it had never received in the past, and he helped to train most of its practitioners who then went off to teach in Canadian universities.[165] And while writers have spent the last forty years taking paragraphs in the official histories and turning them into articles, dissertations, and books, it is clear that no historian can even begin to contemplate the war without first confronting what was initially written by Canada's Second World War official historians. Despite their few flaws, the official histories must rank with the finest historical works ever produced in this country.

6
Forging the Canon of Canadian World War History, 1960-2000

> *War makes rattling good history; but Peace is poor reading.*
> – Thomas Hardy
>
> *History would be an excellent thing, if only it were true.*
> – Leo Tolstoy

The official historians laid the foundation for the study of the two world wars in Canada. Despite influencing the creation of records and providing a solid basis for postwar study, this contribution was nearly curtailed as they struggled against indifference, cutbacks, interference, and the sheer size of their own monumental tasks. Success was not always achieved, as with Great War historian A.F. Duguid; however, his successor, C.P. Stacey, forged an international reputation on the strength and breadth of his work. Nevertheless, both men and their official peers left a crucial legacy in the area of Canadian military history. From 1915 to 1960, it was the official historians, augmented by only a few others – memoirists, regimental historians, and a handful of journalists – who controlled this burgeoning field.

That control began to loosen by the 1960s. Professors, students, and universities expanded rapidly as the baby-boom generation grew up and won greater influence. At the same time, new historians and scholars examined the two world wars, challenging existing interpretations by using the now-open government archives. Nevertheless, the role of the official historians in driving the study of the two world wars is ongoing, even if it is being met forcefully by the essential work of academic historians who have refined and strengthened the canon of world war history in Canada. By the end of the century, the latter eclipsed the former, but both official history and academic history have formed integral parts in constructing the historical memory of the two world wars.

UNTIL THE 1960s, J.L. Granatstein observed, "the number of academic experts in Canadian foreign and defence policy could be counted on two hands – with fingers to spare."[1] Few academic historians had moved into the field despite the work by the official historians of laying the foundation for the study of the two world wars. The three historical sections had also undergone significant changes. Stacey and Wing Commander Fred Hitchins retired from their historical sections in 1959, and Stacey's successor, G.W.L. Nicholson, left only two years later.

There still remained a couple of veteran Second World War historical officers such as J.M. Hitsman and T.M. Hunter and newer official historians such as D.J. Goodspeed and John Swettenham, but it was a far different section. The navy and air force historical sections were now headed by E.C. Russell and Wing Commander Ralph Manning, respectively; however, neither were accomplished historians, and those units continued to define themselves as support groups for their larger services through the management of records and the answering of inquiries, rather than the writing of official histories.[2] The Royal Canadian Air Force (RCAF) Historical Section grew from two to four historians in the early 1960s, but the eight-volume official history that the section and the service wanted could barely be started, let alone completed, for lack of historians.[3] With more than double the staff of the air force, but still only a third that of the army, the Naval Historical Section published in 1965 two volumes, a history of naval aviation and a history of naval forces in Korea, neither of which was well received by the historical profession. The section also produced a series of excellent narratives and ships' histories, but these remained unavailable to most scholars.[4] Russell's long-standing desire to replace Schull's operational history with an official one based on a close study of archival records, both Allied and Axis, remained a distant hope due to a lack of resources and experienced historians.

The Army Historical Section built on its earlier publishing success and embarked on a lengthier Korean War history. Captain F.R. McGuire had presented a brief history of the Korean conflict in 1956, but Lieutenant Colonel H.F. Wood, a former battalion commander, was ordered to complete a new history in 1961.[5] This was clearly a conflict of interest. Wood had a bias against the first brigade of volunteers who enlisted, portraying them as less disciplined soldiers than the professionals he commanded later in the war. It is now clear, however, that those first units, consisting largely of combat veterans from the Second World War, performed more efficiently than the professionals who followed.[6] Nonetheless, in 1966 this "forgotten war" received its historical due, even if it did not match the world war official histories in length or quality. The army's involvement in the Korean War would rarely be visited again in an academic history until the late 1990s.[7]

Despite these commendable publications, the most important challenge for the Army Historical Section, now called the Directorate Historical Section (DHS), was to meet the still-present demand for a Great War series. To follow that story, however, one must return to the previous decade. Veterans of the Great War had continued to urge successive governments to produce an official history of their war after the cancellation of Duguid's series in 1947. A history, they noted, would be a "benefit to the Canadian people as a whole and we, the old vets, in particular."[8] The government, in June 1956, entrusted a new Great War history to Stacey, hoping that his proven record would avoid the "expensive fiasco" of the previous series.[9]

Although anxious to promote his historical section and the study of the Great War, Stacey was deeply engaged in managing his unit and in writing the third volume in the Second World War series, and so he passed the history to his experienced and efficient deputy director, G.W.L. Nicholson. Nicholson had proven his worth to Stacey by authoring many narratives and the Italian campaign history, but he was no expert on the Great War and had not, of course, served in the Canadian Expeditionary Force (CEF). Moreover, there had been little work done on producing Great War narratives since 1938, and most of the records were now boxed up in the Public Archives. Even Duguid's expert researchers, such as Edwin Pye or J.F. Cummins, had long since retired. Nonetheless, Great War veterans were overjoyed. While the public voice of the veterans, *The Legionary*, still reminded its constituents and politicians that "it seemed utterly incongruous ... that a nation which had played a proud and victorious role in that conflict should have no official history of famous battles fought by her gallant soldiers," it also noted that any history was better than nothing.[10]

With neither the time nor the resources, Duguid's plan for an eight-volume history was not renewed. Instead, the 1948 historical summary would act as a model. Stacey offered a general directive to Nicholson, as he had with the Italian campaign history: the work had to be "attacked energetically," as "many people are going to be watching us." Instead of Duguid's challenge of dealing with reputations, Nicholson's greatest pressure was now time. The history would have to be a "rather broad treatment" that did not go into tactical detail and would have to remain, for the most part, at the brigade level or higher. This was to be an operational history, but some summary of policy, organization, administration, and home front politics, would be necessary. The bitter legacy, for example, of the conscription debates would have to be covered, with Stacey warning that he "need not say that this portion of the book will receive special public attention."[11] Nicholson was instructed to produce a high-level overview, but he would go far beyond that in coming years.

While Nicholson began researching both the CEF and how it fit into larger British operations, he was no doubt aware of the contested official history legacy of the Great War in Britain. The British program had taken thirty-three years to complete, but it consisted of twenty-nine volumes. The year after Duguid's series was cut in 1947, British official historian Sir James Edmonds completed his final book at the age of eighty-seven. Edmonds had supervised the entire process and wrote nearly half the volumes, including three quarters of those that documented the fighting on the Western Front.[12] However, as Edmonds got older and spent more time pondering the past, he saw himself as a protector of reputations and more willing, in the words of Sir Basil Liddell Hart, to "whitewash" the errors of the high command out of "regard for old friends and professional loyalty."[13] Although Edmonds had secretly confided to Liddell Hart that Field Marshal Sir Douglas

Haig was one of the stupidest men he had ever met, by the late 1930s and 1940s, he vigorously defended Haig in print against his rising critics, especially Winston Churchill and David Lloyd George, who had condemned Haig in their bestselling books as an incompetent martinet who sacrificed the youth of the Empire in his "bloodstained stagger to victory."[14] Edmonds even proved willing to blame other generals to save Haig's reputation, and Sir Hubert Gough, the Fifth Army commander, was thrown to the wolves to satisfy the public for the failures of Passchendaele and the British retreat during the March Offensive.[15] Edmonds's steadfast defence of Haig, which, contrary to some critics, still included sustained criticism of his actions over several volumes, brought on decades of denunciation. But recent historiographical trends suggest that the official historian and Haig's later supporter, John Terraine, were not blindly protecting Haig's reputation and that he deserved some credit for having commanded the greatest series of battles ever fought by the British armies. If both Edmonds and Terraine *were* wearing blinkers, they were right in suggesting that if Haig is to be condemned for his unimaginative handling of the war in 1916 and 1917, he deserves credit for the victories of 1918. After all, the field marshal had commanded his armies to victory, despite what some critics would have the public believe.[16]

Whatever the final judgment on Haig, Edmonds was equally damned by critics for his bland, detached, "official" prose. Military theorist and tank advocate J.F.C. Fuller was no fan of most British generals or those who attempted to protect their reputations, and he sniped at Edmonds, "The atmosphere of reality is completely wanting [in his histories]."[17] Several decades later, military historian John Keegan remarked that the Great War British official historians "achieved the remarkable feat of writing an exhaustive account of one of the world's greatest tragedies without the display of any emotion at all."[18] Edmonds's histories were indeed clinical and cautious. They lacked empathy for the men engaged in the fighting because his volumes were intended to explore higher levels of command and operations. With monumental battles spanning dozens of miles and involving tens of thousands of men, there was little space for the experience of combat. However, the equally prolific Charles Bean, the Australian official historian, had taken a different approach by focusing on the individual "Diggers," who made up the Australian and New Zealand Army Corps (ANZAC), to tell his nation's military history. One can condemn Edmonds for his failure to devote space to the "poor bloody infantry," but one can also realize that he was writing a more sweeping history than either the Australians or the Canadians, who needed only to focus on a handful of infantry divisions. It would have been beneficial to compare Duguid with both Bean and Edmonds, but since the Canadian official historian failed to produce his multi-volume series, there is nothing from which to begin. As Major General H.K. Kippenberger, the senior editor of the multi-volume New Zealand official history series, remarked to Stacey after receiving complimentary copies of Canada's Second World War official histories, their value only increased his "regret that Colonel Duguid frittered away twenty years on that volume and that a dreadful gap has been left in Canada's history."[19] Nicholson was to fill that dreadful gap.

Nicholson began drafting an outline for the monograph and set his small team to work in 1956. Captain F.R. McGuire, Captain J.A. Swettenham, and Lieutenant A.M.J. Hyatt were the primary narrators, and they, with Nicholson, spent months analyzing the archival records at the Public Archives.[20] In attempting to draw what they could from Duguid's decades of research and his enormous number of files, they were disappointed to find that very little had been written on the second volume, which had less than half of its chapters drafted, and almost nothing on the succeeding books.[21] Still, Nicholson condensed Duguid's first volume to form the basis of two chapters.

By late 1957 Nicholson also began to correspond with surviving CEF officers and critical figures such as Lord Beaverbrook, who informed the official historians of his role in England during the war, his support of Sam Hughes, and even of General E.A.H. Alderson's dismissal. While Beaverbrook was less than genuine in recounting some of his underhanded meddling on behalf of Hughes, much of what he presented was new to both Stacey and Nicholson, since while Duguid undoubtedly knew the stories, he had left few paper trails to follow. Equally important for deciphering the contentious civil-military relationship were Sir Robert Borden's papers, which revealed much about the Canadian war effort. Stacey wrote to Beaverbrook in December 1957 that Nicholson and his historians had completed a number of chapters on the operational side of the war, but surprisingly opined that he did "not expect to be able to add a great deal to the story of operations in France, though it will be a good thing to have an account in print based on Canadian official records."[22] This was a serious understatement. Nicholson was in fact establishing for the first time in nearly fifty years the operational history of the CEF based on a close study of the archival sources.

Nicholson toured the battlefields in 1959 and conducted additional research into British records, including Haig's diaries. His historical officers were completing final research into German records, and Swettenham was concluding the contentious chapter on conscription. But Nicholson's team was racing against time. Veterans' reunions continued to receive coverage in newspapers, and it was not uncommon to be reminded: "If the history of the Canadian Corps is not finished in reasonable time, all will be dead before it goes to the publishers."[23]

In 1960 the Treasury Board began to investigate the historical sections, and especially the discrepancies in staff between the army, air force, and navy branches. Professor Stacey, now at the University of Toronto, used all his political contacts with soldiers and politicians to ensure that the army section was not cut, as that would most likely mark the end of the Great War history, which was nearly complete. In corresponding with one minister, Stacey returned to Duguid's "minor national scandal," feeling that there would be "serious criticisms from the Legion and the 1914-18 veterans generally if this second history were shot down by the Government when close to completion." Stacey also believed that "it would be a genuine disaster if Canada were deprived of this last chance of getting a history of her part in the First World War based on her official records."[24] The Army Historical Section was cut – but not substantially – and the Great War history was prepared for publication in 1962.

Nicholson made final revisions in that year and incorporated the comments from surviving veterans. But since he was no longer writing contemporary history, some of the concerns and restraints of the interwar years could be relaxed. For instance, one British official historian, who was reading the history on behalf of his government, suggested that the Canadians might downplay the role of Sam Hughes and his meddling in military affairs. Nicholson declined, believing that the story of the minister had been told many times, and it was not his role to cover up the past.[25] As Nicholson fiddled with the final draft, he was waiting on only one last correspondent: Duguid. But ever consistent with his career, Duguid sent in his notes too late to be incorporated into a finished text that had already gone to the printers.[26] The question remained as to how much credit he should receive publicly. Stacey argued strongly that Duguid had "wasted years of time and thousands of dollars of public money and produced very little ... Duguid's shortcomings came close to being a national scandal, and as his successor as Director I found them a millstone around my neck for years."[27] These were harsh words with which Nicholson did not agree, remarking instead, "We owe a great debt to [his] contribution." Although Duguid had written little, his research files were extensive, and the final version of the preface contained a generous reference to his work and that of his section.

Nicholson's *Canadian Expeditionary Force* (1962) was well received by the critics. British military historian Cyril Falls wrote that it rightly proved that the "Canadian Corps was the best in the best army in the world" and was "good-mannered" enough not to be "glib at British divisions which did not keep up." Other reviewers believed that Canada had finally paid homage to its Great War veterans. The history did that, but Reginald Roy, a former Canadian official historian and professor at the University of Victoria, remarked that it was also "carefully written for fear of giving offence."[28]

Canada's Great War history was indeed cautious, but it was not bland. In summing up the Somme, Nicholson did not mince words. He tried to come to grips with the casualty figures, which were notoriously hard to quantify since both sides used different methods (the Germans, for instance, did not include minor wounds), and posited that the Somme ultimately dealt a devastating and unrecoverable blow to the German Army. Nonetheless, "after all this has been said in vindication of

Haig's achievements at the Somme, we cannot close our eyes to the horror of mass butchery to which the C.-in-C.'s tactics had condemned the troops under his command."[29] Nicholson had written an operational history, but he had taken pains to situate the Canadian story within the larger war context. Furthermore, while Stacey had instructed him to keep the narrative to the level of brigades and divisions, Nicholson expertly folded the operational history of battalions, companies, and on occasion, individual Canadians into the more sweeping storyline. Even the home front was examined in a number of chapters with some space devoted, in accordance with Stacey's orders, to the conscription crisis and the contentious 1917 federal election. Once again and with rare exceptions, the experience of the common soldier went unrecorded, with readers learning little about how soldiers endured the trials of the trenches; questions of discipline, morale, culture, and a host of other important issues were ignored in the short history. But Nicholson had also avoided any impression that inherent racial characteristics had produced elite Canadian soldiers; he allowed notions of leadership, training, tactics, and organization to speak to the Canadian success as a fighting force. Following Duguid's lead, Nicholson left Beaverbrook's romantic history in the past where it belonged.

Yet perhaps Nicholson's greatest accomplishment was condensing the war effort of the Canadian Expeditionary Force into a single volume of 600 pages. It was not perfect, but it was a start. One Australian historian has noted that the "dead-hand of the official histories" had for many years controlled and constrained analysis of the Australian Great War experience.[30] It was the exact opposite in Canada, with barely a finger to point the way along the ever-fading path of inquiry. After nearly fifty years, then, Nicholson's *Canadian Expeditionary Force* finally provided a foundational history that allowed other historians to explore more fully the Canadian war effort.

DESPITE NICHOLSON's significant accomplishment in preparing the official history, it followed a traditional view of the war for the most part. Canada had played an essential role in the British Expeditionary Force (BEF) as its Corps matured on the harsh Western Front. Even conscription, among the most volatile events in Canadian history, was handled deftly and judiciously, as those scars were still not fully healed. But as Nicholson and his team had begun to research and write their volume, a new wave of Great War histories would soon change how the war was conceptualized and remembered.

Leon Wolff, an officer in the United States Army, wrote *In Flanders Fields* (1959), the first salvo in a new battle of the ongoing war of reputations. While his history broke no new ground with archival research and in fact relied heavily on published sources, it offered a harsh interpretation of the war. Wolff used the Passchendaele campaign in late 1917 as an example of the Great War's futile nature. Amid the callous slaughter, Wolff documented the crushing horror of conflict for the common soldier. Seemingly abandoned to a muddy death by generals who did not know any better or did not care, he contended that the campaign, and perhaps the entire war, was a crime committed against the *frontsoldaten*. Wolff even offered a poignant, but probably apocryphal story of a senior British staff officer who visited the front and broke down into tears after viewing the muddy wasteland where he had ordered his soldiers to fight while he rested blissfully unaware miles behind the lines. The message was clear: uncaring British generals were homicidally culpable for sending off the best and brightest to be slaughtered by machine guns as they struggled forward through waist-deep mud and uncut barbed wire. "We used to wonder in the trenches whether the real dirt on our bugbears, the generals and the politicians, would ever come out while we were still alive," wrote one of the most erudite of the war's veterans, Robert Graves. "It seemed improbable, and when the guns stopped, the church bells rang, and the bugbears were exalted to heaven, it seemed positively impossible. Yet here is a shocking shovelful of dirt at last, presented to us with excellent documentation and as little display of passion as a generous nature can achieve in the circumstances."[31] A seemingly dispassionate historian, as opposed to the memoirists or poets, was now taking aim at the leaders of the Allied, and especially British, war effort.

Wolff's history was followed two years later by Alan Clark's *The Donkeys* (1961), which attacked the same senior British generals as uncaring, vain old men who could not understand modern war and therefore killed off soldiers in futile and unending attacks. Building on these antiwar histories, the most popular account of the Great War, A.J.P. Taylor's *The First World War: An Illustrated History* (1963), would sell more than a quarter of a million copies by the end of the century.[32] Accompanying the poignant images, the text noted, for instance, that "Third Ypres [Passchendaele] was the blindest slaughter of a blind war." These histories, when combined with irreverent, anti-authoritarian productions such as *Oh, What a Lovely War!* which debuted on stage in 1963 and was later made into a film, shaped the popular memory of the war as a disaster of monumental proportions that was perpetrated by ossified, incompetent generals on an innocent generation. There was a rejuvenation of interest in the Great War in the 1960s, but it was a far different war from what Duguid or Nicholson had portrayed in their official histories.

Long before, of course, a literature of disillusionment in the 1920s had emanated from the able pens of the war poets and fiction writers. That was the history of the individual, which proved far more evocative and authentic than that of the first generation of historians who documented the collective experience. At the same time, by making the war personal through the writing of memoirs and novels, these "historians of their own experiences" reduced the very nature of the war to the personal.[33] Issues such as the balance of power in Europe, the protection of Belgian neutrality, which drove Great Britain and Canada to war, or common bonds of culture and blood all paled in comparison to a moving account of a poor Tommy who just watched his best mate get killed, his brains sprayed on the trench wall. How could war be viewed as anything else but a senseless slaughter?[34] Despite the poignant prose of memoirists, these were not and cannot be accepted as the only narratives relating to the war. Yet these antiwar writers achieved a lasting legacy because they were adopted by another generation – one from the 1960s – and their deft narratives became literary memorials to the fallen and to the futility of war.

The memory of the Great War became a conflict reimagined and reconstructed. A new generation had returned to the war in the 1960s, which was a time of turbulence, change, and anti-authority. In addition, a more militant and idealistic youth culture had emerged. Most things military were viewed with suspicion, or worse, seen as immoral by a large number of liberal-minded individuals living under the threat of thermonuclear warfare. The baby-boom youth that was coming of age during the decade was particularly strident. Events such as the 1962 Cuban Missile Crisis had brought the superpowers to the brink of planet-killing war. Only a couple of years later, with the Americans sending military personnel to Vietnam, it appeared that the Great War, which was in its fiftieth anniversary, would be an important symbol for the utter wastefulness and futility of war. The Great War had been a mistake or, worse, a cruel trick played on a hapless and trusting generation, or so it seemed fifty years later. It had meant nothing and achieved nothing: there was no Hitler to defeat, no Pearl Harbor to avenge, no Churchillian words to rally the nation – only nine million battlefield dead and a century of unfettered slaughter ushered in its wake. The new antiwar histories did not at first feed off the energy of the 1960s, as they were conceived and written before that, but they helped to fuel this discontent later in the decade. The antipathy towards war meant indiscriminately protesting all war, whether Vietnam or the 1914-18 conflict.

Against this backdrop of change and growing antiwar sentiment in Canada, as in Great Britain, there was a revival in the study of the Great War. The fiftieth anniversary also coincided with Canada's centennial celebrations. With veterans now retired and reflecting on their own past, as well as conscious that their companions were dying in increasing numbers, there was a new desire to explore Canada's part in the Great War.

With bestselling British histories and a renewed interest in presenting the war in popular culture – especially the widely viewed twenty-six-part British Broadcasting Corporation (BBC) series, *The Great War* (1964), Canadians, not just historians, began to take notice.[35] The Canadian Broadcasting Company (CBC) responded to this interest with a major, multi-part radio series on the Great War, *Flanders' Fields* (1964), which was based largely on 600 interviews with veterans. At the time this series was the largest "tape recording and editing assignment ever handled by the Corporation." The "human side of the conflict," as expressed through first-hand accounts by old veterans formed the core of the programs, providing an immediacy that could not be grasped through histories such as the *Canadian*

Expeditionary Force.[36] And while the 1964 CBC program provided an assortment of shocking stories relating to trench warfare and the terrible attrition of men, the sense of futility from recent British war historians was not evident. Rather these were stories of "sacrifice and endurance and an indomitable cheerfulness; of hardship and of victory; of trust in their comrades and pride in their Corps and their country."[37] For Canada, the Great War was still a coming-of-age event; it was a narrative about a colony that had become a proud nation by enduring tremendous hardship. This was the kind of story that would not be easily replaced with one that emphasized the futility of war. Additionally, the fiftieth anniversary of Vimy Ridge coincided with the centennial of Confederation in 1967. This was a time of cultural renewal and national celebration. Nationalists, mythmakers, and historians linked the Great War to larger nation-building myths, while overlooking the fact that the extremity of the war effort nearly tore the country apart along linguistic, cultural, and regional lines. The horrible losses were indeed nearly unthinkable, but the brilliant record of the Canadian Corps and the progression from colony to nation helped to balance the staggering casualty lists. With many veterans hardly receptive to another generation using their collective sacrifice to question all war, most of the new Canadian histories, such as the CBC series, offered more positive appreciations than their British counterparts.

With Nicholson's work providing the essential overview, a number of histories were published between 1965 and 1967.[38] John Swettenham's *To Seize the Victory* (1965) was the best. He incorporated the knowledge he garnered as one of Nicholson's narrators in addition to extensive groundbreaking work by other narrators such as A.M.J. Hyatt, who had examined the newly available Sir Arthur Currie papers, to present an excellent overview history. In fact, *To Seize the Victory* was another barrage in the Currie-Hughes war of reputations, with Currie as the mistreated hero and Hughes as the meddling, malignant conspirator, whose conflict was set against the backdrop of the CEF's operations. Ex-DHS historians such as D.J. Goodspeed, Herbert Wood, and G.W.L. Nicholson, who remained Canada's most prolific Great War historian, published several additional histories in the 1960s and 1970s.[39] As Herbert Wood noted to one veteran while preparing his history, "I want to make this book something that the Vimy veteran can call his own, by bringing to life those days and making them glow for a new generation."[40] Despite the rising anti-Vietnam War movement in major Canadian cities, there was a new impetus to understand and, in some cases, memorialize Canada's role in the Great War.

While most of these Canadian histories were not, for the most part, based on extensive archival research, they offered new perspectives on the war. The soldiers' war was now revealed, and this time it was accomplished in historical works, rather than in personal memoirs, primarily through the use of first-hand accounts. It would be tempting to link this new-found interest in the soldiers' experience to the rise of the "new social history" in universities, but since these histories were almost written exclusively by soldiers or former official historians, this does not seem plausible. Instead, since these histories were generally for the veterans, it made sense for authors to "speak to them" with their own words and experiences.

Academic history was itself undergoing momentous changes during the decade. Political, economic, biographical, and national historians who had ruled the academic profession since the turn of the century began to be joined in the later 1960s by a younger generation of scholars who were anxious to pose new questions and make new connections based on issues of ethnicity, class, gender, culture, and identity. The practitioners of this "history from below," with its desire to reclaim the many voices of those silenced by the mainstream, began to push out the profession's boundaries, especially with their collective hiring into academia to meet the educational needs of the baby-boom generation. Like political and national history, military history was definitely not associated with these new historical movements. Most of the new academics regarded it as a "marginal enterprise or as a lurid fascination of war-watchers and those who simply want to extol the virtues of the military profession; others dismiss it as the narrow and unexciting hobby of the technical and military buffs."[41] The deepening quagmire and brutality of the Vietnam War provided ammunition for new leftists who accused military historians of being warmongers, providing little more than the "military indoctrination of young minds."[42] With many of the military history courses offered as part of, or in conjunction with, university officer training programs, the accusers were not too far off the mark. As well, the old "drum and trumpet" history that emphasized tradition and glory through brave Loyalists, noble or savage natives, and great heroes such as Wolfe, Montcalm, or Brock did not sit well with critical academic historians. All were themes of early romantic historiography of the previous century, where much Canadian military history found its origins. Seen as didactic and narrative, military history was dismissed as being uncritical and untheoretical, and therefore even more out of step with the march of academic historians. That many of these new historians were also liberal socialist commentators in the media or politics, or involved in the antiwar student movements, also helps to explain the palpable dislike of military history by the end of the 1960s.[43]

Despite the new pressures from the Left, the 1960s represented a curious paradox for Canadian military history. More and more of the official historians, trained in the rigorous work of interrogating archival records and writing narratives, were entering academia than ever before. Reg Roy, Charles Stacey, George Stanley, D.J. Goodspeed, T.M. Hunter, and more recent DHS staff such as Desmond Morton and J.L. Granatstein all moved to academia in the 1950s and 1960s, publishing and offering courses in military history, or showing more sympathy to students who wished to explore military topics in theses. John Swettenham became the historian at the Canadian War Museum where he helped to professionalize that institution and establish a respected military history publishing program.[44] Yet at the same time, military history in the academy was gradually becoming marginalized. So even as the academy had attracted some of the best practitioners, the field was increasingly becoming a sub-discipline, isolated from the mainstream of historical studies as a separate activity to which other historians – and most students of history – seemingly needed to pay little attention.

Despite the backlash from the Vietnam War that seeped into Canadian consciousness and became a combustible force on Canadian university campuses, in 1968 a study commissioned by the Canadian Forces College in Toronto concluded that military historians were no longer a "rare breed in Canada" and that their history was "neither despised nor neglected."[45] That was an overly optimistic assessment, but it was true that a growing number of universities offered instruction in academic military history and the Department of National Defence had, in 1967, endowed a number of university research centres in military history. Still, Ronald Haycock, then a university student, later a professor of history at the Royal Military College of Canada, could remember asking one of his professors "why Canadian military history was not taught at most universities; the answer came back that there simply was not enough of it to talk about."[46]

While there were few histories beyond the official volumes, University of Toronto Professor James Eayrs offered the most significant unofficial military history series in the 1960s, *In Defence of Canada*. It explored Canadian military and foreign affairs history from 1914 to the 1960s. Building on the operational official histories, Eayrs probed the impact of war on Canadian society, as well as strategic and political decisions relating to national security.[47] As a result of his thorough reading of available primary and secondary sources, Eayrs also pushed hard for the declassification of government records since most of the essential documents remained closed. Many declassification issues rested with the departmental historical sections.

With Stacey and Nicholson both having moved on, the three military historical sections went through a difficult period in the early 1960s, and it was clear that the government was looking to integrate them. This had been avoided in 1963 when the RCAF and RCN historians had rallied their service commanders to support their operational roles, but Minister of National Defence Paul Hellyer would not be deterred. In attempting to ease the eventual transition, Stacey was enticed to return in 1965 and coordinate the amalgamation. His managerial expertise, international scholarly reputation, and political savvy (often overlooked because of his awe-inspiring historical record) ensured that the new Directorate of History (DHist) had a relatively problem-free transition. Since 1964, however, the army felt that any future Director of DHist would have to be a civilian because the services had now "exhausted the wartime crop of academics"; it was decided that only a professional historian should head the section in order to ensure the high quality of leadership that Stacey had provided almost continually since 1945.[48] After a year, Stacey picked his successor, S.F. Wise, a RCAF veteran, history professor, and co-author of the acclaimed *Men at Arms* (1956), a work praised by Field Marshal Viscount Montgomery of Alamein as one of only two books he found useful in the preparation of his *A History of Warfare* (1968), which perhaps says a little about the importance of *Men at Arms* and a lot about Montgomery.[49]

With Wise at the helm of DHist in 1966, Stacey briefed him on the difficulties of three independent military cultures coming together, and the clash of personalities between senior historians, especially D.J. Goodspeed (army) and E.C. Russell (navy). Most important, Stacey believed that a RCAF official history series had to be a priority, for "we shall never get this unless it is produced officially."[50] Wise also had to deal with the nagging and ongoing question of access to the defence archives of the nation.

"In the field of historical research of defence records, scholars and journalists are every bit as much in the dark as the custodians of defence records regarding what papers are available to the public and what credentials an investigator must hold," wrote Russell in 1966.[51] Stacey had attempted to provide a liberal access policy to the war archives in the mid-1940s, but this had resulted in only limited use of operational records and had attracted almost no scholars to take up the study of the two world wars. For the most part, access to the records depended on whether one belonged to the club of respected academics, and even then it was mediated. When Wise became director, Stacey, who returned to his professorship at the University of Toronto, suggested "normal Second World War documents" be opened to "respectable people," but "not sensitive Second World War documents or *any* records later" than September 1945.[52] Canadian records were governed by a fifty-year rule, but in reality most government departments held on to their records until a lack of space forced them to transfer the materials to the Public Archives. The essential records of the Department of External Affairs from 1909 to the end of the Second World War, for instance, were only transferred to the Public Archives in 1972.[53]

Dominion Archivist Sir Arthur Doughty had called archives "of all our national assets the most precious."[54] However, access to these national assets for researchers and academics had always been problematic and fraught with bureaucratic hurdles. Even at the DND, the three services followed different policies. The air force section claimed to open all records except personnel files. The navy gave access to all records before 1939, and in the early 1960s had made available a number of Second World War records. The army aimed to follow Stacey's recommendations of opening up records to "reputable journalists and authors," but some researchers continued to be turned down. In 1949 former officer Larry Henderson had attempted to write his memoirs of the Italian campaign, but he had not been allowed to read his unit's War Diaries; and in 1955 a graduate student was denied access to records documenting the role of the Militia in the 1913 Nanaimo strike because it was considered too "controversial." More senior scholars such as James Eayrs, who was definitely a "reputable author," were given access to records of the interwar period, except for intelligence records. When he attempted to delve into defence records for the 1940s onward, however, DHist sent him "a rather blunt negative answer."[55] Eayrs eventually accessed many of the records by using documents gathered as part of personal papers, especially those in the W.L.M. King collection, but his work suffered from serious gaps due to his uneven access to archival records. However, the historical profession was not easily shunted aside, and by the late 1960s the Canadian Historical Association (CHA) pushed for more rapid declassification of defence and foreign affairs records, which had been opened slowly but rather, sneered Eayrs, at the "speed of a heavily tranquilised snail."[56]

The struggle by Canadian historians to access government records had been a long one, and largely a failure. Successive governments were not anxious to open up the documents of their deeds to public scrutiny. But in March 1965 the Treasury Board reduced the fifty-year rule to thirty-five years. It also stipulated that departments should transfer their records to the Public Archives.[57] Few followed the guidelines. Access to government records was being parcelled out gradually during the decade, but it was still considered a privilege rather than a right.

Just two years later, the United Kingdom passed the Public Record Act of 1967, which reduced the fifty-year rule to thirty years, and in 1968 most Great War records were opened. This had already been the case in Canada since the retirement of Duguid in 1947, but few scholars availed themselves of these essential documents. In May 1969 Prime Minister Pierre Trudeau, building on his promise of an open and transparent governance process, reduced restrictions on most records from thirty-five years (many departments were still following the fifty-year rule) to thirty years. A few years later the British opened up significant Second World War strategic records, and Canada followed suit. A 1972 press release from the Office of the Prime Minister announced that Cabinet War Committee records would be opened in exception to the thirty-year rule policy, as "it would clearly be undesirable for the press, the academic community, and other interested parties in Canada not to have equal access to the material of such great historic interest."[58] These essential documents were evidence of Canadian wartime policy decisions, but much of that information had been revealed two years earlier in Stacey's final Second World War official history.

When Stacey retired in 1959 he still had to complete one final volume in the official history series. This most demanding multi-service policy volume could only have been written by Stacey, and the chairman of the chiefs of staff, Charles Foulkes, endorsed Stacey's suggestion that he continue to work on the history from Toronto. Foulkes was also able to ensure that George Pearkes, the new Conservative minister of National Defence would have no responsibility to "vet" the book, as had been Claxton's wont, since that was "really the job of the historian."[59] And so Stacey embarked on his research, which would take him across the three services, into the highest policy records of the government, and through the private papers of significant Canadians.

The former official army historian first had to familiarize himself with both government and policy records. Prime Minister King had given Stacey access to government records in the late 1940s, but when King died in 1950 he had ordered the destruction of his personal diaries. These diaries, spanning several decades, were probably the most important single record ever created by any Canadian. Fortunately, they were saved by King's literary executors and became an essential source for Stacey in understanding the complicated decisions made during the war years. In fact, Stacey found them to be "extraordinary" on all aspects of King's life, as they revealed that the pudgy, uncharismatic leader was interested privately in the occult and "rescuing" prostitutes, and that he possessed a tendency to speak to the dead or his dog just as he was publicly dispatching political opponents and holding the country together during an intense and difficult trial by fire.[60] It is no wonder that Stacey later felt driven to write about King's private life.[61] Stacey's normally cautious style was for once immediately abandoned, and he focused on the secret and sensational life of King that involved séances, sexual repression, and ruthless political ambition. Stacey's work was widely reported on and attracted some condemnation by critics who thought the respected historian had wantonly and unfairly revealed King's foibles, with all the warts magnified and his public contributions over a long and illustrious career minimized. But back in the summer of 1960, Stacey was vigorously researching the records of External Affairs and the Cabinet War Committee to understand the overall Canadian policy of the war.[62] These were the records that, even five years earlier, had caused such consternation among Liberal politicians who feared that Stacey's use or even acknowledgment of their existence might unleash some terrible condemnation of the government.

In addition to Stacey's own research, T.M. Hunter and D.J. Goodspeed were writing narratives, and the naval and air force historians were supplying additional information on issues such as the British Commonwealth Air Training Program (BCATP), Canadianization, and naval discipline. To understand the complicated story of the BCATP, for instance, the official historian used RCAF official historian Fred Hatch's excellent narrative to guide the way. "I consider myself greatly in his debt," wrote Stacey. "I simply did not know the air force detail."[63] Much of what Stacey was examining was new to him, since his expertise was with army history. Furthermore, the machinations in Cabinet all had to be pieced together from records and interviews. He was even finding new aspects to the operational history, such as the terrible losses to Bomber Command during the war – something he was largely unaware of before. He noted that the nearly 10,000 casualties were almost on par with what the Canadian Army suffered in Northwest

Europe, and that "some comment must be made on this in our book."⁶⁴ But one should not confuse Stacey's ability to draw from other historians as mere copying or condensing of information; it was only an historian of Stacey's enormous stature and skill who could have drawn the factual narrative together, understanding complex ideas and how the pieces, countless pieces, fit into the larger story.

Stacey continued at his regular breakneck pace and wrote his history during the academic year and through the summers – vacations, it would seem, were not necessary. He had finished most of the chapters by the mid-1960s. His was a history based on previously closed government and personal archives: for instance, he was able to convince Defence Minister J.L. Ralston's son to give him access to his father's papers. Stacey was not as successful with the widow of Angus Macdonald, the minister of National Defence for Naval Services. Despite the official historian's pleading that "it might be considered unfair to his memory to publish an official history of these events which takes account of Mr. King's records, but not of his," Macdonald's wife refused to grant Stacey access, as she did not want someone picking through "bits and pieces of his papers."⁶⁵ Despite these occasional setbacks, Stacey was comfortable with the evidence he had seen, although he never knew of the Ultra intelligence intercepts, which would not be revealed until 1974. It may seem surprising that none of the senior generals ever revealed the secret of Ultra, although it appears that only Crerar, Simonds, and Foulkes were privy to the secret knowledge. But this is perhaps an indication of the powerful oaths they swore during the war, and which, for the most part, all participants abided by for several decades.⁶⁶ These Ultra intercepts had little impact on the story of Canada's handling of the war effort, however, and even after the revelation of these secret records, Stacey's histories and his sound judgments have not suffered.

Stacey circulated draft chapters among surviving senior officers and politicians in 1967; he received accolades, and some, such as General Maurice Pope, chairman of Canada's Joint Staff Mission in Washington during the war, called it "magnificent."⁶⁷ But the distribution of the history produced another skirmish in the war of reputations. Simonds again pressured Stacey to condemn Crerar for the Dieppe operation. Stacey turned to other generals and admirals for advice, and even went through the Dieppe records again, which he knew better than anyone else in the world at that point in his career, but could find no damning evidence. Although he knew there was much about the disastrous raid that had never been committed to paper, he bravely wrote to Simonds in February 1969 that the "Canadians have a good deal of responsibility for the Dieppe plan ... I do not propose to saddle them with other people's responsibility as well."⁶⁸ After several interviews and letters, Simonds refused to give up, and so Stacey concluded that the general had a personal vendetta against Crerar in his "paranoid pursuit" to stake his claim on history against his despised former commander.⁶⁹ "Personalities," wrote Stacey, cause "serious difficulty for the historian, official or unofficial, particularly when dealing with living people." The "feuds between generals" were among the most difficult to judge, and the historian had to "hold the balance" and "tell the truth as he sees it."[70] It is a credit to Stacey that he did not bend to Simonds, a man of forceful personality, much charisma, and a strong patron of the Historical Section since the first years of the war. Would Stacey have been able to stand his historical ground if he had still been a serving officer?

Arms, Men and Governments was published in 1970 and was radically different from the three previous army histories. Stacey revealed the military policies of Canada during the Second World War and, in his words, "interpreted the word 'military' loosely," so that the history offered much insight into events outside the traditional spectrum of military study.[71] Difficult and divisive issues such as conscription, the naval equipment crisis, Canadianization in the RCAF, and finally the firing of General McNaughton, were all presented to the reader. Accuracy and fairness were watchwords for Stacey, and even if the criticism was restrained at times, it always carried the weight of judgment from the official historian. Richard Preston described the history as "fully documented, packed with detailed information, [and] a masterpiece of readability." He would add that it was a "fitting conclusion" to the Army Historical Section's official history program.[72] Stacey's policy history volume is more than an official history: it is a master work that has stood for three decades and remains one of the most impressive single volumes ever written in Canadian history.

With these official history series, and several pivotal unofficial histories to follow – most notably the two-volume *Canada and the Age of Conflict* (1977, 1981) – historian Michael Bliss was right to suggest that Charles Stacey was Donald Creighton's "successor as dean of Canadian historians."[73] Stacey was a leader in the historical profession, moving easily from military to political to national history. While his method – rigorous research aimed at understanding the complexities of the past by piecing together a multitude of facts – may no longer be held in such high esteem in a profession now steeped in cultural theory, at the height of his career, Stacey was the epitome of the Canadian historian. His final policy volume was not the end of the official histories, but it was the end of the official histories written by contemporaries of the events described. The RCN and RCAF histories that were to follow would have different challenges to overcome.

THE ASSOCIATION OF UNIVERSITIES AND COLLEGES OF CANADA formed a committee headed by T.H.B. Symons in 1975 to conduct a benchmark survey on the state of Canadian studies in Canada, including a look at historical writing and the archival sources that were its foundation. It concluded that much work was needed in the field of military history, as well as in a number of other sub-disciplines such as labour, urban, native, and intellectual history. Indeed, the report noted that while army history was covered in some detail in a number of official monographs, there "had been a tendency to treat naval and air force history as an antiquarian pastime." Echoing Richard Preston's call in 1949 for a new military history that examined the impact of war on societies, Symons also observed: "Many aspects of Canadian military policy between the two world wars and during the Second World War have yet to be investigated by scholars. Detailed case studies have yet to be done on the employment of our armed forces in peacetime and on the influence of the armed forces on national policy in both peace and war ... Francophone aspects of Canadian history deserve much more attention."[74] The Directorate of History was singled out for promoting the study of military history, and it was suggested that more resources be put into the Public Archives of Canada to promote access to military records. As in the past, official histories and the war records were essential in supporting the study of military history.

John Gellner echoed the Symons Report in 1976 when he noted in *Canadian Defence Quarterly*, which was revived in the early 1970s as a journal for military history and strategic thought, that the growth and interest in the study of political-military subjects in universities had "been astonishing," as "not long ago the very word 'war' was taboo."[75] For some, the spectre of nuclear war seemed to negate all military history of the past. What was the point of studying trench warfare if entire armies could be vaporized in seconds? But the threat of Mutual Assured Destruction and the various revolutions or evolutions in warfare did not negate the study of military history, especially with the awareness that conventional warfare was still a viable and rather likely scenario for possible combat in Europe between NATO and Warsaw Pact forces. Amid this renewed interested in military and war studies, the mid-1970s marked a number of important publications in Canada that would add new dimensions to the canon of world war writing.

This also occurred against the background of an increasing international turn towards writing "new military history" in the previous decade. The new military history examined the impact of wars and military institutions on nations, rather than simply operational history, which was occasionally derided as being little more than heroic accounts of "drums and trumpets." Influenced by more mainstream academic methodologies, the new military history also provided greater analysis of the impact of war on political, economic, and social history. British historian John Keegan's groundbreaking study, *The Face of Battle* (1976), offered key insights into examining the nature of combat, forcing historians to reappraise some of the early, cherished myths surrounding the motivations and actions of soldiers in battle.[76] Yet with so many topics unexplored or underexplored in Canadian historiography, in many cases the new military history was not offering fresh interpretations of the past because, for the most part, the topics had never been studied enough to be subject to reinterpretation. While the official histories laid the framework for understanding various army, navy, or air force campaigns in the two world wars, second generation military historians in the 1970s were not yet deeply influenced by this "new military history." Moreover, Stacey had written more than "drum and trumpet" history, and for that matter so too had the regimental historians with their focus on the Canadian soldier; however, the major gap that became evident was in analyzing the impact of the two world wars on Canadian society.

The CEF in battle had received increasing coverage over the last five decades, but few military historians had turned to Canada's response to the war on the home front. There were general overview histories, of course, but only the multi-volume history from 1917 to 1921, *Canada in the Great World War*, and the *Canadian Annual Review* had afforded significant space to what the war had meant to the more than seven million Canadians at home. A more scholarly account by Elizabeth Armstrong, *The Crisis of Quebec* (1937), examined the difficult relationship between Quebec and the rest of Canada during the war, with Armstrong relying on newspapers, published reports, and interviews to craft a very fine history of the conscription crisis.

In the mid-1970s, however, Canadian historians returned to the Great War: John Thompson's *Harvest of War* (1978), Michael Bliss's *A Canadian Millionaire* (1978), and Robert Brown and Ramsay Cook's *Canada, 1896-1921* (1974) were insightful academic works that explored the impact of the war on the West, the munitions industry, and Canada as a whole.[77] While these professors would not call themselves military historians, their books were based on an intense reading of recent scholarship, archival sources, and the personal papers of politicians and ordinary Canadians. J.L. Granatstein and J.M. Hitsman, both former officers who had served under Stacey at the DHS, offered *Broken Promises* (1977), a history of the conscription crises in the two world wars. It was the first full-length monograph to delve into the archives and explore these contentious issues. The Quiet Revolution in Quebec, the Vietnam War, and the flow of draft dodgers into Canada all played a part in shaping interpretations underpinning the history. The historians concluded that conscription had been unnecessary and too costly to the unity of the nation. Interestingly, though, Granatstein, who would continue over the next three decades to write books as quickly as most people read them, re-evaluated his position in later work, culminating in a 2001 reflective article where he concluded that conscription could have played a far greater part in influencing the wars had they gone on longer, as contemporaries suspected at the time. Granatstein acknowledged candidly, "The present shapes our understanding of our past."[78] Evidence does not change over time, only how historians view it.

The Second World War was still too recent to engage many military historians during these years, but oral histories avoided the necessity of digging into the enormous archives of the nation. Building on his earlier bestselling oral history of the Depression, *Ten Lost Years* (1973), Barry Broadfoot published *Six War Years,*

1939-1945 to much acclaim in 1974. His history revealed the personal aspects of war and was appreciated readily by veterans and their families, even if it was, by its very nature, episodic.[79] Yet oral history was also proving a useful tool for those interested in the Great War: veterans were dying in greater numbers, and one final codification of personal history through interviews allowed many fading experiences to be captured. Daphne Read's *The Great War and Canadian Society* (1978) and Gordon Reid's *Poor Bloody Murder* (1980) were two of the best examples. While historian A.J.P. Taylor uncharitably called oral history little more than "old men drooling over their youth ... forget[ting] truth and manufactur[ing] myth," there was more than anecdote and emotion that could be drawn from these personal histories with respect to both the experience of combat and life in Canada.[80] But oral history has to be treated with caution, as even the sharpest memories dull over time, change with numerous retellings, or are subject to other external influences.

Although historical writing about the Second World War was still in its infancy, the tradition of regimental histories continued to provide an impetus for understanding the collective experience of individual regiments while lending insight into the operations of war. These regimental historians were assisted by the DHS, and perhaps more important, many of the official historians or former official historians were entrusted to write these cherished works. Reginald Roy, D.J. Goodspeed, and George Stanley authored histories in the 1960s.[81] Stanley and Roy, for instance, took over previously unfinished manuscripts and brought them to fruition. As was the case after the Great War, it was not easy to find military historians in Canada. Many of the regiments also drew upon earlier regimental historians or veterans such as Kim Beattie, Will Bird, and even A.F. Duguid.[82] While one historian noted, "It had been said that there is nothing so dull for the general reader as a regimental history – unless one has served with the regiment concerned," he also pointed out that there are "literally thousands still living who have passed through its ranks and many thousand more who are friends of the Regiment."[83] These works continued to serve as items of commemoration, tools to strengthen regimental ties, and notable historical monographs. As part of the canon of Second World War writing (although many of the histories often covered a century or more of service), the historians drew not only from regimental sources, including the War Diaries and operational logs, but also from first-hand accounts, diaries, and letters from private archives. These were, then, more than "drum and trumpet" accounts or examples of vainglorious chest thumping over drinks in legion halls.

Yet the most important Second World War contribution of the 1970s came from two historians at the Directorate of History, Brereton Greenhous and W.A.B. Douglas, in *Out of the Shadows* (1977). Greenhous had written a number of narratives for the first volume of S.F. Wise's RCAF official history, which would not be published until 1980, and Lieutenant Commander W.A.B. Douglas had been recruited from the navy to become an official historian. Wise had achieved the difficult task of rebuilding DHist during the late 1960s. With most of the experienced narrators having left, he reinforced the principles of academics as official historians, slowly bringing in new historians and instigating a peer promotion system, which benefited historical researchers throughout the government and kept them from returning to universities. Douglas replaced Goodspeed as senior historian in 1970 and later resigned his commission as a naval officer in order to oversee DHist as director in 1973, when Wise became a professor of history at Carleton University. Wise essentially followed Stacey's footsteps; he was elected president of the CHA in 1973 and recognized as a leader in the historical profession, producing salient scholarly works in the fields of military, intellectual, and early political history.

Douglas continued to support the RCAF official history series that Stacey and Wise had mandated as a priority. At the same time, however, the new director was laying the framework for the study of naval history in Canada, which had drifted listlessly for years. Under Wise and Douglas, civilian official historians such as Brereton Greenhous, Norman Hillmer, William McAndrew, Carl Christie, Owen Cooke, and in the early 1980s, Stephen Harris, Jean-Pièrre Gagnon, Serge Bernier, Roger Sarty, and Marc Milner would bring a renewed vigour to the writing of official histories. All trained as academics rather than soldiers, although some had served in uniform. Under Douglas, DHist became almost a Faculty of Military Studies in Canada, and no university could rival this expertise of military historians. Equally important, although the progress on the official histories was slow, all of these historians contributed scholarly articles, conference papers, and were involved in historical organizations such as the CHA or the Canadian Committee for the Study of the Second World War. The official historians were again driving the profession of academic military history, proving that the field was more than simply soldiers, sailors, and air personnel writing for one another.

The brainchild of Greenhous and Douglas, *Out of the Shadows*, was the first academic unofficial publication of the Second World War that covered all three services. It was written outside of daily "official" work, but based on newly opened official records and the personal papers of servicemen and women as well as politicians. Despite these new sources, the authors noted that when they began to write this overview history, "the amount of historical research that still need[ed] to be done is even greater than we had imagined." The air force and navy had no "adequate histories," and although something had been written on politics and personalities, "the social and intellectual history of this period is a void waiting to be filled." Notwithstanding the deficits in the historiography, the official historians were far less constrained in their judgments, feeling that both the gallant deeds and the errors of war needed to be presented. Take, for example, their view of strategic bombing: many Canadian flyers found themselves "committed to a malevolent, technological, impersonal battle waged primarily against women and children."[84] The Second World War was indeed coming out of the shadows, and this work began to shed some light on a new era of critical, analytical, academic military history.

THE RESURGENCE of academic military history in the 1970s had been heavily influenced by the DND's historical sections, which trained many of the historians who had entered academia. But the 1980s saw a new generation of students and young professors rise through the ranks and delve into the now opened war archives of the nation. The British military historian, John Childs, wrote in the early 1980s, "Until very recently, military history has been looked down upon by the historical profession and regarded as not quite respectable." S.F. Wise was even less optimistic, observing that it was "not easy to teach military history in Canadian universities."[85] The paradox of academic military history was that while the profession was pushing out its bridgehead into academia with more professors teaching courses and more historians publishing academic works, the rise of other academic historians, under the broad rubric of social, gender, ethnicity, class, or labour, were gaining control over university departments and influencing the hiring of similar historians. While the top academic journals such as *Canadian Historical Review* (*CHR*) were still controlled by political-national historians – Robert Bothwell, David Bercuson, J.L. Granatstein, and John English among them – by the late 1980s increasing room was devoted to articles exploring gender, labour, business, and social history.

Despite these changes in academia, A.M.J. Hyatt, in an overview of the profession, was right to note in 1982 that the state of military studies in Canada "could be much worse." Graduate students such as Stephen Harris, Roger Sarty, and Marc Milner had all completed doctoral theses on underexplored aspects of military history – the professionalization of the Canadian forces and officers, coastal defence, and the Royal Canadian Navy during the Second World War, respectively – and all three had become historians at DHist by the early 1980s.[86] There were other dissertations completed on military topics at the masters and doctoral level, but most of these successful candidates turned to life outside academic history. Yet academia still seemed largely uninterested in the burgeoning scholarship in the field. Whining was not the solution, opined Stacey, who insisted instead, "Active research and writing on the part of interested and competent people is the activity most likely to encourage interest in the subject among larger members of scholars."[87] And the directorate remained a sanctuary that allowed for the development of a core of military historians who were instrumental in furthering the field.

"The unofficial historian's debt to the official histories is bound to be great, whether or not he has the candour and the courtesy to admit it," wrote John Connel in 1965.[88] That debt had not changed by the 1980s, and almost every interpretation of the two world wars had come, up to that point, from the official historians. But candour and courtesy are not always the most obvious characteristics of professional historians. A new generation of historians was reworking the interpretations of the foundational official histories through new methodologies and newly unearthed archival sources, and they were not always eager to acknowledge the debts to their predecessors. The challenge of the 1980s was to re-examine and reinterpret the official histories, wrote Kenneth Taylor, a professor at the University of Alberta. Showing little courtesy to historians such as Stacey or Nicholson, Taylor suggested that the official histories were compromised works that had been influenced to suit military superiors and guard reputations. Taylor assumed that the official historians, as serving officers, were obliged to craft histories that did not embarrass the government, the services, or Canadians, and therefore were unable to prevent powerful senior officers from foisting postwar justifications on to them, thus corrupting their works.[89] Richard Preston, a professor of military history at Royal Military College of Canada and later Duke University, attacked Taylor in print for misrepresenting the role of the official historians as well as that of the senior officers, arguing forcefully that the historians were not sycophants attempting only to please their service masters. Their findings "might be open to valid challenge," as all scholarly contributions are, but they "should not be impugned by implication or innuendo." In short, Preston admonished that "all writing on, and all teaching of, Canadian military must refer to" the official histories and Stacey's work specifically.[90] Despite the thrashing, Taylor was partially correct. The official historians had been constrained in what they could write in contemporary histories, especially in regard to personalities or military debacles such as Hong Kong or Dieppe. The "dirty linen" of the forces had not been hung out for all to see, and so it was time for historians to critically reappraise these foundational works, while acknowledging the enormous contributions they represented.

History is constructed in layers – written, reworked, revised, reappraised, added to, and then dismembered, each generation viewing the past in a different way from the next or the last. But without the first foundation of official histories and archival records, it is far more difficult to develop all subsequent analyses of the broader experiences of war. The history of the army in the two world wars continued to prosper from the strong base laid by Stacey and Nicholson, but now the history was being re-examined in a number of first-class works during the 1980s. Desmond Morton published a series of important books that re-evaluated aspects of the two world wars, from a much-needed overview of Canadian military history and the overseas administration of the CEF to the trials and difficulties of Great War veterans reintegrating into Canadian society.[91] Morton and Granatstein also provided excellent surveys of the two world wars, which expertly wove the operational warfare with the home front experience.[92] Both historians could write critically, even if their sympathy was with a generation of Canadians called on to sacrifice all for their nation and the ideals that underpinned it. A.M.J. Hyatt offered a discerning reading of Sir Arthur Currie that focused more on his influence on the CEF rather than providing a standard biography, and Ronald Haycock produced a similar assessment of Sir Sam Hughes. Both were willing to pass judgment when necessary, writing candidly about Currie's lack of charisma or Hughes's unbalanced actions, enormous ego, and interference with CEF operations. And although Charles Stacey had retired and was suffering from severe arthritis, he and archivist Barbara Wilson co-authored *The Half Million* (1987), which built upon Stacey's 1946 monograph *Canadians in England* by presenting a lively history that explored complex social and military issues relating to the half million Canadians stationed in the United Kingdom during the war years.

The navy, too, was finally receiving some academic coverage. For much of the century, it had been a field left to seafaring buffs and veterans. Marc Milner, for instance, remembered mastering the entire body of literature on the Royal Canadian Navy at the time by the end of high school.[93] Yet starting in 1980 with Jim Boutilier's "The RCN in Retrospect," a series of conferences brought together serving officers, veterans, and scholars, and later published these papers in a number of anthologies.[94] These conferences created a new intellectual climate where veterans began to draw out their locked-away personal archival papers and pass them over to the Naval Historical Section. Equally important, the Naval Officers' Association of Canada started an oral history process that captured the wartime experiences of veterans in the multi-volume *Salty Dips* series.[95] It was a good start at reclaiming the past, but by the mid-1980s W.A.B. Douglas tallied the thin score of writing on the navy: five official histories relating to the RCN and Coast Guard, a book of collected essays, a handful of theses, several articles, and less than a dozen additional books had been published in the seventy-four years since the establishment of the RCN.[96]

But that was changing. Marc Milner, an official historian and later a professor of history at the University of New Brunswick, offered an impressive and much-needed re-evaluation of the RCN during the Battle of the Atlantic. With so little written on the RCN, many international scholars viewed the navy's role through the eyes of Captain Donald Macintyre, Royal Navy, who painted a harsh and critical picture in his 1956 memoir *The U-Boat Killer*.[97] In two pivotal books, Milner responded to British critics who had labelled the Canadian navy in the Second World War a failure during the convoy battles to keep open the lifeline to the United Kingdom. Milner indeed acknowledged the problems of the RCN (more merchant ships were lost while the RCN acted as convoy protection than when other nations' navies acted in the same role), but he also examined the technological deficit of Canadian warships and the growing pains of a navy that expanded fifty-fold during the course of the war.[98] Historians Michael Hadley and David Zimmerman broadened the understanding of the navy in the Second World War with their works on the German U-boat threat to Canada and the wartime administrative struggle to equip Canadian ships with the latest technology.[99] Meanwhile, Douglas continued his significant work in bringing together interested parties to study Canadian naval history, involving historians in international organizations and pushing for the greater integration of maritime and naval historians. Douglas's involvement in the Canadian Nautical Research Society and its journal, *Northern Mariner*, created an accessible avenue for presenting original research while strengthening ties between naval and military historians. He also encouraged links with university history departments, hoping to draw students to the field of military history. But this was slow work and until the late 1980s there were still only a few academic naval historians pushing the profession in new directions.

The air force, in contrast to the strong army history and the newly emerging naval scholarship, lagged far behind. The lack of official histories had stifled academic historians in the field, although there was a very strong and knowledgeable base of public and amateur historians who kept traditions and stories alive in conferences and print. Nevertheless, the first two official histories were finally published in the 1980s: S.F. Wise's *Canadian Airmen and the First World War* (1980) and W.A.B. Douglas's *Creation of a National Air Force* (1986). As with official publications of the past, both the primary authors had been greatly assisted by a number of official historians who wrote narratives for the volumes, such as Brereton Greenhous, D.J. Goodspeed, Norman Hillmer, W.J. McAndrew, Stephen Harris, Roger Sarty, and Marc Milner. And this "faculty" of military historians passed the chapters around, editing, critiquing, writing, and rewriting to ensure the proper nuances were obtained, not to mention upholding the legacy of meticulous scholarship passed down from C.P. Stacey.[100] It was assiduous work, but quite simply there were few other academic publications that covered the breadth of research and human involvement in these enormous affairs.

Wise and his staff had the enormously difficult task of reconstructing the stories of more than 10,000 flyers and then assessing their impact on the air war. Much time was spent in the Public Record Office (London), attempting to write the national and personal story of Canadian flyers as well as how they fit into the British flying services. With its painstaking research and ability to reach beyond the national narrative, *Canadian Airmen* has often been praised as one of the finest aviation histories ever written. The second volume, Douglas's *The Creation of a National Air Force*, was equally crucial in its assessment of civil-military relations during the interwar period, the production of aircraft in Canada, the role of the BCATP, and the heretofore misunderstood task of aircraft in not only assisting in coastal defence, but also in defeating the U-boat menace. Both were works of the highest scholarship, and while many hands were involved in their shaping, it was the primary authors, Douglas and Wise, who wove together the myriad strands of narratives and analyses to craft these groundbreaking studies.[101]

Military history was being interpreted widely, and the considerable work exploring the impact of war on Canada was done by academics, most of whom would not call themselves military historians. Thomas Socknat studied the difficult role of conscientious objectors in the two world wars, Robert Bothwell and William Kilbourn revealed the importance of the "minister of everything" in their biography of C.D. Howe, and Ruth Roach Pierson explored women's wartime work. The government component of Stacey's *Arms, Men and Governments* was reappraised in J.L. Granatstein's far-reaching political history, *Canada's War* (1975). Employing an extensive range of government and personal papers, many of which had been unavailable to Stacey, Granatstein revealed that the waffling weirdo, Mackenzie King, was also a ruthless politician who kept his country together during a time of intense strain. Granatstein also explored issues of social welfare, diplomacy, finance, and their implications on Canada, which emerged from the war a far different country from the one that responded to Britain's call in 1939. As well, some darker periods of Canadian history were being brought into the light, such as the evacuation of Japanese Canadians in the Second World War, although such issues still remained politically charged since first governments and then courts were dealing with claims for restitution and official apologies. Building on the work in the 1970s, then, the writing of the two world wars was moving from the operational history phase to a fuller appreciation of their impact on Canada and all Canadians.[102]

Along with, and often borrowing from, these academic works, popular histories flourished. The best of these practitioners, Pierre Berton and Daniel Dancocks re-examined the Great War, while Tony German and decorated veteran Denis Whitaker provided excellent overviews of the navy and the army in the Second World War.[103] All these historians had conducted research in the archives to support their histories, but it was their skill at writing rather than new scholarship that distinguished their work. At the same time, they knew that the secret of connecting with readers was to highlight the story of individual Canadians: ordinary men and women in extraordinary times of turmoil and sacrifice. And while academic historians often seemed to delight in poking fun at bestseller Pierre Berton's occasional historical gaffes or hyper-nationalistic interpretations, they did so while realizing that he was reaching hundreds of thousands of Canadians, compared with the few thousand readers for which they might hope. In turn, Berton and others like him regretted that professional historians had allowed their writing to degenerate into passionless prose more akin to railway timetables than literature. There was much that academic historians could learn from Berton and historians like him; whatever the divide between scholars and popularizers, these popular historians, who relied heavily on the work of scholars, both official and unofficial, made significant contributions in disseminating military history to the Canadian public. Yet these popular histories rarely drove the profession in new directions, as most were repackaged, lively interpretations of previous works.

By the 1980s, therefore, military historians had reached far beyond the narrow boundaries of the official histories. J.M. Hitsman identified only twenty-three Canadian titles relating to Canadian military history in 1969; a revised article by Ronald Haycock in 1987 cited 248 sources.[104] Owen Cooke, the senior archivist at DHist, compiled a bibliography of Canadian works in 1984 that spanned several hundred pages.[105] The trickle of writing from the 1960s had become a torrent. If this new wave of military history was largely ignored by most academic historians and their students, who were focusing on gender, class, and other aspects of social history, it certainly stimulated the sub-discipline of military history scholarship and, through various popularizations, engaged a broad range of Canadians.

HISTORIANS, MUSEOLOGISTS, ARCHIVISTS, and even popular writers are not the only interpreters of the past: there is no monopoly on history. The two world wars had been presented to the Canadian public through a number of documentaries and radio programs since 1918 and 1945. And just as historians were re-examining the narratives of war in the 1980s, so too were a new generation of filmmakers. In 1982 the National Film Board (NFB) produced and aired Paul Cowan's *The Kid Who Couldn't Miss*. The film questioned whether Great War national hero W.A. "Billy" Bishop faked the raid of 2 June 1917 that earned him the Victoria Cross. Cowan offered many points of conjecture, but did not build a convincing case against Bishop, largely because the evidence no longer existed to definitively prove or disprove Bishop's actions. Nonetheless, veterans groups viewed the act of merely questioning the incident as an outrage – an attack against one of Canada's war heroes was an attack against all veterans.

Second World War veteran Clifford Chadderton, chief executive officer of the War Amputations of Canada, led the counterattack on Cowan and the NFB in a media blitz that spanned newspapers and television. He also pressured a Senate committee to examine the film, and he hoped they would recall it and then have it destroyed. The NFB was accused of "tampering with history" in their attempt to "hang a legend." The film, Chadderton derided, was based on the work uncovered by Phil Markham, who despite his dogged research into untapped resources in British and German archives and a detailed understanding of the air war, was dismissively labelled an "amateur historian." Markham and others like him, according to Chadderton, were "not qualified to express any expert opinion." Instead, using decades of hagiographic history such as George Drew's *Canadian Airmen*, the veterans stressed that professional historians supported their case. Most important, the recent volume of the RCAF official history, Wise's *Canada's Airmen*, came down strongly in favour of Bishop's claims, despite two footnotes that raised questions about the veracity of the dawn raid that earned Bishop the Victoria Cross; this "official" support was used as further evidence to justify the veterans' actions. In this instance, it would appear that Markham had bested the official historians in research, as surely Bishop's claim of seventy-two kills had been over exaggerated. But the eventual Senate subcommittee of 1985 did little except draw more attention to the film.[106] The veterans felt wounded that the taxpayer-funded NFB had supported this revisionist film, and many Canadians supported the veterans with an amazing 3,000 letters of protest.[107] But this flare of anger over how history should be interpreted would pale in comparison to the outrage unleashed a decade later.

"It is no exaggeration to claim that history and revisionism are central motifs of the 1990s, on both personal and social levels," wrote social critic Steven Dubin.[108] In 1992 a three-part revisionist documentary aired on the CBC under the title *The Valour and the Horror*. Award-winning documentary filmmaker brothers Terrence and Brian McKenna wrote and produced the series that examined three controversial events of the Second World War: the Canadians at Hong Kong and their subsequent suffering as prisoners of war, the Normandy campaign, and the role of Bomber Command. Attesting to the interest of Canadians in their military history, the three programs attracted audiences of several millions. The films were visually appealing, employing vivid archival footage, contemporary footage, and actors to convey the discourse of wartime participants. But almost immediately there was a "ground-swell of protest" from veterans furious over the seemingly distorted portrayal of their actions during the war, which in many cases were questioned against the moral relativism of the early 1990s.[109] Most grievous from the veterans' perspective was the program *Death by Moonlight*, which dealt with Canada's No. 6 Group and the strategic bombing campaign.

Death by Moonlight presented Canadian flyers as the victims of Sir Arthur Harris, commander in chief of the Royal Air Force's Bomber Command, who sent them out night after night to pound German cities and civilians. Although the McKennas rightly pointed out the terrible losses inflicted on Canadian flyers, the veterans appeared as guileless innocents sent to their death by maniacal senior commanders. Dropping high-explosive bombs on cities from great heights remains a controversial aspect of the Second World War, but no part of the operation could be understood without the contextual historical background that explained why the bomber war was being unleashed against civilians. The reasons were these: German attacks first on British cities; the nightly firebombing of London in the Blitz, which lasted for months; the technological inability at the time of the Allies to precision bomb, which they had tried and failed with terrible casualties; the political and military need to open a "Second Front" against Germany to help relieve the incredible pressure on the Russians; the necessity in an unlimited war to destroy war materiel and civilian morale; and the concrete effects of the bombing, which forced the Germans to pull back hundreds of thousands of defenders and thousands of anti-aircraft guns, all of which could have been used to devastating effect on the Eastern and Western Fronts. All these factors were either underemphasized or ignored in the film. Instead, *Death by Moonlight* portrayed the bombing campaign in moralistic terms, imposing 1990s hindsight on actions taken fifty years earlier. The bombing campaign was reduced to little more than the wanton destruction of cities from the sky; and those cities, it seemed, were filled only with innocents. As one angry veteran, Walter Thompson, DFC and Bar, complained, there was no attempt to understand the desperate situation of the Allies; instead, the film "criticized a strangulation victim for 'reaching for and using a club rather than a rapier.'"[110] Notwithstanding claims of "bulletproof" research made by the McKennas, the film presented numerous errors of fact and interpretation, which seemed to suggest to some that the brothers were launching an all-out polemical assault against the memory of the war.[111]

Cliff Chadderton again led the charge to censure the film. Unlike the debate over the Great War memoirs in the late 1920s in which the war was contested among men "who had been there," this time it was veterans pitted against civilians. Of course, not all veterans agreed with Chadderton, and certainly the McKennas had their supporters, including fellow media commentators who circled the wagons under the banner of journalistic freedom. Angry diatribes were unleashed between journalists and veterans. As historians S.F. Wise and David Bercuson observed, the veterans usually did not fare well in these exchanges, falling prey to their emotions, confusing facts, and often resorting to questioning the right of the McKennas to re-evaluate "their" history.[112] However, using their "militarized grey power," veterans again convinced a sympathetic Senate committee to call hearings over the films. Chadderton pleaded that the message of *The Valour and the Horror* must not go "unchallenged" for fear of "misleading future generations of Canadians in relation to the contributions made by Canadian veterans in time of war."[113] Veterans, journalists, and professional historians were called before the committee, with the testimony passionate, angry, and at times absurd. The whole affair starkly revealed that the history of the Second World War was very much still contested ground. It also reinforced a sense of proprietary identity on the part of the veterans: this was their history, and revisionists were not welcome to investigate and call into question the actions of a generation that had sacrificed so much for the defence and liberty of Western democracies against the exterminating evils of the Axis Powers.

To be fair to the McKennas, a two-hour film has a script much smaller than the shortest history books, even if a picture speaks a thousand words. There is not a lot of space for contextual information that would allow the viewer to piece together why an event took place. Nonetheless, good history can be presented on film, although it requires writers, producers, and directors to spend the time to engage fully in the nuances of the topic, and not seek out ahistorical cheap shots at the expense of balance and detail. The McKennas failed in that regard because they clearly prejudged the bombing campaign as an immoral operation and therefore aimed to present just that conclusion. Documentarians are not required to present all sides equally in a film, but it is poor history to pretend to do so. Historians must not try to hold the past accountable to the present: it must be understood in its own contextual system of values and historical events.

Writing history is difficult, and the public tends not to realize that long, grinding years of graduate school are required to produce historians who can evaluate the past through the compromised records left behind. Historians are still tricked by evidence or their own desire to believe something, but generally far less so than journalists, who seem ready to pounce on any controversial issue. The McKennas were right in their final message for the film: that the bombers attacked civilian cities night after night and that both the flyers and those on the ground suffered the terror of chance and death. But the McKennas failed to provide the proper context and even to get the basic facts right in many places. The supposed unearthing of new insights or never-before-seen issues that the filmmakers insinuated had been buried to protect reputations over the years, only betrayed a lack of understanding of the historiography.[114] The contentious issue of terror-bombing civilians during the Second World War was, as official historian Stephen Harris rebuked, "a secret only to the McKennas."[115] The films were shorn of complexities and nuances, with difficult issues presented in absolute terms: good or bad, black or white. That is not how history unfolded at the time, nor how it should be portrayed especially long after the event. With these issues, however, the fiery debate put military history back into public discourse.

In 1994 the historians at the Directorate of History, after a decade of intense study, published the third volume of the RCAF official history, entitled *Crucible of War, 1939-1945*.[116] It appeared in the immediate aftermath of *The Valour and the Horror*. The official history was based on the same sound scholarship of the first two volumes, and it presented operations overseas and the contentious issue of RCAF policy. During the war it had been the policy of Canadianization – the various attempts and failures of the government and military to draw Canadian flyers together into national squadrons and commands – that was so difficult to write about with contemporaries still alive. The policy had been roundly criticized by many of the flyers themselves, who did not want the disruption and disintegration of their close friendships with other international flyers. The three popular RCAF histories of the late 1940s steered clear of the issue, focusing almost solely on operations. As such, there was a significant gap in the historiography of the RCAF in the Second World War and all questions relating to overseas policy. As one aviation historian noted in the 1990s, the writing on the RCAF was in its "infancy."[117] While excellent popular histories such as Larry Milberry's *Aviation in Canada* (1979) or J.A. Foster's *For Love and Glory* (1989) were among the best works in print, Stephen Harris, Brereton Greenhous, and the RCAF official historians still had to construct their narratives from the war archives of not only Canada, but also of many other nations.¹¹⁸ That is precisely what the historians did, and *Crucible of War* offered new interpretations of Fighter Command, the largely ignored role of aircraft in supporting sea operations and, of course, strategic bombing. Although the conclusions were sometimes starkly laid out and not in guarded "official history language," the most contentious issues of strategic bombing were similar to those raised by British official historians Noble Frankland and Sir Charles Webster in 1961. Both the British and the Canadian official historians had concluded that bombing had not met the high expectations ascribed to it and, towards the end of the war, was used as a terror weapon against civilians. The McKennas had revealed the same conclusions, but shorn of all the nuances and complexities. Thus, when the reviews of *Crucible of War* appeared to support the McKennas' conclusions (and that of the largely forgotten Webster and Frankland series), many veterans, still deeply hurt from the perceived attack by filmmakers, immediately lashed out at DHist and the government. *Crucible of War* was hit by flak before it left the ground.¹¹⁹

Senator Jack Marshall, a D-Day veteran, noted that *The Valour and the Horror* spawned a "surge of patriotism" among veterans.¹²⁰ In fact, it militarized them. Those veterans interested in how their history would be portrayed became more willing to intervene against revisionist history they found distasteful. *Crucible of War* was as eagerly anticipated as official histories in the past. Yet advance reviews indicated some seemingly startling conclusions: almost none of the reviews focused on the contentious issue of Canadianization (it was condemned in the history), or even the denunciation of offensive fighter sweeps of 1941-42, which had been costly and ineffective; instead, almost all highlighted the several hundred pages devoted to bomber command.¹²¹ Headlines and remarks such as "RCAF historians reopen WWII bombing row" and "War veterans are outraged by an official history that says Canadian airmen took part in terror raids on German civilians during World War II," set the tone for the debate.¹²²

Anxious to pre-empt the distribution of this "revisionist" history, many veterans attacked the book even before reading it. A combative book launch had veterans questioning the right of civilian official historians to pass judgment on their history. Without a copy in his hands, Cliff Chadderton demanded an immediate official inquiry by "responsible military historians." "Like me," Chadderton charged, "I believe most Canadians would be under the impression that a government published work of history should be scrupulously objective!"¹²³ That the history was "official" and prepared by the Department of National Defence rankled other veterans. Not all agreed with these outbursts, however. Other academics, journalists, and even veterans accused Chadderton and his supporters of attacking the history because it did not conform to their accepted perception of the past. This was also reflected in letters to the editor, with even Pierre Berton wading into the debates and accusing Chadderton and others like him of "never taking their blinkers off."¹²⁴

But media commentators did not have a uniform view either: pro-veteran journalists simply saw the authors of *Crucible of War* as armchair generals, or air marshals in this case, applying hindsight history to defame a generation of heroes.[125] The fact that a team of expert historians had spent almost a decade on the history appeared to be of little significance in questions of re-evaluating the past.

There is never total agreement regarding history. No two historians will read it the same way. To the veterans, however, their own perspective was reinforced when some other military historians also seemed uncomfortable with the official history's conclusions. Respected military historian J.L. Granatstein, who reviewed an advance copy, added fuel to the fire by commenting, "This account, astonishingly opinionated for official history, too often seems like nothing so much as the TV series with footnotes."[126] But the controversy hit new heights when the *Toronto Star* had Brian McKenna review the book. McKenna used the opportunity to write a long review that suggested this "courageous addition" to academic scholarship supported his film's interpretations. The two, in his eyes, appeared linked, and burdened by the telling of "terrible truths."[127] Veterans were not impressed. His review provoked another series of attacks, but this time the veterans focused again on the more comfortable target of *The Valour and the Horror*.

When the angry veterans finally read *Crucible of War* and saw the scholarship that underpinned the conclusions – none of which were as damning as anything suggested in the vitriolic reviews – the furor began to die down. Marshall said in the Senate that the history written by "respect[ed] ... official military historians" was far different from *The Valour and the Horror*.[128] Even Chadderton, after having read the history, retracted his call for a commission of experts to review the work.[129] However, the controversy over *Crucible of War* was more than just a question of contested memory, with veterans realizing that they had to be more active in the defence of their perceived past, it also spoke to the nature of writing official history fifty or sixty years after events. *Crucible of War* would be a "wonderful guide to the sources for all who follow," wrote J.L. Granatstein, but "to see politicians labelled as drunks and fools with such abandon and to see the venom with which some senior officers are assailed is surprising ... This is not the usual official history and, after a half-century, the untypical may be necessary."[130] Indeed, what was the role of official historians in documenting the two world wars by the end of the twentieth century?

During the fiercest part of the controversy, journalist Peter Worthington wrote, "There's something vaguely irrelevant about 'official' histories published 50 years after a war, when most of its participants and all of its planners and strategists are dead." His suggestion was to "quit rewriting war history."[131] That, of course, is unacceptable, as it implies that history is only relevant to those who took part in it – this is the exact opposite of what veterans' organizations have been trying to impart to Canadians throughout the twentieth century with their multi-faceted educational and memorial programs. But the larger question is whether official histories are still needed. The answer, judging from the most recent products, is yes. When the official program was cut in 1948, Canadians did not receive their RCAF series for many decades, and academic writing in that field had been stunted as a result. The enormous and complicated story of Canada's aerial contributions during the Second World War was beyond the resources of a single scholar; a team of historians over an extended period of time was needed to subject the enterprise to the rigours of serious intellectual inquiry. Records were scattered throughout archives in Canada, Germany, the United Kingdom, and the United States. Without the official histories, one wonders who would have ever been able to carry out the essential research needed to fully explain the exceedingly complex story of higher policy and the air war. Moreover, the intricately detailed official history maps, based on countless hours of plotting the movement of aircraft in this case, or units and ships in previous official histories, are essential tools for all subsequent historians, and one of the most important and enduring aspects of official work. At the same time, these official histories cast wide their interpretative nets, providing new insight into national politics, regionalism, economic development, and of course, the effect of war on Canadian society. In the end, all three RCAF histories had considerable impact on international air force scholarship. With this foundation now laid, future historians can build upon and, if necessary, reinterpret the work of the official historians.

In addition to the necessity of an ongoing official history program is the challenge of writing official history fifty years after the event. There was a difference between the army official histories and the more modern works on the RCAF. Stacey and Duguid were writing official histories, but they were also contemporary histories. The first and second generation of official historians had far less time to absorb all the records available (Duguid being the exception, but he buried himself so deeply that he was never able to dig himself out). Powerful contemporaries were also alive and interested in how their history would be codified in print. This, as noted earlier, was a significant obstacle, but so too was the struggle of crafting official histories without the benefit of other works to establish contextual information. The vast majority of issues that affected the army, even peripheral ones or questions relating to international forces, had to be researched and reconstructed from the primary records. The advantage to this first generation writing, though, was that the official historians were not beholden to a particular interpretation. Duguid was able to break away from the Beaverbrook school, while Stacey fashioned the first critical interpretation of the Second World War.

The concerns for the RCAF official historians were far different: they had to deal with nearly a half-century of hindsight, historical writing, and popular memory. Moreover, after *The Valour and the Horror*, veterans wanted a celebratory history, not a critical one. The fiftieth anniversary in 1994 marked the heroic

D-Day landings, as well as the ongoing assault against German forces on the sea, in the air, and on land in other theatres. It was a time for commemoration. For those who thought they knew their own history, there was already an accepted interpretation of the meaning and memory of the war, centred on acknowledging the veterans' sacrifices. But the official historians were not willing to eulogize the air war, and these different expectations provided much of the tension in the conflict over how the air war would be captured in history.

Only professional, academically trained historians could have accomplished the enormous task of writing the official history. But as Elizabeth Muenger observed while analyzing American service historians, "History will often disclose unexpected and perhaps unwished-for knowledge."[132] After enlisting some of the finest civilian historians in the country, it was not possible to then control what they were to write. The Directorate of History had fought for and won its academic freedom under Stacey, and it would not easily relinquish that to pressure from politicians, senior officers, or veterans' groups. During the crisis, Director W.A.B. Douglas and his successor, Serge Bernier, along with primary editor Brereton Greenhous, refused to bend to the pressures of these stakeholders, even when there were sharp and sometimes hysterical questions about taxpayers' money supporting revisionist history. There were even searching questions by veterans about how a team of historians, none of whom had flown in the war, could possibly write the RCAF's history. With the mass of evidence available, from firsthand accounts to archival records, historians could reconstruct the past through intense study, just as, for instance, historians continue to write medieval history. That kind of response was unconvincing to some angry veterans, even as it rang true to academics.

While Stacey and Duguid dealt with fresh battles of reputations among powerful contemporaries, the more recent official historians had to deal with the memory of the war that had calcified over time and, in this particular case, with veterans who had been wounded by *The Valour and the Horror*. Some veterans now saw any questioning of the accepted past as an indictment of their collective deeds and their comrades' sacrifices. Writing official history fifty years later had its own particular set of demands that were different but no less challenging than those faced by Stacey, Tucker, or Duguid.

Historical work that assumes some sort of impartial, official tone is likely to be viewed as the exact opposite. Official history, Christopher Moore observed, has often been considered state-sponsored propaganda.[133] If this study has proven anything, however, it is that despite enormous pressure, both overt and covert, the official historians have effectively resisted any tampering with their histories. Compromises were made, but rarely did concessions substantively change the nature of the history. Yet as Ken Roberts Greenfield, who played an essential role in overseeing the production of the United States Army official histories, observed: the only way to remove "the curse that lies on official history is to leave no doubt that qualified historians will be allowed to get at all the facts, and, subject only to the requirements of national security, call the shots as they see them."[134] That was certainly the case with the *Crucible of War*, and if it was the most critical of any Canadian official military history, it has proven that official historians would not temper their judgments to produce happy history. At the same time, senior departmental and Canadian Forces' personnel refused to intervene and reverse the judgments derived from intense study. Had they wanted "cooked history," they could have handed the work over to public relations branches. Yet senior department officials understood that though history may make us uncomfortable and we may not like the conclusions derived from its study, we rewrite it at our peril.

The Second World War veterans are still a powerful force, and they should be reckoned with when historians examine their history. But no veteran or group should control how that history is interpreted. Despite all the drawbacks to the historical craft, it is usually historians, rather than other chroniclers such as journalists or filmmakers, who offer the most balanced portrayals. Certainly historians have shown through their extensive research of primary archival sources that they are the most diligent in determining how the past unfolded, with its many nuances, contradictions, and uncomfortable revelations. But there is no getting it "right" in history. The past cannot be recaptured and represented "as it was," for the writing of history is always about drawing conclusions from insufficient evidence.

Through the work of historians, veterans, and journalists, who were all questioning, reappraising, or defending interpretations, the wars of reputations revealed jagged fault lines between history and memory. There are multiple meanings and truths surrounding every event; and anyone telling the story of the past must choose, select, and filter the evidence. Canada's military history will continue to provide fertile ground for debate, posturing, and full-out controversy, as it remains a contested field of battle.

THE 1990S WERE A DECADE OF UNCERTAINTY, as Canada struggled with a massive debt, its declining place in the world, the mixed effects of free trade, and even the survival of the country. These were difficult times for Canadians, and they culminated in the explosive 1995 Referendum that would have set the stage for Quebec's separation from Canada. By only the narrowest of margins Canada avoided immediate divisive constitutional discussions and possible fragmentation. The potential destruction of the country spawned countless books, documentaries, media stories, and deep ponderings on what it meant to be Canadian. This self-reflection, which ranged from the profound to the banal, coincided with the fiftieth anniversary of the Second World War, which stimulated a renewed appreciation of Canada's rich military history.

Veterans in the 1990s were exerting a stronger influence than they had for decades. "Militarized grey power" made them a force to be reckoned with in society. With massive anniversary celebrations in Canada and Europe, for a brief time Canadians awoke to their history. Equally important, though, Canadians seemed willing to listen to veterans, acknowledging their sacrifices. Striking while the iron was hot, journalists and historians lamented how poorly history was taught in our schools, with CBC newscaster Peter Mansbridge noting during the ceremonies that "there is no shortage of Canadian history ... Our history is NOT dull. But we are dull-witted when it comes to learning about it. We cheat ourselves. We cheat our children. We cheat our country." During those heady commemorations, Canadians shed the powerful but blinkered myth of being solely peacekeepers, acknowledging that Canada had also been a country of warriors.[135]

Perhaps it takes fifty years to come to grips with events as traumatic and epochal as the world wars. Some aspects of the Second World War are still raw; the wounds have not yet fully closed for events such as the Holocaust, the French collaboration during the occupation, the enormous Russian losses, or the Japanese atrocities.[136] But the fiftieth anniversary celebrations were marked with a sense of urgency by many Canadians and provided another impetus for the appreciation of military history. Academic military history was undoubtedly stimulated by these events as well, but the profession had, since the 1980s, profited from a number of critical studies that continued to explore the world wars and Canada's complex military past.

"To date the army's Second World War experience seems mired in its memoir, nostalgia and operational phase," wrote Marc Milner in 1989, and the navy and air force were far worse.[137] But in the 1990s, military historians would broaden their analysis of the world wars, continuing to work at understanding the complicated nature of operational history, which for the army had not been substantially re-evaluated since Stacey's monumental official histories. Historians Terry Copp and Robert Vogel had begun their reappraisal a decade earlier, drawn to the supposedly poor performance of the Canadian Army during the Northwest Europe campaign in 1944 to 1945, where international scholars had lamented its uninspired leadership, cautious tactics, and failure to defeat quickly its German opponents.[138] General Montgomery's claims of the Canadian operations being "badly handled and very slow" did not help.[139] But the Canadian Army, argued Copp and Vogel in a series of histories under the title of the *Maple Leaf Route*, had a low force ratio when attacking the enemy, had to face some of the toughest panzer units in the Normandy fighting, and were allocated the least glamorous fighting in clearing the coastal towns and the Scheldt. A re-evaluation was required, although even in the 1980s the authors had been forced to self-publish these works in order to include the appropriate maps, photographs, and word length to explore the complicated operational history. Their reappraisal made little initial impact among

Canadian and international historians, who still preferred to ignore the Canadian Army or deride it in relation to its Allies, the opposing Germans, or even the memory of the Great War CEF shock troops. But the slow swing of the pendulum had begun.

John A. English's *The Canadian Army and the Normandy Campaign* (1991) offered a new assessment of the army's fighting capabilities. In trying to explain the uneven performance of the Canadians in Normandy, Stacey had blamed junior regimental officers. Acknowledging his debt to Stacey, English offered that his work "illustrates the cumulative nature of history, for its arguments could not have been raised up without the firm foundations provided by Colonel C.P. Stacey's official and unofficial histories ... The more one reads Stacey, the more one is struck by the sheer magnitude of his scholarly achievement."[140] Intensive research into the war records and his own appreciation of command after more than thirty years in the Canadian Forces allowed English to conclude that the Canadian soldier had been poorly served by his high command, despite years of pre-invasion training. His work turned the interpretation of the Canadian Army on its head, even if English relied too heavily on the judgments of Montgomery. English was no doubt influenced by the writing that, since the late 1970s, had a greater sympathy for the fighting man at the front, but he was also unencumbered by having to deal with the personalities of powerful men such as McNaughton, Crerar, Simonds, or Foulkes.

Complementing English's important study, J.L. Granatstein offered a collective biography of senior Canadian commanders in *The Generals* (1993). His assessment of the high command was closer to English than to Stacey, and Granatstein freely passed judgment on Canadian battlefield failures, although the book's strengths were on questions of leadership, command, and policy. In 2002 he published *Canada's Army*, the finest overview history of ground forces in the two world wars, which also opened up new pathways for research into the postwar years.[141] Granatstein had produced another bestseller, but one with a polemical tone as he warned Canadians that the price they had paid for forgetting their military history was the neglected state of the Canadian Forces in the twenty-first century: either we "pay now in dollars for competent soldiers or we pay later in dollars *and* our sons and daughters."[142] It was refreshing to see academic history used as a tool for understanding the past and charting a path for the future.

Terry Copp continued to assess the Canadian Army and, with Bill McAndrew, an official historian from DHist, produced *Battle Exhaustion* (1990). It was a truly innovative study that analyzed battlefield stress and military psychiatry during sustained combat operations. Copp and McAndrew wove morale, discipline, and medicine into an analysis that personalized the carnage of battle and shed light on the nature of combat for the men who must take part in it. *Battle Exhaustion* stimulated new avenues of research in Canada and around the world. McAndrew also offered a number of studies of the Italian campaign, which continued to remain in the shadow of the Northwest European fighting, just as it had during the war.[143]

After two decades of studying the Canadian Army in the Second World War and producing almost a dozen books, Terry Copp offered a culminating work, *Fields of Fire* (2003).[144] It was a significant re-evaluation, concluding that the army was far more combat effective than earlier historians had allowed. His rehabilitating claims were based on the absorption of more than sixty years of literature, but primary sources from both Canadian and international archives allowed him to build his history from the bottom up. He walked the battlefields, studied the ground, and compared his observations against the available documentation. It is worth recalling Stacey's remark in 1964 that perhaps he had been too hard on the Canadian Army and that other nations' official historians had not been critical enough about their own forces. To prove the assertion, Stacey had opined, an historian would have to study all the armies in order to draw any final conclusions. Copp's work offered a deep appreciation of Canadian, British, American, and German forces, and *Fields of Fire* stands as a benchmark. Not all will agree with Copp's conclusions, but as a result of his work, the debate surrounding the effectiveness of the Canadian Army has moved beyond Stacey's long established views.[145]

The RCAF had been well served with the publication of the three official histories after 1980, but few academic works had yet been inspired by these groundbreaking histories. Spencer Dunmore continued to offer academically respectable and readable works on 6 Group and the British Commonwealth Air Training Program, but these interpretations differed little from those of the official historians: Greenhous, Harris, or Hatch.[146] A more innovative history was Allan English's *The Cream of the Crop* (1996), which built upon the work of Copp and McAndrew by examining underexplored issues of manpower allocation, air-crew selection, aviation psychology, and the controversial "Lack of Moral Fibre" designation for those who could not continue to fly in the attritional air battles over Europe. Hugh Halliday, Larry Milberry, John Griffin, Wayne Ralph, and Carl Vincent (whose company, Canada's Wings, published many histories and memoirs), produced popular, scholarly histories underpinned by archival scholarship.[147] In fact, many of these books were squadron or aircraft histories akin to the army's regimental histories, and were essential in tracking the achievements of individual squadrons and flyers within the larger aerial war effort. Despite these useful histories, the literature was often overshadowed by technical eulogies to aircraft, and as Allan English noted in 1996, "RCAF history today is a generation behind the work done by the historians of the Canadian Army."[148] The army's lead can be directly attributed to the lasting influence of Stacey and the essential work of the Army Historical Section.

The navy made the most significant leap forward in academic military history from the 1980s onward. Douglas's directorship at DHist had not only supported the mandated RCAF official histories, but he had also worked at reviving the moribund study of naval history. He hired naval historians Roger Sarty and Marc Milner, and through a series of academic conferences, which brought together veterans, serving officers, and scholars, he encouraged the study of all manner of naval issues that had been ignored or understated in the Tucker and Schull official histories. Michael Hadley and Roger Sarty also offered the first scholarly reappraisal of the naval debates, coastal defence, and the role of the Royal Canadian Navy in the Great War with *Tin-Pots and Pirate Ships* (1991).[149] With Milner having left for a professorship at the University of New Brunswick, Sarty continued to work in writing narratives and drafting plans for what was then a one-volume Second World War operational naval history.

A significant addition to the canon of Canadian naval history seemed likely with the authorization by the DND in 1989 of a three-volume official naval history, which subsequently became four volumes. A new team of naval historians, consisting of veterans of the naval section such as J.D.F. Kealy and P.A.C. Chaplin along with new historians straight from graduate school such as Robert Fisher and Shawn Cafferky, produced an astonishing number of detailed narratives. These were subsequently condensed and rewritten into book chapters by Douglas and Sarty, and later Michael Whitby. Equally important, the naval historians were encouraged to disseminate their findings in academic articles, of which almost fifty were published, thereby stimulating the field both in Canada and internationally.[150] In Ottawa the naval team was forced to reconstruct the Second World War records, since their provenance had been lost over the years, and it fell to them to ferret out old records such as the Ultra decoded intercepts that had been squirrelled away in the vaults of the Canadian Security Establishment. Overseas work in the United Kingdom and Washington helped to draw out German U-boat strategy and tactics, and this, when combined with detailed plotting of every contact between aerial spotting airplanes and submarine-hunting ships with U-boats, produced a clearer picture of the enemy threat to Canada. By incorporating enemy records and cross-referencing the information with records compiled at home, naval historians had been able to construct the kind of history that Gilbert Tucker had been anxious to write in the 1940s.

The Second World War official naval history was about two-thirds completed when government cutbacks savaged DHist in the mid-1990s, reducing the staff from thirty-two to ten. Only six of the newest historians were able to keep their jobs.[151] With the official history program in jeopardy, it was decided that the research completed to date had to be presented to the public. Roger Sarty published *Canada and the Battle of the Atlantic* (1998), which was a well-written, high-production book with vivid images and maps of the kind that usually adorn the work of more journalistic accounts.[152] His work was a tour de force that has been called by one naval historian, "the best single-volume history of Canada's role in this great campaign."[153]

With Douglas retired but still working on the reduced official history program, Sarty and Whitby led the now depleted team until, much to the surprise of the Directorate of History and Heritage (DHH), the department supplied an essential infusion of capital to hire contract workers. The first half of the Second World War naval history was published to public acclaim a few years later; *No Higher Purpose: The Official Operational History of the Royal Canadian Navy in the Second World War, 1939-1943* (2003) offered an impressive reappraisal of the RCN's fighting capabilities during the Second World War, ultimately concluding that the essential Battle of the Atlantic could not have been won without Canadian naval support.[154] It was a striking work of synthesis and original research that drew on the scholarship of the profession and deep forays into international archives. In the late 1940s, Vice Chief of the Naval Staff Frank Houghton had remarked that an attempt to finish Tucker's operational history was "unlikely to be written unless someone does it off his own bat."[155] Academic naval historians had uncovered significant naval aspects of the world wars since the 1980s, but it had required official historians to draw together this enormous corpus of research and writing. The three succeeding volumes, which are scheduled to appear before the navy's one-hundredth anniversary in 2010, will, one suspects, further open new avenues of research for academic naval history in Canada and internationally. *No Higher Purpose* was stark testimony to the essential and ongoing work carried out by Canada's official historians.

With such academic strides made in exploring the Second World War, in the words of historian J.M. Bourne, the Great War "struggled for visibility in the glare."[156] But by the 1990s, some of the most innovative work in Canadian military history was found in the ranks of Great War historians. Desmond Morton continued his prolific writing career; in addition to exploring issues surrounding prisoners of war, he offered *When Your Number's Up* (1993), a seminal publication that analyzed the Canadian soldier through a number of thematic issues, including questions of discipline and punishment, medicine, and the experience of combat. It was a groundbreaking study built on more than three decades of research, with Morton even wisely incorporating some of Duguid's unpublished reports, and it remains the starting point for historians attempting to understand the trials of trench warfare for the Canadian soldier. Currently, there is no counterpart to Morton's work for the Second World War. One of Morton's graduate students, Bill Rawling, another productive DHH historian, provided an invaluable guide to the evolution of tactical warfare within the CEF; *Surviving Trench Warfare* (1992) is cited frequently by international scholars attempting to come to grips with the constant evolution of victory within the mostly static nature of stalemated trenches. I analyzed gas warfare, the evolution of battlefield doctrine, and soldiers' morale in *No Place to Run* (1999), and Shane Schreiber's *Shock Army of the British Empire* (1997) was a welcome addition from a serving officer in the Canadian Forces, providing a significant study of the last Hundred Days battles. All these new interpretations were constructed through an intensive reading of the war records, as well as an examination of personal archives from General Currie to the lowest-ranking private.[157]

Yet perhaps the most distinguished work of Canadian military history from the last decade was Jonathan Vance's *Death So Noble* (1997), a critical reading of how the Great War was remembered and reconstructed over the twentieth century. Drawing on cultural theory and a close reading of texts and images – not just those created by the high-brow artists but everything from the infantry's trench doggerel to the patriotic jingles produced on the home front, as well as photographs, war posters, art, ephemera, stained glass windows, rituals, and traditions – Vance demonstrated that the memory of the war had been constructed to fit the needs of a grieving population trying to find closure and understanding in its 60,000 slain.[158] The wider historical profession acknowledged Vance's work with the Sir John A. Macdonald prize for best book in Canadian history, and it has already stimulated a number of graduate students to explore related issues.

This new Canadian historiography was also influenced by international scholarship, largely from the United Kingdom, which had begun to reappraise all aspects of war, but especially long-standing myths surrounding the supposed "butchers and bunglers" who led the Allies to victory. Despite these important advances to the canon of Great War literature, the home front still remains poorly explored by military historians, who for the most part have abdicated that study to specialist Canadian historians who have hived off the various topics of gender, labour, and politics. There is much more that military historians could offer in assessing the impact of the war on Canadian society, although there has recently been some movement in the field.[159]

Despite historians exploring the impact of the war on individuals in greater detail and listening more attentively to their discourse to provide insight into the war experience, arguably the memoirs of servicemen continue to offer a sharper perspective of the nature of combat, even if the larger contextual information on battles, campaigns, logistics, or leadership is sacrificed. The difficulty in writing war memoirs was to craft a work that reflected events, not just how events were remembered fifty years later. The use of official records, the bread and butter of the academic historian, was nearly useless for conveying these experiences, and George Blackburn, in his bestselling trilogy of the early 1990s, which explored a gunner's view of the fighting in Normandy, believed that the inability of official record makers to capture the essence of battle, left much past military history without value. Official war diarists, wrote Blackburn scathingly, offered "little recognition of the conditions under which the fighting soldier existed, which, more often than not, were dreadful." As such, the histories based upon these records has led "to inaccurate, irresponsible conclusions bordering on outright dishonesty – even in the works of our own official historians – regarding the training and fighting qualities of Canadians officers and men of World War II." Certainly, historians that rely only on the official records will present a sterile view of war, where the sheer brutality, fear, and chaos of battle are subsumed to the clearly written reports of higher officials. Yet few historians have relied exclusively on such records. Blackburn's comments, and other memorialists who echo him, miss the fact that official records that form the government archives, whether War Diaries, medical reports, or after-battle reports, not to mention photographs, film, and art, can still offer insight into the experience of battle at the sharp end.[160] Recent scholarly writing in the last two decades has incorporated these official sources, as well as first-hand testimonials and experiences, which accounts for the profession's greatest progression since the writing of the first generation of official historians.

The profusion of memoirs since the 1980s also reflects the nostalgia of Second World War veterans who, after completing their careers and moving into retirement, had begun to look back on the events of "their" war. Personnel from all three services began to pen insightful and valuable memoirs. Many of these sold well and were far more accessible than academic tomes. They offered a vibrant portrayal of the men and women who confronted the vast world at war. Moreover, the flood of memoirs – and even a surprising number still from the Great War – was evidence of the popularity of military history throughout the country. That so many of these personal histories were issued by small publishers also seemed to indicate that the market was strong enough to support these works. Even when it was not, that did not stop veterans or, increasingly, the children or grandchildren of wartime participants from publishing the memoirs or collected letters of family members that were a form of commemoration, remembrance, and personal fealty, much like the regimental histories of the interwar years.

With this avalanche of popular and academic military history, one might think that Canadians now understand better the two world wars. Yet periodic polls by the Dominion Institute indicating the abysmal knowledge that Canadians have about their history quickly, if sadly, puts that notion to rest. Much of the new academic military history still sells as academic history, which means press runs in the hundreds. Nor have these new interpretations been transmitted to general textbooks used in high schools or undergraduate Canadian history courses, which remain written by historians with an apparent disdain or ignorance of military scholarship. Textbooks hundreds of pages in length that cover post-Confederation history might have only a handful of pages devoted to the world wars. Even then the focus is on decontextualized tragedies such as Dieppe and Hong Kong, with rarely a mention of Canadian operations, let alone the astounding accomplishments and victories. This tends to be accompanied by a sort of national flagellation over issues such as the evacuation of Japanese Canadians or the divisive French-English relations.[161] These are important topics, no doubt, but ones that leave a skewed view of Canadian world war history when divorced from operations, tactics, strategy, the experience of combat, the legacy of commemoration and memory, or the host of other themes and events that weave through Canada's military history writing.

Despite the influence of the official histories and the subsequent academic monographs in strengthening the canon of Canadian military history, one must be careful not to claim too much for these works. It still remains populist writers such as Pierre Berton, Peter C. Newman, or Charlotte Gray who reach the widest audience, although some military historians, most notably Desmond Morton and J.L. Granatstein, have had an impact well beyond academia. But Timothy Findley's novel *The Wars* (1977) and the subsequent movie based on it have probably shaped a generation's thought concerning the Great War more than Nicholson's painstaking official history.[162] And the new History Television channel – for a while dubbed the Hitler Channel for all the Second World War documentaries shown on it – influences far more Canadians than the latest cutting-edge scholarly history. Luckily, Canadian-content television programs are beginning to be infused with and backed by recent scholarship, even if it is sometimes curtailed to fit hour-long episodes.[163] Nevertheless, the sensational continues to find much currency on television, and only brave historians can watch their field being covered without cringing.

Yet there is obvious value in attempting to get the history right. The popular writers of Canadian history build their much-read works from academic treatises. If professional or official historians do not lay this interpretative foundation in a principled fashion, few others will spend the agonizing hours in the archives doing so. And so the world wars continue to be re-evaluated. There remains much to be explored, comfortable assumptions to be shaken, myths to be reappraised. Although battles are fought on all fronts by all types of academic historians, today, contrary to previous decades, the explosive material usually comes from a deep mining of archives. Yet there remains a large gap between the new scholarship and long-held popular perceptions, especially in sensitive areas such as the supposed criminal futility of donkey-like Great War generals or the decontextualized condemnation of the Second World War bombing campaign. Historical memory constructed and accepted over several decades does not change quickly, and cutting-edge scholarship presented in academic monographs and journals can take years before it is processed and distilled into general histories.

WHILE ACADEMIC HISTORIANS have slowly superseded the importance of official historians in the profession since the 1980s, the DND's historians still play a supportive part in the study of military history. The directorate emerged from the battle over Bomber Command in 1994 and was met squarely with funding cuts.

Although unrelated to the controversy, the staff reduction of more than 50 percent greatly curtailed work on a number of future official history series. Nonetheless, having anticipated cost-cutting measures for some time and wanting to prove its worth to the department, much as Stacey had done during the 1950s, the DHH repositioned itself in the early 1990s by expanding its work to include peacekeeping official histories and staff studies for use in the instruction of officers. Responding to further departmental requests for accessible works, the DHH produced a number of excellent popular histories on Vimy, Dieppe, aviation in Canada, the Northwest Campaign, and the aforementioned naval history by Roger Sarty.[164] All were crafted by teams of historians with a deep knowledge of the two world wars, and these works once again highlight the important, if understated, role of the DHH in disseminating the study of military history within the Canadian Forces and to the academic and broader reading public. Additionally, these were some of the first scholarly publications to appear in their subject areas in French Canada since Stacey's translated official histories.

Before this, however, Douglas had been slowly repositioning the DHH to play a greater role in preserving the institutional memory of the department. In the early 1990s, new command historians with the air force, and later with the navy, were established.[165] As well, the 1990-91 Gulf War was documented through the deployment of field historian Major Jean Morin to that theatre. Like the historical officers of the Second World War, Morin worked with the forces to document Canada's involvement in the conflict and to ensure that adequate records were created and preserved, including electronic ones.[166] He returned to Canada and with Lieutenant Commander Rich Gimblett, a senior officer aboard the HMCS *Protecteur* and naval historian, published *Operation Friction* (1997).[167]

This renewed need to support the department also coincided with the spectacle of the Somalia Affair, which splayed the Canadian Forces on the front pages of newspapers across the country in 1994 and 1995. The incident produced seemingly unending revelations of the torture and murder of an adolescent in Somalia by supposed elite troops. The resulting cover-up, alleged destruction of official documents, and the succeeding controversies rained continuous blows on the forces' reputation. Committees, inquiries, and recommendations – some supplied by military historians such as Desmond Morton, J.L. Granatstein, and David Bercuson – first pushed the Canadian Forces to the brink of disaster and then brought it back. Suddenly there was a renewed impetus to craft a sense of professionalism in the Canadian Forces that would be based, among other guiding factors, on a firm understanding of Canada's military history. In the decade since the Somalia Affair, the DND has reacted positively to most of the recommendations and a greater emphasis has been placed on the study of military history, which has benefited those universities near military units, bases, or headquarters.[168] The DHH fully supports these renewed operational requirements, realizing that educated service personnel are a storehouse of memory when it comes to assisting the Canadian Forces in understanding its past in order to better shape its future.

The DHH also contributes to the ongoing dissemination of military history to Canada's French-speaking population. Douglas had established a section within DHist in 1974 to work on a number of histories that would be more relevant to French Canadians. With the world wars leaving deep scars, French Canadians had received a far different appreciation of the country's military history, one that had always been viewed through the cracked lens of the conscription debates. A 2002 survey asking Canadians to associate Vimy Ridge as a Canadian battle received a positive response from 54 percent of respondents in British Columbia, 42 percent in Ontario, but only an astonishing 6 percent in Quebec.[169] Throughout the twentieth century, there had been surprisingly few academic military histories written in French, and the world wars remain largely ignored in Quebec's school curriculum. Although tens of thousands of French Canadians served their country in the two world wars, this remained, as one commentator noted, a "secret de famille honteux" – a shameful family secret.[170]

Since the mid-1970s, Jean Pariseau, Jean-Pièrre Gagnon, Serge Bernier, and a small group of official historians have helped to produce a more balanced vision of Canada's past, building historical bridges with French-speaking academics.[171] They were, for most of the century, the only "francophones practising in the field."[172] These official historians prepared a number of unique works, including a social history of the 22nd Battalion during the Great War and a two-volume history of bilingualism in the Canadian Forces – histories that attracted much attention in English and French circles.[173] Yet there remained many unexplored topics relating to the world wars.

The exploration into "shameful secrets" began to change in the 1990s, especially with the closing of Collège Militaire Royal, and the appointment of many of its professors to Quebec universities. They began to offer additional courses, even if there were few publications. Serge Bernier, the director of the DHH since 1994, remains a principal figure in bringing together new scholars in Quebec, and an annual military conference at Université du Québec à Montréal established by Robert Comeau has created an academic stimulus for military historical scholarship by a growing group of professors, students, and independent writers. Two Quebec publishers, Athéna and VLB, have begun to issue a series of books and translations of English histories, which are slowly creating a foundation for the study of the military history in that province. Of course, there is much work to be done by French-Canadian historians in telling their own stories; however, sound scholarship has begun to elucidate the impact of military history on the lives of French-speaking Canadians as both a force of repression and resentment, but also as an example of duty and sacrifice during the two world wars. Both facets of wartime service must be better understood in English and French Canada.

The DHH has continued to carry out the equally vital function of control and influence over war records. By the 1980s most of the department's central registry files were covered under disposition plans with the National Archives of Canada, resulting in the transfer of records – paper, electronic, cartographic, and photographic – to the nation's central archival depository. But some of these older disposition plans were loosely written and often outdated, and it fell to the historians and archivists to interpret them. In effect, the DHH was again determining the fate of military records – those that would be saved for posterity at the National Archives and those that would be incinerated. Without historically minded guardians in the department, important records had been destroyed in the past, such as many of the court martial records relating to the twenty-five Canadians executed during the Great War or the equally contentious conscription tribunal records, which Supreme Court Justice Lyman Duff, the final appeals judge for the local tribunals, thought were so "full of hatred and bitterness and would have been a living menace to national unity" that they had to be burned.[174] With these two series, and possibly others, destroyed before they even reached the Historical Section, it is worth remembering that historians and archivists are not always able to intervene in defence of Clio. Yet more often they did, and records were saved. Even the act of determining which series of records received detailed finding aids influenced accessibility and how historians might use the records. The DHH also continued to manage operational records such as War Diaries and the Annual Historical Report, and like the official historians of the past, it impressed on units the necessity to create fuller, more descriptive records.[175] These official records remained an administrative burden for most units, and the DHH acted as watchdog to ensure that the records were created.

With respect to access, while DHH historians no longer had the same control over the records as Duguid, Stacey, or the official historians of the past, they continued to assist researchers and students in further exploring Canada's military history by answering inquiries and opening some records still in DHH custody before their transfer to the National Archives. For instance, the directorate has the authority to declassify Canadian defence documents up to 1980, but other records, especially those regarding current operations or information from foreign governments, remain closed. While since 1983 researchers have employed Access to Information and Privacy Act (ATIP) requests to dig out closed material from the archives, there is much that remains unavailable. "Researchers who choose current topics in sensitive areas," wrote former DHH archivist Isabelle Campbell, "are likely to be working with very incomplete records."[176] Yet in this field and all other aspects of Canadian military history, the DHH archivists and historians provide generous assistance to researchers by locating and opening records as well as sharing knowledge. The DHH remains an important centre for historical research.

In the case of the world wars, the work of the official historians is coming to an end, although, as evidenced most recently by the official naval history, these volumes continue to offer distinguished contributions to the canon of military history. There also remains a role for official historians to mobilize strong teams of researchers to access the archives of other nations and to encourage the study of military history. One wonders if the DHH will turn back to the abandoned Great War series or perhaps the South African War, neither of which received adequate histories. And though historians have begun to piece together aspects of our recent martial history, it is still the official historians, notwithstanding the Access to Information and Privacy Act, who have access to many national and international records that will still not be opened for decades.[177] It is not quite the same as Stacey's warning in 1946 – the stark choice between official history or nothing at all – but ATIP so far has precluded any unfettered opening of the nation's archives. In all likelihood, then, official history will still have an influential role in reconstituting Canada's military past, even if it is in closer partnerships with academic historians. And perhaps as Gilbert Tucker had remarked after the war, in writing Canadian Forces' contemporary history the official histories will be closer to the "last word" than the first. Sean Maloney of the Royal Military College, for instance, has been providing a solid historical foundation for a number of key Canadian Forces' operations for the last half of the twentieth century.[178] Political scientists and graduate students are exploring other facets of the Canadian Forces, such as its structure, personnel, and operations. One wonders if the official historians are passing into a new phase: of waiting for foundational academic or journalistic histories to revise and provide the "last word," or to be less positivist, a more developed work on contemporary events after consultation in various national archives, with access to closed documents and with the full intellectual firepower of a team of historians.

AFTER EXAMINING the rise of academic history and the ongoing importance of official historians, there remain some concluding comments on the state of Canadian military history at the beginning of the twenty-first century. A number of universities now offer students the choice of courses in military history, but many of the senior professors are close to retirement. One can only wonder if Ronald Haycock, Desmond Morton, David Bercuson, Carman Miller, and David Facey-Crowther, to name only some of the best-known military historians, will be replaced as they retire, or if their positions and courses will be allowed to wither away. Universities have had to do more with less during the last decade, and history departments have been forced to cut their permanent staff and rely more on sessional teachers. However, the recent hiring of several military historians is an encouraging sign for academics.[179] In addition, the military history profession has received ongoing support from the Department of National Defence, which has readily acknowledged the value of teaching about Canada's martial past, and since the late 1960s has provided grants for both students and research directed towards that end. As a result, nationwide research centres have been established and have attracted many of the profession's most productive historians and students, and they encourage a less centralized view of military history. At the University of New Brunswick, for instance, the national histories of Stacey and Nicholson have been challenged, since much of the maritime history does not find a place in those official works.[180] The universities of Victoria, Calgary, Waterloo, Western Ontario, and Ottawa, plus McGill University, Wilfrid Laurier University, and the Royal Military College of Canada all have thriving military history programs. This broadening of perspectives, with military history being taught across the country and with each faculty or centre playing to its strengths, also emphasizes different aspects of our shared past.

Military history remains popular among students, with most undergraduate classes being oversubscribed. Some institutions, such as the University of Calgary, boast nearly a fifty-fifty ratio of men and women in undergraduate survey courses.[181] The fact that many students have family members who served in the world wars encourages them to seek out the past.[182] Yet the continued relevance of military matters is not hard to trace to the present day: the Gulf Wars, the Second World War anniversaries, the building of a new Canadian War Museum, the return of the Unknown Soldier to Canada in 2000, and the twenty-first century "War on Terrorism," as well as renewed peacekeeping missions from Afghanistan to Haiti, are all indicators that Canadians cannot escape conflict, and many have taken a renewed interest in their military history. One need only look at the shelves devoted to military history in most bookstores, especially in comparison to, say, social or labour history, to see how the subject resonates with those outside of academia. Despite this relevance, most of these books are written by popular writers and journalists, and academic military historians might be a little less smug when they crow about the market share of military history in comparison to that of their academic colleagues.

Yet certainly part of that crowing comes from military historians who feel under siege, believing that many academics continue to view their field as an irrelevant and morally questionable area of inquiry. Terry Copp, a professor for over thirty years who produced a groundbreaking social history before turning to the study of the Second World War, observed that mainstream academics consider military history "as a marginal area of little relevance to the profession's agenda."[183] Ronald Haycock, former dean of War Studies at the Royal Military College, has written that many academics regard military history as a "marginal enterprise or as a lurid fascination of war-watchers who simply want to extol the virtues of the military profession."[184] With military history having little to do with "finding one's cultural roots, castigating the endless immorality of the effervescent middle classes, illustrating the recently discovered moral superiority of the current generation or raising the consciousness of the present with regards to the past and the continuing destruction of the environment," chided professor Robert Vogel of McGill University, the study of war and military history can be viewed with disdain.[185] "War is out," opined J.L. Granatstein, "abuse is in."[186] Others across Canada and abroad have repeated these assessments. And while some history departments embrace the teaching of Canadian military history, especially "War and Society" studies (operational history is still a hard sell in any history department), there remains a strong undercurrent of mistrust towards military historians in academia.

An equally helpful evaluation on the academic status of military history is the number of articles that have been published in the flagship journal of the historical profession, the *Canadian Historical Review*. There have been only a handful relating to military history since the late 1980s and, until recently, it appeared that few if any military – or political, national, or foreign affairs – historians would ever again grace its pages. So bad was the situation in the 1990s that J.L. Granatstein and Norman Hillmer felt compelled to establish a scholarly splinter group, The Organization for the Study of the National History of Canada, to address these now neglected studies, and to provide a venue to present new findings in publications or at conferences. Both had been intimately involved in the CHA, with Granatstein a former editor of the *Canadian Historical Review* and Hillmer a long-serving member of the secretariat. While the *National History* journal eventually folded, this deliberate strategy of confrontation within the history wars of academia forced the CHA to confront their increasingly exclusionary policies. But military historians had other avenues of publication. *Canadian Military History*, which was started at Wilfrid Laurier University by Terry Copp in 1992, is an essential journal and contains the newest Canadian military history scholarship. With approximately 1,000 subscribers, *Canadian Military History* remains an essential venue for the ongoing discussion of world war historiography. As well, Laurier and the Royal Military College of Canada have hosted annual military history conferences since 1989 and 1980, respectively, where new scholars can present their research and engage in a dialogue with like-minded historians. In 2000 a significant military history conference was convened in Ottawa, and it included over 100 presenters and more than 400 attendees. Finally, an assessment of the number of articles, theses, and books in the *Canadian Historical Review*'s "recent publications section" is also a clear indication that while some predicted Canadian military history as a casualty of the "new" social-cultural academic history, the profession is alive and thriving.[187]

With History Television devoting so much of its programming to military issues, with bookstores stocking large military history sections, and with its relevance continually reinforced in the daily media with each new war and terrorist attack, it appears that military history is of interest to almost everyone but those in academia. That military history remains far more narrative- and archives-centred, and less reliant on theory than other academic disciplines, often leaves the field open to attack or dismissal. Military historians continue to be viewed by some academics as narrators, who neither understand nor care about the latest theoretical undercurrents and are more intellectually challenged than challenging.

But surely good narrative history based on solid research has its place in the academic profession. It forces historians out from behind the jargon-laden prose that both hedges statements and occasionally obfuscates the historian's message. At its core, history is about exploring and sharing the past. Experts analyze the available archival documentation within the context of past events and attempt to show linkages, lessons, or even tell a story. While the truth may never be fully discovered nor the past completely reconstructed, there is value in attempting to present insight into the challenges, threats, exertions, stupidity, and bravery of those who have come before us. Narrative history certainly accounts, in part, for the popularity of military history among non-academics.

The undeniable brutality of war is off-putting for some, and many have chosen not to spend their professional time reading it and certainly not teaching it. The necessary knowledge of military organizations, structures, ranks, and weapon systems makes the history complex and inaccessible for many. But all except the most militant pacifists must believe that war is sometimes necessary to defeat intransigent dictators, abolish slavery, or end genocidal regimes.[188] For those who want to develop strategies for global security and the abolition of war, how can they accomplish that if they have no detailed understanding of what they oppose? With so many of today's conflicts rooted in the past, a fragmented appreciation of contemporary events must result if military history is ignored in the academy. War is horrible and to be avoided, but not at all costs; little is gained by burying one's head and hoping it will simply go away. Even if studying the world wars, or military history in general, is unpalatable for some, these unlimited conflicts affected every man, woman, and child in the Canadian context. War is an integral part of Canadian history in the twentieth century, and one is always better able to situate the contemporary with the aid of the historical lens.

If war and society studies have expanded the boundaries of military history, it is also true that there is still much work to be done, and Canadian historians seem far behind in relation to other countries. Canadian military historians must look outside their intellectual borders: both to make better use of international archives and to draw on scholarship from the broader field of history. This is not so easily managed. Few scholars have the resources of the official historians to hire language experts, most notably, A.G. Steiger, an army intelligence officer who translated German documents relating to both world wars for Stacey. For the most part, academic historians have not been willing or able to pursue this same rigorous approach to research. Comparative history also offers valuable insights, but has been little practised. For example, Canadians celebrate one of their defining moments of nationhood with the victory at Vimy Ridge in the Great War; Australians do so with their defeat at Gallipoli, even though Canadians have a series of defeats and Australians their share of victories that could have been substituted in both cases. Why then do nations adopt the myths, memories, and discourse that they do? Military history is as much about memory, identity, and community as any other field of history, and because of the intensity of events, even more so. Yet just as military history encompasses aspects of political, economic, and social history, so too must it now push into the realms of gender, cultural, and intellectual history and become fully interdisciplinary. Postmodernist discourse and analysis, little of which has yet found its way into Canadian military publications, can offer new approaches and conceptual tools for exploring military history. The profession will only continue to grow and expand by employing new methodologies from other academic disciplines in order to continue piecing together the elusive past. Warfare is almost completely dominated by issues of gender as an almost exclusive masculine activity, yet there is no dialogue between historians of gender and the military. If military historians complain that "mainstream" academic historians ignore their work, they should not return the favour, but rather embrace much of value in the "new" history, which may help to blur the artificial lines between the various historical disciplines.

There is also a tendency for Canadian military historians to engage in heavy lifting for nation-building myths, especially the colony-to-nation paradigm, with wars, battles, and military events as weighty signposts along that Whiggish road towards full autonomy. Although few historians worth their salt are willing to accept anything that has stood the test of nearly half a century in print, this colony-to-nation idea has attracted much attention because it is largely true. Yet both scholarly and popular military history tends to range from self-congratulatory to outright cheerleading, and current practitioners might best turn back to the official historians led by Stacey, who were successful in restraining themselves from supporting larger national myths with their deeply analytical historical treatises.

In contrast to this nation-building historiography and despite the new wave of much needed revisionist Canadian military history, there remains a tendency to display colonial attitudes. When British generals or prime ministers praised Canadian forces, such rhetoric is frequently held up as proof of fighting efficiency. If an imperial leader spoke positively of the Canadians, then that counts as weighty evidence. Too often, though, little analysis is applied to such discourse or the reasons and motivations behind it. For instance, the elevation of the Canadian Corps to shock troops in the Great War by British Prime Minister David Lloyd George was often done to embarrass his own hated British generals.[189] That is not to say that the Canadian Corps did not deserve these accolades, but Canadians, perhaps betraying their past imperial dependencies, swoon heavily before such praise. In contrast to the praise earned in the Great War, the criticism by Second World War British generals, especially Montgomery, or by the British admiralty, which had left the Canadian navy to escort the war-winning merchant vessels across the Atlantic and then condemned it for failing to excel at U-boat killing, were accepted with a deferential nod and good grace. Recent works by Milner or Copp are considerably less willing to adopt these condemnations as the defining evidence in assessing Canadian forces. While it is high time for re-evaluating past events and long-defended beliefs, it will be interesting to see how historians in the next generation view these reputation-restoring conclusions.[190]

The writing of history with contemporaries alive, or with reputations still sensitive, also remains a challenge. The interpretation of the world wars is still contested ground. While the Great War has slipped into history, there remain thousands who either fought in the Second World War or supported it from the home front. While historians continue to interpret the wars, there can be a terrible sense of frustration, even helplessness, for some veterans or their family members to have non-combatants pick through "their" history, like scavengers through bones, and to arrive at conclusions that question their accepted stories. Yet others have spoken warmly of finally knowing why a battle unfolded as it did or how things had gone wrong, such as the revelation of technical failures in the Battle of the Atlantic. Either way, the veterans' past has been recognized as a key component of Canadian history. Those stories must be told and remembered, and the skills that make a soldier, sailor, nurse, or pilot are far different from those that make a good military historian. While historians are not infallible, they do spend years delving through the war records to try to piece together the divergent narratives of Canadians in the world wars. And if military history has become more critical and willing to pass judgment, that is perhaps a useful sign that the profession is continuing to evolve.

Yet academic military historians still have both internal and external burdens to overcome. In 2003 former official historian Brereton Greenhous was confronted by one of Billy Bishop's family members after a public lecture, where Greenhous had challenged the veracity of Bishop's Victoria Cross-winning raid: "I wouldn't say these things about your grandfather," complained the hurt family member.[191] Is that how history is viewed by the public? Is history to be the celebration of heroes or the dispassionate study of the available records? Is it an exercise in name calling or defending reputations? Must any historian who arrives at unpopular conclusions, such as the contrarian Greenhous, be accused of being little more than a better-educated McKenna-like muckraker, tearing down Canadian heroes? Should the past remain unappraised if it involves shaking loose the foundations on which heroes are placed? One hopes not, for the evolving historical reappraisal is the historian's most significant contribution to society. As Soviet premier Nikita Khrushchev once remarked, "Historians are dangerous people. They are capable of upsetting everything."[192]

Conclusion: An Ongoing Dialogue

> *History has a habit of bequeathing to us disastrous legacies.*
> — Gertrude Himmelfarb

> *History is an altogether stranger and far more difficult discipline than it is often envisioned.*
> — W.H. Walsh

> *It has been said that although God cannot alter the past, historians can. It is perhaps because they can be useful to him in this respect that He tolerates their existence.*
> — Samuel Butler

Canada was formed in 1867, but forged during the Great War. Yet the sacrifice of the country and its citizens nearly destroyed the country. Scarred and weary, Canadians hobbled towards full autonomy over their foreign affairs. In Britain the public and, until recently, most historians could only envision the Great War as a senseless bloodletting of unfathomable proportions that was mitigated only slightly by Allied victory. It was treated differently in Canada by first and second generations of military historians, who produced nationalistic histories that focused on the operational success and the well-earned reputation of the Canadian Corps. All agree that 60,000 dead and double that number of wounded and maimed was a great tragedy for a small nation. But the colony-to-nation narrative is a powerful one, and therefore the historical memory of the Great War remains less tragic than in Britain, even if conscription was perhaps the single, most damaging event in English-French relations in the twentieth century.

The Second World War is less problematic, almost universally viewed as the good war. After the slaughter of 1914-18, Canadians did not want to be involved in another war, with "never again" being the postwar mantra. Yet they realized by the end of the 1930s that Hitler and his minions would never listen to reason, and so Canadians again marched to war, although some were more willing than others. With the fall of France, Canada was Great Britain's closest and strongest ally. Even with the entry into the war of the Soviet Union and the United States relegating Canada to a more junior partnership, the mobilization of one in ten into the three services and the equally important work on the industrial home front proved the nation was willing to fight this just war to the fullest extent. The Canadian Army in the Second World War supposedly failed to emulate the legacy of Currie's Canadian Corps; the nature of the bombing war left little room for knights of the sky such as William Barker or Billy Bishop; and the navy failed to shine in its unglamorous "sheep dog" role of ensuring convoys survived the deadly Atlantic crossing. Yet the nation survived the divisive strains of unlimited conflict under Mackenzie King's cautious, guiding hand. The postwar prosperity and revelations of Nazi barbarity made the Canadian sacrifice more palatable.[1]

After the defeat of the Axis powers in 1945, a generation of Canadians could look back on the first half of the twentieth century and see that their "Peaceful Kingdom" had been at war for no fewer than ten years in two of the most destructive conflicts the world has ever witnessed, another three years of fighting in South Africa at the turn of the century, and in a short time, another three years of static warfare in Korea from 1950 to 1953.[2] Twentieth-century wars shaped Canadian society. Profound social, cultural, demographic, and industrial changes occurred as a result of the two world wars. Yet how had the emerging professional historical community responded to these nation-changing events?

Until the 1960s the task of capturing and conveying immediately this military history fell to the official historians, since the war records that were needed to support authentic, professional histories were under their control. As guardians of memory, they guided their readers through the difficult battles of reputations that erupted among senior officers, politicians, and even nations after the world wars. But who was watching the official historians? Who could legitimately evaluate their work? Buttressed by the war records, the official historians had significant control over how the wars would be interpreted. And since no one could rival their knowledge or access the war records, it would take several decades before professional historians had a chance to re-evaluate the work of the official historians, and only then after the opening of the war archives.

Charles P. Stacey wrote of the official histories: "Everyone hates them and suspects the people who write them. Nobody nowadays wants to be caught writing one. Perhaps, this is quite right!" Despite his self-deprecating statement, Stacey felt that even this "form of history has its humble uses."[3] Yet official histories have more than such humble uses, for they established the very foundation for all subsequent study of the world wars in Canada. But it was no easy task. Overt pressure from senior officers, politicians, veterans, and even other nations, as well as the more subtle pressures of being responsible for capturing the "official" authentic memory of these momentous wars, were balanced against the desire to present the history to all Canadians.

E.H. Carr believed that one should study the historian before studying the facts of the history.[4] Echoing Carr, Umberto Eco admonished: "Books are not made to be believed but to be subjected to inquiry."[5] This work has gone beyond the study of military historians or the deconstruction of texts, however, by attempting to unravel the history behind the history. Not only are the official historians situated within their society, which helps to explain and acknowledge the pressures exerted on them, but they are explored through an analysis of their surviving discourse, everything from official reports and memoranda to private correspondence. Only then can the struggle of the official historians be placed in context with their published work. The undercurrent of battle that raged behind the printed words is important in assessing the role of the official historians in shaping the canon of world war academic writing.

It has been said that he who pays the piper, calls the tune. Few imagine that official historians can be anything other than court chroniclers. Yet if this work has shown anything, it is that the official historians relentlessly, and for the most part successfully, withstood pressures that could have perverted their enormously important historical series. The official histories ought to be praised, not buried, even if they were the first, rather than the last, word on the wars. While some historians view their "official" designation as broadly tainting the work, others have held the histories up as sacrosanct. As such, subsequent generations of historians seem positively gleeful to find fault with the official histories.

That the official histories need full reappraisals every generation is beyond doubt, and the recent work of Terry Copp and Marc Milner is important proof of this. Certainly, most of the official historians themselves never expected their works to last for decades unexplored. Yet instead of ignoring the official histories or using them as straw men, it is worth remembering that these were significant works produced under the most trying of conditions. From Lord Beaverbrook's heroic histories and record gathering, which helped to shape the reputation of the Canadian soldier, through to Duguid's painstaking work as a champion in the war of reputations, to the professionalism of the Second World War academic professional historians, these were important histories that not only reached Canadians, but also established the footing for all subsequent historical work.

Understanding the skirmishes fought by the official historians in the name of history provides insight into the integral role they played in more than simply writing history. In the war of reputations, it was the official historians who were in the front lines defending Canada's interest. Duguid, and to a lesser extent Stacey, fought for the reputation of the Canadian soldier, rebuffing the British, Americans, and even fellow Canadians. And while this was considered one of Duguid's primary duties, his work has been forgotten, overshadowed by the "dreadful gap" of his never-completed series. It is ironic that Duguid's most damning critic was Stacey, who excoriated the former official historian in his memoirs. Duguid may have failed as an author of the official histories, but he succeeded in guarding the Canadian Corps' reputation, which was won through blood and battles on the Western Front, and in organizing many of the records that underpin subsequent scholarship. It is unlikely that Canadian historians will ever again hold such a prominent role in the Department of National Defence, or in the Canadian government for that matter.

In Canada, Great Britain, and Australia, the Great War official historians helped to pave the way for their Second World War counterparts. This later generation built on the successes and failures of the Great War histories, but their mandates were by no means frictionless. The fact that in Canada the Second World War historians were trained civilian academics, with more experience and skill in completing their tasks, and therefore more secure in themselves and their ability to stand behind the war record to safeguard the authenticity of their accounts, was an important evolution in the professionalism of writing official histories. Led by Stacey, the official historians carved out their positions in a postwar Department of National Defence, ensuring that their histories were written without censorship from a host of constituents. At the same time, Stacey's frequently repeated phrase that the soldiers wanted "honest history" must be questioned. Generals McNaughton, Crerar, Simonds and Foulkes all influenced Stacey's interpretations; while they were keen to divine the lessons of war, it was not to be at their own expense. Yet sycophants and superficial histories may be popular at first, but their weaknesses are soon revealed. That the Second World War official histories still remain essential reading is perhaps the strongest proof of how the official historians carefully crafted their volumes, followed the findings revealed in the war records, and balanced their roles as historians and guardians of memory.

While these key historical monographs form the canon of Canadian military writing, equally important is the role of archives and war records in allowing for the writing and rewriting of the world wars. The archival records must be analyzed and deconstructed. Archives are the bearing walls of academic history, but too many historians fail to understand the contested nature of the records they use to craft their works. Archives are not replicas or mirrors of past deeds. Records are constructed and shaped by the pressures of time, place, and authorship, much like any other forms of documentation. This does not mean that archives or records are so unreliable that the history based on them is little more than a fictionalized account, but historians must devote as much time to deciphering, analyzing, and deconstructing the history of the record, as they spend on the information contained in these historical texts. Although it is impossible to prove what the records might have been had they not been influenced by historical officers, their regulations, or a host of other factors, there often remain telling clues in the archives themselves. An analysis of war records is essential to understanding the history that we have and, perhaps, the history that has yet to be written.

"History does not repeat itself," goes the adage. "Historians repeat one another."[6] There are certainly enough bland, uninspired retellings of Canada's past to support that assertion. But with the opening of the war archives in the decades following the world wars, a new generation of academic military historians had the opportunity to return to the primary sources and question the interpretations within the seminal official histories. The war records, which had often been collected and preserved by the official historians and later by archivists, allowed for the ongoing refining and re-evaluation of world war writing.

With the facts established on the world wars, C.P. Stacey observed in his brilliant memoir *A Date with History* (1983), other historians could now turn to asking the question why.[7] Historians indeed have done just that, but in many cases the facts of Canada's world wars continue to be questioned, and many new ones are uncovered among the millions of pages and images in archives. Even when facts are established, historians still need to interpret them. The world wars have been shaped and constructed over time: contested, imaginary terrain, where angles of approach change from historian to historian and generation to generation. But all have been built upon the studies of their predecessors. That does not mean that history is an idiosyncratic construction of factual building blocks leading to enlightenment, for most historians disagree with some or most of what came before, and offer completely new ideas and conclusions in their works. Yet it would be naïve to think that the influence of historians and their works disappear as their books go out of print. Rather, they remain part of the canon of historical literature, forever preserved in the lengthening discourse of support and refutation.

The strengthening of the profession since the 1960s reveals several dozen practicing military academic historians, a cyclical flow of at least that many graduate students, a vibrant group of popular historians, expert collectors, military museologists, government historians, military archivists, veterans, Canadian Forces' members, and a public that continues to be fascinated by the world wars. And while this work has dealt almost exclusively with the two world wars, there are military scholars who have reappraised the warfare of early centuries. Historians such as S.F. Wise, Ian Steele, Donald Graves, Jane Errington, Carman Miller, and Fernand Ouellet have made the greatest impact, but there are many more, often not calling themselves military historians, who continue to explore our understanding of Canada's wars. In fact, Canada's colonial warfare is part of the very fabric of the societies in question, from conflicts with First Peoples through to the competition between the French and British Empires, and finally the resulting American and Canadian nations. The artificial divide of post-Confederation military historians with their colleagues is far less evident in the field of colonial history, where warfare determined the very nature of the country. "War has shaped Canadians more than most of them realize ... Indeed, it is hard to find an institution, from family to trade unions, whose history was not transformed by either or both world wars," wrote historian Desmond Morton.[8] Military historians do not study war because it is fun to re-fight old battles, or to marvel at military hardware, or because it glorifies violence and killing. They study war because it matters.

The new academic military history, which goes beyond campaign history to include the assessment of war's impact on society, offers new insight into deciphering Canada's rich martial history. But it remains in its infancy, partially because of the difficult relationship between academics and academic military historians and, more damaging, the inaccessibility of the archives for much of the twentieth century. The new military history, which is no longer "new," has further advances to make into the analysis of the past; at the same time, an examination of the canon of Canadian military history reveals that "old" history was not nearly as archaic, simplistic, and rigid as many believe. Progress has been made, and military historians are drawing increasingly on the disciplines of social, economic, and cultural history. Yet in expanding our intellectual borders, military historians must not turn their back on the study of battles, the raison d'être of the field. With the new military historians bounding down these profitable paths, it is worth repeating that military history is, ultimately, about examining the terrifying, brutal, and exhilarating experience of battle: preparing for it, fighting it, cleaning up the mess, and dealing with the consequences. The role of women in support roles or the impact of income tax on soldiers' dependents are all crucial areas of study, but battles make military history unique from everything else studied by historians. There is much to explore in the realm of tactics, doctrine, weapon systems, military ethos, biography, discipline, command, and morale to name but a few of the factors that form the combat efficiency of armies, navies, or squadrons. While historians understand the sum, it is time to go back and explore the parts, which then will surely require a re-evaluation of the whole. And so the historiographical circle goes around. Since military historians cannot even agree on the past, there is no predicting the many axes of advance on which the profession of Canadian military historians will move in the future. But it is clear that it will be based on the past work of military historians and archivists.

"We know the future only by the past we project into it," suggests historian John Gaddis. "History, in this sense, is all we have."[9] But the past can never be fully reclaimed. Historians try, but will invariably fail. Still, that does not mean historians should abandon their inquiries simply because the answers cannot be made perfect. Without question, the past can be imagined and reconstructed into comprehensible patterns through the evidence left behind. With more than 102,000 Canadians having given their lives in the world wars, and countless others affected by its outcome, military historians still have much to explore, and Canadians still have a great stake in the results of defining their national identity. We are not yet finished with the world wars, and they, it would appear, are not yet finished with us.

Notes

Introduction

1 David French, "'Official but not History'? Sir James Edmonds and the Official History of the Great War," *RUSI Journal* 133, 1 (1986): 58-63.
2 Christopher Moore, "The Legacy of Colonel Stacey," *The Beaver* (April-May 1994): 52.
3 Herbert Butterfield, *History and Human Relations* (St. James Place: Collins, 1951), 198.
4 Captain S.W. Roskill, "Some Reasons for Official History," in *Official Histories: Essays and Bibliographies from around the World*, ed. Robin Higham (Manhattan, KS: Kansas State University Library, 1970), 11.
5 For accusations of this sort, see Denis Winter, *Haig's Command: A Reassessment* (London: Penguin Books, 1991).
6 There has been recent important work by Canadian archivists regarding these questions. For an introduction and useful summary, see Terry Cook, "Archival Science and Postmodernism: New Formulations for Old Concepts," *Archival Science: International Journal of Recorded Information* 1, 1 (2001): 3-24; Terry Cook, "What Is Past Is Prologue: A History of Archival Ideas since 1898, and Future Paradigm Shift," *Archivaria* 43 (Spring 1997): 17-63; Tom Nesmith, "Still Fuzzy, But More Accurate: Some Thoughts on the 'Ghosts' of Archival Theory," *Archivaria* 47 (Spring 1999): 136-50.
7 For some of the best Canadian military historiographical writing, see, in chronological order, Wilfrid Kerr, "Historical Literature on Canada's Participation in the Great War," *Canadian Historical Review* 14, 4 (1933): 412-36; Donald Schurman, "Writing about War," *Writing about Canada: A Handbook for Modern Canadian History*, ed. John Schultz (Scarborough, ON: Prentice Hall, 1990); W.A.B. Douglas, "The Prospects for Naval History," *Northern Mariner* 1, 4 (1991); W.A.B. Douglas, "Marching to Different Drums: Canadian Military History," *Journal of Military History* 56 (April 1992): 245-60; Jeff Keshen, "Review Essay: The New Campaigns of Canadian Military Historians," *American Review of Canadian Studies* 23 (Autumn 1993): 425-37; Ronald Haycock, *Teaching Military History: Clio and Mars in Canada* (Athabasca, AB: Athabasca University Press, 1995); Owen A. Cooke, *The Canadian Military Experience, 1867-1995: A Bibliography* (Ottawa: Department of National Defence, 1997); Serge Bernier, "Se hâter lentement – l'historiographie militaire canadienne, 1988-1999," *Bulletin d'histoire politique* 8, 2-3 (2000): 11-24; Denis Whitaker, *Victory at Falaise: The Soldiers' Story*, with an historiographical chapter by Terry Copp (Toronto: HarperCollins, 2000); David Zimmerman, "New Dimensions in Canadian Naval History," *American Neptune* 60, 3 (2000): 263-72.
8 For Canadian and international histories that have offered profitable examples to follow, see Carl Berger, *The Writing of Canadian History: Aspects of English-Canadian Historical Writing since 1900*, 2nd ed. (Toronto: University of Toronto Press, 1986); C.P. Stacey, *A Date with History: Memoirs of a Canadian Historian* (Ottawa: Deneau, 1983); Wesley C. Gustavson, "Missing the Boat? Colonel A.F. Duguid and the Canadian Official History of World War I" (MA thesis, University of Calgary, 1999); Beverly Boutilier and Alison Prentice, eds., *Creating Historical Memory: English-Canadian Women and the Work of History* (Vancouver: UBC Press, 1997); and M. Brook Taylor, *Promoters, Patriots and Partisans: Historiography in*

Nineteenth-Century English Canada (Toronto: University of Toronto Press, 1989). For international histories, see Robin Prior, *Churchill's "World Crisis" as History* (London: Croom Helm, 1983); Jeffrey Grey, ed., *The Last Word? Essays on Official History in the United States and British Commonwealth* (Westport, CT: Praeger, 2003); Brian Bond, ed., *The First World War and British Military History* (Oxford: Clarendon Press, 1991); Brian Bond, *The Unquiet Western Front: Britain's Role in Literature and History* (Cambridge: Cambridge University Press, 2002); Andrew Samuel Green, "Sir James Edmonds and the Official Military Histories of the Great War" (PhD diss., University of Leeds, 1999), later published as *Writing the Great War: Sir James Edmonds and the Official Histories, 1915-1948* (London: Taylor and Francis, 2004).

9 For a brief sample of postmodernist historical theory, see Keith Jenkins, *On "What Is History?": From Carr and Elton to Rorty and White* (London: Routledge, 1995); Joyce Appleby, Lynn Hunt, and Margaret Jacob, *Telling the Truth about History* (New York: W.W. Norton, 1994); and Georg G. Iggers, *Historiography in the Twentieth Century: From Scientific Objectivity to the Postmodern Challenge* (Hanover, CT: Wesleyan University Press, 1997). For a vituperative rebuttal to postmodernist historical theory, see Keith Windschuttle, *The Killing of History: How a Discipline Is Being Murdered by Literary Critics and Social Theorists* (Paddington, New South Wales: Macleay Press, 1994); and the more balanced views of Richard J. Evans, *In Defence of History* (New York: W.W. Norton, 1997); and Gertrude Himmelfarb, *The New History and the Old: Critical Essays and Reappraisals* (Cambridge, MA: Harvard University Press, 2004).

Chapter 1: Documenting War and Forging Reputations, 1914-18

1 Donald F. Harris, "The Presentation of a British Canada in Shropshire c. 1890-1914," in *Imperial Canada, 1867-1917*, ed. Colin M. Coates (Edinburgh: University of Edinburgh, 1997), 196.
2 R.G. Moyles and Doug Owram, *Imperial Dreams: British Views of Canada, 1880-1914* (Toronto: University of Toronto Press, 1988), 7-8.
3 Carl Berger, *The Sense of Power: Studies in the Ideas of Canadian Imperialism, 1867-1914* (Toronto: University of Toronto Press, 1970), 53. See ch. 5, "The Canadian Character," for an analysis of the perceived characteristics of Canadians.
4 Desmond Morton, *When Your Number's Up: The Canadian Soldier in the First World War* (Toronto: Random House of Canada, 1993), 17, 278.
5 Carman Miller, "The Crucible of War: Canadian and British Troops during the Boer War," in *The Boer War: Army, Nation and Empire,* ed. Peter Dennis and Jeffrey Grey (Canberra: Army History Unit, 2000).
6 For the best account of Aitken during this period, see Gregory P. Marchildon, *Profits & Politics: Beaverbrook and the Gilded Age of Canadian Finance* (Toronto: University of Toronto Press, 1996).
7 Library and Archives Canada (hereafter LAC), Lord Beaverbrook papers (BP), MG 27 II G 1, Series E, reel A-1764, Aitken to Hughes, 28 December 1914. These are microfilmed copies of the Beaverbrook papers held in the Beaverbrook library.
8 LAC, Records of the Department of External Affairs (RG 25), v. 259, file P-3-19, Order-in-council 3117, 6 January 1915.
9 See Desmond Morton, *A Peculiar Kind of Politics: Canada's Overseas Ministry in the First World War* (Toronto: University of Toronto Press, 1982); and Stephen Harris, *Canadian Brass: The Making of a Professional Army, 1860-1939* (Toronto: University of Toronto Press, 1988).
10 BP, A-1765, Report by Sir Max Aitken to Rt. Hon. Sir Robert Borden on the Joint Establishment of the Canadian Representative at the Front and the Canadian War Records, n.d. [ca. 19 May 1916].

11 BP, reel A-1764, Aitken to Hughes, 26 September 1915; Hughes to Aitken, n.d., received 1 December 1915; Hughes to Aitken, letter including Hughes's speech in the House of Commons on 30 January 1917; BP, reel A-1765, Aitken to Borden, 3 December 1915; LAC, Sir Robert Borden papers (Borden papers), MG 26 H, reel C4311, 32478, Aitken to Borden, 4 March 1916.
12 BP, A-1765, Report by Sir Max Aitken to Rt. Hon. Sir Robert Borden ... Canadian Representative at the Front and the Canadian War Records, n.d. [ca. 19 May 1916].
13 LAC, Records of the Department of Militia and Defence (hereafter RG 9), v. 4746, folder 175, file 5 (hereafter 175/5), Canadian War Records Office (hereafter CWRO), Report Submitted to ... Sir Robert Borden, 11 January 1917.
14 Lord Beaverbrook, *Politicians and the War, 1914-1916*, vol. 1 (London: Thornton Butterworth, 1928), 189.
15 On the problems of war journalists, see Keith Grieves, "War Correspondents and Conducting Officers on the Western Front from 1915," in *Facing Armageddon: The First World War Experienced*, ed. Peter Liddle and Hugh Cecil (London: Leo Cooper, 1996), 719-35; Martin Farrar, *News from the Front: War Correspondents on the Western Front 1914-18* (Thrupp, UK: Sutton Publishing, 1998).
16 BP, reel A-1764, Aitken to Hughes, 13 October 1916. For Aitken's violations of censorship rules, see Peter Buitenhuis, *The Great War of Words: Literature as Propaganda, 1914-1918 and After* (London: B.T. Batsford, 1989), 80.
17 For problems with Alderson, see RG 9, v. 4676, 4/3, Aitken to Alderson, 14 February 1916.
18 Tom Driberg, *Beaverbrook: A Study in Power and Frustration* (London: Weidenfeld and Nicolson, 1956), 84.
19 Sir Max Aitken, *The Official Story of the Canadian Expeditionary Force* (London: Hodder and Stoughton, 1916), 4.
20 A.J.P. Taylor, *Beaverbrook* (New York: Simon and Schuster, 1972), 88; Lord Beaverbrook, *Men and Power, 1917-1918* (London: Hutchinson, 1956), 268.
21 BP, reel A-1765, Aitken to Borden, 1 January 1915. A similar letter had been sent to Hughes to garner his support.
22 BP, reel A-1765, Borden to Aitken, 14 September 1915; Aitken to Borden, 25 August 1916; Borden to Aitken, 11 July 1917. Borden was also very supportive of Aitken, and he was particularly pleased with the historical legacy that Aitken was gathering for future generations of Canadians.
23 RG 9, v. 4746, 175/1, CWRO, Report, 11 January 1917. Denis Winter has gone so far as to say that the Dominions' control over their records allowed them to keep more documents than the British, who culled many of the war records. Although Winter's arguments are sometimes based on conjecture or negative evidence, and are coloured by his palpable dislike for British senior commanders, his point on the Canadian control of their own records is important. Denis Winter, *Haig's Command: A Reassessment* (London: Penguin Books, 1991), chs. 14 and 15.
24 RG 9, v. 4746, 175/5, CWRO, [draft history, 21 February 1918].
25 For Beaverbrook's career as an historian, see John O. Stubbs, "Beaverbrook as Historian: 'Politicians and the War, 1914-1916' Reconsidered," *Albion* 14, 3-4 (1982): 235-53; and J.M. McEwen, "Lord Beaverbrook: Historian Extraordinary," *Dalhousie Review* 59, 1 (1979): 129-43.
26 One report claimed that 250,000 copies were sold by May 1916. BP, reel A-1765, Report by Sir Max Aitken to Rt. Hon. Sir Robert Borden on the Joint Establishment of the Canadian Representative at the Front and the Canadian War Records, n.d. [ca. 19 May 1916].
27 Reviews collected in RG 9, v. 4732, 140/7, Extracts from Press Opinion of *Canada in Flanders*, n.d. [ca. March 1916].

28 RG 25, v. 259, file P-3-19, Aitken to Herbert Samuel [of the Home Office], 22 May 1916; BP, A-1764, Aitken to Hughes, 13 October 1916; Aitken to Hughes, 27 October 1916.
29 RG 9, v. 4746, 175/1, CWRO, Report submitted to ... Sir Robert L. Borden, 11 January 1917.
30 Quotation from RG 9, v. 4746, 175/5, CWRO, [draft history, 21 February 1918]; RG 9, v. 4732, 140/7 Aitken to Leckie, 15 March 1916.
31 Quotation from RG 9, v. 4746, 175/1, CWRO, Report submitted to ... Sir Robert L. Borden, 11 January 1917; also see RG 9, v. 4732, 140/8, CWRO to Colonel F.A. Gascoigne, 29 May 1918.
32 RG 9, v. 4720, 114/18, Aitken to Major General J.W. Carson, 27 December 1916.
33 Henry Beckles Willson, *From Quebec to Piccadilly* (London: Jonathan Cape, 1929), 201.
34 At this point in the war, the Canadian Corps consisted of the 1st and 2nd Divisions. The 3rd and 4th Divisions had been added by the end of 1916.
35 RG 9, III-D-3, v. 4676, 4/3, Aitken to Manly Sims, 9 February 1916.
36 RG 9, v. 4770, 143/7, CWRO in France, n.d. [ca. 1918].
37 For Aitken's role in the removal of Alderson, see BP, reel A-1764, Aitken to Hughes, 24 April 1916; Morton, *A Peculiar Kind of Politics*, 72-5.
38 For examples of Aitken's power in Canadian war politics until Hughes was asked to resign, see BP, reel A-1764, Aitken to Hughes, 19 September 1915; Aitken to Hughes, 26 September 1915; Hughes to Aitken, 28 September 1915; Aitken to Hughes, 6 October 1915; Hughes to Aitken, 2 November 1915. For Aitken's role in bringing down the Asquith government, see Driberg, *Beaverbrook: A Study*, 86-109; and the more recent book by Anne Chisholm and Michael Davie, *Beaverbrook: A Life* (London: Hutchinson, 1992).
39 LAC, MG 30 E52, Talbot Papineau papers, v. 4, Papineau to Dear B., 26 October 1916.
40 See Jeffrey Williams, *Byng of Vimy: General and Governor General* (Toronto: University of Toronto Press, 1983, 1992), xiv.
41 LAC, Records of the National Archives of Canada (RG 37), v. 195, Doughty to Hughes, 16 February 1916.
42 Ian E. Wilson, "Shortt and Doughty: The Cultural Role of the Public Archives of Canada, 1904-1935" (MA thesis, Queen's University, 1973), 26.
43 For the best account of Doughty in the war, see Robert McIntosh, "The Great War, Archives and Modern Memory," *Archivaria* 46 (Fall 1998): 1-31.
44 Maria Tippett, *Art at the Service of War: Canada, Art and the Great War* (Toronto: University of Toronto Press, 1984), 17.
45 See LAC, MG 30 D 26, Sir Arthur Doughty papers (DP), v. 8, diary, 19 March 1916; 3 May 1916.
46 Beckles Willson, *From Quebec to Piccadilly*, 210-11.
47 RG 9, v. 4746, 175/5, CWRO, [draft history, 21 February 1918].
48 Borden papers, 32523-4; Doughty to Borden, 11 August 1916; LAC, DP, v. 8, diary, 3 May 1916.
49 DP, diary, v. 8, 3 May 1916.
50 Ibid.
51 LAC, MG 30 E 300, Victor Odlum papers, v. 3, T.G. Roberts, "I remember Currie," pt. 2, *The Ottawa Journal*, 9 April 1940.
52 BP, A-1765, Manly Sims to Aitken, 5 June 1916.
53 RG 9, v. 4458, 19/4, Aitken to Byng, 25 July 1916; RG 9, v. 4746, 176/2, Report on War Diaries, 8 February 1917.
54 RG 9, v. 4458, 19/3, G.40, 30 March 1917.
55 LAC, T-10721, War Diary, 18th Battalion, p. 2, September 1916.
56 LAC, T-10750, War Diary, 73rd Battalion, Aitken to Byng, 25 July 1916.
57 RG 9, v. 4746, 175/1, CWRO, Report submitted to ... Sir Robert L. Borden, 11 January 1917. The CWRO representatives at the front often "stimulated" battalion officers to craft better testimonials of their unit's actions; see RG 9, v. 4740, 159/1, CWRO memorandum, 19 February 1918; and RG 9, v. 4741, 161/2, Roberts to Watkins, 24 May 1917.

58 Official historian A.F. Duguid wrote in 1938, after having used the CWRO-shaped records to craft his history, that the Canadian War Diaries were at least twice as detailed as that of the British and Australians; "this excellence ... must in fairness be laid to Beaverbrook and his emissaries at the front 'urging upon units in the field the historical importance of making their own war diaries complete.'" LAC, Records of the Department of National Defence (RG 24), v. 1755, DHS 10-10, pt. 2, Duguid to Sir Andrew Macphail, 8 February 1938.
59 LAC, MG 30 E52, Talbot Papineau papers, Papineau to Dear B., 9 October 1916.
60 Quotation from RG 9, v. 4741, 162/4, Robertson to C.H. Hastings, 28 December 1917; RG 9, v. 4740, 159/1, Doughty to Beaverbrook, 21 June 1917.
61 The CWRO undertook a rigorous analysis of all Canadian battalion War Diaries after the battle of the Somme. See RG 9, v. 4746, 175/4, Memorandum on the Supply of Reports and Narratives on Recent Fighting, n.d. [ca. late 1916, early 1917]. On the improvement of War Diaries, see RG 9, v. 4741, 161/2, Report to Lord Beaverbrook from Capt. G.E.G.T. Roberts, 16 May 1917, and RG 9, v. 4740, 159/1, CWRO, 19 February 1918.
62 LAC, MG 27, II-D-9, A.E. Kemp papers (hereafter KP), v. 133, file C-27, CWRO, Second Annual Report ... to the Hon. Sir Edward Kemp, 30 March 1918. Also see RG 9, v. 4741, 162/1, CWRO to Manly Sims, 27 June 1917.
63 Borden papers, items 32496-7, 11 May 1916.
64 For basing the Canadian book on the Anzac book, see RG 9, v. 4746, 175/3, Minutes of Meeting, 22 September 1916, which referred to how the CWRO was looking for a publisher for the Canadian "Anzac" Book. Quotation from RG 9, v. 4746, 175/1, CWRO Report, 11 January 1917. It is interesting to note, however, that Charles Bean, the Australian reporter, archivist, and official historian, modelled his Australian War Records Section after Beaverbrook's CWRO. See Ann Millar, "Gallipoli to Melbourne: The Australian War Memorial, 1915-19," *Journal of the Australian War Memorial* 10 (April 1987): 34.
65 RG 9, v. 4732, 140/9, Aitken to Roberts, 30 August 1916.
66 Charles Bean conducted a similar selection of material to conform to his image of the Digger. See D.A. Kent, "The Anzac Book and the Anzac Legend: C.E.W. Bean as Editor and Image-maker," *Historical Studies* 84, 21 (1985); Denis Winter, "The Anzac Book: A Reappraisal," *Journal of the Australian War Memorial* 16 (April 1990); Alistair Thomson, "'Steadfast until Death'? C.E.W. Bean and the Representation of Australian Manhood," *Australian Historical Studies* 23, 93 (1989): 462-79.
67 RG 9, v. 4733, 140/10, "Fact."
68 LAC, KP, v. 52, file 9, Beaverbrook to Kemp, 21 April 1917.
69 The quotations are taken from *Canada in Khaki: A Tribute to the Officers and Men Now Serving in the Canadian Expeditionary Force, No. 1* (London: CWRO, 1917).
70 RG 9, v. 4746, 175/1, CWRO, Report submitted to ... Sir Robert L. Borden, 11 January 1917.
71 For photography, see RG 9, v. 4746, 175/1, CWRO, Report submitted to ... Sir Robert L. Borden, 11 January 1917; Peter Robertson, "Canadian Photojournalism during the First World War," *History of Photography* 2, 1 (1978): 371; W. Rider, "With a Camera at the Front," in *Canada in Khaki: A Tribute to the Officers and Men Now Serving in the Canadian Expeditionary Force, No. 3* (London: CWRO, 1917). For films, see KP, v. 133, file C-27, Second Report of the War Office Cinematography Committee, September 1918; Nicholas Reeves, *Official British Film Propaganda Film during the First World War* (London: Croom Helm, 1986); Peter Morris, *Embattled Shadows: A History of Canadian Cinema, 1895-1939* (Montreal and Kingston: McGill-Queen's University Press, 1978): 58-61. For the CWMF and the war artist program, see Tippett, *Art at the Service of War*; and Laura Brandon, "Shattered Landscape: The Great War and the Art of the Group of Seven," *Canadian Military History* 10, 1 (2001): 58-66.
72 RG 9, v. 4770, 143/7, draft article, CWRO in France, n.d. [ca. 1918].

73 Quotation from diary of Lieutenant Colonel John J. Creelman, a bitter enemy of Hughes. LAC, MG 30 E8, John J. Creelman papers, diary, 19 November 1916.
74 Robert Craig Brown and Ramsay Cook, *Canada, 1896-1921: A Nation Transformed* (Toronto: McClelland, 1974), 217.
75 For the most even-handed account of Hughes, see Ronald G. Haycock, *Sam Hughes: The Public Career of a Controversial Canadian, 1885-1916* (Ottawa: Canadian War Museum, 1986); and, more recently, Ronald G. Haycock, "Sir Sam Hughes: A Canadian General – Why Bother!" in *Warrior Chiefs: Perspectives on Senior Canadian Military Leaders,* ed. Lieutenant Colonel Bernd Horn and Stephen Harris (Toronto: Dundurn Press, 2001), 17-42. The destruction of Hughes's papers has not helped historians reconstruct his accomplishments; see Sam H.S. Hughes, "Sir Sam Hughes and the Problem of Imperialism," *Report of the Annual Meeting of the Canadian Historical Association,* 1950, 30-41.
76 BP, A-1764, Aitken to Hughes, 16 November 1916.
77 RG 9, v. 4769, file CIF-3. It is interesting to note that after the war, A.F. Duguid, the Canadian official historian, uncovered the same damning testimony and was struggling with how to incorporate it into the volume dealing with St. Eloi. See Directorate of History and Heritage (DHH), Duguid Biography file, folder 3, file Colonel A.F. Duguid, pt. 1, Duguid to Turner, 4 August 1923; ibid., Duguid to Lt. Col. D.E. Macintyre, 18 June 1928, and Macintyre to Duguid, 28 June 1928; ibid., file 75 – Relations between General Turner and General Alderson, interview on 14 March 1934 as recorded by Duguid.
78 RG 9, v. 4746, 175/3, Memo, Sir Max Aitken, 19 September 1916.
79 See for example, RG 9, v. 4732, 140/7, correspondence; ibid., J.B. Murphy to Beaverbrook, 25 June 1917; RG 9, v. 4732, 140/8, CWRO to Gascoigne, 29 May 1918; BP, A-1766, Sanders to HQ, 2nd Division, 3 April 1917; Aitken to Manly Sims, 19 April 1917.
80 The Beaverbrook papers contain ample evidence of Aitken's interference in the appointments of senior officers to make way for his friends and ensure that they received plum positions during 1915 and 1916.
81 RG 9, v. 4678, 10/1, Currie to Beaverbrook, 22 May 1917; and RG 9, v. 4732, 140/6, Davy to Aitken, 15 December 1916.
82 LAC, MG 30 E100, Sir Arthur Currie papers (LAC, CP), v. 2, file "M-R," Currie to Perley, 10 December 1917; Smart to Currie, 6 January 1918; A.M.J. Hyatt, "Sir Arthur Currie and Politicians: A Case Study of Civil-Military Relations in the First World War," in *Swords and Covenants,* ed. Richard Preston and Peter Dennis (London: Croom Helm, 1976), 148; Daniel Dancocks, *Sir Arthur Currie: A Biography* (Toronto: Methuen, 1985), 126-7.
83 Hugh M. Urquhart, *Arthur Currie: The Biography of a Great Canadian* (Toronto: J.M. Dent and Sons, 1950), 205-6.
84 For the controversy, see KP, v. 135, file C-48: Currie to Beaverbrook, 3 July 1918; Roberts to Currie, 11 July 1918; Beaverbrook to Currie, 12 July 1918; Currie to Kemp, 4 July 1918.
85 RG 9, v. 4746, 176/1, Extract of Routine Orders by Sir Arthur Currie, 6 September 1918.
86 The CWRO also published a newspaper for the Canadian soldier: the *Canadian Daily Record.* The paper contained general news on Canada and the war, with sporting and social news forming the majority of the content. From mid-1917 onward, the circulation of the paper was more than 15,000 copies a day. The 787th and final issue was published on 31 July 1919. RG 9, v. 4746, 176/7, CWRO – *The Canadian Daily Record,* 31 May 1918. For a few examples, see RG 9, v. 4770, 143/7; and Willson, *From Quebec to Piccadilly,* 204.
87 RG 9, v. 4770, 143/7, CWRO to Roberts, 16 October 1917.
88 LAC, CP, v. 1, file 1, Currie to Brewster, 31 May 1917; Dancocks, *Sir Arthur Currie,* 131.
89 BP, A-1765, Report by Sir Max Aitken to Rt. Hon. Sir Robert Borden on ... Canadian Representative at the Front, n.d. [ca. 19 May 1916].

90 See Shane B. Schreiber, *Shock Army of the British Empire: The Canadian Corps in the Last 100 Days of the Great War* (Westport, CT: Praeger, 1997); Tim Cook, *No Place To Run: The Canadian Corps and Gas Warfare in the First World War* (Vancouver: UBC Press, 1999). Canadian War Museum, Sir Arthur Currie papers (hereafter CWM, CP), file 58A 1 61.4, Currie to Dobie, 9 February 1919.
91 RG 9 III-A-2, v. 353, file 106, Major E. Bristol to Embury, 23 October 1918. Also see LAC, CP, v. 1, file 1, Currie to Borden, 26 November 1918; ibid., v. 1, file 2, Currie to Kemp, 1 November 1918.
92 RG 9 III-A-2, v. 353, file 106, Memo: Re Press Censorship, 31 October 1918; Embury to C.P., GHQ, 1 November 1918; Embury to Bristol, 10 November 1918.
93 Quote from BP, A-1766, William Dennis to Beaverbrook, 28 September 1918.
94 For Dominion anger regarding coverage, see John F. Williams, *ANZACs, the Media and the Great War* (Sydney: University of New South Wales, 1999), 179, 199-201, 245-6.
95 *Manchester Guardian*, 23 December 1919, as cited in Tippett, *Art at the Service of War*, 21.
96 James E. Hahn, *For Action: The Autobiography of a Canadian Industrialist* (Toronto: Clarke, Irwin, 1954), 7.
97 RG 9, v. 4746, 176/1, Memorandum to Lord Beaverbrook by Lieutenant W.H. Wright, n.d. [ca. 31 January 1919].
98 RG 24, v. 1732, file DHS 1-4, Wright to Parkinson, n.d. [early 1919].
99 RG 37, v. 352, file 1-11, Doughty to Foster, 22 March 1917; Order-in-council 67/1209, 2 May 1917. Wood was a prolific military historian of the Seven Years War and had written to Prime Minister Borden in March 1916 to be appointed "War Historian of Canada." Borden forwarded the correspondence to Aitken, who obviously coveted that role for himself – for the moment at least – and politely turned him down. See BP, 32483-5, Wood to Borden, 30 March 1916 and 16 April 1916. Lanctôt had served in the CEF and would later rise to succeed Doughty as Dominion Archivist of Canada (1937-1948).
100 RG 37, v. 11, p 300-302, Doughty to Ashton, 27 May 1918. For an account of the War Archives Survey, see RG 37, v. 352, file 1-11, Private Memoir on the Canadian War Archives Survey ..., 1 January 1918 [revised by Wood on 29 November 1918].
101 RG 9, III-A-1, v. 99, file 10-14-23, War Trophies, 24 June 1918; and the correspondence in RG 9, III-B-1, v. 1033, file W-3-3.
102 RG 37, v. 366, file 1, Report of a Special Committee ... Disposition of War Trophies, 6 November 1918, 3-4; ibid., file: Dominion Archivist, 1916-22, Doughty to E.L. Patenaude, Secretary of State, 26 April 1917, 53-5.
103 See Laura Brandon, "The Canadian War Memorial That Never Was," *Canadian Military History* 7, 4 (1998): 45-54.
104 Before it disbanded in 1919, the CWRO also assisted and published histories: Colonel J.G. Adami's *War Story of the Canadian Army Medical Corps* (1918) and *Thirty Canadian V.C.s* (1919), edited by T.G. Robert.
105 KP, v. 133, file C-27, CWRO Third Annual Report, 31 August 1919; and CWRO to Kemp, n.d. [ca. late 1918]; LAC, CP, v. 2, file "M-R", Parkinson to Currie, 18 October 1918.
106 J.F.B. Livesay, *Canada's Hundred Days: With the Canadian Corps from Amiens to Mons, Aug. 8-Nov. 11, 1918* (Toronto: T. Allen, 1919), 81.
107 J.F.B. Livesay, *The Making of a Canadian* (Toronto: Ryerson Press, 1947), 96.
108 Robert Scott Demill, "The 1928 Cobourg Trial of Sir Arthur Currie and the Port Hope Evening Guide: The Rehabilitation of the Reputation of a Corps Commander," (MA thesis, University of Ottawa, 1989), 65-6.
109 RG 9, v. 4746, 175/4, Supply of Reports and Narratives on Recent Fighting, n.d. [ca. late 1916, early 1917].
110 CWM, CP, file 58A 1 61.4, Currie to Sir Arthur Conan Doyle, 1 February 1919.

111 RG 9, III-B-1, v. 1033, file W-4-3, G.8/6-19, 30 December 1918; also, see the correspondence in RG 24, v. 1733, file DHS-1-13.
112 RG 9, v. 4809, file 196, General directions for guidance in the compilation of detailed narrative of operations of the CANADIAN CORPS, 15 September 1919.
113 LAC, CP, v. 1, file 2, Currie to Lt. Col. W. Ridgway Wilson, 10 December 1918.
114 House of Commons Debates, 1919, v. 1, 3 March 1919, 207.
115 CWM, CP, file 58A 1 61.7, Peck to Currie, 8 April 1919; House of Commons Debates, 1919, v. 1, 14 March 1919, 468.
116 See Tim Cook, "The Butcher and the Madman: Sir Arthur Currie, Sir Sam Hughes and the War of Reputations," *Canadian Historical Review* 85, 4 (2004): 693-719.
117 CWM, CP, file 58A 1 61.4, Currie to Watson, 4 February 1919.
118 CWM, CP, file 58A 1 61.4, M.H. Dobie to Currie, 4 January 1919; Currie to Dobie, 9 February 1919.
119 CWM, CP, file 58A 1 61.5, Currie to First Army, 20 March 1919; Horne to Currie, 27 March 1919. Burstall was also angry because he thought that several "published reports" had ignored his division. He pleaded for Currie to rectify the matter, especially in any official publications. LAC, CP, v. 3, file 1, Burstall to Currie, 8 April 1919.
120 Desmond Morton, *Canada and War: A Military and Political History* (Toronto: Butterworths, 1981), 133.
121 KP, v. 136, file c-90, Canadian War Narrative Section, n.d. [ca. June 1919].
122 Jay Luvaas, "The First British Official Historians," in *Official Histories: Essays and Bibliographies from around the World,* ed. Robin Higham (Manahattan, KS: Kansas State University Library, 1970) 488-505.
123 See the correspondence in RG 24, v. 369, HQ 54-2-3.
124 LAC, CP, v. 39, file 174, Brutinel to Currie, 26 August 1919.
125 RG 9, v. 4732, 140/7, Extracts from Press Opinion of *Canada in Flanders*, n.d. [ca. March 1916].
126 RG 9, v. 4676, 3/5, untitled [memoirs by Colonel J.J. Carrick], n.d. [ca. late 1915].
127 LAC, CP, v. 1, file 1, Currie to Harold Daly, 26 October 1918; v. 1, file 2, Currie to Sir William Hearst, 14 November 1917.
128 RG 9, v. 4746, 175/5, CWRO, [draft history, 21 February 1918]; Aitken, *Canada in Flanders,* vol. 2, vii-viii.
129 See Peter Buitenhuis, *The Great War of Words: British, American and Canadian Propaganda and Fiction, 1914-1933* (Vancouver: UBC Press, 1987), 80, 98-101; and Williams, *ANZACS, the Media and the Great War,* 171, 265 for assertions that Beaverbrook was the war's premier propagandist. For the quotation, see Chisholm and Davie, *Beaverbrook: A Life,* 163.
130 The traditional concept of archives and self-image of archivists concerns notions of neutrality, objectivity, and impartiality. In other words, the archivist is constructed as a kind of invisible, honest broker between original creators and users of records. Such views have been challenged in recent debates in archival theory. For the most significant discussion on the topic, see Terry Cook, "What Is Past Is Prologue: A History of Archival Ideas since 1898, and Future Paradigm Shift," *Archivaria* 43 (Spring 1997): 17-63; Brien Brothman, "The Limits of Limit: Derridean Deconstruction and the Archival Institution," *Archivaria* 36 (Autumn 1993): 205-20; and Richard Brown, "Death of a Renaissance Record-Keeper: The Murder of Tomasso da Tortona in Ferrara, 1385," *Archivaria* 44 (Fall 1997): 1-43.
131 Basil Liddell Hart, *Why Don't We Learn from History?* (London: George Allen and Unwin, 1944), 9.
132 Philip Gibbs, *Realities of War* (London: Heinemann, 1920), 191.
133 Quotation from Arthur R.M. Lower, *My First Seventy-Five Years* (Toronto: Macmillan, 1967), 106; Buchan cited in Tippett, 21.

134 Lord Beaverbrook, *Canada in Flanders*, vol. 2, 4th ed. (London: Hodder and Stoughton, 1917), viii-ix.

Chapter 2: The War of Reputations, 1918-39

1. N.a., "Canadian War Records: The Making of History," *Canada in Khaki: A Tribute to the Officers and Men Now Serving in the Canadian Expeditionary Force*, vol. 1 (London: CWRO, 1917), 114.
2. LAC, Lord Beaverbrook papers (hereafter BP), microfilm reel, A-1765, Aitken to Willson, 22 May 1916.
3. Order-in-council 19, 17 January 1917.
4. J. Mackay Hitsman and C.P. Stacey, *Historical Activities within the Canadian Army: Report No. 1, Historical Officer, Canadian Military Headquarters* (Ottawa: N.p., 1965), 1-2.
5. LAC, MG 27, II-D-9, A.E. Kemp papers, v. 70, file 19, Memo to Kemp, 2 December 1916; P. Whitney Lackenbauer, "The Military and 'Mob Rule': The CEF Riots in Calgary, February 1916," *Canadian Military History* 10, 1 (2001): 31-43.
6. Order-in-council 2814, 15 November 1918.
7. Historical Section, General Staff, *A History of the Organization, Development and Services of the Military and Naval Forces of Canada from the Peace of Paris in 1763 to the Present Time*, 3 vols. (Ottawa: Historical Section, 1919-20).
8. Historical Section, General Staff, *A Narrative of the Formation and Operations of the First Canadian Division, to the end of the Second Battle of Ypres, May 4, 1915*, vol. 1 (Ottawa: Thomas Mulvey, King's Printer, 1920).
9. LAC, MG30 E100, Sir Arthur Currie papers (hereafter LAC, CP), v. 11, file 34, Currie to MacBrien, 12 January 1921.
10. Cruikshank (1892-1940) was the author of numerous histories, including the nine-volume *Documentary History of the Campaigns upon the Niagara Frontier in 1812-1814* (Welland, ON: Lundy's Lane Historical Society, 1896-1908).
11. For Cruikshank's post-military career, see C.J. Taylor, *Negotiating the Past: The Making of Canada's National Historic Parks and Sites* (Montreal and Kingston: McGill-Queen's University Press, 1990).
12. Hitsman and Stacey, *Historical Activities within the Canadian Army*, 3-5.
13. G.W.L. Nicholson, "Archer Fortescue Duguid 1887-1976," *Canadian Historical Association Annual Papers* (1976); RG 24, v. 1734, file DHS 1-22, handwritten account by Duguid on his wartime services, n.d.
14. Order-in-council 1652, 27 May 1921.
15. Wesley C. Gustavson, "Missing the Boat? Colonel A.F. Duguid and the Canadian Official History of World War I" (MA thesis, University of Calgary, 1999), 17.
16. RG 24, v. 1732, file DHS 1-4 (pt. 2), Guthrie to Lougheed, 12 May 1921.
17. RG 24, v. 1733, file DHS 1-12 (pt. 1), Report of the Director, 1 June-31 December 1921.
18. Duff Crerar, *Padres in No Man's Land* (Montreal and Kingston: McGill-Queen's University Press, 1995), 5, 254. The manuscript is in LAC, MG 30 E4, William Beattie papers, History of the Canadian Chaplain Services.
19. It is unclear why the engineer history failed, but Hitsman and Stacey suggest it was due to the controversy that erupted over his brother's medical history in 1925. Alexander Macphail was also sick in the late 1920s and that may have put paid to the history. Hitsman and Stacey, *Historical Activities within the Canadian Army*, 7.
20. RG 24, v. 1733, file DHS-1-12 (pt. 2), Report of the Director, April-June 1923.
21. I would like to thank Dr. Susan Mann for sharing her research on Margaret Macdonald.
22. John Ross Matheson, *Canada's Flag: A Search for a Country* (Boston: G.K. Hall, 1980), 103.
23. RG 24, v. 1733, file DHS-1-12 (pt. 2), Report of the Director, October-December 1923.

24 LAC, Records of the National Archives of Canada, RG 37, v. 352, file 1-11, Doughty to Sir George Foster, 22 March 1917.
25 Harold R. Peat, foreword to *Private Peat* (New York: Grosset and Dunla, 1917).
26 W.A. Bishop, *Winged Warfare: Hunting the Huns in the Air* (Toronto: Hodder and Stoughton, 1918).
27 Wilfrid Kerr, "Historical Literature on Canada's Participation in the Great War," *Canadian Historical Review* 14, 3 (1933): 417.
28 William Breckenridge, foreword to *From Vimy to Mons: A Historical Narrative* (self-published, 1919).
29 RG 24, v. 1740, DHS 4-4, pt. 4, Manager of United Publishers of Canada Limited to McNaughton, 4 July 1922.
30 Frank H. Underhill, "The Canadian Forces in the War," in *The Empire at War*, vol. 2., ed. Sir Charles Lucas (London: H. Milford, 1924). Underhill had access both to war records and senior generals such as Sir Arthur Currie. LAC, CP, 27/7, Currie to Underhill, 8 September 1920 and 17 September 1920. On restricted access to other historians, see RG 24, v. 1740, DHS 4-4, pt. 4, Duguid to Major J.M. Macdonnel, 4 September 1931.
31 LAC, CP, 27/7, Underhill to Currie, 8 September 1920.
32 Underhill, "The Canadian Forces in the War," 30.
33 Mary Vipond, "Best Sellers in English Canada: 1919-1928," *Journal of Canadian Fiction* 35-6 (1986): 84-5.
34 LAC, CP, Livesay to Currie, 23 December 1922.
35 For quotations see Annika Mombauer, *The Origins of the First World War: Controversies and Consensus* (London: Longman, 2002), 68-9; also see George Kent, "Editing Diplomatic Documents: A Review of Official U.S. and German Document Series," *American Archivist* 57, 3 (1994).
36 A.F. Duguid, *Official History of the Canadian Forces in the Great War, 1914-1919*, General Series, vol. 1 (Ottawa: J.O. Patenaude, 1938), v.
37 RG 24, v. 6990, file: Introduction, handwritten notes, n.d.
38 For the nature of amateur writing in Canadian history, see Beverly Boutilier and Alison Prentice, eds., *Creating Historical Memory: English-Canadian Women and the Work of History* (Vancouver: UBC Press, 1997); and M. Brook Taylor, *Promoters, Patriots and Partisans: Historiography in Nineteenth-Century English Canada* (Toronto: University of Toronto Press, 1989).
39 There is no exact figure in the archival records as to how many veterans Duguid corresponded with, but he did so at every opportunity, arranging interviews, sending off letters, and chatting informally at the many postwar reunions.
40 See T.H.E. Travers, "From Surafend to Gough: Charles Bean, James Edmonds, and the Making of the Australian Official History," *Journal of the Australian War Memorial* 27 (October 1995): 15, 23; and RG 24, v. 2680, file HQC 4950 (pt. 1), Duguid to Major General Sir C.F. Romer, 12 May 1926. The correspondence between Bean and Edmonds offers fascinating reading and also speaks to Edmonds's occasionally disdainful attitude towards the Australians. See, for example, Australian War Memorial (AWM), 3DRL 3954/34.
41 John Lukacs, *The History of Hitler* (New York: Knopf, 1997), 32.
42 G.W.L. Nicholson, *Canadian Expeditionary Force, 1914-1919* (Ottawa: Queen's Printer, 1964), 92.
43 Sir Andrew Macphail wrote to the British Colonial Secretary that the British official history drafts were "discussed between the 200 officers present at the Governor General's annual Vimy Dinner on 9 April ... if the book is published, even in its present form, it will let loose wrath and recrimination." The correspondence relating to the draft histories bears out Macphail's observation. LAC, CP, v. 11, file 33, Macphail to Currie, 26 April 1926.

44 RG 24, v. 2680, file HQC 4950 (pt. 1), T.V. Anderson to Duguid, 10 May 1926.
45 LAC, CP, v. 8, file 22, Currie to MacBrien, n.d. [ca. 1926].
46 RG 24, v. 1738, DHS 3-17 (vol. 1), Duguid to Edmonds, 18 May 1925.
47 RG 24, v. 1738, DHS 3-17 (vol. 2), MacBrien to Chief of the Imperial General Staff, 24 November 1925.
48 LAC, CP, v. 15, file 44, MacBrien to Currie, 4 June 1926.
49 Andrew Samuel Green, "Sir James Edmonds and the Official Military Histories of the Great War" (PhD diss., University of Leeds, 1999), 16-17; RG 24, v. 1738, DHS 3-17 (vol. 1), Edmonds to Duguid, 3 June 1925.
50 RG 24, v. 1755, DHS 10-10, pt. 1, Tuxford to Duguid, 15 April 1926.
51 See correspondence in RG 24, v. 1755, DHS 10-10, pt. 20.
52 RG 24, v. 1738, DHS 3-17 (vol. 2), Extracts from letters of officers on staff of Canadian Division April and May 1915, Gordon Hall, 9 December 1925.
53 Tim Travers, "Allies in Conflict: The British and Canadian Official Historians and the Real Story of Second Ypres (1915)," *Journal of Contemporary History* 24 (1989): 303-4.
54 RG 24, v. 2680, file HQC 4950 (pt. 1), Brown to MacBrien, 25 November 1925.
55 RG 24, v. 1755, DHS 10-10, pt. 2, Duguid to Alderson, 15 May 1926.
56 RG 24, v. 1738, DHS 3-17 (vol. 2), Duguid to Edmonds, 9 December 1925.
57 I would like to thank Dr. Patrick Brennan for sharing with me his research on Currie and his generals.
58 Tim Travers, "Currie and 1st Canadian Division at Second Ypres, April 1915: Controversy, Criticism and Official History," *Canadian Military History* 5, 2 (1996): 13.
59 Daniel G. Dancocks, *Sir Arthur Currie: A Biography* (Toronto: Methuen, 1985), 231. For a similar Australian reaction, see Alistair Thompson, "'The Vilest Libel of the War'? Imperial Politics and the Official Histories of Gallipoli," *Australian Historical Studies* 25, 101 (October 1993): 628-36.
60 Travers, "Allies in Conflict," 308.
61 RG 24, v. 1738, DHS 3-17 (vol. 3), Duguid to CGS, 13 March 1928.
62 Ibid., Duguid to CGS, 11 May 1928.
63 Directorate of History and Heritage (DHH), Duguid Biography file, folder A, file 2, Duguid to Megill, Canadian Official History, 18 February 1947.
64 Macphail had finished writing most of his history by the summer of 1922, but it was delayed three years before publication. See RG 24, v. 1733, DHS-1-12 (pt. 1), Report of DHS, 1-7-22 to 30-9-22. Sir Andrew Macphail, *The Medical Services* (Ottawa: King's Printer, 1925).
65 David Campbell, "Politics, Polemics, and the Boundaries of Personal Experience: Sir Andrew Macphail as Official Historian." 81st Annual Meeting of the Canadian Historical Association, Toronto, 28 May 2002.
66 Professor J.C. Adami, F.R.S., of McGill University had been appointed Medical Historical Recorder of the CEF on 5 March 1917. In 1918 he published *War Story of the Canadian Army Medical Corps* (London: Rolls House, 1918), but it recounted the story of the CAMC only up to 1915. In 1924 A.E. Snell, another CAMC veteran, published *The C.A.M.C. with the Canadian Corps during the Last Hundred Days of the Great War* (Ottawa: King's Printer, 1924). This was a semi-official publication, but might be considered more of a textbook for medical training than an historical work.
67 A review in the *British Medical Journal* in September 1925 rightly noted that Macphail's history, and especially his view on shell shock, was "sweeping and dogmatic." RG 24, v. 5942, file HQ 393-9-17.
68 DHH, unprocessed registry files (URF), box 58, file 10-4, pt. 1, MacBrien to Minister, 22 February 1922; Macphail to MacBrien, 30 January 1923; box 58, file 10-4, pt. 2, Macphail and Medical History, MacBrien to Private Secretary, Minister of National Defence, 18 January 1924.

69 For the disclaimer, see RG 24, v. 1739, file DHS 3-17A, Neal to Duguid, 23 July 1924. For the reviews, see RG 24, v. 1872, file 13, History of the Canadian Forces Medical Services, Reviews, Remarks and Comments Culled from Various Sources. This collection of reviews was created by the AHS.
70 LAC, MG30 E300, Victor Odlum papers, v. 3, file Duguid, Duguid to Odlum, 4 October 1938. For the ongoing demand for an official history, see Douglas Mackay, "Canada's Official War History," *Maclean's Magazine*, 15 February 1926, 15.
71 Editorial, *Evening Guide of Port Hope*, 13 June 1927.
72 RG 24, v. 448, HQC 54-21-1-210, Currie to Duguid, 22 June 1927.
73 LAC, CP, v. 18, file 60, Currie to Duguid, 22 June 1927.
74 RG 24, v. 448, HQC 54-21-1-210, List of Killed – 3rd Cdn Division, Mons, 1918.
75 LAC, CP, v. 18, file 60, Currie to Ralston, 22 June 1927.
76 RG 24, v. 448, HQC 54-21-1-210, Currie to Duguid, 22 September 1927. Currie had received a few letters from veterans stating this after the war; see, for example, LAC, CP, v. 18, file 60, Captain Harry T. Cock to Currie, 29 March 1928; and ibid., Lt. Col. B.O. Hooper to Currie, 2 April 1928.
77 RG 24, v. 448, HQC 54-21-1-210, Duguid to Bovey, 8 October 1927.
78 Dancocks, *Sir Arthur Currie*, 251.
79 Keith Wilson, ed., *Forging the Collective Memory: Government and International Historians through Two World Wars* (Oxford: Berghahn Books, 1996), 22.
80 RG 24, v. 448, HQC 54-21-1-210, Memo by Colonel R.J. Orde, Judge Advocate-General, 13 March 1928.
81 It is likely that these figures include the dead and wounded from the battle of Valenciennes, the last set-piece Canadian engagement of the war that was fought on 1-2 November 1918.
82 RG 24, v. 448, HQC 54-21-1-210, "Claims Records Deliberately Falsified and Will Call Men Engaged at Mons to Prove It," *The Ottawa Citizen*, 19 March 1928.
83 Trial transcript, 33.
84 Trial transcript, 712.
85 Robert J. Sharpe, *The Last Day, the Last Hour: The Currie Libel Trial* (Toronto: The Osgoode Society, 1988), 133-5.
86 RG 24, v. 448, HQC 54-21-1-210, Orde to Minister, 22 May 1928.
87 Trial transcript, 2122-3.
88 Dancocks, *Sir Arthur Currie*, 235.
89 RG 24, v. 2732, HQS 5393, Thacker to Deputy Minister, 17 January 1928.
90 RG 24, v. 1738, file DHS 3-17 (vol. 3), Duguid to Thacker, 16 March 1928.
91 RG 24, v. 2732, HQS 5393, Thacker to Deputy Minister, 17 January 1928.
92 DHH, Duguid Biography file, folder A, file 2, Tory to Ralston, 2 January 1929.
93 LAC, CP, v. 41, file 186, A draft of the instructions to the Committee on the Official History, n.d.; DHH, Duguid Biography file, folder A, file 10, McNaughton to Minister, 22 January 1929.
94 Green, "Sir James Edmonds," 32, 109-10.
95 The selection and destruction of the war records was carried out by the DND, and specifically the AHS, rather than the Dominion Archives. Hundreds of thousands of administrative records were destroyed, and it appears from the file titles at least that these included few valuable records. One cringes, however, when one comes across a reference such as the following by one of the AHS researchers who examined a number of files in 1937, and after finding a file relating to a First Contingent officer who deliberately shot himself at Givenchy on 6 June 1915, the AHS officer felt it not worth keeping because "the sketch of the trench was not particularly good." The most important case of destroying files came in the early 1920s when senior officials decided to destroy the "shot at dawn" courts-martial records

relating to the twenty-five Canadians executed during the war. For DND destruction of records, see the correspondence in RG 37, vol. 41, 60-3-NAT DEF (vol. 4). For the self-inflicted wound record destroyed, see RG 24, v. 1733, DHS 1-8-8, Pye to Duguid, 25 September 1937. For courts-martial records, see Andrew Godefroy, *For Freedom and Honour?: The Story of the 25 Canadian Volunteers Executed in the First World War* (Nepean, ON: CEF Books, 1998).

96 DHH, Duguid Biography file, folder A, file 7, Duguid draft memo to Sir Andrew [Macphail], 23 May 1928. For the official order to allow only "properly accredited" historians, see RG 24, v. 1502, file HQ 683-1-29 (pt. 6), Duguid to CGS, Access to Official Documents, 4 May 1935.
97 In addition, there are more than thirty souvenir books and another twenty or more post-1945 regimental histories. These figures have been compiled from O.A. Cooke, *The Canadian Military Experience 1867-1995: A Bibliography*, 3rd ed. (Ottawa: Directorate of History and Heritage, 1995).
98 CWM, 58 C 1.1.9, Cummins to Spreckley, 15 September 1935.
99 CWM, 58 C 1.1.8, Nineteenth Battalion History, Questionnaire No. 1, n.d. [ca. April 1936].
100 CWM, 58 C 1.1.9, Link to V.E., 21 September 1936.
101 CWM, 58 C 1.1.8, Nineteenth Battalion History, Questionnaire No. 1, n.d. [ca. April 1936].
102 CWM, 58 C 1.1.9, Thompson to Spreckley, 6 February 1937.
103 Ibid., Knott to Spreckley, 31 January 1937.
104 See the correspondence in LAC, MG 30 E153, 38th Battalion papers; and Kevin R. Shackleton, preface to *Second to None: The Fighting 58th Battalion of the Canadian Expeditionary Force* (Toronto: Dundurn Press, 2002).
105 E.S. Russenholt, *Six Thousand Canadian Men: Being the History of the 44th Battalion Canadian Infantry, 1914-1919* (Winnipeg: De Montfort Press, 1932), vii.
106 Fetherstonhaugh would eventually write three regimental histories, as well as several histories and biographies. He was confined to a wheelchair throughout his life and was considered medically unfit for service in the Great War. DHH, file 000.9 (D4), biography file for R.C. Fetherstonhaugh. For the assistance to Fetherstonhaugh from the AHS, see RG 24, v. 1733, DHS-1-12 (pt. 3), Quarterly Report ending March 1927.
107 RG 24, v. 1754, DHS 9-1, Duguid to Major Gordon Thornton, 2 February 1933; LAC, MG 30 D252, Alan Beddoe papers, v. 22, file Duguid, British and Canadian Official Histories of the Great War, 1914-1919, 6 April 1932.
108 RG 24, v. 1504, HQ 683-1-30-5, Loomis to Duguid, 27 January 1937.
109 RG 24, v. 1754, DHS 9-1, Duguid to Major Gordon Thornton, 2 February 1933.
110 Lieutenant Colonel C. Beresford Topp, *The 42nd Battalion, CEF: Royal Highlanders of Canada in the Great War* (Montreal: Gazette Printing, 1931), vii.
111 CWM, A.F. Duguid papers, Unprocessed material, Hamilton Gault to Duguid, 4 June 1924.
112 Will R. Bird, *The Communication Trench: Anecdotes & Statistics of the Great War, 1914-1918* (1933; reprint, Nepean, ON: CEF Books, 2000), 58.
113 Topp, *The 42nd Battalion*, iv.
114 See, for example, Charles Yale Harrison, *Generals Die in Bed* (New York: Morrow, 1930).
115 The caption read: "In preparing this work the author was allowed access by the Department of National Defence to all official diaries, orders, messages, maps, and other relevant documents." See RG 24, v. 1502, file HQ 683-1-29 pt. 3, Duguid to CO, 5th Battery, 22 September 1928; DHH, 113.302009 (D72), Colonel F.A. Lister to Military District No. 2, 2 August 1932.
116 RG 24, v. 1875, file 23 (18), Duguid to Corrigall, 2 December 1929.
117 Ibid., file 23 (12), Duguid to Major K. Weatherbe, 19 September 1928.
118 R.C. Fetherstonhaugh, *The 13th Battalion Royal Highlanders of Canada, 1914-1919* (Montreal: 13th Battalion, Royal Highlanders of Canada, 1925), 209.

119 J.F.C., review of *Six Thousand Men: Being the History of the 44th Battalion Canadian Infantry,* by E.S. Russenholt, *Canadian Defence Quarterly* 9 (1931-32): 555.
120 Captain S.G. Bennett, MC, *The 4th Canadian Mounted Rifles, 1914-1919* (Toronto: Murray Printing, 1926), 8.
121 RG 24, v. 1504, HQ 683-1-30-5, Duguid to Sir Richard Turner, 5 February 1937.
122 Bennett, *The 4th Canadian Mounted Rifles,* 154-5.
123 RG 24, v. 1874, file 23, *Chronicle-Telegraph,* "The Fourteenth Battalion," 26 May 1927.
124 LAC, CP, v. 15, file 43, Currie to H.M. Urquhart, 8 October 1931.
125 For a view of the war as a great rift marking the birth of the modern age, see Modris Eksteins, *Rites of Spring: The Great War and the Birth of the Modern Age* (Toronto: Lester and Orpen Dennys, 1989) and Samuel Hynes, *A War Imagined: The First World War and English Culture* (London: The Bodley Head, 1990). For the postwar process of grieving that drew on traditional forms of commemoration, see Jay Winter, *Sites of Memory, Sites of Mourning: The Great War in European Cultural History* (Cambridge: Cambridge University Press, 1995) and Jonathan Vance, *Death So Noble: Memory, Meaning, and the First World War* (Vancouver: UBC Press, 1997).
126 E.S. Russenholt, *Six Thousand Canadian Men: Being the History of the 44th Battalion Canadian Infantry, 1914-1919* (Winnipeg: De Montfort Press, 1932), v; also see H.M. Urquhart, *The History of the 16th Battalion (The Canadian Scottish)* (Toronto: Macmillan, 1932), xx.
127 Captain W.L. Gibson, *Records of the Fourth Canadian Infantry Battalion in the Great War* (Toronto: Maclean Publishing, 1924) is interesting because it is only an honour roll. Gibson had hoped for a more detailed history, but a number of factors delayed and eventually cancelled the history. See Andrew Iarocci, "The 'Mad Fourth': The 4th Canadian Infantry Battalion in the Great War, 1914-1916" (MA thesis, Wilfrid Laurier University, 2001), ii-iv. Other regimental histories, such as that for the 77th, which was mobilized in Ottawa and then disbanded to provide reinforcements for England, concern individuals and not the battalions themselves. But they too are largely based on honour rolls. See War Publications, comp., *An Historical Sketch of the Seventy-Seventh Battalion, Canadian Expeditionary Force* (Ottawa: War Publications, 1926).
128 Topp, *The 42nd Battalion,* 316.
129 For an exploration of this issue, see Thomas W. Laqueur, "Memory and Naming in the Great War," in *Commemorations: The Politics of National Identity,* ed. John R. Gillis (Princeton: Princeton University Press, 1994).
130 Ralph Hodder-Williams, *Princess Patricia's Canadian Light Infantry, 1914-1919* (London: Hodder and Stoughton, 1923), viii, xvi.
131 Vance, *Death So Noble,* 116.
132 RG 24, v. 2732, file HQS 5393, Memorandum on the Historical Section, H.Q.C.650-16-6, 5 January 1928.
133 AWM, Series 38, Charles Bean papers, 7953/item 34, Edmonds to Bean, 26 July 1935.
134 RG 24, v. 1740, DHS 4-4, pt. 5, R.C. Fetherstonhaugh to Duguid, 8 January 1929.
135 See J. Castell Hopkins, *Canadian Annual Review 1919* (Toronto: Canadian Annual Review, 1920), 63-5, for an early counterattack by a high-profile Canadian against the American claims that they had won the war for the Allies.
136 Brigadier General Henry J. Reilly, "Who Won the War?" extract from *Liberty,* 29 January 1927. For support of Drew by the AHS, see DHH, Pye papers, 74/672, folder 18; RG 24, v. 1838, GAQ 10-17, Duguid to Brown, 21 February 1927.
137 Vance, *Death So Noble,* 178-9.
138 RG 24, v. 1733, DHS-1-12 (pt. 3), Report of the Director for the fiscal year ending 31 March 1927; and correspondence and notes in LAC, MG 30 E15, W.A. Griesbach papers, v. 1, file 2.

139 Major George A. Drew, "The Truth about the War," *Maclean's*, 1 July 1928.
140 *Ottawa Journal*, 14 November 1928.
141 *Montreal Star*, 6 December 1929.
142 For air-minded Canadians and the myths and imagery surrounding flight in Canada, see Jonathan Vance, *High Flight: Aviation and the Canadian Imagination* (Toronto: Penguin Canada, 2002).
143 RG 9, III-C-14, v. 4612, 14/3, McAdam to CWRO, (n.d., ca. July 1919).
144 The figure of 12,000 is given in ibid., McAdam to James, 10 December 1919.
145 Alan Sullivan, *Aviation in Canada, 1917-1918: Being a Brief Account of the Work of the Royal Air Force, Canada, the Aviation Department of the Imperial Munitions Board and the Canadian Aeroplanes Limited* (Toronto: Rous and Mann, 1919).
146 DHH, Duguid Biography file, folder A, file 3, documentation relation to PC 1652, 27 May 1921.
147 RG 24, v. 1733, DHS-1-12 (pt. 2), Notes on the Collection and Compilation ... Canadians Who Served in the British Flying Services, Appendix B, 24 July 1924. Also see RG 24, v. 1732, DHS 1-4 (vol. 2), Department of Militia and Defence, Historical Section, 7 September 1921; RG 24, v. 1733, DHS-1-12 (pt. 1), Report to DHS, 28 June 1922.
148 The RAF official historians had their own problems and suffered interference from senior air officers. See Robin Higham, "Air War History: The State of the Art," in *Military History and the Military Profession*, ed. David A. Charters, Marc Milner, and J. Brent Wilson (Westport, CT: Praeger, 1992), 91-104; and Williamson Murray, "Strategic Bombing," in *Military Innovation in the Interwar Period*, ed. Williamson Murray and Allan R. Millett (Cambridge: Cambridge University Press, 1996).
149 S.F. Wise, *Canadian Airmen and the First World War: The Official History of the Royal Canadian Air Force*, vol. 1 (Toronto: University of Toronto Press, 1980), x.
150 Sydney Wise, "Canadian Military History: A Comparative Report," *Journal of the Australian War Memorial* 7 (October 1985): 5.
151 K.B. Conn, "The Royal Canadian Air Force Historical Section," *Canadian Historical Review* 26, 3 (1945): 246.
152 Lieutenant Colonel George A. Drew, *Canada's Fighting Airmen* (Toronto: Maclean Publishing, 1930), 2; F.V.H., review of *Canada's Fighting Airmen*, by George A. Drew, *Canadian Defence Quarterly* 8, 3 (1931): 422. Also see Wayne Ralph, *Barker VC* (Toronto: Doubleday Canada, 1997), 245-6.
153 LAC, CP, v. 12, file 35A, Editor of *Maclean's* [H. Napier Moore] to Currie, 12 September 1928.
154 Richard Preston and Peter Dennis, *Swords and Covenants* (London: Croom Helm, 1976), 14.
155 LAC, CP, v. 5, file "P-R," Currie to Paterson, 8 March 1920.
156 On Byng's point of view, see editorial, *Canadian Defence Quarterly* 12, 4 (July 1935): 384. The Currie papers contain several references to his desire to write his memoirs, but also to his inability to find the time. Sir Richard Turner would have been a good candidate to write his memoirs, as he outlived all his contemporaries, and he was angry with some of Duguid's interpretations in the first volume of the official history; however, he never published anything.
157 LAC, CP, v. 15, file 43, Tuxford to Currie, 20 March 1922.
158 LAC, CP, v. 8, file 22, Currie to Dyer, 4 July 1922.
159 LAC, MG 30 E 300, Victor Odlum papers, v. 3, Odlum to Currie, 17 May 1930.
160 Walter S. Herrington and Rev. A.J. Wilson, preface to *The War Work of the Country of Lennox and Addington* (Napanee, ON: Beaver Press, 1922).

161 Pierre Van Paassen, *Days of Our Years* (New York: Hillman-Curl, 1939), 91.
162 Brian Bond, *The Unquiet Western Front: Britain's Role in Literature and History* (Cambridge: Cambridge University Press, 2002), 31. For a discussion of why soldiers write memoirs, see Samuel Hynes, *The Soldiers' Tale: Bearing Witness to Modern War* (Allen Lake: Penguin, 1997).
163 Jeffrey A. Keshen, *Propaganda and Censorship during Canada's Great War* (Edmonton: University of Alberta Press, 1996), 195. Also see Dagmar Novak, *Dubious Glory: The Two World Wars and the Canadian Novel* (New York: Peter Lang Publishing, 2000).
164 RG 24, v. 1734, file DHS 3-2, Kerr to Minister of National Defence, 3 March 1930.
165 Wilfred Kerr, foreword to *Shrieks and Crashes: Being Memories of Canada's Corps, 1917* (Toronto: Hunter-Ross, 1929).
166 See review by J.F.C. in *Canadian Defence Quarterly* (January 1930) in RG 24, v. 1734, file DHS 3-2.
167 Kerr, "Historical Literature," 420, 422.
168 Will Bird, *And We Go On* (Toronto: Hunter Rose, 1930).
169 RG 24, v. 1740, DHS 4-4. pt. 4, "Nova Scotian Tells of War as it was on the Western Front," 13 December 1930.
170 For the reception of Harrison's work, see Jonathan Vance, "The Soldier as Novelist: Literature, History, and the Great War," *Canadian Literature* 179 (Winter 2003): 22-37.
171 Vance, *Death So Noble*, 186-97.
172 H.M. Urquhart, *The History of the 16th Battalion* (Toronto: Macmillan, 1932), 342.
173 Vance, *Death So Noble*, 193-4; Vance, "The Soldier as Novelist," 22-37. The reviews in *Canadian Defence Quarterly*, the soldiers', sailors', and aviators' journal, is replete with references to the unrepresentative works of "neurotics" and "foreign filthy minds" who sullied the name of the Canadian Corps with their dirty memoirs. See, for example, E.L.M. Burns's review of Major T.V. Scudamore, "Lighter Episodes in the Life of a Prisoner of War," *Canadian Defence Quarterly* (1933-34): 238; Sir Andrew Macphail, "Review of A.J. LaPointe, *Soldier of Quebec*," *Canadian Defence Quarterly* (1931-32): 282. For a British historian's view along the same lines, see Cyril Falls, *War Books: A Critical Guide* (London: P. Davies, 1930).
174 LAC, CP, v. 11, file 33, Macdonell to Currie, 26 June 1930.
175 Ibid., Currie to Macdonell, 25 June 1930.
176 James Pedley, *Only This: A War Retrospect* (Ottawa: Graphic, 1927); Peregrine Acland, *All Else Is Folly* (Toronto: McClelland and Stewart, 1929).
177 Martin Stephen, *The Price of Pity* (London: Leo Cooper, 1996); Hugh Cecil, *The Flower of Battle: How Britain Wrote the Great War* (Vermont: Steerforth Press, 1996); Rosa Maria Bracco, *Merchants of Hope: British Middlebrow Writers and the First World War, 1919-1939* (Oxford: Berg, 1993).
178 LAC, CP, v. 7, file 21, Currie to H. Clendining, 13 November 1929.
179 Duguid was obviously only partially successful, as any perusal of the Currie, Odlum, Turner, or McNaughton private papers at the LAC would indicate a rich collection of government records.
180 On collecting material, see RG 24, vol. 1501, HQ 683-1-28, Duguid to Lt. Col. W. Bovey, 14 April 1923; The editor of *The Legionary* to Duguid, 15 March 1939. On the quote, see RG 24, v. 1501, file HQ 683-1-28, Duguid to Gunn, 7 October 1938.
181 RG 24, v. 1755, file DHS 10-10, pt. 2, Extract from *The Legionary,* December 1929; RG 24, v. 2732, file HQS 5393, LaFleche to Prime Minister Mackenzie King, 17 March 1930.
182 RG 24, v. 1755, file DHS 10-10, pt. 2, McNaughton to Desbarats, 5 February 1930.
183 J.F.B. Livesay, "Canada's Black Watch, 1914-1918," *Ottawa Evening Journal*, 13 February 1932.
184 LAC, CP, v. 15, file 44, Livesay to Currie, 28 March 1933.
185 LAC, MG 26 K, R.B. Bennett papers, 500609, Roper to Bennett, 17 February 1932.
186 RG 24, v. 1755, file DHS 10-10, pt. 2, Production of Canadian Official History, 26 April 1932.

187 LAC, MG 30 E133, A.G.L. McNaughton papers, v. 9, file 39, Duguid to McNaughton, 30 April 1932.
188 See a number of newspaper accounts in RG 24, v. 1813, file G.A.Q. 4-15; Vance, *Death So Noble*, 166-7.
189 McNaughton papers, v. 9, file 39, Currie to McNaughton, 13 May 1932; McNaughton to Currie, 17 May 1932.
190 S.F. Wise, "Canadian Official Military History: The End of an Era?" in *The Last Word? Essays on Official History in the United States and British Commonwealth*, ed. Jeffrey Grey (Westport: Praeger, 2003), 10.
191 Bird, preface to *The Communication Trench*.
192 A.M.J. Hyatt, "Military Studies in Canada: An Overview," *Revue Internationale d'Histoire Militaire* 51 (1982): 328.
193 CWM, A.F. Duguid Accession, unprocessed material, R.C. Fetherstonhaugh to Duguid, 28 Feb 1934. Fetherstonhaugh was referring to Kerr's 1933 review article in the *Canadian Historical Review*.
194 Danielle Lacasse and Antonio Lechasseur, *The National Archives of Canada, 1872-1997*, Historical Booklet no. 58 (Ottawa: Canadian Historical Association, 1997), 6-9; Ian E. Wilson, "Shortt and Doughty: The Cultural Role of the Public Archives of Canada, 1904-1935" (MA thesis, Queen's University, 1973), 91.
195 Donald Schurman, "Writing about War," in *Writing about Canada: A Handbook for Modern Canadian History*, ed. John Schultz (Scarborough, ON: Prentice Hall, 1990), 234.
196 DHH, 917.009 (D1), v. 1, Stanley to Stacey, 29 January 1946.
197 RG 24, v. 1756, file DHS 10-10 – E, pt. 1, Duguid to James Kirkcaldy, 13 December 1934.
198 Colonel A.F. Duguid, *Official History of the Canadian Forces in the Great War, 1914-1919*, General Series, vol. 1 (Ottawa: J.O. Patenaude, 1938), viii.
199 LAC, MG 30 E300, Victor Odlum papers, file, A.F. Duguid, Duguid to Odlum, 4 October 1938.
200 Denis Winter, ed., *Making the Legend: The War Writings of C.E.W. Bean* (Brisbane: University of Queensland Press, 1992), 2.
201 RG 24, v. 1756, file DHS 10-10 – E, pt. 1, Notes by D.H.S. on letter from General Turner dated 2nd September 1936; RG 24, v. 2732, file HQS 5393, Memorandum on the Historical Section, H.Q.C.650-16-6, 5 January 1928.
202 Wise, "Canadian Official Military History"; and C.P. Stacey, *A Date with History: Memoirs of a Canadian Historian* (Ottawa: Deneau, 1983), 66. For a revisionist view of Duguid that comes to more positive conclusions, see Wes Gustavson, "Fairly Well Known and Need Not Be Discussed: Colonel A.F. Duguid and the Canadian Official History of the First World War," *Canadian Military History* 10, 2 (2001): 41-54.
203 CWM, A.F. Duguid Accession, unprocessed material, file: comments by individuals, Duguid to Reg, 9 April 1937.
204 RG 24, v. 1756, file DHS 10-10-N, Official Reply of Duguid to the comments from Major General G.B. Hughes, 16 April 1934; Duguid to Turner, 2 October 1934; Duguid memo on rebuttal to General Turner's comments on Ypres chapters, n.d. [ca. 17 October 1934].
205 Bennett papers, 500635-6, Garnet Hughes to Bennett, 10 April 1934.
206 McNaughton papers, v. 9, file 39, Hughes to Bennett, 10 April 1934.
207 Ibid., Duguid to McNaughton, 13 April 1934; McNaughton to Bennett, 14 April 1934; Duguid to McNaughton, 20 November 1934.
208 For quotation in text: RG 24, v. 2680, file HQC 4950 (pt. 2), Appendix to above: Points Raised by Turner and Hughes on 2nd Battle of Ypres, 19 June 1936.
209 RG 24, v. 2680, file HQC 4950 (pt. 2), Duguid to C.C.S., 23 June 1936.
210 RG 24, v. 1756, file DHS 10-10 – E, pt. 1, Notes by D.H.S. on letter from General Turner dated 2 September 1936.

211 RG 24, v. 1501, HQ 683-1-28, Duguid to H.H. Matthews, 18 May 1936.
212 DHH, Duguid Biography file, folder A, file 73, Duguid to CGS, n.d. [ca. 13 December 1934].
213 John English, "Afterword: The Mark of the Heretic," in *Military Heretics: The Unorthodox in Policy and Strategy*, ed. B.J.C. McKercher and A. Hamish Ion (Westport, CT: Praeger, 1994), 197.
214 RG 9, v. 4746, 175/1, CWRO Report, 11 January 1917.
215 Bean wrote six volumes of the official history, and also edited the others and a volume of historical photographs. Quotation from E.M. Andrews, "Bean and Bullecourt: Weaknesses and Strengths of the Official History of Australia in the First World War," *Revue Internationale d'Histoire Militaire* 72 (1990): 25.
216 Alistair Thomson, "'Steadfast until Death'? C.E.W. Bean and the Representation of Australian Manhood," *Australian Historical Studies* 23, 93 (1989): 462-78; John Barrett, "No Straw Man: C.E.W. Bean and Some Critics," *Australian Historical Studies* 23, 89 (1988): 102-14.
217 C.P. Stacey, *Canada and the British Army 1846-1871: A Study in the Practice of Responsible Government* (London: Longmans, 1936); George Stanley, *The Birth of Western Canada: A History of the Riel Rebellions* (London: Longmans, 1936).
218 On Halifax, see John Armstrong, *The Halifax Explosion and the Royal Canadian Navy: Inquiry and Intrigue* (Vancouver: UBC Press, 2002); for Canada's role on the east coast, see Michael L. Hadley and Roger Sarty, *Tin-Pots and Pirate Ships: Canadian Naval Forces and German Sea Raiders, 1880-1918* (Montreal and Kingston: McGill-Queen's University Press, 1991).
219 RG 24, vol. 1755, DHS 10-10, pt. 2, Duguid to Naval Secretary, 17 June 1937; ibid., Duguid to CGS, 17 December 1937; CWM, A.F. Duguid Accession, unprocessed material, file: comments by individuals, Duguid to Reg, 9 April 1937.
220 The AHS collected dozens of reviews and published them in a small pamphlet, see DHH, box 1, folder A, file 2.
221 RG 24, v. 1506, file HQ 683-1-30-18, "Canada's Immortal Story," *Sudbury Star*, 29 June 1938.
222 Ibid., "First Two Issues," *St. Catharines Standard*, 29 June 1938.
223 Ibid., "Valcartier to Ploegsteert," *Calgary Albertan*, 28 June 1938.
224 Ibid., "Canada's Part Told Officially," *Ottawa Journal*, 29 June 1938.
225 C.P. Stacey, "Canada's Last War – And the Next," *University of Toronto Quarterly* (April 1939); CWM, A.F. Duguid Accession, unprocessed material, file: comments by individuals, Edmonds to Duguid, 26 January 1939.
226 "Review of *The Canadian Brass: The Making of a Professional Army, 1890-1939*, by Stephen J. Harris," *Queen's Quarterly* 97 (Spring 1990): 187.
227 RG 24, v. 1756, file DHS 10-10 – E, pt. 2, Duguid to Loomis, 4 February 1937.
228 Duguid, *Official History of the Canadian Forces*, xv.
229 Editorial, "Canadian War History," *Evening Times-Globe*, 24 June 1938.
230 Z.Z., "Canada's First Year of the War," *Winnipeg Free Press*, 30 June 1938.
231 Brian Bond, *Liddell Hart: A Study of his Military Thought* (London: Cassell, 1977), 82.
232 RG 24, v. 6990, file: Introduction to Preface, n.d. [ca. 1938].
233 On the heraldry question, see Wise, "Canadian Official Military History," 9; Stacey, *A Date with History*, 67.
234 David French, "'Official but not History'? Sir James Edmonds and the Official History of the Great War," *RUSI Journal* 133, 1 (1986): 59.
235 Tim Travers, *The Killing Ground: The British Army, the Western Front and the Emergence of Modern Warfare, 1900-1918* (London: Allen and Unwin, 1982); Denis Winter, *Haig's Command: A Reassessment* (London: Penguin Books, 1991).
236 Bennett papers, 506037, Bennett to Hughes, 11 April 1934.

Chapter 3: Clio in the Service of Mars, 1939-45

1. Library and Archives Canada (LAC), Records of the Department of National Defence (RG 24), v. 12339, 4/HISTORY/1, Crerar to Defensor, 28 November 1939 and Burns to GS 100, 3 January 1940.
2. For general biographical information on Stacey, see C.P. Stacey, *A Date with History: Memoirs of a Canadian Historian* (Ottawa: Deneau, 1983); and D.G. Creighton, "Introduction: C.P. Stacey," in *Policy by Other Means: Essays in Honour of C.P. Stacey*, ed. Michael Cross and Robert Bothwell (Toronto: Clarke, Irwin, 1972), 3-17. C.P. Stacey, *The Military Problems of Canada: A Survey of Defence Policies and Strategic Conditions Past and Present* (Toronto: Ryerson Press, 1940).
3. University of Toronto Archives (UTA), Charles P. Stacey papers (hereafter Stacey papers), box 10, file Official History Appointment, Crerar to Stacey, 11 October 1940.
4. Stacey, *A Date with History*, 71.
5. RG 24, v. 10752, 220C1.009 (D35), Turner to McNaughton, [no date, but a reply to M.A. Pope's initial, more positive review of Stacey position was dated 14 November 1940]; see also Stacey, *A Date with History*, 74, 79.
6. Ibid., Historical officers, CMHQ, Statement of Duties and Instructions, December 1940. For additional support by General McNaughton, see RG 24, v. 6918, McNaughton to Stacey, 27 April 1942.
7. RG 24, v. 17508, War Diary, Army Historical Section (hereafter AHS War Diary), Canadian Military Headquarters, 27 January 1942; 16 April 1942; quote from RG 24, v. 10431, 210.051 (D1), memo by Stacey, n.d. [ca. January 1941].
8. AHS War Diary, 4 January 1941; RG 24, v. 12751, 24/GEN/1/2, Harrison to Stacey, 20 June 1945; RG 24, v. 12747, 24/Diaries/1, Crerar to Burns, 30 January 1940.
9. AHS War Diary, 13 January 1944.
10. Most of these reports have been digitized and are now online at the Directorate of History and Heritage website.
11. RG 24, v. 12747, 24/DIARIES/1, War Diaries, 13 January 1940.
12. There are countless examples of how the historical officers influenced the war record; see, for example, RG 24, v. 12747, 24/DIARIES/1, "War Dairies," 16 September 1942.
13. RG 24, v. 6918, Historical officer report no. 76, 2 July 1942.
14. Ibid., 2 July 1942; AHS War Diary, 11 March 1942, 28 July 1942.
15. Stacey had initially wanted Gerald Graham of Queen's University, but he was already teaching naval recruits. He would, however, join the Historical Section later in the war.
16. RG 24, v. 12754, 24/NARRATIVES/1, Project for Preliminary Narrative ..., 1939-1940, 26 September 1942.
17. For Stanley quote: UTA, Stacey papers, box 10, file: CPS – Personnel, Stacey to Rex, 24 October 1943; for words, see RG 24, v. 12754, 24/ NARRATIVES/3, Stanley to Stacey, 2 June 1945.
18. For Stacey's warning, see RG 24, v. 12752, 24/LIAISON/1, Stacey to BGS, 26 November 1943.
19. C.P. Stacey, *Six Years of War* (Ottawa: Queen's Printer, 1955), 389.
20. Stacey interviewed survivors and asked participants to put their memories on paper. See AHS War Diary, 24 August 1942.
21. For a discussion of the historiographical debates, see Brian Villa, *Unauthorized Action: Mountbatten and the Dieppe Raid* (Oxford: Oxford University Press, 1994), chs. 1, 2, and epilogue.
22. Stacey, *A Date with History*, 92.
23. For an account of Stacey's hard work, see AHS War Diary, 2-5 September 1942; RG 24, v. 6918, Historical officer report no. 83. Ralston later met with Stacey and "spoke kindly of the 'White

278 Notes to pages 100-4

Paper' on Dieppe, and mentioned that it had had a good press in the U.S." AHS War Diary, 5 October 1942.
24 Quentin Reynolds, *Dress Rehearsal: The Story of Dieppe* (New York: Blue Ribbon, 1943).
25 UTA, Stacey papers, box 54, file: correspondence, 1964, Stacey to Simonds, 25 February 1969; ibid., file: historical research, 1962-3, McNaughton to Stuart, 13 March 1943.
26 AHS War Diary, 27 January 1943; for the best analysis of the cover-up of Mountbatten's actions, see Villa, *Unauthorized Action*.
27 RG 24, v. 12756, 24/OPERATIONS/1, Stacey to BGS, 28 September 1942; Montague to HQ, First Army, 26 September 1942; Brigadier C.R. Stein to Senior Officer, CMHQ, 1 October 1942.
28 AHS War Diary, 12 February 1943.
29 As in the Great War, film and photographic records were also created, although these were not administered by the Historical Section. See Sarah Klotz, "Armed with Cameras: The Canadian Army Film Unit during the Second World War" (MA thesis, University of Ottawa, 2004).
30 Quote from Stacey, *A Date with History*, 119; Sam Hughes, *Steering the Course: A Memoir* (Montreal and Kingston: McGill-Queen's University Press, 2000), 94.
31 For Sesia's dismay, see RG 24, v. 10878, 233C1.011, Sesia's daily diary of the Sicilian campaign (hereafter SD), 19 May 1943. For Simonds, see SD, 29 June 1943. For Ogilvie's duties, see RG 24, v. 12756, 24/OPERATIONS/1, Montague to 1st Divisional HQ, 24 May 1943.
32 RG 24, v. 12756, 24/OPERATIONS/2, Stacey to Sesia, 7 August 1943.
33 SD, 20 July 1943.
34 SD, 26 July 1943.
35 RG 24, v. 12756, 24/OPERATIONS/2/2, Sesia to Stacey, 8 July 1943; Historical officer report no. 126, CMHQ, paragraph 5.
36 SD, 17 August 1943; RG 24, v. 12756, 24/OPERATIONS/1, Simonds to CMHQ, n.d. [ca. August 1943].
37 AHS War Diary, 31 August 1943.
38 AHS War Diary, November 1943, Appendix B, Montague to 1st Canadian Corps Headquarters, 18 November 1943; RG 24, v. 12756, 24/OPERATIONS/2, Stacey to Hughes, 12 October 1943.
39 RG 24, v. 17505, War Diary, Eric Harrison, 23 January 1944.
40 Ibid., 30 June 1944.
41 RG 24, v. 12752, 24/LIAISON/1, Stacey, memo, 2 February 1944. For details on the use of sources to construct the narrative, see RG 24, v. 12754, 24/NARRATIVES/1, Project for Preliminary Narrative of the History of the Canadian Army Overseas, 1939-1940, 26 September 1942.
42 RG 24, v. 12744, 24/AAI/1/4, Stuart to Secretary, Department of National Defence, 27 July 1944.
43 RG 24, v. 17505, No. 1 CFHS War Diary, 15 November 1943.
44 AHS War Diary, 29 August 1943.
45 RG 24, v. 12744, 24/AAI/1, In Canadian Operations – Mediterranean Area, Extract no. 6; Extract no. 4.
46 RG 24, v. 12744, 24/AAI/1/3, Extracts from War Diary and Memoranda, Distribution, 4 May 1944. Also see positive remarks by the chief of staff in AHS War Diary, 11 May 1944, and the No. 2 Operational Research Section in RG 24, v. 17506, No. 2 CFHS War Diary, 10 August 1944.
47 RG 24, v. 12744, 24/AAI/1/2, Stacey to BGS, 31 December 1943; RG 24, v. 12756, 24/OPERATIONS/1, Stacey to Penhale, 29 December 1943.
48 Ibid., Stuart to GHQ, 21 January 1944.

49 Directorate of History and Heritage (DHH), unprocessed registry files (URF), box 20, file 4-0-2, part 1, Whitelaw to Duguid, 10 January 1944.
50 For Stacey's warning, see RG 24, v. 11750, CS 632-3, Preliminary Narrative, 1 September 1943. On the actions of senior officers, see RG 24, v. 12754, 24/NARRATIVES/1, McNaughton to Stacey, 16 February 1943; Spry to Stacey, 24 June 1943; Mann to Senior Officer, CMHQ, 17 March 1943. On historical guidelines, see RG 24, v. 12752, 24/LIAISON/1, Provisional Notes for the Guidance of Narrators, 15 September 1941.
51 DHH, Duguid Biography file, box 1, folder 1, file 16, Duguid, Preliminary Narratives, 27 January 1944.
52 John Ross Matheson, *Canada's Flag: A Search for a Country* (Boston: G.K. Hall, 1980), 103.
53 RG 24, v. 12754, 24/NARRATIVES/2, Crerar to Stacey, 30 June 1944.
54 For further examples, see the comments by senior officers in RG 24, v. 12754, 24/NARRATIVES/1; C.P. Stacey, "The Life and Hard Times of an Official Historian," *Canadian Historical Review* 51, 1 (1970): 22-3.
55 UTA, Stacey papers, box 17, file: military personalities, 1945, notes on McNaughton, 21.
56 RG 24, v. 12744, 24/ARTICLES/1/2, C.P. Stacey, draft copy of "The Historical Program of the Canadian Army Overseas."
57 Interview with Dr. W.A.B. Douglas, 8 November 2004.
58 On Engler, see RG 24, v. 12756, 24/OPERATIONS/2, Sesia to Stacey, 5 October 1944.
59 Historical officer report No. 135, CMHQ, paragraph 2.
60 Historical officer report No. 127, CMHQ, paragraph 62.
61 RG 24, v. 12756, 24/OPERATIONS/2, Harrison to Stacey, 13 June 1944.
62 RG 24, v. 17506, War Diary, J.R. Martin, see entries for June 1944. On the extracts, see RG 24, v. 12756, 24/OPERATIONS/2/2, Sesia to Stacey, 8 January 1945.
63 Charles Comfort, foreword to *Artist at War*, (Pender Island, BC: Remembrance Books, 1995), xiii. Stacey also referred to the important role of the historical officers in preserving war records, "which might otherwise have been destroyed." C.P. Stacey, "The Historical Program of the Canadian Army Overseas," *Canadian Historical Review* 26 (September 1945): 232.
64 DHH, URF, box 17, file 3-5-3, Harrison to Stacey, 20 June 1945; RG 24, v. 12756, 24/OPERATIONS/2, Harrison to Stacey, 24 September 1944; ibid., Harrison to Stacey, 9 October 1944; ibid., Harrison to Stacey, 24 September 1944.
65 RG 24, v. 12756, 24/OPERATIONS/2, Stacey to Sesia, 10 June 1944; ibid., Sesia to Stacey, 16 June 1944; No. 2 CFHS War Diary, 6 June 1944.
66 RG 24, v. 12756, 24/OPERATIONS/2/2, Gray to Stacey, 24 March 1945.
67 RG 24, v. 17505, War Diary, Eric Harrison, 23 May 1944; AHS War Diary, Appendix 1 of August 1943.
68 RG 24, v. 12756, 24/OPERATIONS/2/2, Sesia to Stacey, 2 January 1945.
69 RG 24, v. 17505, No. 1 CFHS War Diary, 8 May 1944; 16 June 1944.
70 RG 24, v. 17505, War Diary, historical officer, 5th Canadian Armoured Division, 12 and 18 August 1944.
71 RG 24, v. 17506, War Diary, historical officer, 3rd Canadian Infantry Division, 1 and 7 December 1944.
72 Stacey acknowledged this after the war, see C.P. Stacey, "Writing the History of the Canadian Army," *Canadian Army Journal* 2, 1 (1948): 30-1, but he never explored the issue of his historical officers specifically influencing and authoring war records.
73 See S.L.A. Marshall, *Men against Fire* (New York: William Morrow, 1947). For a reassessment of Marshall's method, see Roger S. Spiller, "S.L.A. Marshall and the Ratio of Fire," *RUSI Journal* 133, 4 (1988): 63-71. Marshall and Stacey met three times and discussed methodological

historical practices at least once. See AHS War Diary, 21 November 1944, 22 November 1944, 16 May 1945.
74 RG 24, v. 5231, HQS 19-57-37, pt. 2, Historical Section, 6 June 1946.
75 DHH, 74/494, "Lecture Performed for Staff College," [ca. 1945].
76 RG 24, v. 17673, file 046-10, pt. 2, Radio Program from Clair Wallace's, *They Tell Me*, 21 July 1944
77 RG 24, v. 5231, file 19-15-37, pt. 1, Royal Canadian Air Force, Historical Records, December 1943; ibid., Conn to A.M.C., 21 September 1942.
78 The phrase "on barbed wire" belongs to Winston Churchill. For the BCATP plan, see F.J. Hatch, *The Aerodrome of Democracy: Canada and the British Commonwealth Air Training Plan, 1939-1945* (Ottawa: Department of National Defence, 1983).
79 Kenneth Conn, "The Royal Canadian Air Force Historical Section," *Canadian Historical Review* 27 (September 1945): 247.
80 DHH, F.H. Hitchins biography file, 75/514, file B6, Historical Section – R.C.A.F., 23 June 1941.
81 DHH, 181.003 (D5219), Breadner to Air Officer Commanding, RCAF HQ in Great Britain, 29 July 1941.
82 RG 24, v. 5231, file 19-15-37, pt. 1, RCAF Historical Section, 14 July 1943. Hitchins was born in London, Ontario, on 10 July 1904, received B.A. and Masters degrees from the University of Western Ontario, and completed his PhD at the University of Pennsylvania. His thesis, "The Colonial Land and Emigration Commission (1840-1878)," was published by the University of Pennsylvania Press in 1931. He taught at the New York University until 1941. During the 1930s, he researched and wrote about early balloon history and the role of the Canadians in the British Flying Services in the Great War. See F.J. Hatch, "In Memoriam: Wing Commander Fred Harvey Hitchins," *CAHS Journal* 11, 1 (1973): 24.
83 Quote from RG 24, v. 5231, file 19-15-37, pt. 1, Conn, Survey of Central Registry Overseas HQ, 7 September 1942.
84 RG 24, v. 5231, file 19-15-37, pt. 1, Overseas Historical Organization, 20 August 1942; RG 24, 1983-84/216, box 2967, file 895-DAFH, pt. 1, Historical Section, RCAF, 23 July 1942.
85 DHH, 75/514, file B6, 11 September 1941.
86 Brian Bond, introduction to *The Burning Blue: A New History of the Battle of Britain*, ed. Paul Addison and Jeremy Craig (London: Pimlico, 2000), 1-2.
87 DHH, 75/514, Hitchins to Air Officer in Charge, 27 May 1942.
88 A "rhubarb" was a fighter sweep across occupied France, which aimed at drawing the Luftwaffe into combat.
89 RG 24, v. 5231, file 19-15-37, pt. 1, L.H. Jenkins, Operational Record Books – In General, 18 May 1943.
90 DHH, 75/514, file B6, Operations Record Books, 4 May 1943.
91 RG 24, 1983-84/216, box 2967, file 895-DAFH, pt. 1, Conn, Historical Section, RCAF, n.d. [ca. between Jan-July 1942]; DHH, 75/514, file B6, McGregor to Secretary, Department of National Defence for Air, 10 April 1942; DHH, 181.003 (D5219), Operations Record Books, 12 December 1944.
92 DHH, 181.003 (D5219), Hitchins to Crozier, 19 November 1942; DHH, 75/514, file B6, Campbell to Hitchins, 25 November 1942.
93 DHH, 75/514, file B6, Fifteenth Monthly Report on Progress of Historical Research, 9 February 1943.
94 RG 24, v. 5231, file 19-15-37, pt. 1, RCAF Ottawa to ROYCANAIRF, 12 July [1943]. For long quotation, see DHH, 79/445, Historical Narrative, RCAF Overseas (to 31 August 1942). For short quotation, see DHH, 181.003 (D5219), Hitchins, R.C.A.F. Historical Section, 12 April 1943.

95 RG 24, v. 17673, file 046-10, pt. 3, Martin to Conn, 14 May 1945.
96 RG 24, v. 17673, file 046-10, pt. 2, Radio program transcript: Clair Wallace: *They Tell Me*, 21 July 1944.
97 Quotations from *The RCAF Overseas: The First Four Years* (Toronto: Oxford University Press, 1944), 13, 165, 166. For more on the Lubeck raid, see Brereton Greenhous, Stephen J. Harris, William C. Johnston, and William G.P. Rawling, *The Crucible of War, 1939-1945*, vol. 3 of *Official History of the Royal Canadian Air Force* (Toronto: University of Toronto Press, 1994), 223.
98 RG 24, v. 17673, file 046-10, pt. 3, Popular Narrative, 18 October 1943.
99 *The RCAF Overseas*, ix.
100 RG 24, v. 17673, file 046-10, ROYCANAIRF to RCAF Ottawa, 7 January 1944.
101 Torchy Anderson, "A Story to Be Read," *Ottawa Citizen*, 18 October 1944.
102 On the Militia myth, see Jack Granatstein, *Canada's Army: Waging War and Keeping the Peace* (Toronto: University of Toronto Press, 2002), ch. 1.
103 *Owen Sound Sun Times*, 26 October 1944. By September 1946 over 12,000 copies had been sold. It is likely that even more would have been bought had Oxford not been delayed in issuing second and third editions. RG 24, v. 5231, HQS 19-57-37, pt. 2, Supporting Data – Official History of the RCAF, 4 September 1946.
104 RG 24, v. 17673, file 046-10, pt 2, clipping of letter in *Toronto Globe and Mail*, 22 November 1944.
105 For Duguid's work during the Second World War, see his recently unearthed date books at the CWM, 58A 1.97. For the CGS's order, see DHH, Duguid Biography file, box 1, folder A, file 2, CGS to DHS, 15 September 1939.
106 RG 24, v. 5231, file 19-15-37, pt. 1, Conn to AOC-C, 9 December 1943.
107 Of the original 6,500 press run, only 700 copies were still in stock by June 1946. Flying Officer W.S. Large, *The Diary of a Canadian Fighter Pilot* (Toronto: Reginald Saunders, 1944).
108 See DHH, 72/372, Conn to Saunders, 31 January 1945; and the correspondence in RG 24, v. 17674, file 046-15; file 046-16.
109 Richard Overy, *Why the Allies Won* (London: Pimlico, 1996), 101.
110 W.A.B. Douglas and Brereton Greenhous, *Out of the Shadows: Canada in the Second World War*, rev. ed. (Toronto, Dundurn Press, 1995), 191.
111 RG 24, v. 5231, file 19-15-37, pt. 1, ROYCANAIRF to AFHQ, 31 December 1943.
112 RG 24, v. 5263, file 24-13-10, Monthly Resume, June 1944.
113 DHH, 181.009 (D6513), Instructions on Keeping Operations Record Books Daily Diaries. It appears that the RCAF Historical Section simply followed the already successful instructions that the RAF issued to its squadrons.
114 RG 24, v. 5263, file 24-13-10, Monthly Resume, June 1944.
115 RG 24, 1983-84/216, box 2967, file 895-DAFH, pt. 1, RCAF Detachment, 19 June 1945; DHH, 72/372, RCAF Detachment, Rockcliffe, 19 June 1945.
116 Peter G. Tsouras, ed., *The Greenhill Dictionary of Military Quotations* (London: Greenhill Books, 2000), 235.
117 Marc Milner, *Canada's Navy: The First Century* (Toronto: University of Toronto Press, 1999), 156-7.
118 DHH, URF, box 16, file 3-4-5, Duguid to Youle, 12 February 1940.
119 RG 24, v. 1756, file DHS 10-10-G, Memo by Duguid, 18 March 1940.
120 "Maureen O'Sullivan's Husband Joins Canadian Navy in Ottawa," *Ottawa Journal*, 19 March 1940. For his activities, see Gilbert Tucker, "The Royal Canadian Naval Historical Section and Its Work," *Canadian Historical Review* 26 (September 1945): 239-40; RG 24, v. 6917, Historical Officer, Report of Interviews in Ottawa, 2 November 1940.

121 Farrow went on to serve as a lieutenant commander in the Royal Navy, but was injured and returned to Hollywood by 1942. He won an Academy Award nomination for his direction of *Wake Island* (1942). He later converted to Catholicism and wrote several books and screenplays.
122 DHH, NHS 1000-5-18, Nelles to Deputy Minister, 20 September 1940.
123 Ibid., Maclachlan to CNS, 6 November 1940.
124 J.M. Hitsman, "Canadian Naval Policy" (MA thesis, Queen's University, 1940).
125 DHH, NHS 1700/100/78A, typed obituary of Professor Gilbert Tucker, 1896-1955.
126 W.A.B. Douglas, "Filling Gaps in the Military Past: Recent Developments in Canadian Official History," *Journal of Canadian Studies* 19, 3 (1984): 113.
127 Robert C. Fisher, "Heroism: On the North Atlantic," *The Legion*; interview with Robert Fisher, 3 March 2003.
128 RG 24, 1983-84/167, box 498, file 1700-N/HIST (pt. 1), N.Hist to DNI, 30 October 1942.
129 RG 24, v. 3842, file NS 1017-10-23, Agnew to Secretary of the Naval Board, 13 May 1942.
130 RG 24, 1983-84/167, box 498, file 1700-N/HIST (pt. 1), Agnew to Secretary of the Naval Board, 9 October 1942.
131 DHH, Interview with James George, 15 November 1989. I would like to thank Dr. Roger Sarty for sharing with me the interview transcripts.
132 DHH, NHS 1700/100/78A, Memo by Tucker, n.d. [handwritten, ca. 1943]; RG 24, v. 11749, file C.S. 632-2, handwritten instructions, no title, n.d. [written by Tucker, ca. 1943].
133 DHH, Interview with James George, 15 November 1989.
134 DHH, NHS 1700/100/78A, George to Tucker, 10 May 1944.
135 RG 24, v. 11749, file C.S. 632-2, George to Loaring, 6 May 1943.
136 Ibid., George to Tucker, 4 August 1943; George to Tucker, 28 May 1943.
137 DHH, Interview with James George, 15 November 1989.
138 Sir Ian Hamilton, preface to *A Staff Officer's Scrap Book* (London: Edward Arnold, 1905).
139 Ibid., George to SCNO (L), 2 February 1944; DHH, NHS 1700/100/78A, George to Tucker, 10 May 1944.
140 DHH, interview with Professor Freeman Tovell, 12 May 1988. For a full account of this engagement and the controversy behind the supposed sinking of the *Athabaskan* by a British Motor Torpedo Boat, see Michael Whitby, "The Case of the Phantom MTB and the Loss of the HMCS *Athabaskan*," *Canadian Military History* 11, 3 (2002): 5-14.
141 RG 24, v. 11749, file C.S. 632-2, George to Little, 4 January 1943 [sic, 1944].
142 Ibid.; George to Tucker, 11 April 1944.
143 DHH, NHS 1700/100/78A, Naval Historian to Senior Canadian Naval Officer (London), 21 April 1944. Quotation from W.A.B. Douglas, "The RCN Official History: Some Comments," *Starshell* (Spring 2003): 19.
144 DHH, 81/520/1443-249/96, box 70, file 1, The Sinking of the *U-744* by C.2. on 6 March 1944, report by Lieutenant George.
145 DHH, NHS 1700/100/78A, Historical Records Officer to N.A. (P.P.), 18 May 1944. Also see, RG 24, v. 11749, file C.S. 632-1, Historical Coverage of Forthcoming Operations by J. George, 7 April 1944.
146 RG 24, 1983-84/167, box 498, file 1700-N/HIST (pt. 1), Tucker to DNI, 29 July 1944; DHH, NHS 1700/100/78A, Tucker to George, 24 January 1945.
147 DHH, 81/520/1443-249/96, box 70, file 1, Report by Lt. James George, Work of RCN L.S.I.'s Reviewed, 20 November 1944.
148 DHH, NHS 1700/100/78A, George to Tucker, 17 January 1945.
149 Ibid., George to Tucker, 16 November 1944.
150 Gilbert Tucker, preface to *The Naval Service of Canada*, vol. 2, *Activities on Shore during the Second World War* (Ottawa: King's Printer, 1952).

151 DHH, NHS 1700/100/78A, Tucker to George, 24 January 1945.
152 Stephen Leacock and Leslie Roberts, *Canada's War at Sea* (Montreal: Alvan M. Beatty, 1944).
153 W.A.B. Douglas, *The Creation of a National Air Force*, vol. 2 of *The Official History of the RCAF* (Toronto: University of Toronto Press, 1986).
154 Review by Eric Harrison, *Canadian Historical Review* 29, 3 (1948): 301-6.
155 Liddell Hart cited in Harold C. Deutsch, "The Matter of Records," *The Journal of Military History* 59, 1 (1995): 137.

Chapter 4: History Wars and War History, 1945-48

1 RG 24, v. 17508, Army Historical Section War Diary (AHS War Diary), 6 September 1945.
2 RG 24, v. 20272, 932.002 (D1), Harrison to Stacey, 2 June 1945; RG 24, v. 12756, 24/OPERATIONS/2/2, Stacey to Harrison, 26 May 1945.
3 Ibid., Disposal of Personnel Files – Senior Officers by C.P. Stacey, [ca. 27 June 1945].
4 AHS War Diary, 25 July 1945; University of Toronto Archives (UTA), C.P. Stacey papers, box 17, file: Military Personalities, 1945, notes on General Crerar, p. 6; UTA, box 21, file misc. 1945-58, Stacey to Stanley, 26 July 1945.
5 UTA, Stacey's personal diary, 23 October 1945.
6 RG 24, v. 12752, 24/LIAISON/1, Suggestions for Keeping Operational Journals [ca. April 1944].
7 RG 24, v. 20271, 916.016 (D3), Historical Section, General Staff Branch, CMHQ by Stacey, 13 September 1945.
8 RG 24, v. 12751, 24/GEN/1/2, Stacey to All Narrator Officers, Historical Section, 7 August 1945.
9 Directorate of History and Heritage (DHH), file 917.009 (D1), v. 1, Harrison to Stacey, 24 May 1946.
10 Ibid., Harrison to Stacey, 15 June 1946.
11 DHH, Historical officer's report no. 101, CMHQ; ibid., no. 107.
12 AHS War Diary, 2 June 1945.
13 RG 24, v. 12752, Harrison to Stacey, 21 December 1945; AHS War Diary, 31 July 1945.
14 DHH, file 917.009 (D1), v. 1, Nicholson to Stacey, 14 October 1946; RG 24, v. 12752, Philips to Historical Section, 8 October 1946.
15 DHH, unprocessed registry files (URF), box 16, file 3-4-22, Duguid to CGS, 24 December 1942.
16 RG 24, v. 20302, file 948.002 (D1), Policy: Official History, Canadian Army, 16 December 1944.
17 Library and Archives Canada (LAC), MG 30 E 157, H.D.G. Crerar papers (hereafter Crerar papers), v. 3, file Historical, Stacey to DCGS, 10 May 1945.
18 UTA, Stacey papers, box 6, file: CPS – Personnel file, Montague to Crerar, 16 May 1945; Crerar papers, v. 3, file Historical, COS to Crerar, 30 January 1945.
19 UTA, Stacey's personal diary, 16 April 1945.
20 For Stacey's view of this affair, see C.P. Stacey, *A Date with History: Memoirs of a Canadian Historian* (Ottawa: Deneau, 1983); and Stacey, "The Life and Hard Times of an Official Historian," *Canadian Historical Review* 51, 1 (1970): 23-5.
21 For Duguid's involvement, see DHH, URF, box 1, file 1-0, Duguid to DCGS, 13 July 1945. For Stacey's refusal, see ibid., Murchie to Foulkes, army message 141200A, September 1945.
22 J.L. Granatstein, *The Generals: The Canadian Army's Senior Commanders in the Second World War* (Toronto: Stoddart, 1993), 160-3, 174-5.
23 Stacey, *A Date with History*, 171-5; DHH, file 917.009 (D1), v. 1, Stacey to Hughes, 11 October 1945.
24 UTA, Stacey papers, box 58, file: Date with History, early draft, ch. 14, p. 10.
25 See Robert A. Spencer, *History of the Fifteenth Canadian Field Regiment, Royal Canadian Artillery, 1941 to 1945* (Amsterdam: Elsevier, 1945). A number of regimental histories were

written after the war by members of their respective units with the support of the Historical Section. However, few of them were published.
26 Interview with Robert A. Spencer, 17 February 2005.
27 DHH, 112.21009 (D137), Brigadier DCGS(B) to DM(R), 12 September 1945.
28 C.P. Stacey, *The Canadians in Britain, 1939-1944* (Ottawa: King's Printer, 1945); C.P. Stacey, *From Pachino to Ortona: The Canadian Campaign in Sicily and Italy, 1943* (Ottawa: King's Printer, 1946); C.P. Stacey, *Canada's Battle in Normandy: The Canadian Army's Share in the Operations, 6 June-1 September 1944* (Ottawa: King's Printer, 1946).
29 UTA, Stacey's personal diary, 5 July 1945. Simonds met with Stacey and informed him that he could "add a great many points from personal knowledge." Stacey wrote, "Some units have not got proper credit because they did not keep good records. And often General Simonds recalls the events of a conference of which no record was made."
30 DHH, CMHQ Report No. 150, Operation Spring, with comments from Lt. Gen. G.G. Simonds (Ottawa, 1946).
31 Stacey's War Diary, 30 July 1945 and 15 August 1945.
32 Terry Copp, *Fields of Fire: The Canadians in Normandy* (Toronto: University of Toronto Press, 2003), 148.
33 DHH, 83/269, Comments Regarding Official History ..., folder 3, General Charles Foulkes, 24 April 1959.
34 UTA, Stacey papers, box 41, file: Dir., Historical Section, 1968-74, Stacey to Wise, 9 February 1972.
35 Stacey, *A Date with History*, 175. See C.P. Stacey, *Canada's Battle in Normandy: The Canadian Army's Share in the Operations, 6 June-1 September 1944* (Ottawa: King's Printer, 1946), 97.
36 UTA, box 5, file: general, 1982-89, Stacey to J.A. English, 4 November 1987. For an account of the battle, see C.P. Stacey, *The Victory Campaign: The Operations in North-West Europe, 1944-1945* (Ottawa: Queen's Printer, 1960), 191-2.
37 DHH, URF, box 3, file 1-2-2, Stacey to Crerar, 30 April 1946.
38 Ibid., file 1-2-2, pt. 2, Stacey to Creighton, 16 April 1947; UTA, Stacey papers, box 21, file: Correspondence historical research ..., 17 June 1955.
39 Typed reviews from *The Fighting Forces* (October 1946) and *The Legionary* (August 1946) in DHH, URF, box 3, file 1-2-2, pt. 2.
40 DHH, 72/372, Conn to Masters, 16 October 1945.
41 RG 24, 1983-84/216, box 2967, file 895-DAFH, pt. 1, Air Historian Detachment – RCAF Station, Rockcliffe, 27 February 1945; DHH, 75/514, file B6, Air Historian, 18 October 1945.
42 RG 24, v. 5231, HQS 19-57-37, pt. 2, Organization of the RCN and Canadian Army Historical Section, 5 July 1946.
43 DHH, 75/514, file A-20, National Defence Archives, 20 November 1945.
44 RG 24, v. 5263, file 24-13-10, Monthly Resume for February 1946.
45 RG 24, v. 5231, HQS 19-57-37, pt. 2, Historical Section, 6 June 1946.
46 Ibid., Projected Outline for a History, 15 October 1945; ibid., Official History of the RCAF, 15 October 1945.
47 DHH, 72/372, History of the RCAF, 28 June 1945; Quote in RG 24, v. 5231, HQS 19-57-37, pt. 2, Organization Post War RCAF – UK Historical Section, 29 May 1946.
48 *The R.C.A.F. Overseas: The Fifth Year* (Toronto: Oxford University Press, 1945), vii-x.
49 Ibid., 13-16, 18, 127.
50 RG 24, vol. 17673, file 046-11, pt. 2, John Yocom, *Saturday Night*, 22 June 1946.
51 Ibid., Apedaile to Sellers, 9 May 1947.
52 RG 24, vol. 17673, file 046-11, pt. 2, Hichins, memo, 16 October 1947.
53 Ibid., Johnson to Secretary, DND Air, 29 June 1946; 18 June 1946.

54 Ibid., Supporting Data for Air Members Meeting, 5 July 1946; Justification for an RCAF History, 5 July 1946; Official History of the RCAF, 4 September 1946.
55 RG 24, v. 5231, HQS 19-57-37, pt. 2, Royal Canadian Air Force History, [25 September 1946].
56 DHH, 112.21009 (D137), Brigadier DCGS(A) to CGS, Comments on Official History of the RCAF, 12 October 1946.
57 Andrew Samuel Green, "Sir James Edmonds and the Official Military Histories of the Great War" (PhD diss., University of Leeds, 1999), 19.
58 For Claxton's career, see David J. Bercuson, *True Patriot: The Life of Brooke Claxton, 1898-1960* (Toronto: University of Toronto Press, 1993), chs. 8 and 9.
59 DHH, 917.009 (D1), v. 2, Stacey to Nicholson, 18 January 1947.
60 Stacey, "The Life and Hard Times," 29.
61 For both quotations on saving the history, see UTA, Stacey papers, box 58, file: Date with History, early draft, ch. 14, pp. 3-4. See also, UTA, Stacey's personal diary, 28 April 1947.
62 DHH, URF, box 1, file 1-0, pt. 2, Official History of the Canadian Army, War of 1939-45, 23 January 1947; Stacey, *A Date with History*, 194-5.
63 DHH, URF, box 1, file 1-0, Plan for the Production of the Official History of the Canadian Army, 13 October 1945.
64 RG 24, 1983-84/216, box 2967, file 895-DAFH, pt. 2, RCAF HS to Acting Chief of Staff, 7 February 1947.
65 Stacey, "The Life and Hard Times," 32-3.
66 DHH, 75/514, file A-15, Hitchins to Nerney, 10 March 1947.
67 Ibid., file A-4, Burchill to Hitchins, 7 March 1947.
68 Ibid., 22 March 1947.
69 RG 24, 1983-84/216, box 2499, file 801-P405, Board of Officers, 2 February 1946; Hitchins to Halliday, 20 June 1946; DHH, 72/372, Coulson to Conn, 6 September 1945.
70 RG 24, 1983-84/216, box 2967, file 895-DAFH, pt. 2, RCAF HS to Acting Chief of Staff, 7 February 1947.
71 W.A.B. Douglas, "Naval History: The State of the Art," in *Military History and the Military Profession*, ed. David A. Charters, Marc Milner, and J. Brent Wilson (Westport, CT: Praeger, 1992), 73.
72 Gilbert Tucker, "The Royal Canadian Naval Historical Section and Its Work," *Canadian Historical Review* 26 (September 1945): 241.
73 DHH, URF, box 1, file 1-0, pt. 2, Meeting of Service Historians, 2 April 1947.
74 Ibid., Tucker to DNPI, 22 May 1946; RG 24, 1983-84/167, box 498, file 1700-N/HIST (pt. 1), Tucker to DNPI, 22 May 1946.
75 DHH, NHS 1700/100/78A, Minute from Director of Planning to Naval Historian, 30 June 1945.
76 "What Is Military History?" *History Today* 34 (December 1984): 7.
77 DHH, URF, box 1, file 1-0, pt. 2, Tucker to CNS, 30 July 1945.
78 RG 24, 1983-84/167, box 498, file 1700-N/HIST (pt. 1), Deputy Minister to Tucker, 27 August 1946.
79 Ibid., Foulkes to Minister, 5 October 1945; Duguid to CGS, 15 January 1946.
80 Ibid., Foulkes to Minister, 21 December 1946.
81 Ibid., Duguid to DCGS(A), 20 January 1947; ibid., Duguid to Foulkes, 15 January 1946.
82 Ibid., Duguid to DCGS(A), 18 July 1946.
83 DHH, Duguid Biography file, box 1, folder A, file 2, Duguid to Megill, Canadian Official History, 18 February 1947.
84 LAC, MG 30 D252, Alan B. Beddoe papers (hereafter Beddoe papers), v. 22, file: Canadian Forces, Duguid, draft letter by Duguid to Bovey, ca. 25 February 1947. Duguid would publish

a regimental history before his death: A.F. Duguid, *History of the Canadian Grenadier Guards, 1760-1964* (Montreal: Gazette Print, 1965).
85 Harold Dingman, "Report to the Nation," *New Liberty*, 6 December 1947.
86 DHH, Duguid Biography file, folder A, HQC 650-16-6, FD 4, 19 February 1947; "Popular Histories of Forces To Be Issued by March 31," *The Ottawa Journal*, 7 February 1947.
87 Beddoe papers, v. 22, file: Canadian Forces, Duguid, draft letter by Duguid to Bovey, ca. 25 February 1947.
88 Jeffrey Grey, ed., introduction to *The Last Word? Essays on Official History in the United States and British Commonwealth* (Westport, CT: Praeger, 2003), xii.
89 DHH, file 917.009 (D1), v. 1, Stacey to Foulkes, 7 September 1946.
90 Hughes remained in that role until he was replaced in 1946 by Lieutenant Colonel G.W.L. Nicholson, who was brought back to Canada in 1947 to write the Italian history. Nicholson was replaced by Major T.M. Hunter, who remained in that role until the early 1950s. See Tim Cook, "Sam Hughes: Historical Officer," *Canadian Military History* 12 (Winter-Spring 2003): 56-9
91 RG 24, v. 12756, 24/OPERATIONS/2/2, Harrison to Stacey, 27 September 1945.
92 AHS War Diary, 12 December 1945.
93 RG 24, v. 12744, 24/AAI/1/6, Present State of Work of Canadian Operations in Italy [by Sam Hughes], 14 March 1946; RG 24, v. 12752, 24/LIAISON/1, Hughes to Kittoe, 1 February 1946.
94 RG 24, v. 12752, 24/LIAISON/1, Memorandum [written by Stacey], 2 February 1944; ibid., Memorandum [written by Stacey], 17 August 1944.
95 DHH, 917.009 (D1), pt. 1, Stacey to Stanley, 12 March 1946; RG 24, v. 12752, 24/LIAISON/1, Murchie to Foulkes, 15 March 1946.
96 DHH, DO 127/81, Dixon to Molson, 6 May 1947.
97 DHH, URF, box 1, file 1-0, pt. 1, Foulkes to Minister, 13 January 1950.
98 DHH, 917.009 (D1), pt. 3, Stacey to Hunter, 3 October 1947. For a broad study of British, Canadian, and American relations, see Jack Granatstein, *How Britain's Weakness Forced Canada into the Arms of the United States* (Toronto: University of Toronto Press, 1989).
99 John E. Jessup and Robert W. Coakley, "A Century of Army Historical Work," in *A Guide to the Study and Use of Military History* (Washington, DC: United States Army Center of Military History, 1982), 290.
100 Australian War Memorial, AWM 77, 6/2, Minutes of the Joint Meeting of the Advisory Committee ..., 4-6 February 1948. Quotation from DHH, DO 127/81, Document 16536, Appendix A, Draft Agreement.
101 UTA, Stacey's personal diary, 15 January 1948 and 23 January 1948.
102 UTA, Stacey papers, box 21, file: misc. 1945-58, Notes on Matters Discussed during Meeting of U.S. and Commonwealth Military Historians, Washington, 4-7 February 1948.
103 DHH, 917.009 (D1), v. 4, Stacey to Hunter, 12 February 1948.
104 UTA, Stacey's personal diary, 7 February 1948.
105 DHH, DO 127/81, Aide Memoir, n.d. [ca. December 1949]; Brook to Clutterbrook, 8 August 1949.
106 DHH, 917.009 (D1), pt. 6, Memorandum of Discussion of Combined Records, 22 August 1950; DHH, DO 127/81, Dixon to Clutterbuck, 19 April 1948.
107 UTA, Stacey papers, box 58, file: DWH, 1983-6 (1), Murray Hunter to Stacey, 12 June 1983.
108 For Stacey's access, see J. Mackay Hitsman and C.P. Stacey, *Historical Activities within the Canadian Army: Report No. 1, Historical Officer, Canadian Military Headquarters*, 2 July (Ottawa: N.p., 1965), 19. For the quotation, see DHH, 917.009 (D1), v. 6, Hunter to Stacey, 3 February 1950.
109 LAC, MG 30 E133, A.G.L. McNaughton papers, Stacey to McNaughton, 11 November 1946.

110 See Annika Mombauer, *The Origins of the First World War: Controversies and Consensus* (London: Longman, 2002), 55-69; and Keith Wilson, ed., *Forging the Collective Memory: Government and International Historians through Two World Wars* (Oxford: Berghahn Books, 1996).
111 RG 24, v. 12752, 24/LIAISON/1/2, Liaison Visit – Historical Division, W.D.S.S. Washington, memo by Stacey, 11 June 1946.
112 RG 24, v. 20270, Colonel C.P. Stacey, "The Nature of an Official History," n.d. [ca. 1946], 4. Another official historian made a similar observation: see Captain S.W. Roskill, "Some Reasons for Official History," in *Official Histories: Essays and Bibliographies from around the World*, ed. Robin Higham (Manahattan, KS: Kansas State University Library, 1970), 11.
113 Stacey, "The Nature of an Official History," 10.
114 Ibid., 7.
115 RG 24, v. 12747, 24/DIARIES/3, Stacey to DCGS, 21 February 1946.
116 C.P. Stacey, "Writing the History of the Canadian Army," *Canadian Army Journal* 2, 1 (1948): 30; RG 24, vol. 20270, Colonel C.P. Stacey, The Nature of an Official History, n.d. [ca. 1946], 7.
117 Crerar papers, v. 3, file Historical, Crerar to Stacey, 11 June 1944; UTA, Stacey's personal diary, 23 October 1945.
118 Dominick Graham, *The Price of Command: A Biography of General Guy Simonds* (Toronto: Stoddart, 1993), 60-2.
119 Stacey, *The Canadian Army*, 86.
120 UTA, Stacey's personal diary, 23 October 1945.
121 DHH, URF, box 3, file 1-3-0-3, pt. 1, Stacey to Kent Greenfield, 15 September 1947 and Stacey to Hughes-Hallett, 3 October 1947.
122 RG 24, vol. 20270, Colonel C.P. Stacey, "The Nature of an Official History," n.d. [ca. 1946], 8.
123 "Nazi War Training Near Miss – Stacey," *The Varsity*, 14 November 1951.
124 UTA, Stacey's personal diary, 16 July 1946.
125 Jeffrey Grey, *A Commonwealth of Histories, The Trevor Reese Memorial Lecture, 1998* (London: Institute of Commonwealth Studies, 1998), 15.
126 RG 24, v. 12752, 24/LIAISON/1/2, Latham to Hunter, 12 December 1947; DHH, URF, box 1, file 1-0, pt. 2, Progress Report, January 1949 and Progress Report, January 1950.
127 Ibid., Stacey to DMI, 14 April 1948.
128 Stacey, *The Canadian Army, 1949-1945*, 285, 288.
129 DHH, URF, box 3, file 1-3-0, Stacey to Crerar, 24 July 1947.
130 For Stacey's intervention, see Brereton Greenhous, *"C" Force to Hong Kong: A Canadian Catastrophe, 1941-1945* (Toronto: Dundurn Press, 1997), 51; "The Controversy over Maltby's Hong Kong Dispatch," *Canadian Military History* 2, 2 (1993): 111-16; Kent Fedorowich, "'Cocked Hats and Swords and Small, Little Garrisons': Britain, Canada and the Fall of Hong Kong, 1941," *Modern Asian Studies* 37, 1 (2003): 151-7.
131 McNaughton papers, v. 325, file Comment on Chapters IV and V of Canadian Official Historical Sketch, by General A.G.L. McNaughton, 30 June 1947; ibid., McNaughton to Stacey, 30 July 1947.
132 C.P. Stacey, *Arms, Men and Governments* (Ottawa: Queen's Printer, 1970), 201; RG 24, v. 20409, 958.009 (D53), paper by C.P. Stacey, "The Great Aberrations of Canadian War Policy, 1939-45." Stacey believed the other colossal error in judgment by the Canadian government was "the failure to take control of our own airforce early in the war."
133 DHH, URF, box 1, file 1-1-0, pt. 1, Stacey to Feasby, 9 January 1948.
134 UTA, Stacey's personal diary, 11 August 1947, 29 September 1947.
135 Stacey, "The Life and Hard Times," 33-4; DHH, URF, box 3, file 1-3-0-3, pt. 1, Memo of Interview with Hon. Brooke Claxton, 11 August 1947.

136 Stacey, *The Canadian Army*, 92-3.
137 McNaughton papers, v. 325, file: History of the Canadian Armies overseas, Stanley to Stacey, n.d. [ca. January 1947]; DHH, 917.009 (D1), v. 1, Stanley to Stacey, 12 September 1946. Dick Malone, *Missing from the Record* (Toronto: Collins, 1946), 129-38.
138 DHH, 917.009 (D1), v. 2, Nicholson to Stacey, 21 December 1946.
139 C.P. Stacey, *The Canadian Army, 1939-1945: An Official Historical Summary* (Ottawa: King's Printer, 1948); Tim Creery, "Home Comes the Colonel," *Varsity Graduate* 8, 1 (1959): 52.
140 John Hundevad, *The Legionary*, May 1948, 20-2.
141 Major General R.H. Keefler, "Balanced Picture," *The Gazette* (Montreal), 15 May 1948.
142 Review by "M.G.B.," *Pelican Record*, Corpus Christi College, Oxford (December 1948): n.p.
143 Eric Harrison, "Review of *The Canadian Army, 1939-1945: An Official Historical Summary*, by C.P. Stacey," *Canadian Historical Review* 29, 3 (1948): 301-6.
144 Quoted in Captain S.W. Roskill, "Some Reasons for Official History," in *Official Histories: Essays and Bibliographies from around the World*, ed. Robin Higham (Manhattan, KS: Kansas State University Library, 1970), 11.
145 "The Story of the Canadian Army, One of Splendid Achievement," *Saturday Night*, 15 May 1948.
146 DHH, URF, box 3, file 1-3-0-6, pt. 2, Palmer to Stacey, 2 February 1949.

Chapter 5: Official History, Contested Memory, 1948-60

1 C.P. Stacey, "The Life and Hard Times of an Official Historian," *Canadian Historical Review* 51, 1 (1970): 33.
2 Directorate of History and Heritage (DHH), unprocessed registry files (URF), box 1, file 1-0, pt. 2, Meeting of Service Historians, 2 April 1947.
3 RG 24, v. 5231, HQS 19-57-37, pt. 2, Review of Status of RCAF Historical Section, Appendix A, [ca. 23 February 1948]; RG 24, 1983-84/216, box 2967, file 895-DAFH, pt. 2, Chairman, Chiefs of Staff Committee, 30 July 1947.
4 RG 24, 1983-84/216, box 2967, file 895-DAFH, pt. 2, Organization of Air Historian, 25 February 1948.
5 RG 24, v. 17674, file 046-12, pt. 1, Hitchins to A/CAS, 5 August 1947.
6 Ibid., Sorel to RCAF Historical Section, 17 January 1949.
7 Royal Canadian Air Force Historical Section, preface to *The R.C.A.F. Overseas, The Sixth Year* (Toronto: Oxford University Press, 1949).
8 Ibid., 83.
9 Review, *Saskatoon Star-Phoenix*, 20 August 1949.
10 John Yocom, *Saturday Night*, 5 September 1949.
11 *Calgary Herald*, 20 August 1949; J.H.S. Reid, review of *The R.C.A.F. Overseas, The Sixth Year*, by Royal Canadian Air Force Historical Section, *Canadian Historical Review* 41, 1 (March 1950): 79.
12 George Stanley, review, *Queen's Quarterly* (Winter 1949-50).
13 Yocom, *Saturday Night*, 5 September 1949.
14 RG 24, v. 17674, file 046-12, memorandum 23 January 1950; Sales, 22 June 1950.
15 DHH, 81/520/1440-10, v. 3, pt. 2, box 64, file 3, VCNS to CNS, 6 April 1948.
16 DHH, URF, box 1, file 1-0, pt. 2, Meeting of Service Historians, 2 April 1947.
17 DHH, 81/520/1440-10, v. 3, pt. 2, box 64, file 3, Mills to Brown, 22 December 1947.
18 RG 24, 1983-84/167, box 614, file 1834-54, Stacey to Captain Dillon, 18 October 1949.
19 DHH, 81/520/1440-10, v. 3, pt. 2, box 64, file 3, Claxton to CNS, 12 January 1948; ibid., Memo to Chief of Naval Staff, 23 July 1948; UTA, Stacey's personal diary, 11 January 1948.
20 DHH, 81/520/1440-10, v. 3, pt. 2, box 64, file, 3, Northhrup to Raby, 3 February 1947.

21 On Schull, see ibid., DNI to ACNS, 2 September 1947. On the history, see ibid., Schull to DNI, 13 December 1947.
22 DHH, URF, box 7, file 1-7-0, Stacey to Schull, 1 February 1949.
23 LAC, MG 31 D 5, Joseph Schull papers, Mainguy to Schull, 23 February 1949; Godfrey to Schull, 10 March 1949; Audette to Wright, 19 April 1949.
24 Joseph Schull, *Far Distant Ships: An Official Account of Canadian Naval Operations in the Second World War* (Ottawa: King's Printer, 1950), 55.
25 UTA, C.P. Stacey papers, box 41, file D Hist Correspondence, 1980-88, clipping, n.a., "Canada Kept Atlantic Open for Supplies to Britain," review of *Far Distant Ships*, by Joseph Schull, n.d.
26 David Zimmerman, review of *Canada and the Battle of the Atlantic, Canadian Historical Review* 81, 2 (2000): 322-4.
27 RG 24, 1983-84/167, box 498, file 1700-N/HIST (pt. 3), Russell to Naval Secretary, 19 January 1952.
28 UTA, Stacey papers, box 58, file: Date with History, early draft, ch. 14, p. 5; and Stacey, "The Life and Hard Times," 31.
29 Gilbert Tucker, "The Royal Canadian Naval Historical Section and Its Work," *Canadian Historical Review* 26 (September 1945): 245.
30 Gilbert Tucker, preface to *The Naval Service of Canada*, vol. 1, *Origins and Early Years* (Ottawa: King's Printer, 1952).
31 RG 24, v. 12747, 24/DIARIES/3, Canmilitary to Defensor, December 1945.
32 George W. Brown, "The Problem of Public and Historical Records in Canada," *Canadian Historical Review* 25 (March 1944): 3.
33 Archives Committee, "The Discussion of the Problem of Public and Historical Records in Canada," *Historical Papers of the Canadian Historical Association* (1-2 June 1944): 40.
34 LAC, RG 37, v. 305, file: Public Records Committee, Report of the Advisory Committee on Public Records, 16 July 1945.
35 Ibid., Committee on Public Records, ca. July 1945. Archivists now aim to retain between 3 to 5 percent of all created government records.
36 DHH, URF, box 26, file 6-0-14-1, pt. 1, Committee on Public Meetings, Minutes, 13 December 1945.
37 C.P. Stacey, The Problem of Canadian Archives: A Special Study to the Royal Commission on National Development in the Arts, Letters and Sciences, brief (Ottawa, 2 June 1950).
38 RG 24, v. 12751, 24/GEN/1/2, Stacey to DCGS, 9 August 1945.
39 RG 24, v. 12747, 24/CORPS & REGT/1, NOTES ON THE PREPARATION OF REGIMENTAL HISTORIES, 14 September 1945.
40 RG 24, v. 12747, 24/CORPS/1, Corps and Regimental histories, 14 September 1945; DHH, URF, box 8, file 1-13-0, Nicholson to Bell-Irving, 20 May 1953.
41 DHH, 917.009 (D1), v. 1, Stanley to Stacey, 29 January 1946. Stanley had been one of those academics who had received a "chilly" reception in 1938 when he had visited the DHS to conduct research.
42 DHH, URF, box 20, file 4-0-2, pt. 1, Stacey to Rye, 7 May 1946; ibid., file 4-0-2, pt. 2, Drury to Goldring, 31 March 1950; ibid., Stacey to DMI, 20 April 1951; UTA, Stacey's private diary, 4 July 1949.
43 DHH, 917.009 (D1), v. 3, Stacey to Hunter, 10 October 1947.
44 DHH, 917.009 (D1), v. 6, Interview with General Burns, 18 August 1950.
45 E.L.M. Burns, *Manpower in the Canadian Army, 1939-1945* (Toronto: Clarke, Irwin, 1956). Historians would not revisit the issue in detail for almost fifty years; see Michael D. Stevenson, *Canada's Greatest Wartime Muddle: National Selective Service and the Mobilization of Human*

Resources during World War II (Montreal and Kingston: McGill-Queen's University Press, 2001).
46 DHH, 917.009 (D1), v. 3, Stacey to Nicholson, 15 May 1947; UTA, Stacey's private diary, 6 May 1948 and 24 November 1948.
47 Ibid., 11 August 1950; Royal Commission on National Development in the Arts, Letters, and Sciences, 1949-1951, *Report* (Ottawa: King's Printer, 1951), 338.
48 C.P. Stacey, "Harry Hopkins and the General Eisenhower," *Canadian Army Journal* 3, 2 (1949): 32.
49 UTA, Stacey's private diary, 22 November 1945; DHH, 917.009 (D1), Stacey to Stanley, 25 January 1946.
50 RG 24, v. 17670, file 045-12, v. 1, Defence Council Minutes, 7 March 1947.
51 DHH, URF, box 1, file 1-1-0, pt. 1, Stacey to CGS, 14 February 1947.
52 DHH, 917.009 (D1), pt. 2, Stacey to Nicholson, 21 March 1947; DHH, URF, box 1, file 1-1-0, pt. 1, Feasby to Claxton, 15 February 1947.
53 DHH, URF, box 1, file 1-1-0, pt. 1, Stacey to Feasby, 12 July 1947.
54 Ibid., Stacey to Feasby, 9 January 1948.
55 Ibid., Stacey to Feasby, 9 January 1947; UTA, Stacey's personal diary, 8 January 1948.
56 DHH, 917.009 (D1), pt. 7, Stacey to Cunningham, 12 October 1951.
57 There has been some work, however; see Charles G. Roland, *Long Night's Journey into Day: Prisoners of War in Hong Kong and Japan, 1941-1945* (Waterloo: Wilfrid Laurier University Press, 2001).
58 DHH, URF, box 7, file 1-8-0, Memorandum to DHS file, 6 October 1949; UTA, Stacey's personal diary, 5 October 1949.
59 DHH, URF, box 8, file 2-1-2, Comments by Historical Section on The Raid on Dieppe by Christopher Buckley, 5 December 1949; DHH, 917.009 (D1), v. 5, Stacey to Hunter, 16 November 1949.
60 DHH, URF, box 1, file 1-0, pt. 2, Progress Report, Historical Section, January 1950; DHH, URF, box 8, file 2-1-2, Stacey to VCGS, 3 February 1950.
61 DHH, URF, box 1, file 1-0, pt. 2, Foulkes to Minister, 13 January 1950.
62 DHH, URF, box 1, file 1-0, pt. 3, Approximation of Cost of Salaries, n.d. [ca. 1955]; UTA, Stacey papers, box 21, file: official history, Stacey to Nicholson, 15 March 1949.
63 LAC, RG 24, Accession 1983-84/167, box 4957, file 3201-5, pt. 1, Memo, Study of Military History in the Army, 20 January 1950.
64 UTA, Stacey papers, box 45, speech by C.P. Stacey, The Study of Military History By Service Officers, 28 May 1957.
65 For the didactic value of military history, see *A Guide to the Study and Use of Military History*, ed. John E. Jessup and Robert W. Coakley (Fort McNair, DC: United States Army Center of Military History, 1982); David A. Charters, Marc Milner, and J. Brent Wilson, eds., *Military History and the Military Profession* (Westport, CT: Praeger, 1992).
66 LAC, RG 24, Accession 1983-84/167, box 4957, file 3201-5, pt. 2, Macdonald to Rutherford, 23 March 1955.
67 Ibid., file 3201-5, pt. 1, HQ 3201-5, 8 September 1954.
68 T.M. Hunter, *Marshal Foch: A Study in Leadership* (Ottawa: Queen's Printer, 1961); G.W.L. Nicholson, *Marlborough and the War of the Spanish Succession* (Ottawa: Directorate of Military Training Army Headquarters, Queen's Printer, 1956); Department of National Defence, *The Western Front, 1914* (Ottawa: Directorate of Military Training: Queen's Printer, 1957); J. Mackay Hitsman, *Military Inspection Services in Canada, 1855-1950* (Ottawa: Department of National Defence, Inspection Services, [1962]); D.J. Goodspeed, *The British Campaigns in the Peninsula, 1808-1814* (Ottawa: Army Headquarters, 1958).

69 Sir Michael Howard, "The Use and Abuse of Military History," *Royal United Service Institute* 107 (February 1962), reprinted in *The Army Doctrine and Training Bulletin* 6, 2 (2003): 18.
70 Louis Morton, "The Historian and the Study of War," *The Mississippi Valley Historical Review* 48, 4 (March 1962): 612.
71 Richard Preston, "The Teaching of Military History in Canada," *Canadian Army Journal* 3, 1 (April 1949): 14-15, 30
72 George F.G. Stanley, *Canada's Soldiers: The Military History of an Unmilitary People* (Toronto: Macmillan, 1960), 359.
73 C.P. Stacey, "The Myth of the Unguarded Frontier, 1815-1871," *American Historical Review* 56, 1 (1951): 1-18. This later became the inaugural subject of the Canadian Historical Association booklet series: C.P. Stacey, *The Undefended Border: The Myth and Reality* (Ottawa: Canadian Historical Association, 1953).
74 DHH, 917.009 (D1), pt. 1, Stacey to Foulkes, 7 September 1946.
75 Quote from DHH, URF, box 1, file 1-0, pt. 2, Stacey to Nicholson, 15 March 1949. See also, DHH, 83/269, folder 4, General Specifications [for the official history], 21 April 1948.
76 UTA, Stacey papers, box 21, file: official history, Stacey to Nicholson, 3 May 1949.
77 LAC, MG 31 G19, G.W.L. Nicholson papers, v. 6, The Writing of an Official History, speech, 26 October 1956.
78 See, for example, Historical Report no. 121.
79 UTA, Stacey papers, box 45, draft notes to Introduction to the Study of Military History.
80 Quote from LAC, G.W.L. Nicholson papers, v. 6, The Writing of an Official History, speech, 26 October 1956. LAC, RG 24, v. 20270, 903.003 (D2), Topographical Notes during visit by DDHS to Italy, Sept-Nov 1948, contains Nicholson's sixty page report on terrain, with photographs and maps.
81 DHH, URF, box 8, file 1-13-0, Nicholson to McCarter, 10 January 1952.
82 UTA, Stacey's personal diary, 22 September 1952.
83 DHH, URF, box 8, file 1-13-0, Nicholson to McCarter, 10 January 1952; Nicholson to Bell-Irving, 20 May 1953.
84 UTA, Stacey papers, box 21, file: Official History (proper), Stacey to Nicholson, 24 January 1950.
85 DHH, URF, box 4, file 1-5-8, pt. 2, Stacey to CGS, 19 February 1951.
86 DHH, URF, box 1, file 1-0, pt. 2, Progress Report, Historical Section, Army Headquarters, January 1950.
87 UTA, Stacey's personal diary, 15 March 1949.
88 DHH, 917.009 (D1), v. 7, Stacey to Cunningham, 21 April 1952; Robert Sherwood, *Roosevelt and Hopkins* (New York: Harper and Bros., 1948); Chester Wilmot, *The Struggle for Europe* (London: Collins, 1952).
89 LAC, RG 24, v. 20415, 959.009 (D26), Memo of interview with CGS, 20 December 1954.
90 DHH, 917.009 (D1), v. 7, Stacey to Cunningham, 11 September 1951.
91 DHH, URF, box 1, file 1-0, pt. 3, Simonds to Minister, 5 April 1954.
92 UTA, Stacey's personal diary, 26 February 1954, 2 March 1954.
93 Ibid., 2-4 March 1954.
94 C.P. Stacey, "The Canadian-American Permanent Joint Board of Defence, 1940-1945," *International Journal* 9, 2 (1954): 107-24.
95 Stacey, "The Life and Hard Times," 37.
96 DHH, URF, box 7, file 1-12-0, pt. 2, UTA, Stacey's personal diary, 13 October 1954.
97 Stacey to CGS, 7 July 1955; DHH, 83/269, folder 5, Interview with Lt. Gen. G.G. Simonds [by Stacey], 20 December 1954.
98 DHH, URF, box 1, file 1-0, pt. 3, Stacey to CGS, Interview with the Minister, 18 July 1955.

99 UTA, Stacey's personal diary, 19 April 1955, 11 May 1955, and 15 July 1955.
100 DHH, URF, box 1, file 1-0, pt. 3, Official Histories, 3 August 1955.
101 Ibid., Simonds to Campney, 21 March 1955; DHH, URF, box 2, file 1-1-2, Record of Cabinet Conclusion, 16 August 1955.
102 UTA, Stacey's personal diary, 12 August and 16 August 1955.
103 C. P. Stacey, *A Date with History: Memoirs of a Canadian Historian* (Ottawa: Deneau, 1983), 153.
104 C.P. Stacey, *Official History of the Canadian Army in the Second World War*, Vol. 1, *Six Years of War: The Army in Canada, Britain and the Pacific* (Ottawa: Queen's Printer, 1955).
105 Stacey, *Six Years of War*, 461 for the problem with sources, and 477 for the resolute defence.
106 DHH, URF, box 4, file 1-5-8, pt. 2, Stacey to CGS, 19 February 1951.
107 Stacey, *Six Years of War*, 490.
108 Ibid., 490.
109 Ibid., 397-404.
110 Ibid., 393.
111 G.W.L. Nicholson, *Official History of the Canadian Army in the Second World War*, Vol. 2, *The Canadians in Italy, 1943-45* (Ottawa: Queen's Printer, 1956).
112 Arnold Edinborough, "Of Battles Old and New," *The Kingston Whig Standard*, 29 September 1956.
113 Editorial, "Well Worth Owning," *County Herald*, 16 November 1956.
114 Forrest C. Pogue, review in the *Journal of Modern History* (June 1957).
115 Michael Howard, "Official History of the Canadian Army in the Second World War," *History* 42 (October 1957).
116 DHH, URF, box 1, file 1-0-1-1, Nicholson to Stacey, 18 March 1960.
117 RG 24, 1983-84/216, box 2967, file 895-DAFH, pt. 2, Slemon to Graham, 5 October 1956.
118 Ibid., Hitchins to A/VCAS, 2 May 1953.
119 Air Historical Section, *Among the Few: A Sketch of the Part Played by Canadian Airmen in the Battle of Britain* (Ottawa: King's Printer, 1948); Historical Section, RCAF, *RCAF Logbook: A Chronological Outline of the Origin, Growth and Achievement of the Royal Canadian Air Force* (Ottawa: E. Cloutier, King's Printer, 1949).
120 UTA, Stacey's personal diary, 17 August 1955.
121 Farley Mowat, *The Regiment* (1955; reprint, Toronto: McClelland and Stewart, 1973), vi.
122 Ibid., 141, 147.
123 Ross Munro, *Gauntlet to Overlord* (Toronto: Macmillan, 1946) and Peter Simonds, *Maple Leaf Up, Maple Leaf Down* (New York: Island Press, 1946), 1, 2, 20, 29. For wartime journalistic writing, see Ross Munro, *Red Patch in Sicily* (Toronto: Canadian Press, 1943); Lionel Shapiro, *They Left the Back Door Open* (Toronto: Ryerson, 1944); Edgar McInnis, *The War*, 6 vols. (Toronto: Oxford University Press, 1940-46).
124 Dick Malone, *Missing from the Record* (Toronto: Collins, 1946), v, vi-vii.
125 Ibid., v.
126 On McNaughton, see ibid., 129-34, 137-8; on Crerar, see ibid., 65-73.
127 For an example, see George Harsh, *Lonesome Road* (New York: W.W. Norton, 1971).
128 Murray Peden, *A Thousand Shall Fall: A Pilot for 214* (Stittsville, ON: Canada's Wings, 1979), 478-81.
129 William H. Pugsley, foreword to *Saints, Devils and Ordinary Seamen: Life on the Royal Canadian Navy's Lower Deck* (Toronto: Collins, 1945). Alan Easton, *50 North: Canada's Atlantic Battleground* (Toronto: Ryerson Press, 1963) has also remained a classic in the genre. Dr. W.A.B. Douglas, interview with author, 8 November 2004.
130 Peter G. Tsouras, ed., *The Greenhill Dictionary of Military Quotations* (London: Greenhill Books, 2000), 294.

131 E.L.M. Burns, *General Mud: Memoirs of Two World Wars* (Toronto: Clarke, Irwin, 1970).
132 Maurice A. Pope, *Soldiers and Politicians: The Memoirs of Lt.-General Maurice A. Pope, C.B., M.C.* (Toronto: University of Toronto Press, 1962); George Kitching, *Mud and Green Fields: The Memoirs of Major General George Kitching* (Langley, BC: Battleline Books, 1986); Chris Vokes and John P. Maclean, *Vokes: My Story* (Ottawa: Gallery Books, 1985).
133 John Swettenham, *McNaughton*, 3 vols. (Toronto: Ryerson Press, 1968-69).
134 DHH, URF, box 8, file 1-15-0, Stacey to Crerar, 25 October 1956.
135 C.P. Stacey, *Official History of the Canadian Army in the Second World War*, vol. 3, *The Victory Campaign: The Operations in Northwest Europe, 1944-1945* (Ottawa: Queen's Printer, 1960).
136 Ibid., 118-19.
137 UTA, Stacey papers, box 21, file: misc. 1945-58, Stacey, memo [on McNaughton's removal], 21 July 1958.
138 Extract from *U.S.I. Journal* (July-September 1960) in DHH, URF, box 8, file 1-15-3; *Montreal Star*, 4 February 1960.
139 DHH, URF, box 1, file 1-0-1-1, Nicholson to Stacey, 18 March 1960.
140 UTA, Stacey papers, box 41, file: DHist Correspondence, 1959-60, Nicholson to Stacey, 5 February 1960.
141 J.L. Granatstein, *The Generals: The Canadian Army's Senior Commanders in the Second World War* (Toronto: Stoddart, 1993), ch. 4.
142 For Simonds on Foulkes, see George Kitching, *Mud and Green Fields: The Memoirs of Major-General George Kitching* (Langley, BC: Battleline Books, 1986), 189.
143 For Simonds's complex plans, see Roman Jarymowycz, "General Guy Simonds: The Commander as Tragic Hero," in *Warrior Chiefs: Perspectives on Senior Canadian Military Leaders*, ed. Lieutenant Colonel Bernd Horn and Stephen Harris (Toronto: Dundurn Press, 2001).
144 DHH, URF, box 8, file 1-15-0, Stacey, "Removal of Commanding Officers in Normandy," 28 January 1959.
145 Stacey, *The Victory Campaign*, 275.
146 DHH, URF, box 8, file 1-15-0, Crerar to Stacey, 10 January 1958.
147 Stacey, *The Victory Campaign*, 275.
148 Ibid., 132-3.
149 UTA, Stacey papers, box 5, file: general, 1982-89, Stacey to J.A. English, 4 November 1987. See Stacey, *The Victory Campaign*, 274-5, for the suggestion that it was not just the Canadians who were inexperienced, but also the British and the Americans.
150 S.M. Lett, "Falaise Gap Vets Deny Laxity Lengthened War," *The Telegram*, 19 January 1960.
151 See Terry Copp, *Fields of Fire: The Canadians in Normandy* (Toronto: University of Toronto Press, 2003); and Russell A. Hart, *Clash of Arms: How the Allies Won in Normandy* (Boulder: Lynne Rienner, 2001).
152 Stacey, *The Victory Campaign*, 271-7; UTA, Stacey papers, box 44, file: books on WWII, Clipping, *The Gazette*, 6 October 1956; Denis Whitaker, *Victory at Falaise: The Soldiers' Story* (Toronto: HarperCollins, 2000), 297.
153 Stacey, *The Victory Campaign*, 150-1.
154 UTA, Stacey papers, box 5, file: Inquiries, 1961-75, Stacey to J.D. Holmes, 16 August 1964.
155 UTA, Stacey papers, box 45, draft notes on Introduction to the Study of Military History.
156 A.M.J. Hyatt, "Official History in Canada," *Military Affairs* 30, 2 (Summer 1966): 91.
157 C.P. Stacey, *Quebec, 1759: The Siege and Battle* (Toronto: Macmillan, 1959); *Records of the Nile Voyageurs 1885-1885: The Canadian Voyageur Contingents in the Gordon Relief Expedition* (Toronto: The Champlain Society, 1959).
158 See the compiled bibliography in Michael Cross and Robert Bothwell, eds., *Policy by Other Means: Essays in Honour of C.P. Stacey* (Toronto: Clarke, Irwin, 1972).

159 Donald Wright, *The Canadian Historical Association: A History* (Ottawa: Canadian Historical Association, 2003), 21-4.
160 Interview with Roberts Spencer, 17 February 2005.
161 Reginald Roy, who had been one of Stacey's junior narrators in the early 1950s, testified before a 1992 Senate Committee investigating *The Valour and the Horror* that Stacey had told him that he had no idea that Ultra existed until it was revealed in Winterbotham's 1974 history. Senate of Canada Standing Senate Subcommittee of Social Affairs, Science and Technology – Proceedings of the Subcommittee on Veterans Affairs, No. 9, 6 November 1992. For the revelation of Ultra to the world in 1974, see F.W. Winterbotham, *The Ultra Secret* (New York: Harper and Row, 1974); and John Keegan, *The Battle for History: Re-Fighting World War Two* (Canada: Vintage Books, 1995), 86-7.
162 Ronald Spector, "Public History and Research in Military History: What Difference Has It Made?" *The History Teacher* 26, 1 (1992): 91.
163 UTA, Stacey papers, box 45, speech by C.P. Stacey, "Generals and Historians," 21 March 1960.
164 Stacey, "The Life and Hard Times," 45-6.
165 Sydney Wise, "Canadian Military History: A Comparative Report," *Journal of the Australian War Memorial* 7 (October 1985): 5.

Chapter 6: Forging the Canon of Canadian World War History, 1960-2000

1 Cited in Jeff Keshen, "Review Essay: The New Campaigns of Canadian Military Historians," *American Review of Canadian Studies* 23 (Autumn 1993): 425.
2 LAC, RG 24, 1983-84/216, box 3075, Supporting Data for Defence Council by the Naval and Air Historian, 2 May 1963; LAC, MG 32 B19, Douglas Harkness papers, v. 25, file 41-73, Stacey to Churchill, 10 August 1960.
3 LAC, RG 24, 1983-84/216, box 2967, file 895-DAFH, pt. 2, ND-AF-Min-1, 4 April 1961; ibid., Revision of Function and Increase in Staff, 12 June 1961; ibid., file 895-DAFH, pt. 3, Publication of the First Volume of an Official RCAF History, 27 September 1963.
4 Thor Thorgrimsson and E.C. Russell, *Canadian Naval Operations in Korean Waters, 1950-1955* (Ottawa: Naval Historical Section, 1965); and J.D.F. Kealy and E.C. Russell, *A History of Canadian Naval Aviation, 1918-1962* (Ottawa: Naval Historical Section, 1965).
5 Canadian Army Historical Section, *Canada's Army in Korea: The United Nations Operations, 1950-1953 and the Aftermath* (Ottawa: Queen's Printer, 1956).
6 William Johnson, *A War of Patrols: Canadian Army Operations in Korea* (Vancouver: UBC Press, 2003).
7 Herbert Fairlie Wood, *Strange Battleground: The Operations in Korea and Their Effects on the Defence Policy of Canada* (Ottawa: Queen's Printer, 1966). For recent Korean War Canadian studies, see D.J. Bercuson, *Blood on the Hills: The Canadian Army in the Korean War* (Toronto: University of Toronto Press, 1999); Ted Barris, *Deadlock in Korea: Canadians at War, 1950-1953* (Toronto: Macmillan, 1999); Brent Watson, *Far Eastern Tour: The Canadian Infantry in Korea, 1950-1953* (Montreal and Kingston: McGill-Queen's University Press, 2002); and Johnson, *A War of Patrols*.
8 C.A. Masters, "Letter to Editor," *The Legionary*, March 1956, 32.
9 LAC, RG 24, v. 17673, file 046-1, Record of Cabinet Decision, 21 June 1956. Quote from DHH, unprocessed registry files (URF), box 5, file 1-6-1, pt. 1, CGS to minister, n.d. [ca. 22 November 1955].
10 "At Long Last: An Official History of World War I," *The Legionary*, August 1956, 5.
11 DHH, URF, box 5, file 1-6-1, pt. 1, Stacey to Nicholson, 8 January 1957.
12 For an examination of Sir James Edmonds's prolific work and struggles, see Andrew Samuel Green, "Sir James Edmonds and the Official Military Histories of the Great War" (PhD diss.,

University of Leeds, 1999); David French, "'Official but not History'? Sir James Edmonds and the Official History of the Great War," *RUSI Journal* 133, 1 (1986): 58-63.
13 *The Memoirs of Captain Liddell Hart*, vol. 1 (London: Cassell, 1965), 211.
14 Brian Bond, *The Unquiet Western Front: Britain's Role in Literature and History* (Cambridge: Cambridge University Press, 2002), 46-7.
15 For a critique of Edmonds and his work, see T.H.E. Travers, *The Killing Ground: The British Army, the Western Front, and the Emergence of Modern Warfare, 1900-1918* (London: Allen and Unwin, 1987); and Denis Winter, *Haig's Command: A Reassessment* (London: Penguin, 1991).
16 For supporters of Haig, see John Terraine, *Douglas Haig: The Educated Soldier* (London: Hutchinson, 1968); for his most vitriolic critics, see Winter, *Haig's Command*, and John Laffin, *British Butchers and Bunglers of World War One* (London: Sutton Publishing, 1988). For a most recent assessment, see the collection of essays in Brian Bond and Nigel Cave, eds., *Haig: A Reappraisal 70 Years On* (London: Leo Cooper, 1999).
17 Quoted in Jay Luvaas, "The First British Official Historian," in *Official Histories: Essays and Bibliographies from around the World*, ed. Robin Higham (Manhattan, KS: Kansas State University Library, 1970), 504.
18 John Keegan, *The Face of Battle* (London: Jonathan Cape, 1976), 31.
19 DHH, URF, box 8, file 1-12-3, Kippenberger to Stacey, 3 April 1956.
20 DHH, URF, box 5, file 1-6-1, pt. 1, Nicholson, Official History – First World War, 15 November 1957.
21 DHH, URF, box 5, file 1-6-0, Short History, First World War, 22 June 1955.
22 DHH, URF, box 5, file 1-6-1, pt. 1, Stacey to Beaverbrook, 5 December 1957.
23 "The Quick and the Dead," *Ottawa Journal*, 14 August 1958; LAC, MG 31 G19, G.W.L. Nicholson papers, v. 1, Nicholson to Sprung, 5 December 1961.
24 LAC, MG 32 B19, D.S. Harkness papers, v. 25, file 41-73, Stacey to Churchill, 10 August 1960. The DHS had 38 staff members, the navy had 9 staff members, and the air force had 4 staff members. The DHS was cut from 38 to 34. Figures cited in ibid., Armstrong to Roberts, 18 August 1960.
25 DHH, URF, box 7, file 1-6-6, pt. 1, Nicholson to Latham, 17 March 1961.
26 Nicholson papers, v. 1, Sprung to Duguid, 16 May 1962.
27 UTA, Stacey papers, box 41, file: DHist Correspondence, Stacey to DHist, 30 July 1962.
28 W.H.S. Macklin, "A Belated War History Does Canada Justice," *Ottawa Citizen*, 26 January 1963; Reginald Roy, "An Official War History at Last," *Victoria Daily Times*, 8 February 1964; Cyril Falls, review, *International Journal* (June 1963): 229.
29 G.W.L. Nicholson, *Canadian Expeditionary Force, 1914-1919* (Ottawa: Queen's Printer, 1964), 200.
30 Peter Dennis, "Introduction," *Revue Internationale d'Histoire Militaire* 72 (1990): ix.
31 Alex Danchev, "Bunking and Debunking: The Controversies of the 1960s," in *The First World War and British Military History*, ed. Brian Bond (Oxford: Clarendon Press, 1991), 267-8.
32 Bond, *The Unquiet Western Front*, 61.
33 Stephane Audoin-Rouzeau and Annette Becker, *1914-1918: Understanding the Great War* (London: Profile Books, 2002), 37-9.
34 See the discussion of personal history in Samuel Hynes, *The Soldiers' Tale: Bearing Witness to Modern War* (New York: A. Lane, 1997).
35 Gary Sheffield, *Forgotten Victory. The First World War: Myth and Realities* (London: Headline Book Publishing, 2001), 20-4.
36 A.E. Powley, "Flanders' Fields," *Radio-TV: The Canadian Broadcasting Corporation Staff Magazine*, October 1964.

37 *Flanders' Fields* promotional advertisement, copy held at Canadian War Museum library, Ottawa.
38 Larry Worthington, *Amid the Guns Below* (Toronto: McClelland and Stewart, 1965); Kenneth Macksey, *The Shadow of Vimy Ridge* (London: William Kimber, 1965); John Swettenham, *To Seize The Victory: The Canadian Corps in World War I* (Toronto: Ryerson Press, 1965); Alexander McKee, *The Battle of Vimy Ridge* (New York: Stein and Day, 1966); Herbert Fairlie Wood, *Vimy!* (Toronto: Macmillan, 1967); D.E. Macintyre, *Canada at Vimy* (Toronto: Peter Martin, 1967). For an analysis of the changing significance of Vimy, see Dave Inglis, "Vimy Ridge, 1917-1992: A Canadian Myth over 75 Years" (MA thesis, Simon Fraser University, 1995).
39 After his retirement from the DHS in the early 1960s, Nicholson wrote a number of other histories: *The Fighting Newfoundlander: A History of the Royal Newfoundland Regiment* (St. John's: Government of Newfoundland, 1964); *The Gunners of Canada: The History of the Royal Regiment of Canadian Artillery* (Toronto: McClelland and Stewart, 1967); *Canada's Nursing Sisters* (Toronto: A.M. Hakkert, 1975); *Seventy Years of Service: A History of the Royal Canadian Army Medical Corps* (Ottawa: Borealis Press, 1977).
40 RG 24, v. 20409, 958.009 (D40), Wood to Draycot, 22 October 1965.
41 Ronald Haycock, *Teaching Military History: Clio and Mars in Canada* (Athabasca, AB: Athabasca University Press, 1995), 1.
42 Ronald H. Spector, "Military History and the Academic World," in *A Guide to the Study and Use of Military History*, ed. John E. Jessup and Robert W. Coakley (Washington, DC: United States Army Center of Military History, 1982), 435.
43 John English, "National Politics and Governments," in *Canadian History: A Reading Guide*, vol. 2, *Confederation to the Present*, ed. Doug Owram (Toronto: University of Toronto Press, 1994), 3-5; Louis Morton, "The Writing of Official History," in *Official Histories: Essays and Bibliographies from around the World*, ed. Robin Higham (Manhattan, KS: Kansas State University Library, 1970), 37; Marc Milner, introduction to *Canadian Military History: Selected Readings* (Toronto: Copp Clark Pitman, 1993).
44 Fred Gaffen succeeded Swettenham as the editor of the Canadian War Museum series, which continued until the mid-1990s. W.A.B. Douglas, "In Memoriam, G.W.L. Nicholson and J.A. Swettenham: History and the Military," *Canadian Defence Quarterly* 10, 1 (1980): 43-6.
45 M.G. Dyer, *Military History and War Studies in Canadian Universities* (Toronto: Canadian Forces College, 1968), 2, 24.
46 Haycock, *Teaching Military History*, 14.
47 James Eayrs, *In Defence of Canada*, 6 vols. (Toronto: University of Toronto Press, 1964-83).
48 DHH, NHS 1700/100/78A, Director of History – Army Headquarters, 4 May 1964.
49 Field Marshal Viscount Montgomery of Alamein, *A History of Warfare* (London: Collins, 1968), 12.
50 UTA, Stacey papers, box 41, file: DHist Correspondence, 1963-64, Stacey to Major General W.A.B. Anderson, 15 April 1964.
51 Ibid., box 38, file: DHist Correspondence, 1966-67, 19 August 1966.
52 Ibid., Stacey to Wise, 7 September 1966. There was no definition of who was "respectable," but a researcher probably needed to produce a letter of introduction from a notable figure.
53 UTA, Stacey papers, box 38, file: Access to Records, 1972, Department of External Affairs Communiqué, 22 February 1972.
54 A.G. Doughty, "Canada's Record of the War," *University Magazine* 15 (December 1916): 471.
55 Information drawn from UTA, Stacey papers, box 41, file: DHist Correspondence, 1966-67, Access to Historical Records, 19 August 1966. After several requests, Crerar gave Eayrs access to his files in late 1964, but only the 1931-39 period. UTA, Stacey papers, box 41, file: DHist Correspondence, 1963-65, Stacey to Hunter, 6 December 1964.

56 Greg Donaghy, "Documenting the Diplomats: The Origins and Evolution of Documents of Canadian External Relations," *Public Historian* 25, 1 (2003): 22.
57 UTA, Stacey papers, file: DHist Correspondence, 1966-67, Access to Historical Records, 19 August 1966.
58 UTA, Stacey papers, box 38, file: Access to Records, 1972, Press Release, Office of the Prime Minister, 28 April 1972; Don Page, "Unlocking Canada's Diplomatic Record," *International Journal* 24, 2 (1979): 251-80.
59 DHH, URF, box 2, file 1-1-2, Foulkes to Minister, 26 January 1959.
60 See the Stacey correspondence in UTA, Stacey papers, box 55, file: A Very Double Life correspondence.
61 C.P. Stacey, *A Very Double Life: The Private World of Mackenzie King* (Toronto: Macmillan, 1976).
62 DHH, URF, box 2, file 1-1-2, Stacey to Manning, 7 July 1960; Policy Volume – Progress, 4 August 1961.
63 UTA, Stacey papers, box 54, file: correspondence, 1971-73, Stacey to Douglas, 20 September 1973.
64 UTA, Stacey papers, box 5, file: historical research, 1962-63, Stacey to Goodspeed, 27 November 1961.
65 UTA, Stacey papers, box 54, file: policy volume, Stacey to Macdonald, 3 June 1966.
66 David O'Keefe, "'A Most Difficult Bit of History': Re-examining the Historiography of Operation Spring, Normandy, July 25, 1944," MS, based on "Bitter Harvest: A Case Study of Allied Operational Intelligence for Operation Spring, Normandy, July 25, 1944" (MA thesis, University of Ottawa, 1996).
67 UTA, Stacey papers, box 54, file: correspondence, Pope to Wise, 28 September 1968.
68 Ibid., file: correspondence, Stacey to Simonds, 25 February 1969.
69 Ibid., file: Documents on Dieppe, 1948-69, Stacey to Admiral [Hughes-Hallett], 8 March 1969; box 5, file: correspondence, 1962-66, Stacey to Alice [Sorby], 27 February 1969.
70 UTA, Stacey papers, box 46, file: C.P. Stacey, Writing War History, 10 November 1978.
71 C.P. Stacey, *Arms, Men and Governments: The War Politics of Canada, 1939-1945* (Ottawa: Queen's Printer, 1970), vi.
72 Richard Preston, review, *American Historical Review* 77, 1 (1972): 233.
73 Michael Bliss, "Privatizing the Mind: The Sundering of Canadian History, the Sundering of Canada," *Journal of Canadian Studies* 26, 4 (1991-92): 10. C.P. Stacey, *Canada and the Age of Conflict: A History of Canadian External Policies*, 2 vols. (Toronto: Macmillan, 1977, 1981).
74 T.H.B. Symons, *To Know Ourselves: The Report of the Commission on Canadian Studies* (Ottawa: Association of Universities and Colleges of Canada, 1975), 61-4.
75 John Gellner, "Browsing," *Canadian Defence Quarterly* 6, 2 (1976): 56.
76 John Keegan, *The Face of Battle* (London: J. Cape, 1976).
77 Elizabeth Armstrong, *The Crisis of Quebec* (New York: Columbia University Press, 1937); John Thompson, *Harvest of War: The Prairie West, 1914-1918* (Toronto: McClelland and Stewart, 1978); Michael Bliss, *A Canadian Millionaire: The Life and Times of Sir Joseph Flavelle, Bart. 1858-1939* (Toronto: Macmillan, 1978); Robert Brown and Ramsay Cook, *Canada, 1896-1921* (Toronto: McClelland and Stewart, 1974). Also see Barbara M. Wilson, ed., *Ontario and the First World War, 1914-1918: A Collection of Documents* (Toronto: Champlain Society, 1977).
78 J.L. Granatstein and J.M. Hitsman, *Broken Promises: A History of Conscription in Canada* (Toronto: Oxford University Press, 1977); J.L. Granatstein, "Conscription and My Politics," *Canadian Military History* 10, 4 (2001): 35-8.
79 Barry Broadfoot, *Six War Years, 1939-1945* (Toronto: Doubleday, 1974), viii.

80 Quote in John A. English, *Failure in High Command: The Canadian Army and the Normandy Campaign*, rev. ed. (Ottawa: Golden Dog Press, 1995), 2.
81 D.J. Goodspeed, *Battle Royal: A History of the Royal Regiment of Canada 1862-1962* (Toronto: Royal Regiment of Canada Association, 1962); George Stanley, *In the Face of Danger: The History of the Lake Superior Regiment* (Port Arthur: Lake Superior Scottish Regiment, [1960]); Reginald Roy, *The Seaforth Highlanders of Canada, 1919-1965* (Vancouver: Seaforth Highlanders of Canada, 1969).
82 Will R. Bird, *North Shore (New Brunswick) Regiment* (Fredericton: Brunswick Press, 1963); A.F. Duguid, *History of the Canadian Grenadier Guards, 1760-1964* (Montreal: Gazette Print, 1965); Kim Beattie, *Dileas: History of the 48th Highlanders of Canada 1929-1956* (Toronto: 48th Highlanders of Canada, 1957).
83 Paul Hutchinson, *Canada's Black Watch: The First Hundred Years, 1862-1962* (Montreal: The Black Watch of Canada, ca. 1962).
84 W.A.B. Douglas and Brereton Greenhous, *Out of the Shadows: Canada in the Second World War* (Toronto: Dundurn Press, 1977), 6-7, 193.
85 N.a., "What Is Military History?" *History Today* 34 (December 1984): 9; Sydney Wise, "Canadian Military History: A Comparative Report," *Journal of the Australian War Memorial* 7 (October 1985): 6.
86 All three would publish their theses and make significant additions to the historiography. For their books, see Stephen J. Harris, *Canadian Brass: The Making of a Professional Army, 1860-1939* (Toronto: University of Toronto Press, 1988); Milner and Sarty are noted below.
87 Dyer, *Military History and War Studies*, 25.
88 John Connel, "Official History and the Unofficial Historian," *The Royal United Service Institutions Journal* (November 1965): 329.
89 Kenneth Taylor, "The Challenge of the Eighties: World War II from a New Perspective, the Hong Kong Case," in *Men at War: Politics, Technology and Innovation in the Twentieth Century*, ed. Timothy Travers and Christon Archer (Chicago: Precedent, 1982), 197-212.
90 Richard Preston, "Review Essay: Canadian Military History: A Reinterpretation Challenge of the Eighties?" *American Review of Canadian Studies* 19, 1 (1989): 97.
91 See Desmond Morton, *A Military History of Canada* (Edmonton: Hurtig Publishers, 1985); *A Peculiar Kind of Politics: Canada's Overseas Ministry in the First World War* (Toronto: University of Toronto Press, 1982); Desmond Morton and Glenn Wright, *Winning the Second Battle: Canadian Veterans and the Return to Civilian Life: 1915-1930* (Toronto: University of Toronto Press, 1987).
92 Desmond Morton and J.L. Granatstein, *Marching to Armageddon: Canadians and the First World War, 1914-1918* (Toronto: Lester and Orpen, 1988); J.L. Granatstein and Desmond Morton, *A Nation Forged in Fire: Canadians and the Second World War, 1939-1945* (Toronto: Lester and Orpen, 1989).
93 Dr. Marc Milner, interview with the author, 12 June 2004.
94 James A. Boutilier, ed., *The RCN in Retrospect, 1910-1968* (Vancouver: UBC Press, 1982); W.A.B. Douglas, ed., *The RCN in Transition, 1910-1985* (Vancouver: UBC Press, 1988).
95 Naval Officers' Association of Canada, *Salty Dips*, 8 vols. (Ottawa: privately published, 1979-2001).
96 W.A.B. Douglas, "The Prospects for Naval History," *The Northern Mariner* 1, 4 (1991): 19.
97 Marc Milner, *Canada's Navy: The First Century* (Toronto: University of Toronto Press, 1999), 96. Donald Macintyre, *The U-Boat Killer: Fighting the U-Boats in the Battle of the Atlantic* (London: Donald Macintyre, 1956).
98 Marc Milner, *North Atlantic Run: The Royal Canadian Navy and the Battle of the Convoys* (Toronto: University of Toronto Press, 1985); *The U-Boat Hunters: The Royal Canadian Navy*

and the *Offensive against Germany's Submarines* (Toronto: University of Toronto Press, 1994). Milner has also offered in *Canada's Navy* an excellent and much needed overview history of the RCN, from its establishment through the two world wars, and perhaps most important, the postwar years.

99 Michael Hadley, *U-Boats against Canada* (Montreal and Kingston: McGill-Queen's University Press, 1985); David Zimmerman, *The Great Naval Battle of Ottawa* (Toronto: University of Toronto Press, 1989).

100 Dr. Norman Hillmer and Dr. Roger Sarty, interview with the author, 22 February 2005.

101 W.A.B. Douglas, *The Creation of a National Air Force: The Official History of the RCAF* (Toronto: University of Toronto Press, 1986); and S.F. Wise, *Canadian Airmen and the First World War* (Toronto: University of Toronto Press, 1980).

102 Thomas Socknat, *Witness against War: Pacifism in Canada, 1900-1945* (Toronto: University of Toronto Press, 1987); Robert Bothwell and William Kilbourn, *C.D. Howe: A Biography* (Toronto: McClelland and Stewart, 1979); J.L. Granatstein, *Canada's War: The Politics of the Mackenzie King Government, 1939-1945* (Toronto: Oxford University Press, 1975); Ann Gomer Sunahara, *The Politics of Racism: The Uprooting of Japanese Canadians during the Second World War* (Toronto: James Lorimer, 1981); Ruth Roach Pierson, *"They're Still Women After All": The Second World War and Canadian Womanhood* (Toronto: McClelland and Stewart, 1986).

103 Pierre Berton, *Vimy* (Toronto: McClelland and Stewart, 1986) and *Marching as to War: Canada's Turbulent Years, 1899-1953* (Toronto: Doubleday Canada, 2001); Daniel Dancocks, *The D-Day Dodgers: The Canadians in Italy, 1943-1945* (Toronto: McClelland and Stewart, 1991), *Welcome to Flanders Fields: The First Canadian Battle of the Great War: Ypres, 1915* (Toronto: McClelland and Stewart, 1988), *Spearhead to Victory: Canada and the Great War* (Edmonton: Hurtig, 1987); Tony German, *The Sea Is at Our Gates: The History of the Canadian Navy* (Toronto: McClelland and Stewart, 1990); Denis Whitaker, *Dieppe: Tragedy to Triumph* (Toronto: McGraw-Hill Ryerson, 1992), *Tug of War: The Canadian Victory that Opened Antwerp* (Toronto: Stoddart, 1984), and *Rhineland: The Battle to Win the War* (Toronto: Stoddart, 1989).

104 Haycock, *Teaching Military History*, 13.

105 Cooke reissued his bibliography in 1997, and it had increased in size by one third since the 1984 edition. Owen A. Cooke, *The Canadian Military Experience, 1867-1995: A Bibliography* (Ottawa: Department of National Defence, 1997).

106 This paragraph drawn from H. Clifford Chadderton, *Hanging a Legend: The NFB's Shameful Attempt to Discredit Billy Bishop, VC* (Ottawa: War Amputations of Canada, [1986]), 29, 77. For the Bishop footnote, see Wise, *Canadian Airmen*, 413, 414.

107 Tim Travers, "Canadian Film and the First World War," in *The First World War and Popular Cinema*, ed. Michael Paris (New Brunswick, NJ: Rutgers University Press, 2000), 109.

108 Steven Dubin, *Displays of Power: Memory and Amnesia in the American Museum* (New York: New York University Press, 1999), 4.

109 Quoted in David O'Keefe, "'A Most Difficult Bit of History': Re-examining the Historiography of Operation Spring, Normandy, July 25, 1944," MS, from evidence given by Reg Roy in the Veterans Affairs subcommittee investigating *The Valour and the Horror*.

110 Canada, Senate, *Proceedings of the Subcommittee on Veterans Affairs* (Ottawa, 1993), 10:19

111 Ibid., 10:12.

112 David J. Bercuson and S.F. Wise, eds., *The Valour and the Horror Revisited* (Montreal and Kingston: McGill-Queen's University Press, 1994), 6. See also Ernest Dick, "History on Television: A Critical Archival Examination of 'The Valour and the Horror,'" *Archivaria* 34 (Summer 1992): 199-216.

113 H. Clifford Chadderton, *The Morality of Bomber Command in World War II* (N.p., 1992), 9.
114 In *Desperate Battle: Normandy 1944*, one of the other two films that formed the trinity of *The Valour and the Horror*, it was claimed that the "true story of those battles has never really been told." Canada, Senate, *Proceedings of the Subcommittee on Veterans Affairs* (Ottawa, 1993), 10:35.
115 George Koch, "Direct Hit on the McKennas," *Alberta Report*, 20 June 1994.
116 Brereton Greenhous, Stephen J. Harris, William C. Johnston, and William G.P. Rawling, *The Crucible of War, 1939-1945*, vol. 3 of *Official History of the Royal Canadian Air Force* (Toronto: University of Toronto Press, 1994).
117 Allan English, *The Cream of the Crop: Canadian Aircrew, 1939-1945* (Montreal and Kingston: McGill-Queen's University Press, 1996), 214.
118 Milberry has produced a number of excellent histories; see *Sixty Years: The RCAF and the CF Air Command 1924-1984* (Toronto: CANAV Books, 1984); *The Royal Canadian Air Force at War 1939-1945* (Toronto: CANAV Books, 1990); *Canada's Air Force at War and Peace* (Toronto: CANAV Books, 2000).
119 For the British official history, see Noble Frankland, *History at War: The Campaigns of an Historian* (London: DLM, 1998); and Sir Charles Webster and Noble Frankland, *The Strategic Air Offensive Against Germany, 1939-1945* (London: HMSO, 1961).
120 Joseph Owen, "Canadian Landing: Controversy Continues," *Stars and Stripes*, Summer 1994.
121 See the correspondence by the official historians in DHH, 94/168, file 4/01 for the difficult question of how to address Canadianization in the RCAF.
122 Gordon Barthos, "RCAF Historians Reopen WWII Bombing Row," *Toronto Star*, 18 May 1994; Desmond Bill, "War Vets Irate as Book Revives Bombing Furor," *Toronto Star*, 19 May 1994.
123 News release from the War Amps, 17 June 1994; Editorial, "War History Infuriates Air Veterans," *Ottawa Citizen*, 19 May 1994.
124 Pierre Berton, "The Valour, the Horror, and the Nagano Syndrome," *Toronto Star*, 28 May 1944.
125 Douglas Fisher, "The Armchair Generals Rave On," *Toronto Sun*, 22 May 1994.
126 J.L. Granatstein, "Warring Aloft 50 Years On," *Quill and Quire*, June 1994. The most sustained academic criticism of *Crucible of War* came from David Bercuson and S.F. Wise in "The Valour and the Horror Controversy and the Official History of the RCAF, Volume 3," *Canadian Military History* 3, 2 (1994): 107-10. Statements such as "The whole thrust of Volume 3 of the official history is that the bomber offensive was a misguided failure, and that the deaths of 9,919 Canadians in Bomber Commander were essentially meaningless in the total picture of the war," were a limited and inaccurate characterization of the almost 350 pages devoted to the bombing campaign.
127 Brian McKenna, "War History 'Heavy with Terrible Truths,'" *Toronto Star*, 18 June 1994.
128 Honourable Jack Marshall, *Debates of the Senate*, 1st session, 35th Parliament, v. 135, no. 27, 25 May 1994; and v. 135, no. 28, 31 May 1994.
129 National Council of Veteran Associations, "Veterans Heritage," Summer 1994.
130 J.L. Granatstein, "Warring Aloft 50 Years On," *Quill and Quire*, June 1994.
131 Peter Worthington, "Quit Rewriting War History," *Ottawa Sun*, 26 May 1994.
132 Elizabeth A. Muenger, "Activities Looking Backward and Planning Ahead," *Journal of Military History* 61 (January 1997): 124.
133 Christopher Moore, "The Legacy of Colonel Stacey," *The Beaver* (April-May 1994): 52.
134 Martin Blumenson, "Can Official History Be Honest History?," in *Official Histories: Essays and Bibliographies from around the World*, ed. Robin Higham (Manhattan, KS: Kansas State University Library, 1970), 40.

135 Mansbridge cited in J.R. Miller, "The Invisible Historian," *Journal of the Canadian Historical Association* 8 (1997): 9. There are few scholarly works devoted to analyzing the 50th Anniversary of the Second World War, but for a discussion on the topic see J.L. Granatstein, "A Half-Century On: The Veterans' Experience," in *The Veterans Charter and Post-World War II Canada*, ed. Peter Neary and J.L. Granatstein (Montreal and Kingston: McGill-Queen's University Press, 1998), 222-31.
136 Erna Paris, *Long Shadows: Truth, Lies and History* (London: Bloomsbury Publishing, 2001).
137 Marc Milner, "Reflections on the State of Canadian Army History in the Two World Wars," *Acadiensis* 18, 2 (1989): 149.
138 Terry Copp and Robert Vogel, *Maple Leaf Route*, 5 vols. (Alma, ON: Maple Leaf Route, 1983-88).
139 Quote in Terry Copp and Robert Vogel, "No Lack of Rational Speed: 1st Canadian Army Operations, September 1944," *Journal of Canadian Studies* 16, 3-4 (1981): 145. For a discussion by international scholars of the First Canadian Army's poor performance during the Normandy campaign, see the historiographical sections in John A. English, *The Canadian Army and the Normandy Campaign: A Study of Failure in High Command* (New York: Praeger, 1991); reissued as *Failure in High Command: The Canadian Army and the Normandy Campaign* (Ottawa: Golden Dog, 1995) 3; Terry Copp, *Fields of Fire: The Canadians in Normandy* (Toronto: University of Toronto Press, 2003), introduction and ch. 1; Denis Whitaker, *Victory at Falaise: The Soldiers' Story*, with historiographical chapter by Terry Copp (Toronto: HarperCollins, 2000).
140 English, *The Canadian Army*, xv.
141 J.L. Granatstein, *Canada's Army: Waging War and Keeping the Peace* (Toronto: University of Toronto Press, 2002).
142 Granatstein, *Canada's Army*, xii.
143 J.L. Granatstein, *The Generals: The Canadian Army's Senior Commanders in the Second World War* (Toronto: Stoddart, 1993); Terry Copp and Bill McAndrew, *Battle Exhaustion: Soldiers and Psychiatrists in the Canadian Army, 1939-1945* (Montreal and Kingston: McGill-Queen's University Press, 1990); Bill McAndrew, *Canadians and the Italian Campaign, 1943-1945* (Montreal: Art Global, ca..1996).
144 Terry Copp, *Fields of Fire: The Canadians in Normandy* (Toronto: University of Toronto Press, 2003).
145 *Fields of Fire* won the Society of Military Historians 2004 Distinguished Book award for a non-American military history. In contrast, see the negative review by Donald E. Graves, *Canadian Military Journal* 4, 3 (2003): 65-7.
146 Fred Hatch, *The Aerodrome of Democracy: Canada and the British Commonwealth Air Training Plan, 1939-1945* (Ottawa: Department of National Defence, 1983).
147 Spencer Dunmore, *Reap the Whirlwind: The Untold Story of 6 Group* (Toronto: McClelland and Stewart, 1991); and *Wings for Victory: The Remarkable Story of the British Commonwealth Air Training Plan in Canada* (Toronto: McClelland and Stewart, 1994); English, *The Cream of the Crop*; Carl Christie, *Ocean Bridge: The History of RAF Ferry Command* (Toronto: University of Toronto Press, 1995); Hugh Halliday and Ben Greenhous, *Canada's Air Forces, 1914-1999* (Montreal: Art Global, 1999); Hugh Halliday, *Typhoon and Tempest: The Canadian Story* (Toronto: CANAV Books, 1992); Carl Vincent, *The Liberator and Fortress* (Stittsville, ON: Canada's Wings, 1975); Wayne Ralph, *Barker VC* (Toronto: Doubleday, 1997). For the work of non-academic aviation historians, see "Recording Canada's Aviation History," updated from CANAV's Spring 1997 newsletter, www.canavbooks.com.
148 English, *Cream of the Crop*, 214.
149 Michael L. Hadley and Roger Sarty, *Tin-Pots & Pirate Ships: Canadian Naval Forces and German Sea Raiders, 1880-1918* (Montreal and Kingston: McGill-Queen's University Press, 1991).

150 Roger Sarty, "Writing Official Naval History, 1939-1945," Royal Military College of Canada, 26th Annual Military History Symposium, 18 March 2005.
151 Dr. Roger Sarty, interview with the author, 22 November 2003; Dr. Serge Bernier to Cook, 2 March 2005.
152 Roger Sarty, *Canada and the Battle of the Atlantic* (Montreal: Art Global, 1998).
153 David Zimmerman, "New Dimensions in Canadian Naval History," *The American Neptune* 60, 3 (Summer 2000): 270.
154 W.A.B. Douglas, Roger Sarty, and Michael Whitby, *No Higher Purpose: The Official Operational History of the Royal Canadian Navy in the Second World War, 1939-1943*, vol. 2, part 1 (St. Catharines, ON: Vanwell Publishing, 2003).
155 Cited in Marc Milner, "No Higher Purpose: A Special Review Section," *The Northern Mariner* (Summer 2004): 52.
156 J.M. Bourne, "A personal reflection on the two world wars," *The Great World War 1914-45*, vol. 2, ed. Peter Liddle, J.M. Bourne, and Ian R. Whitehead (London: HarperCollins, 2001), 16.
157 Desmond Morton, *When Your Number's Up: The Canadian Soldier in the First World War* (Toronto: Random House, 1993); Shane B. Schreiber, *Shock Army of the British Empire: The Canadian Corps in the Last 100 Days of the Great War* (Westport, CT: Praeger, 1997); Bill Rawling, *Surviving Trench Warfare: Technology and the Canadian Corps* (Toronto: University of Toronto Press, 1992); Tim Cook, *No Place To Run: The Canadian Corps and Gas Warfare in the First World War* (Vancouver: UBC Press, 1999).
158 Jonathan Vance, *Death So Noble: Memory, Meaning, and the First World* War (Vancouver: UBC Press, 1997).
159 For recent works, see Jeff Keshen, *Propaganda and Censorship during Canada's Great War* (Edmonton: University of Alberta Press, 1996); Ian Hugh Maclean Miller, *Our Glory and Our Grief: Torontonians and the Great War* (Toronto: University of Toronto Press, 2001); Robert Rutherdale, *Hometown Horizons: Local Responses to Canada's Great War* (Vancouver: UBC Press, 2004); Desmond Morton, *Fight or Pay: Soldiers' Families in the Great War* (Vancouver: UBC Press, 2004).
160 See George Blackburn, *The Guns of Normandy: A Soldier's Eye View, France 1944* (Toronto: McClelland and Stewart, 1995) xiii; and Stanley Scislowski, *Not All of Us Were Brave* (Toronto: Dundurn Press, 1997), introduction.
161 J.L. Granatstein, "Canadian History Textbooks and the Wars," *Canadian Military History* 3, 1 (1994): 123-4. For a short but useful rebuttal, see Margaret Conrad and Alvin Finkel, "TextBook Wars: Canadian Style," *Canadian Issues* (October 2003): 12-15.
162 Timothy Findley, *The Wars* (Toronto: Clarke, Irwin, 1977).
163 Christopher Moore, "History Television: Stay Tuned," *The Beaver* 78, 1 (1998): 50-1.
164 Brereton Greenhous, *Dieppe, Dieppe* (Montreal: Art Global, 1992); Brereton Greenhous and Hugh A. Halliday, *Canada's Air Forces, 1914-1999* (Montreal: Art Global, 1999); Brereton Greenhous and Stephen J. Harris, *Canada and the Battle of Vimy Ridge, 9-12 April 1917* (Montreal: Art Global, 1992); Bill McAndrew, Bill Rawling, and Michael Whitby, *Liberation: The Canadians in Europe* (Montreal: Art Global, 1995).
165 DHH, 99/36, W.A.B. Douglas papers, box 37, file 3, 1991-1993 Annual Reports.
166 Jean Morin, "L'Historien officiel des forces armées, son rôle et sa perspective perçus à travers la guerre du Golfe," *Cahiers d'Histoire Politique* 2 (Winter 1996).
167 Jean Morin and Richard Gimblett, *Operation Friction, 1990-1991* (Toronto: Dundurn Press, 1997).
168 Dr. David Bercuson, interview with the author, 30 December 2004.
169 The poll was conducted by Ipsos-Reid and the Dominion Institute. Kim Honey, "A Once-Proud History, Slipping Away," *Globe and Mail*, 9 April 2002.

170 Pierre Vennat, "Béatrice Richard et le mythe de Dieppe," *La Presse*, 15 September 2002.
171 See Yves Tremblay, "L'histoire militaire officielle au Canada, 1916-1999," *Bulletin d'histoire politique* 8: 2-3.
172 S.F. Wise, "Canadian Official Military History: The End of an Era?" in *The Last Word? Essays on Official History in the United States and British Commonwealth*, ed. Jeffrey Grey (Westport, CT: Praeger, 2003), 17.
173 Jean-Pierre Gagnon, *Le 22e bataillon (canadien-français), 1914-1919: étude socio-militaire* (Ottawa and Quebec: Presses de l'Université Laval and Ministère de la défense nationale et le Centre d'édition du gouvernement du Canada, 1986); Jean Pariseau and Serge Bernier, *Fear of a Parallel Army* (Ottawa: Department of National Defence, 1987); *French Canadians and Bilingualism in the Canadian Armed Forces* (Ottawa: Department of National Defence, 1988).
174 For courts-martial records, see Andrew Godefroy, *For Freedom and Honour? The Story of the 25 Canadian Volunteers Executed in the First World War* (CEF Books, 1998); for the conscription tribunal records, see Granatstein and Hitsman, *Broken Promises*, 98.
175 Carl Christie, "News from the Directorate of History," *Canadian Military History* 1, 1-2 (1992): 99-100.
176 Dr. I. Campbell, "Historical Declassification and Access to Information – A Bureaucrat's Nightmare. Unofficial views on what historians and archivists release in the Department of National Defence," 6 November 2002, posted at Canadian Intelligence Resource Centre, http://circ.jmellon.com.
177 A number of government departments have been embarrassed by revelations resulting from ATIP. Recent scholarship and journalistic investigations suggest that bureaucrats, with their ministers' support, have begun to avoid ATIP requests by not putting important decisions and documents on file. Despite growing protest, there appears to be no attempt to rectify the situation. See Jay Gilbert, "Access Denied: The Access to Information Act and Its Effect on Public Records Creators," *Archivaria* 49 (Spring 2000): 84-123.
178 *Canada and UN Peacekeeping: Cold War by Other Means, 1945-1970* (St. Catharines, ON: Vanwell, 2002); *War without Battles: Canada's NATO Brigade in Germany, 1951-1993* (Kanata, ON: 4 CMBG History Book Association, 1997); *War with Iraq: Canada's Strategy in the Persian Gulf, 1990-2002* (Kingston, ON: Centre for International Relations, Queen's University, 2002).
179 Scott Robertson, Roger Sarty, Serge Durflinger, and Whitney Lackenbauer have all been hired recently in tenure-track positions.
180 Dr. Marc Milner, letter to author, 4 October 2004.
181 Dr. Pat Brennan, letter to author, 14 January 2005.
182 Dr. Geoff Hayes, letter to author, 11 January 2005.
183 Terry Copp, review, *Canadian Historical Review* 73, 4 (December 1992): 551-2. Terry Copp, *The Anatomy of Poverty: The Condition of the Working Class in Montreal, 1897-1929* (Toronto: McClelland and Stewart, 1974). See also, Jeremy Black, *Rethinking Military History* (London: Routledge, 2004), ch. 2.
184 Haycock, *Teaching Military History*, 1.
185 Robert Vogel, "Some Reflections on the Teaching of Military History in Canada," *Canadian Military History* 1, 1-2 (1992): 101-4.
186 J.L. Granatstein, "Canadian History Textbooks and the Wars," *Canadian Military History* 3, 1 (1994): 123-4.
187 Desmond Morton has compared military and labour history dissertations and concluded that there were more students engaged in the former in the 1990s, where previously there had been more engaged in the latter. It should be no surprise that his third category of comparison, under the broad rubric of "social history," had three times as many students engaged in these studies than in military history. Desmond Morton, "Some Millennial Reflections on the State of Canadian Labour History," *Labour/Le Travail* 46 (Fall 2000): 36.

188 See Victor Davis Hanson, "The Utility of War," *Military History Quarterly* 15, 2 (2003).
189 See Winter, *Haig's Command*.
190 For an eloquent and witty discussion of these issues, see Dean Oliver, "Canada: Fact and Fancy," in *The Great World War 1914-45*, vol. 2, ed. Peter Liddle, John Bourne, and Ian Whitehead (London: HarperCollins, 2001), 233-42.
191 Brereton Greenhous, *The Making of Billy Bishop: The First World War Exploits of Billy Bishop, VC* (Toronto: Dundurn, 2002). Accusation in *A Hero to Me*, (Ballinran Productions, 2003).
192 As cited in J.L. Granatstein, *Who Killed Canadian History?* (Toronto: HarperCollins, 1998), 21.

Conclusion: An Ongoing Dialogue

1 See the discussion in Jeff Keshen, introduction to *Saints, Sinners, and Soldiers: Canada's Second World War* (Vancouver: UBC Press, 2004).
2 William Kilbourn, ed., *Canada: A Guide to the Peaceable Kingdom* (Toronto: Macmillan, 1970).
3 UTA, C.P. Stacey papers, box 45, Official Histories, n.d.
4 E.H. Carr, *What Is History* (Harmondsworth, UK: Penguin, 1964), ch. 1.
5 Cited in R.J.B. Bosworth, *Explaining Auschwitz & Hiroshima: History Writing and the Second World War, 1945-1990* (London: Routledge, 1993).
6 Sir Michael Howard, "The Use and Abuse of Military History," *Royal United Service Institute* 107 (February 1962), reprinted in *The Army Doctrine and Training Bulletin* 6, 2 (2003): 19.
7 C. P. Stacey, *A Date with History: Memoirs of a Canadian Historian* (Ottawa: Deneau, 1983), 230.
8 Desmond Morton, *A Military History of Canada* (Edmonton: Hurtig, 1985), ix.
9 John Lewis Gaddis, *The Landscape of History: How Historians Map the Past* (Oxford University Press, 2002), 3.

Select Bibliography of Official and Semi-Official Canadian Histories

Canada, Army Historical Section. *Canada's Army in Korea: The United Nations Operations, 1950-53, and their Aftermath.* Ottawa: Queen's Printer, 1956.

Douglas, W.A.B. *The Creation of a National Air Force: The Official History of the Royal Canadian Air Force.* Vol. 2. Ottawa: Minister of National Defence, 1986.

Douglas, W.A.B., Roger Sarty, and Michael Whitby. *No Higher Purpose: The Official Operational History of the Royal Canadian Navy in the Second World War, 1939-1943.* Vol. 2. Pt. 1. St. Catharines, ON: Vanwell Publishing, 2003.

Duguid, A.F. "From the Outbreak of War to the Formation of the Canadian Corps, August 1914-September 1915." Pt. 1 of *Official History of the Canadian Forces in the Great War, 1914-1919.* Vol. 1. Ottawa: King's Printer, 1938.

–. "Chronology, Appendices, and Maps." Pt. 2 of *Official History of the Canadian Forces in the Great War, 1914-1919.* Vol. 1. Ottawa: King's Printer, 1938.

Feasby, W.R., ed. *Official History of the Canadian Medical Services, 1939-1945.* Vol. 1, *Organization and Campaigns.* Ottawa: Queen's Printer, 1956.

–. *Official History of the Canadian Medical Services, 1939-1945.* Vol. 2, *Clinical Subjects.* Ottawa: Queen's Printer, 1956.

Flying Officer W.S. Large. *The Diary of a Canadian Fighter Pilot.* Toronto: Reginald Saunders, 1944.

Greenhous, Brereton, Stephen J. Harris, William C. Johnston, and William G.P. Rawling. *The Crucible of War, 1939-1945.* Vol. 3 of *Official History of the Royal Canadian Air Force.* Ottawa: Minister of National Defence, 1994.

Historical Section. Royal Canadian Air Force. *R.C.A.F. Logbook: A Chronological Outline of the Origin, Growth and Achievement of the Royal Canadian Air Force.* Ottawa: King's Printer, 1949.

–. *The R.C.A.F. Overseas: The First Four Years.* Toronto: Oxford University Press, 1944.

–. *The R.C.A.F. Overseas: The Fifth Year.* Toronto: Oxford University Press, 1945.

–. *The R.C.A.F. Overseas: The Sixth Year.* Toronto: Oxford University Press, 1949.

Kealy, J.D.F., and E.C. Russell. *A History of Canadian Naval Aviation.* Ottawa: Naval Historical Section, 1965.

Macphail, Andrew. *Official History of the Canadian Forces in the Great War, 1914-1919: The Medical Services.* Ottawa: King's Printer, 1925.

Morin, Jean H., and Richard Gimblett. *Operation Friction, 1990-1991.* Toronto: Dundurn Press, 1997.

Nicholson, G.W.L. *Canadian Expeditionary Force, 1914-1919: Official History of the Canadian Army in the First World War.* Ottawa: Queen's Printer, 1962.

–. *Official History of the Canadian Army in the Second World War.* Vol. 2, *The Canadians in Italy, 1943-45.* Ottawa: Queen's Printer, 1956.

Schull, Joseph. *The Far Distant Ships: An Official Account of Canadian Naval Operations in the Second World War.* Ottawa: Queen's Printer, 1950.

Stacey, C.P. *Arms, Men and Governments: The War Policies of Canada 1939-1945.* Ottawa: Minister of National Defence, 1970.

–. *Canada's Battle in Normandy: The Canadian Army's Share in the Operations, 6 June-1 September 1944*. Ottawa: King's Printer, 1946.
–. *The Canadian Army, 1939-1945: An Official Historical Summary*. Ottawa: King's Printer, 1948.
–. *The Canadians in Britain, 1939-1944*. Ottawa: King's Printer, 1945.
–. *From Pachino to Ortona: The Canadian Campaign in Sicily and Italy, 1943*. Ottawa: King's Printer, 1946.
–. *Six Years of War: The Army in Canada, Britain and the Pacific: Official History of the Canadian Army in the Second World War*. Vol. 1. Ottawa: Queen's Printer, 1955.
–. *The Victory Campaign: The Operations in Northwest Europe, 1944-1945: Official History of the Canadian Army in the Second World War*. Vol. 3. Ottawa: Queen's Printer, 1960.
Thorgrimsson, Thor, and E.C. Russell. *Canadian Naval Operations in Korean Waters, 1950-1955*. Ottawa: Naval Historical Section, 1965.
Tucker, G.N. *The Naval Service of Canada: Its Official History*. Vol. 1, *Origins and Early Years*. Ottawa: Queen's Printer, 1952.
–. *The Naval Service of Canada: Its Official History*. Vol. 2, *Activities on Shore during the Second World War*. Ottawa: Queen's Printer, 1952.
Wise, S.F. *Canadian Airmen and the First World War: The Official History of the Royal Canadian Air Force*. Vol. 1. Ottawa: Minister of National Defence, 1980.
Wood, Herbert F. *Strange Battleground: The Operations in Korea and Their Effects on the Defence Policy of Canada*. Ottawa: Queen's Printer, 1966.

Index

academic historians: access to records, 6, 7, 172; amateurs vs, 49; Duguid as, 86; as historical officers, 106; in historical sections, 129; and military history, 152, 200, 210, 247-8; and official histories, 4, 62, 152, 233; popular historians vs, 225; and war, 81; world war writing, 7. *See also* historians; military historians
academic history, 235; popular histories built from, 242; in 1960s, 210
Access to Information and Privacy (ATIP), 245
access to records, 7, 212, 258; by academic historians, 6, 7, 172, 200, 221; AHS and, 60, 78, 82, 139-40, 155; British-American archives, 139-40; in Canadian Army, 212-13; by civilians, 152, 170-1, 197, 200; Claxton and, 172; Combined, 149-50, 151; and Currie's lawsuit, 60; defence archives, 202; in DHist, 213; DND and, 150, 172, 212; Duguid and, 62-3, 70, 75, 76, 78, 81, 82, 89, 90, 152, 170; Foulkes and, 149-50, 151; government, 213; by historians, 7, 150, 213; by historical officers, 98; Japanese, 155; military, 217; by official historians, 91, 134, 135, 150, 213; and official histories, 6; Public Archives and, 217; RAF, 139; by regimental historians, 81, 82; Stacey and, 96, 131-2, 160, 170-2, 212; Stanley on, 170, 172; strategic records, 140; by Tucker, 145; in UK, 81, 82, 89, 90, 149-52, 150, 213; by veterans, 80
Acland, Peregrine, 77-8
Acton, Lord, 58
Adami, J.C., 44, 55
Admiralty (UK): criticism of Canadian navy, 251; Historical Section, 123, 124; War Room, 125
Agnew, R.I., 122
AHS. *See* Army Historical Section (AHS)
Air Council, 141
air force, Canadian, 71, 72; in Great War compared to Second World War, 254. *See also* Royal Canadian Air Force (RCAF)
aircraft: bombers, 118 (*see also* Bomber Command); histories, 237
airmen. *See* flyers
Aitken, Max. *See* Beaverbrook, Max Aitken, Lord
Alderson, Sir Edmund A.H., 13, 14, 17, 18, 19, 52-3, 204
Aleutian campaign, 181
All Quiet on the Western Front (Remarque), 75, 77
Allied Combined records. *See* Combined records
American Expeditionary Forces (AEF), 71
Amiens, Battle of, 31, 69
Among the Few (Hitchins), 188
And We Go On (Bird), 76, 77-8
Anderson, Torchy, 116-17
antiwar writings, 77-8, 208; memoirs, 191; novels, 66, 191; poetry, 66
Anzac Book, 23
archives. *See* records
Armoured Divisions: 4th, 108; 5th, 109
Armoured Regiment, 12th, 110
Arms, Men and Governments (Stacey), 216, 225
Armstrong, Elizabeth, *The Crisis of Quebec*, 218
Armstrong, Logie, 58
Army Group 21, 170
Army Historical Section (AHS): academic historians and, 81; access to British-American archives, 139-40; and access to Japanese records, 155; and access to records, 60, 78, 82; and Currie's lawsuit, 57, 58-9, 60; cuts to, 205; CWNS combined with, 37; donations of records to, 79; Duguid as head of, 43-4, 79; and Duguid's history, 87; and Edmonds's

history, 50; generals' support of, 96; and historical extracts, 104; historical officers, 148; and history of Great War flyers, 72; and Macphail's history, 55; and military study, 170; narratives produced by, 98; number of personnel, 139; and official histories, 62, 158, 237; overseas section, 148; Public Archives vs, 81; and regimental histories, 63, 65, 66; role of, 100; Stacey and, 95; and Stacey's official histories, 158; staffing of, 83, 147-8; Stanley's visit to, 82; and War Diaries, 97; and war records, 101. *See also* Directorate Historical Section (DHS)
Asquith, Herbert, 12, 19
Assiniboine, 121
Association of Universities and Colleges of Canada, 216-17
Athabaskan, 124
Athéna, 244
Audette, Louis C., 167
Australian and New Zealand Army Corps (ANZAC), 203
Australian soldiers: at Gallipoli, 250; in Great War, 30, 250; image of, 85-6; official histories, 68, 79, 83, 85-6, 90, 146, 203, 206
Authie, 194
Aviation in Canada (Milberry), 229

baby boomers, 208, 210
Barker, William, 71, 254
Bateman, H.M., 24
Bates, Bill, 187
Battalions: 5th, 52; 13th, 64; 16th, 70; 18th, 21; 19th, 63-4; 22nd, 244; 38th, 64; 42nd, 65, 66; 44th, 69; 58th, 64
Battle Exhaustion (Copp, McAndrew), 236-7
The Battle of Britain (British Ministry of Information), 113
Battle of the Atlantic, 115, 119, 123, 126, 144, 239, 251
battles: battlefield messages, 62; field accounts/narratives, 136; honours, 90; in military history, 258; in narratives, 107
Battles Nomenclature Committee, 60
Bean, Charles, 54, 68, 83, 85-6, 203
Beattie, Kim, 219
Beattie, William, 44

Beaverbrook, Max Aitken, Lord: as adviser to Canadian government, 11-12, 13; Alderson and, 14, 18, 19; as archivist, 21; on Battle of Second Ypres, 15, 16; Borden and, 12; Byng and, 19, 21; *Canada in Flanders*, 16-17, 21, 25-6, 27-8, 29, 37, 45-6; as Canadian Records Officer, 16; and Canadian soldiers, 11, 18, 24-5, 38, 41-2; and Canadian War Archives building, 33; and censorship, 16-17; collection of soldiers' writings, 23-4; and Currie's criticisms, 28-9; and CWRO, 11, 17-18, 26-7; documentation of war, 18, 24-5; and Doughty, 20-1; early life, 12; in English society, 12; as Eye Witness, 13-16, 18, 19, 27; following Canadian Division, 13-14; histories, 255; and Hughes, 12-13, 15-16, 19, 25, 27, 37; importance in England, 18, 19; interviews by, 16; liaison with British, 13; and Manly Sims, 13-14; as minister of information in War Cabinet, 28; and Nicholson, 204, 206; and official histories, 42; as propagandist, 37-8; reputation of, 37-8; "school" of, 232; and St. Eloi battle, 26; and Turner, 19; and war archives, 37; war art collection, 78; as war correspondent, 14; and War Diaries, 16; and war records, 11, 16, 21; Willson and, 18-19; on writing contemporary history, 85
Bennett, R.B., 80, 84, 91
Bennett, Stewart, 68
Bercuson, David, 221, 228, 243, 245
Bernier, Serge, 220, 233, 244
Berry, O., 72
Berton, Pierre, 225, 230, 242
Bilbrough, W.H., 139
Bird, Will, 65-6, 70, 80, 219; *And We Go On*, 76, 77-8
The Birth of Western Canada (Stanley), 86
Bishop, W.A. "Billy," 71, 226-7, 251, 254; *Winged Warfare*, 46
Black Watch Regiment, 136-7
Blackburn, George, 240-1
Bliss, Michael, 216; *A Canadian Millionaire*, 218
Blondin, P.E., 20
Bomber Command, 116, 214-15, 227, 230, 242
Book of Remembrance, 83

Borden, Sir Robert, 11, 12, 16, 19, 25, 28, 33, 35, 41, 204
Bothwell, Robert, 221, 225
Bourne, J.M., 239
Boutilier, Jim, "The RCN in Retrospect," 223
Breadner, L.S., 112
Breckenridge, William, 46
Brigades: 2nd, 28, 50, 85; 3rd, 28, 52-3, 84, 85
Britain. *See* United Kingdom
British Broadcasting Corporation (BBC), *The Great War*, 208
British Combined records. *See* Combined records
British Commonwealth Air Training Plan (BCATP), 111, 112, 118, 139, 164, 214, 224
British Divisions: 27th, 51; 50th, 194
British Expeditionary Force (BEF), 206; Canadians within, 11, 15; Dominion operations and, 30-1
British Historical Section, Committee of Imperial Defence, 16
British Ministry of Information, *The Battle of Britain*, 113
Broadfoot, Barry: *Six War Years*, 218-19; *Ten Lost Years*, 218
Broken Promises (Granatstein, Hitsman), 218
Brown, George, 142, 165-6, 168
Brown, J.S. "Buster," 52-3
Brown, Robert, *Canada, 1896-1921*, 218
Brown, Sydney, 117
Brutinel, Raymond, 34, 37
Buchan, John, 39
Buckley, Christopher, *The Raid on Dieppe*, 175
Burchill, Charles, 143
Burns, E.L.M., 96, 171, 180, 185, 187, 191, 199; *Manpower in the Canadian Army*, 171-2
Byng, Julian, Lord, 19, 21, 38, 51, 74

C Force, 185
Cabinet: Defence Committee, 141; records, 134, 149, 151, 181; War Committee, 183, 213, 214
Caen, 193
Cafferky, Shawn, 238
Calgary, University of, 247
Campbell, Isabelle, 245
Campney, Ralph, 183-4

Canada, 1896-1921 (Brown, Cook), 218
Canada and the Age of Conflict (Stacey), 216
Canada and the Battle of the Atlantic (Sarty), 238-9
Canada and the British Army (Stacey), 86, 94
Canada and the War at Sea (Roberts), 127
Canada in Flanders (Beaverbrook), 16-17, 21, 25-6, 27-8, 29, 37, 45-6
Canada in Khaki, 23-4
Canada in the Great War, 46, 218
Canada Lancet, 55
Canada Year Book, 43
Canada's Airmen (Wise), 226
Canada's Army (Granatstein), 236
Canada's Battle in Normandy, 136-8
Canada's Fighting Airmen (Drew), 73, 226
Canada's Hundred Days (Livesay), 33, 47
Canada's Soldiers (Stanley), 178
Canada's Triumph (James), 33
Canada's War (Granatstein), 225
Canada's War at Sea (Roberts), 166
Canada's Wings, 237
Canadian Airmen and the First World War (Wise), 224
Canadian Annual Review, 218
Canadian Army: access to records in, 212-13; within Allied strategic operations, 179; attitude of international historians toward, 236; Canadian Corps compared with, 254; First, 100, 170; historical officer, 93; histories, 136-8, 222-3, 235-7; official histories (*see* official histories); splitting of, 181. *See also* Army Group 21; Army Historical Section (AHS)
The Canadian Army, 1939-1945: An Official Historical Summary (Stacey), 147-60, 163, 175, 181, 182, 185, 202
The Canadian Army and the Normandy Campaign (English), 236
Canadian Army Journal, 176, 177, 191
Canadian Army Medical Corps (CAMC). *See* Royal Canadian Army Medical Corps (RCAMC)
Canadian Army Veterinary Corps, 44
Canadian Broadcasting Corporation (CBC), *Flanders' Fields*, 208-9
Canadian Committee for the Study of the Second World War, 220

Canadian Corps, 10, 209, 253; II, 131; Canadian Army compared with, 254; characteristics of, 86; history of, 33-6; as shock troops, 251
Canadian Defence Quarterly, 217
Canadian Expeditionary Force (CEF), 13, 202-6; coverage of, 218; Duguid as historian, 146
Canadian Expeditionary Force (Nicholson), 202-6, 208-9
Canadian Field Ambulance, 171
Canadian Field Historical Section (CFHS): 1st, 103, 107-8; 2nd, 108
Canadian Forces: bilingualism in, 244; military history and professionalism in, 243; and Somalia Affair, 243; study of, 246; writing of history, 246
Canadian Forces College, 211
Canadian Historical Association (CHA), 86, 152, 168, 169, 172, 197, 213, 220, 248
Canadian Historical Review (CHR), 76, 221, 248
Canadian Military Headquarters (CMHQ), 94, 131, 133, 168
Canadian Military History, 248
Canadian Militia Regiment, 4th, 69
A Canadian Millionaire (Bliss), 218
Canadian Nautical Research Society, 224
Canadian Security Establishment, 238
Canadian soldiers, 24; banding together by, 77; Beaverbrook and, 11, 18, 24-5, 38, 41-2; and *Canada in Flanders*, 27, 37; collected letters of, 74; collection of writings, 23-4; in CWRO accounts, 29-30; Duguid on reputation of, 88-9; Duguid's defence of, 54, 61, 67, 83; Edmonds on, 50-1; as elite soldiers, 39, 86; first-hand accounts of, 209-10; German soldiers compared with, 195-6; during Great War, 239-40; image of, 24, 38, 39; interviews with, 107; legacy of, 41-2; memoirs of, 74-8; memories of, 63; Nicholson and, 180-1, 206; reputation of, 10, 11, 88-9, 255; as shock troops, 39, 58, 72, 236; Stacey on, 156, 195, 198-9; victories, 30-1. *See also* Canadian Army; Canadian Expeditionary Force (CEF)
Canadian War Archives building, 33
Canadian War Committee, 183
Canadian War Museum, 148, 210-11, 247
Canadian War Narrative Section (CWNS), 29, 34-6, 37, 42

Canadian War Records Office (CWRO), 11, 17-18, 21, 29, 36, 42, 71, 72, 78; Air Historical Section, 113; archival vs publicity functions, 38; Beaverbrook and, 11, 17-18, 26-7; Currie and, 29; and CWNS, 36; field historians, 22; historical officers, 22-3; propaganda from, 38; and Public Archives, 20; publicity function, 38, 39; regimental histories published, 33; responsibilities of, 26; Roberts in charge, 26-7; role of, 23; supportive accounts by, 29-30; war records handled by, 32
Canadian-content television programs, 242
The Canadians in Britain, 136
Canadians in England (Stacey), 223
The Canadians in Italy (Nicholson), 187
Canal du Nord, 36
Careless, Maurice, 126, 127, 129
Caribou, 127
Carr, E.H., 254
casualties: Bomber Command, 214-15, 227; D-Day, 182; at Dieppe, 136; Great War, 31, 32, 41, 69-70, 130, 209; at Hong Kong, 136, 156; at Mons, 57, 58, 59; in Normandy campaign, 196; in Northwest Europe campaign, 214-15; of 3rd Canadian Division, 182; Second World War, 130; at Second Ypres, 50; at the Somme, 205-6; at Verrière Ridge, 136; on Western Front, 10
censorship: Aitken and, 14, 16-17; by Americans, 165; by British, 30; and distinction between different forces' operations, 30; and official histories, 5, 105, 134, 135, 256; and *The RCAF Overseas*, 116; and War Diaries, 97
CFHS. *See* Canadian Field Historical Section (CFHS)
CHA. *See* Canadian Historical Association (CHA)
Chadderton, Clifford, 226, 228, 230, 231
Chamberlain, Austen, 48
Chaplin, P.A.C., 238
Chief of Air Staff (CAS), 143, 163
Chief of General Staff (CGS), 117, 136, 175, 184
Chief of the Imperial General Staff (CIGS), 54
Childs, John, 221
chlorine gas, 14-15, 50
Christie, Carl, 220

Churchill, Sir Winston, 9, 12, 118, 183, 191, 203
CIGS. *See* Chief of the Imperial General Staff (CIGS)
Clark, Alan, *The Donkeys*, 207
Claxton, Brooke, 214; and access to documents, 172; attitude toward histories, 142; and *The Canadian Army*, 182, 185; cutbacks by, 142, 147; and Duguid's historical series, 146; forecasting lack of interest in war, 161; letter to CHA, 172; and medical history, 173; and RCAF official history, 163; resignation from Cabinet, 183; and Schull, 166; and Stacey, 143, 157-8, 167, 170, 173, 184; and Tucker's RCN history, 165
Clemenceau, Georges, 145
Collège Militaire Royal, 244
Collishaw, Raymond, 71
colony-to-nation paradigm, 250, 253
combined chiefs of staff, 149
Combined Operations Headquarters (COHQ), 99
Combined records, 149-52, 153, 160, 181
Comeau, Robert, 244
Commission on War Records and War Trophies, 32
comparative history, 250
Conacher, J.B., 106, 107, 129, 179
Confederation, centennial of, 209
Conn, Kenneth: as head of RCAF Historical Section, 93, 111, 113; on history of RCAF, 113; and Hitchens, 122; leaves RCAF, 138; and overseas posting of two historians, 112; and Oxford University Press, 163; and personal accounts of battles, 117; and popular history of RCAF, 115; on public records committee, 169; and RCAF official historian, 139; and *RCAF Overseas*, 118; role of, 133-4
Connel, John, 221
conscription, 3, 93, 112, 135, 171, 182, 202, 204, 206, 218, 245, 253
contemporary history, writing of, 5, 7, 17, 37, 47, 85, 88, 89, 159, 162, 198, 205, 232, 246
Cook, Ramsay, *Canada, 1896-1921*, 218
Cook, Tim, *No Place to Run*, 239-40
Cooke, Owen, 220, 226
Copp, Terry, 235-6, 247, 248, 251, 255; *Battle Exhaustion*, 236-7; *Fields of Fire*, 237
Coulson, H.H., 138, 163

Courcelette, 28
Cowan, Paul, *The Kid Who Couldn't Miss*, 226-7
The Cream of the Crop (English), 237
The Creation of a National Air Force (Douglas), 224
Creighton, Donald, 216
Crerar, Harry D.G.: and *Canada's Battle in Normandy*, 136; as CGS, 94; at CMHQ, 94, 95-6; and Dieppe raid, 99, 153-4, 215; on Duguid, 134; and Foulkes, 135; Harrison as in-house writer, 108; and Hong Kong, 186; importance of historical work to, 103; in Italy, 103; as a leader, 193; in Northwest Europe campaign, 193; personal papers, 156, 171; private war diary, 95; records created by, 131-2; and Simonds, 135, 154; and Stacey, 95-6, 99, 105, 106, 108, 131-2, 153-4, 156, 157, 193, 194-5, 199, 256; and Ultra intercepts, 215
The Crisis of Quebec (Armstrong), 218
Croil, G.M., 111
Crow's Nest, 191
The Crucible of War, 229-31, 234
Cruikshank, Ernest A., 36, 37, 42-3
Cuban Missile Crisis, 208
Cummins, J.F., 202
Currelly, Ralph T., 106, 109, 110
Currie, Sir Arthur: on CAMC history, 55; on *Canada in Flanders*, 27-9, 37; and Canadian Corps, 30, 31, 33-6; criticism of, 91; on Cruikshank's history, 43; and CWRO, 38; and Duguid, 80, 83, 89; and Edmonds, 50, 51, 53; on Harrison's novel, 76-7; Hyatt on, 209, 223; as leader, 27; libel suit against Preston/*Evening Guide of Port Hope*, 56-60, 61; Livesay and, 33, 47; personal account of war, 73-4; and pullback by Hughes and Turner, 85; on recognition of Corps, 78; retirement from Front, 17; and Tuxford's history, 74; Underhill and, 47; on veterans' memories, 69
Curtis, W.A., 163
cutbacks: after Great War, 44; after Second World War, 232; during 1990s, 238-9
CWNS. *See* Canadian War Narrative Section (CWNS)
CWRO. *See* Canadian War Records Office (CWRO)

The Daily Express, 16
Dancocks, Daniel, 225
A Date with History (Stacey), 257
D-Day: dodgers, 180; landings, 125-6, 132, 149, 154, 182, 186, 192, 194, 232-3
De Beck, A.M., 24
Death by Moonlight, 227-8
Death So Noble (Vance), 240
decoding, 7
demobilization, 32, 41, 136
Department of External Affairs, 126, 127, 150, 212, 214
Department of History and Heritage (DHH), 245-6
Department of Militia and Defence, 36, 42
Department of Munitions and Supply, 168, 174
Department of National Defence (DND), 3; and access to British records, 150; and access to records, 172, 212; accused of cover-up of casualties, 59; censorship by, 135; DHH and, 243; and DHS, 176; endowment of university research centres, 211; historians in, 256; historical sections, 221; official historians' support functions at, 162; and official histories, 61, 62, 79, 134, 135, 138, 230, 238; and scheduling of war records, 168; and Somalia Affair, 243; Stacey seen as spy for, 95; and study of military history, 211, 242
Department of Veterans Affairs, 180
departments, federal government, 174
Desbarats, G.J., 79
Dewolf, Harry, 124
DHH. *See* Directorate of History and Heritage
DHist. *See* Directorate of History (DHist)
DHS. *See* Directorate Historical Section (DHS)
diaries. *See* War Diaries
Diary of a Flying Officer (Large), 117-18
Dieppe raid, 101, 114, 149, 243; casualties, 136; Montgomery and, 154; Mountbatten and, 99-100, 154; navy's actions during, 122; in official histories, 158, 181, 182, 185, 186-7; personal narratives regarding, 133; prisoners taken during, 133; responsibility for, 153-4, 215-16; in school textbooks, 241; white paper on, 99-100, 174

Directorate Historical Section (DHS), 170, 171, 176, 201, 219. *See also* Army Historical Section (AHS); Directorate of History (DHist); Directorate of History and Heritage (DHH)
Directorate of History (DHist), 226; access to records, 213; and *Crucible of War*, 229, 230; Douglas as head of, 220, 237; government cutbacks and, 238; head of, 211-12; and histories relevant to French Canadians, 244; Stacey and, 211; and study of military history, 217
Directorate of History and Heritage (DHH): control over war records, 245-6; funding cuts, 242-3; on need for educated service personnel, 243-4; publications, 239, 243; support of DND, 243-4
disasters. *See* failures
Disraeli, Benjamin, 85
Divisions: 1st, 28, 36, 52, 53, 95, 101, 103-4; 2nd, 28, 63, 99, 101; 3rd, 28, 109, 110, 182; 4th, 28, 35, 36; in Battle of Second Ypres, 14-15
Dixon, F.J., 36
DND. *See* Department of National Defence (DND)
Dominion Institute, polls by, 241
The Donkeys (Clark), 207
Doughty, Sir Arthur: Aitken and, 20-1; on *Canada in Flanders*, 45-6; on CWRO, 23; as Dominion archivist, 19-21, 61, 81, 168, 212; on totality of archival material, 32
Douglas, W.A.B., 144, 220, 223, 233, 237-8, 238, 239, 243, 244; *Creation of a National Air Force*, 224; *Out of the Shadows*, 219, 220-1
draft dodgers, 218
Drew, George A., 71; *Canada's Fighting Airmen*, 73; *Canadian Airmen*, 226
Dubin, Steven, 227
Duff, Lyman, 245
Duguid, Archer Fortescue, 4, 146, 199, 200, 204, 219; as academic vs amateur historian, 49, 86; and access to war records, 70, 75, 76, 81, 82, 89, 90, 152, 170; achievements of, 255-6; additions made to records, 78-9; and CAMC official history, 56; as CEF historian, 146-7; and CEF's memory and reputation, 91-2; on

censorship by DND, 135; CHA and, 86; complaints regarding, 84; and Cruikshank, 37, 44; and Currie, 57-9, 60, 83, 89; dedication of, 153; defence of Canadian soldiers, 54, 61, 67, 83; demotion of, 61-2, 135, 146; on distribution of draft narratives, 105; donations of records to, 79; early life and career, 43; and Edmonds, 51-4, 56, 57, 61, 83, 89, 98; as expert on Great War, 89; as failed amateur, 152; faith in, 80-1; Farrow's meeting with, 120; faults of, 90-1; Foulkes and, 146; generals and, 198; as head of AHS, 43-4; and historical officers' mandate, 95; information requests to, 44; on "literary memorials," 70; McNaughton on, 61-2; and Nicholson, 179, 204, 205; as official historian, 232; and other official histories, 45; prioritization of work, 44; on public records committee, 169; qualities of, 47-8, 92; on RCN records during Great War, 119-20; reference inquiries handled by, 90; and regimental histories, 61, 65, 66-7, 68-9, 70; and reputation of CEF and individuals, 88-9, 90, 91-2, 172, 174, 255; and reputations, 233; responsibilities and role of, 44, 60-1, 168, 175-6; and Stacey, 94, 134, 205, 255; Turner's and Hughes's objections to, 84-5; as unbiased, 56; on use of war records, 48-9; work used by Morton, 239
Duguid's official history: cancellation of, 201; committee of inquiry into, 61; decision to shelve, 117; delays, 60, 80, 83, 88, 89-90; draft chapters sent out, 83-4; Duguid's approach to, 89-90; first volume, 82, 83, 87-8, 90; Foulkes' confidence in, 146; goals for, 48; Great War series, 134, 138, 142, 146-7; interviews for, 49; plans for, 45, 61, 82, 134, 202; public demand for, 83; research for, 62; researchers, 202; reviews of volume 1, 87-8; service volumes planned, 45; sources for, 49; and Stacey, 105; veterans' wait for, 79, 80; writing of, 44, 54-5, 56
Dunmore, Spencer, 237

Eayrs, James, 213; *In Defence of Canada*, 211
Eco, Umberto, 254

Edmonds, Sir James, 49-54, 56, 57, 61, 70, 82, 83, 88, 89, 91, 98, 202-3
Eisenhower, Dwight, 149, 150, 172, 182
Engler, Joe, 106
English, Allan, *The Cream of the Crop*, 237
English, John A., 221; *The Canadian Army and the Normandy Campaign*, 236
enlisted men. *See* soldiers
Errington, Jane, 257
Evening Guide of Port Hope, 56-60
The Evening Standard, 16
Ewing, R.L., 66
extracts from records for training, 103-4, 105, 113

The Face of Battle (Keegan), 217
Facey-Crowther, David, 245
failures, 25-6, 39, 105, 136, 150, 251
Falaise Gap, 115, 138, 193, 195
Falls, Cyril, 205
Far Distant Ships (Schull), 166-7
Farrow, John, 120
Feasby, W.R., 172-4
Fetherstonhaugh, Robert C., 64-5, 67, 70, 81
Field Historical Section, 131
Fields of Fire (Copp), 237
Fighter Command, 230
fighter pilots, 46, 230
filmmakers and films, 226-9, 234
The Final Blow of the First Army in 1918, 35-6
Findley, Timothy, *The Wars*, 242
The First Hundred Thousand (Hay), 17
The First World War: An Illustrated History (Taylor), 207
first-hand accounts, 16, 49, 209, 241. *See also* memoirs
Fisher, Orville, 106
Fisher, Robert, 238
Flanders' Fields (CBC), 208-9
flyers: biographical files on, 113; in Great War, 71-3, 111; personal histories, 224; popular history of, 113-14, 115; in Second World War, 118. *See also* Bomber Command; Fighter Command; fighter pilots
flying: services, 71-3, 111; stress of, 140
Foch, Ferdinand, Marshal, 177
Foster, J.A., *For Love and Glory*, 229
Foster, Sir George, 25, 32

Foulkes, Charles: on access to Combined records, 149-50, 151; and Burns, 171; as CGS, 136; on cuts to official histories, 142; and Duguid, 146; on military "failures," 136; in Normandy campaign, 193; operations trailer found, 131; and Permanent Joint Board of Defence article, 183; on RCAF official history, 141; and Simonds, 137, 193; and Stacey, 135, 136, 147-8, 171, 183, 193, 213-14, 256; support for histories, 135, 136, 146; and Ultra intercepts, 215; on Verrières Ridge battle, 137

France: cross-channel attack against, 101; invasion of, 104; official diplomatic publications, 152

Frankland, Noble, 230

French Canadians: historians, 244; service in world wars, 244-5. *See also* Quebec

Fresnes-Rouvray line, 36

Fresnoy, 30

From Pachino to Ortona (Stacey), 136

Fuller, J.F.C., 203

Gaddis, John, 258

Gagnon, Jean-Pièrre, 220, 244

Gallipoli, 250

Gault, Hamilton, 66

Gauntlet to Overlord (Munro), 189

The Gazette, 158

Gellner, John, 217

generals: British, 4, 8, 91, 251; and common soldiers, 207; conflicts among, 132; criticism of, 91; and drafts of reports, 105; feuds between, 216; Great War, 242; and historical officers, 103, 108-9; memoirs of, 74, 78, 191; Stacey and, 105-6, 132, 152, 194-5, 198; value of history for, 96

The Generals (Granatstein), 236

Generals Die in Bed (Harrison), 76-7

George, James, 93, 122-6, 127, 129

German, Tony, 225

German army: and D-Day landings, 194; at the Somme, 205; Stacey on, 195-6

German commanders, interrogation of, 133

German soldiers, 45, 180-1, 195-6, 199

Germany: Admiralty, 145; Air Force, 140; Allied bombing of, 227-8, 229; naval policy, 165; official diplomatic publications, 152; records, 133, 150, 165, 180, 186, 204, 250; strategic bombing campaign against cities, 227-8

Gibbs, Philip, 39; *Now It Can Be Told*, 47

Gimblett, Rich, *Operation Friction*, 243

Glazebrook, George, 169

Godfrey, V.S., 166-7

Gooch, G.P., 48

Goodspeed, Donald, 201, 209, 210, 212, 214, 219, 220, 224

Gordon, Athol, 172

Gough, Sir Hubert, 203

Graham, Gerald, 106, 120, 129

Graham, H.D., 188

Granatstein, J.L., 200, 210, 221, 222-3, 231, 242, 243, 248; *Broken Promises*, 218; *Canada's Army*, 236; *Canada's War*, 225; *The Generals*, 236

Graves, Donald, 257

Graves, Robert, 207

Gray, Charlotte, 242

Gray, R., 109

Great Britain. *See* United Kingdom

Great War: beliefs about, 66; British Empire vs American contribution, 71; casualties, 130, 209; as coming-of-age event for Canada, 209; common soldiers in, 207; courts martial, 245; Dominion forces' contributions, 30-1; Dominion vs BEF initiatives, 30-1; Duguid as expert on, 89; Duguid's series, 142, 146-7; economic and political history and, 81; flyers in, 71, 72-3, 111; and forging of Canada, 253; hidden history, 84; historical profession and, 81-2; histories, 206-10, 239-40; home front, 218, 240; impact on Canada, 41, 45, 240; interpretations of, 38; memoirs resulting from, 191, 241; official historians of, 256; official histories, 37, 113, 135, 138, 159, 160, 201-6; Patriotic Fund, 177; RCN records, 119-20; reappraisal of, 240; reconstruction of memory of, 208, 240; revival in study of, 208; as sacrifice vs slaughter, 69-70; as seen in Britain, 253; social memory of, 66; television programs, 208-9; United States in, 70-1; war industry, 41

The Great War (BBC), 208

The Great War and Canadian Society (Read), 219

Greenfield, Kent Roberts, 154, 233-4

Greenhous, Brereton, 220, 224, 229, 233, 237, 251, 252; *Out of the Shadows*, 219, 220-1
Griffin, John, 237
Gulf Wars, 243, 247
Guthrie, Hugh, 44

Hadley, Michael, 223-4; *Tin-Pots and Pirate Ships*, 238
Hahn, James E., 31-2
Haida, 124
Haig, Sir Douglas, 19, 91, 202-3, 204, 205-6
The Half Million (Stacey, Wilson), 223
Haliburton, R.G., 10
Halifax explosion, December 1917, 87
Hall, G.C. Gordon, 52
Halliday, Hugh, 237
Halliday, W.E.D., 169
Hamilton, Sir Ian, 123
Hancock, W.H., 123
Harris, Sir Arthur, 227
Harris, Stephen, 220, 221, 224, 229, 237
Harrison, Charles Yale. *Generals Die in Bed*, 76-7
Harrison, Eric, 131, 136, 159
Harrison, W.E.C., 102, 103, 106, 107-8, 109-10, 128, 148, 179
Harvest of War (Thompson), 218
Hatch, Fred, 214, 237
Hay, Ian, *The First Hundred Thousand*, 17
Haycock, Ronald, 211, 223, 226, 245, 247-8
Heeney, A.D.P., 185
Hellyer, Paul, 211
Henderson, Larry, 212
High Commission, 140, 149
Hill, Rowland, 31
Hill 70, 30, 43
Hillmer, Norman, 220, 224, 248
Hindenburg Line, 31
historians, 3; academic vs amateur, 49; access to government records, 213; civilian, 62, 64, 83, 152, 170-1, 256; command, 243; DND, 3; documentarians vs, 229; filmmakers vs, 234; French Canadian, 244; impact on war records, 128; journalists vs, 229, 234; and officers, 128-9; and postmodernism, 8; reliance on official records, 241; service, 93-4; unpopular conclusions of, 252. *See also* academic historians; military historians; official historians
historical officers: American, 111; as archivists vs chroniclers, 109; and creation of war records, 114; demobilization of, 136; determination of value of war records, 131; diarists and, 109-10; in field, 107, 109-10, 123, 131; generals and, 103, 109; historical vs operational concerns, 125-6; impact on type of documentation, 97; increase in number, 102; information supplied by, 113; interviewing of soldiers, 107; mandate of, 95, 96; mistaken for spies, 124; overseas, 93, 95, 125; and postwar collection and survival of records, 131; and preservation of records, 131; and projected operations, 100; in RCAF, 112-13, 118; in RCN, 93, 99, 124; reports, 107; role of, 102-3; shaping of war records in field, 109-10; support within divisions, 108-9; training mandate, 104; visits to units by, 102; way of life, 109. *See also* official historians
historical profession: and Great War, 81-2; and military history, 221; official historians' reputation in, 6. *See also* academic historians; historians
histories, 41; British, 26; cutbacks to, 162; of federal departments, 174; first-generation, 46-7; of individuals, 207-8; interest in, 161; oral, 218-19; Royal Navy, 119; sources of, 45; squadron, 237; written by journalists, 46. *See also* official histories; popular histories; regimental histories
history: agreement regarding, 231; behind history, 255; diplomatic, 152; drum and trumpet, 210, 217; from below, 210; ignorance about, 241; interpretation of, 234; memory and, 234; personalization of, 83; records and, 128; unwritten, 133; writing of, 8, 229. *See also* academic history; military history
A History of Warfare (Montgomery), 212
History Television channel, 242, 249
Hitchins, Fred H., 4; as air historian, 139; *Among the Few*, 188; and biographical files on flyers, 113; and cuts to official histories, 143, 160; as historical officer, 122; as official historian, 129, 138; plan for

eight-volume series, 139, 141; on popular history of Canadian flyers, 113-14; publications of, 188; and RCAF official history, 188; and RCAF records, 188; research into RAF archives at Aberystwyth, 113; retirement of, 143-4, 163, 200; and Second World War official history, 113-15; and staff of RCAF Historical Section, 140-1
Hitler Line, 102, 110
Hitsman, J.M., 106, 120, 129, 148, 201, 226; *Broken Promises*, 218
Hoffmeister, Bert, 191
Holocaust, 191, 235
home front: Great War, 206, 218, 240; Second World War, 251, 253-4
Hong Kong, 101, 136, 155-6, 175, 179, 181, 182, 185-6, 227, 241
honour rolls, 69
Horne, Sir Henry, 36
Hose, Walter, 87
Houghton, Frank, 239
Howard, Sir Michael, 177, 187
Howe, C.D., 168, 225
Hughes, Garnet, 27, 29, 84, 85, 105
Hughes, Sam (grandson of Sir Sam), 101, 102, 106, 136, 148, 149, 179
Hughes, Sir Sam, 101; Aitken and, 11, 12-13, 15-16, 204; Alderson and, 18; and British, 13, 15-16, 17; and Canadian war records, 15-16; characteristics of, 47; and command of Canadian Division, 13; Currie and, 29, 35, 56, 57, 59, 209; death of, 47; in Duguid's official history, 84; Haycock biography of, 223; Macphail and, 55, 91; in Nicholson's history of CEF, 205; removal from Cabinet, 25; and Ross rifle, 84; Underhill on, 47
Hundred Days offensives, 30, 240
Hunter, Murray, 106, 148, 151
Hunter, T.M., 171, 177, 201, 210, 214
Huron, 145
Hyatt, A.M.J., 196, 204, 209, 221, 223

identification discs, 68
Imperial War Graves Commission, 60
Imperial War Museum, 32
In Defence of Canada (Eayrs), 211
In Flanders Fields (Wolff), 206-7
industrialization, 41
Infantry Brigade, 11th, 103

Infantry Division, 3rd, 108
Innis, Harold, 62, 86
interviews, 96, 125; with German senior commanders, 133; with officers, 84, 102; with senior commanders, 132; with veterans, 133, 219
Introduction to Military History for Canadian Students, 176
Italian campaign, 101, 102, 148-9, 175, 179, 180, 181, 212, 236-7

James, Fred, 31; *Canada's Triumph*, 33
Japan: records, 155; reports, 185
Japanese: atrocities, 235; in Hong Kong, 155; prisoner of war camps, 186
Japanese Canadians, evacuation of, 225, 242
Jenkins, L.H., 114
Johnson, G.O., 141
Joint Staff Mission in Washington, 215
Jones, H.A., 112
journalists: historians vs, 229, 234; veterans vs, 228; writings of, 8, 46, 189, 200, 238

Kealy, J.D.F., 238
Keefler, R.H., 158
Keegan, John, 203; *The Face of Battle*, 217
Kemp, Sir A.E., 11, 28
Kennedy, John de Navarre, 174
Kerr, Donald, 126, 127, 129, 144
Kerr, Wilfrid, 62, 81; *Shrieks and Crashes*, 75-6, 77-8
Khrushchev, Nikita, 252
The Kid Who Couldn't Miss (Cowan), 226-7
Kilbourn, William, 225
King, Ernest J., 119
King, William Lyon Mackenzie, 19, 93, 112, 151, 214, 225, 254
King's Printer, 163
Kingston Whig Standard, 187
Kipling, Rudyard, 12
Kippenberger, H.K., 203-4
Kiska campaign, 179
Kitching, George, 101, 103, 108, 191
Knott, Ernie, 64
Korean War, 201, 254

"Lack of Moral Fibre," 237
Lanctôt, Gustave, 32, 168, 169
Large, W.S. *Diary of a Flying Officer*, 117-18
Laurier, Wilfrid, 19
Law, Andrew Bonar, 12

Lawson, J.K., 155-6
Leacock, Stephen, 71, 127
Leese, Sir Oliver, 187
Legion, 79, 205
The Legionary, 138, 158, 202
Leonforte, 102
Lessard, F.L., 46
Lest We Forget, 83
Lett, S.M., 195
letters, collected, 46, 74
Liberty magazine, 70
Liddell Hart, Sir Basil, 4, 39, 81, 91, 128, 202-3
Lind, Charlie, 63
Lipsett, Louis, 27
Liri Valley campaign, 103
literature of disillusionment, 207
Livesay, J.F.B., 31, 79-80; *Canada's Hundred Days*, 33, 47
Lloyd George, David, 25, 28, 203, 251
Loomis, F.O.W., 53
Lower, Arthur, 86
Lübeck, 116
Lusitania, 127

McAdams, J.N., 72
McAndrew, William J. (Bill), 220, 224, 237; *Battle Exhaustion*, 236-7
MacArthur, Douglas, 155
McCarter, G.A., 180
MacBrien, J.H., 37, 43, 51, 53, 55, 66, 83
Macdonald, Angus, 215
Macdonald, Margaret, 44, 45
Macdonell, Archibald C., 27, 76, 77
McGill University, 247
McGillicuddy, Betty, 124
McGuire, F.R., 201, 204
McIntyre, D.E., 26
Macintyre, Donald, *The U-Boat Killer*, 223
McKenna, Brian, 227, 228-9, 230, 231
McKenna, Terrence, 227, 228-9, 230
Mackenzie, F.A., 31
Maclachlan, K.S., 120, 121-2
Maclean's, 71
McNaught, Clifford E., 167
McNaughton, Andrew G.L.: biography of, 191; on Canadian forces sent to Mediterranean, 156; as CGS, 61-2, 84; and Dieppe raid, 99, 100; dismissal of, 158, 159, 192, 216; and Duguid, 80, 83, 84; grievances of, 181; Malone on, 190; as Minister of National Defence, 135; and official histories, 46, 61-2, 79; and official Second World War history, 135; personal papers, 171; and Quentin Reynolds, 100; records created by, 131, 132; removal from command, 190; on splitting the army, 100, 181; and Stacey, 95, 96, 98, 99, 100, 106, 153, 156-7, 181, 192, 194-5, 199, 256
Macphail, Alex, 44, 45
Macphail, Sir Andrew, 44, 55, 56, 90, 91, 173
Mainguy, E.R., 166
Makers of Canada (Morang) Limited, 46
Malone, Dick, *Missing from the Record*, 158, 189-90, 198
Maloney, Sean, 245
Maltby, C.M., 156, 174-5, 186
Manly Sims, R.F., 13, 18, 21, 23
Manning, Ralph, 201
Manpower in the Canadian Army (Burns), 171-2
Mansbridge, Peter, 235
The Maple Leaf, 189
Maple Leaf Route, 235
Maple Leaf Up, Maple Leaf Down (Simonds), 189
Markham, Phil, 226-7
Marlborough's campaigns, 177
Marshall, Jack, 230, 231
Marshall, S.L.A., 111
Martin, Chester, 86
Martin, J.R., 106, 108, 110, 132
Martin, Julia, 115
Martin, Julian, 115
Massey Commission, 170, 172
medical histories, 172-4
Mediterranean, Canadian forces in, 101
memoirs, 8, 200, 207, 209; after Great War vs Second World War, 191; air force, 190; antiwar, 191; army, 189-90; of Canadian soldiers, 74-8; difficulty in writing, 240-1; of generals, 67, 74, 78, 171, 191; Great War, 46, 47, 89, 191; naval, 190-1; of officers vs ranks, 63-4; official histories compared to, 5; Second World War, 162, 191, 241; Simonds's, 171; of soldiers, 67, 240-1; Stacey and, 154-5; of veterans, 241. *See also* antiwar writings; first-hand accounts
Memorial Chamber, Peace Tower, 60, 83
memories: veterans', 51, 63, 69, 77, 83-4, 233; war records vs, 93

Men at Arms (Wise), 212
message logs, 109
Milberry, Larry, 237; *Aviation in Canada*, 229
Miles, Wilfrid, 175
military historians, 211, 246-7, 257; academic, 3, 82, 221, 239, 246-7, 257; broadening of outlook, 235, 249-50; English- vs French-speaking, 3; and historians of gender, 250; and impact of war on society, 240; as narrators, 249; naval, 239; reputation of, 161; variety of, 257; and war archives, 221. *See also* official historians
military history: academic historians and, 152, 210, 247-8; as archives centred, 249; battles in, 258; broadening of perspective on, 247; of Canada, 234, 258; colonial attitudes in, 250-1; colony-to-nation paradigm in, 250; conferences on, 248; as contested area, 8, 176-8; dislike of, 210; dissertations on, 221; in French Canada, 243; historical profession and, 221; history of, 200; inclusion of official histories, 222; interdisciplinary, 250, 258; marginalization of, 211; in the media, 249; methodologies, 250; as militarism, 177; as narrative centred, 249; and neglect of Canadian Forces, 236; new, 217-18, 258; official historians' responsibility for, 242, 254; postmodernism and, 250; and professionalism of Canadian Forces, 243; professors of, 246; in Quebec, 3, 244-5; role in shaping Canada, 86; scholarly articles on, 248; study of, 177, 199, 217; teaching of, 221; in textbooks, 241-2; tone of, 250; as training, 176; university courses, 246, 247; war records and, 217. *See also* history; official histories; revisionism
The Military Problems of Canada (Stacey), 94
Miller, Carman, 245, 257
Millett, Allan, 198
Milne, Sir George, 51
Milner, Marc, 220, 221, 223, 224, 235, 238, 251, 255
Missing from the Record (Malone), 158, 189-90, 198
Mons, capture of, 33, 35, 56, 58, 59, 69
Montague, Price J., 94, 134

Montgomery of Alamein, Bernard, Viscount, 108, 154, 181-2, 190, 193, 235, 236, 251; *A History of Warfare*, 212
Montreal Star, 56
Moore, Christopher, 4, 233
Moore, H. Napier, 73, 75
Morin, Jean. *Operation Friction*, 243
Morrison, E.W.B., 74
Morton, Desmond, 210, 222-3, 242, 243, 245, 257; *When Your Number's Up*, 239
Mount Sorrel, battle of, 21, 25, 43, 47
Mountbatten, Louis, Lord, 99-100, 154
Mowat, Farley, 148; *The Regiment*, 188-9, 198
Muenger, Elizabeth, 233
Mulock, R.H., 72
Munro, Ross, *Gauntlet to Overlord*, 189
Mutual Assured Destruction, 217

Nanaimo strike (1913), 213
narrative history, 249
narratives: for *Arms, Men and Government*, 214; on Dieppe raid, 133; for official histories, 96, 98, 104, 105, 132, 136, 160, 179; of operations in field, 102-3; RCAF, 113; from Sicilian and Italian campaigns, 106-7; Stacey's guidelines on, 105; War Diaries vs, 52; writing of, 106, 110
narrators: army, 147-8; military historians as, 249; RCAF, 139, 141, 143; RCN, 144; for Second World War official historians, 132, 134, 136; Stacey and, 136, 197
National Archives of Canada, 245. *See also* Public Archives of Canada
National Defence Headquarters, 104
National Film Board (NFB), 226-7
National War Memorial, 78
NATO, 217
Naval Historical Section. *See* Royal Canadian Navy (RCN): Historical Section
naval history, 220, 223-4
Naval Intelligence (UK), 122-3
Naval Officers' Association of Canada, 223
The Naval Service of Canada: Its Official History (Tucker), 144-5, 160, 165-6, 167-8, 196, 238, 239
Nelles, Percy, 120, 165, 190
New Liberty, 147
New Zealand, Great War official history, 203-4
Newman, Peter C., 242

Nicholson, G.W.L., 199, 200; *Canadian Expeditionary Force*, 202-6, 208-9; *The Canadians in Italy*, 175, 179-81, 187; narratives for *The Canadian Army, 1939-1945: An Official Historical Summary*, 148; Stacey and, 142, 197
Niobe, 87
No Higher Purpose: The Official Operational History of the Royal Canadian Navy, 239
No Place to Run (Cook), 239-40
Normandy campaign, 106, 108, 158-9, 193-5, 196, 198, 227, 235, 236
North Africa, desert war, 101
Northern Mariner, 224
Northwest Europe campaign, 108, 109, 156-7, 180, 193, 214-15, 235, 237, 243
novels, 75, 76-7, 78, 207
Now It Can Be Told (Gibbs), 47
nuclear war, 208, 217

objectivity: in history, 196; in official histories, 184; in recording of war, 96; of records, 7, 38
Odlum, Victor, 74
officers: awareness of value of publicity, 108-9; correspondence with, 84; DHH staff studies for, 243; historians' work and, 128-9; interviews with, 84, 96, 102; privileged in regimental histories, 65; promotion to, 68; records kept by, 97; soliciting narratives from, 63-4; Stacey on, 193-4; stories of, 16
official historians, 36; and access to records, 7, 150; achievement of, 160, 200; British, 112; civilians as, 62; as court chroniclers, 255; and creation of records, 7; as defenders of reputations, 162; development from Great War to Second World War, 256; in DHist, 211-12; entering academia, 210-11; with expeditionary force, 101; Great War, 256; as guardians of reputation, 63; international collaboration, 149; pressures exerted on, 255; RCAF, 138-9; reputation in historical profession, 6; role of, 175-6, 231, 246; of Second World War, 130; Stacey on, 198; and tampering with histories, 233-4; use of narrative accounts, 132; veterans' opinions regarding qualifications, 62; and war records, 5, 6-7, 254

official histories, 4, 129; academic historians and, 4, 152, 233; American, 70; army editorial control over, 135; Australian, 68, 79, 83, 85-6, 90; Beaverbrook on, 42; British, 52, 54, 80, 82, 83, 90, 91; of CAMC, 44; of Canadians in British air services in Great War, 113; censure in, 56; of chaplains, 45; as compromised works, 222; constraints on, 222; as contested sites, 199; cost of, 141-2; cuts to, 130, 141-2; demand for, 142-3; of engineers, 44, 45; fault found with, 255; of flying services, 44, 72-3, 111; as foundational studies, 4-5, 6, 222, 255; funding cuts and, 243; for general reader, 134; Great War, 37, 44-5, 135, 159, 160, 201-6; historians' debt to, 221-2; interpretation battles, 4-5; military history and, 217, 222; need for, 232; of nursing sisters, 44, 45; as opening old wounds, 142; of peacekeeping missions, 243; as propaganda, 233; public and, 6; RCAF, 113, 196-7, 216, 220, 229-30, 232-3; RCN, 87, 144-6, 196-7, 216; reappraisal of, 255; regimental histories compared to, 67; and reputations, 4-5; sources for, 46-7; of South African War, 36; and Stacey, 98-9, 100-1, 184-5; and study of world wars, 4; tone of, 96; uses of, 254; war records and, 39-40, 89, 147; written years after events, 231
Official History of the Canadian Army in the Second World War (Stacey, Nicholson), 182-5, 187-8, 192-6. See also *The Canadians in Italy*; *Six Years of War*; *The Victory Campaign*
Official History of the Royal Canadian Air Force, 229. See also *Canadian Airmen and the First World War*; *The Creation of a National Air Force*; *The Crucible of War*
Ogilvie, Will, 101, 102
Oh, What a Lovely War!, 207
Operation Baytown, 149
Operation Friction (Gimblett, Morin), 243
Operation Switchback, 110
operational histories, 4, 165, 235, 248
operational orders, 99, 136
operational records, 16, 96, 153, 245
operational reports, 21, 179
oral histories, 218-19
Orde, Reginald, 58, 59

orders: operational, 99, 136; routine, 131; written, 109
Organization for the Study of the National History of Canada, 248
Ortona, 102
Osborn, J.R., 155
Ottawa, University of, 247
Ottawa Citizen, 74, 116-17
Ottawa Journal, 55-6, 71
Otter, Sir William, 46
Ouellet, Fernand, 257
Out of the Shadows (Douglas, Greenhous), 219, 220-1
Owen Sound Sun Times, 117
Oxford University Press, 118, 163

Pacific Command, 179
Palmer, Robert, 160
pamphlets, 103
Papineau, Talbot, 19, 22
Pariseau, Jean, 244
Passchendaele campaign, 30, 43, 67, 203, 206-7
Patton, George, 108
pay cards, 143-4
Peace Tower, 60, 78, 83
peacekeeping missions, 243, 247
Pearkes, George, 213
Pearson, Lester B., 142, 183
Peat, Harold, *Private Peat*, 46
Peck, Cy, 35
Peden, Murray, *A Thousand Shall Fall*, 190
Pedley, James, 77-8
Perley, Sir George, 11, 24
Permanent Joint Board of Defence (PJBD), 183, 185
Perth Regiment, 110
Pierson, Ruth Roach, 225
PJBD. *See* Permanent Joint Board of Defence (PJBD)
poetry, 75; antiwar, 66; war, 207
Pogue, Forrest C., 187
policy: decisions of Canadian government, 183; histories, 134; records, 143, 145-6; wartime decisions, 213, 214
Poor Bloody Murder (Reid), 219
Pope, Maurice, 191, 215
popular histories, 113-14, 115, 127, 142, 225, 229, 242, 243
postmodernism, 8, 250
Power, C.G., 116

Preston, Richard, 177, 216, 217, 222
Preston, W.T.R., 57, 58, 59
Prime Minister's Office, 120, 169
Princess Patricia's Canadian Light Infantry, 66
Private Peat (Peat), 46
Privy Council Office, 183
propaganda, 29-30, 37-8, 77, 100; official histories as, 233
Protecteur, 243
Public Archives of Canada: and access to military records, 217; CEF records transferred to, 147; and crafting of monographs and books, 61; and Cruikshank's publications, 42; CWRO records to, 32; departmental records transferred to, 169, 212, 213; Doughty as archivist, 19, 20, 61, 81; Nicholson's works and, 204; and Stacey's publications, 86; on writing from primary sources, 81. *See also* National Archives
Public Record Act of 1967 (UK), 213
Public Record Office (UK), 6, 17, 224
Pugsley, William H. *Saints, Devils and Ordinary Seamen*, 190
Pye, Edwin, 202

Quebec: conscription in, 3; knowledge of military history in, 244; military history in, 3, 243; Quiet Revolution, 218. *See also* French Canadians
Quebec, 1759 (Stacey), 197
Queen-Hughes, R.W., 171
questionnaires, 63-4

radar, 126
The Raid on Dieppe (Buckley), 175
Rainbow, 87
Ralph, Wayne, 237
Ralston, J.L., 57, 58, 61, 100, 156, 215
Rawling, Bill, *Surviving Trench Warfare*, 239
Rayner, Herbert, 145
RCAF. *See* Royal Canadian Air Force (RCAF)
The RCAF in the Aleutians, 118
RCAF Logbook, 188
The RCAF Overseas series, 138; *The RCAF Overseas: The Fifth Year*, 140; *The RCAF Overseas: The First Four Years*, 115-17; *The RCAF Overseas: The Sixth Year*, 164

"The RCN in Retrospect" (Boutilier), 223
Read, Daphne, *The Great War and Canadian Society,* 219
records, 16, 256-7; access to (*see* access to records); accuracy of, 21; administrative flow of, 96; army-level, 179; Beaverbrook and, 11, 37; and British Empire vs American contribution, 71; Cabinet, 134, 149, 151, 181; Cabinet War Committee, 213; collection, and operational requirements of war, 129; combined Allied, 149-52; commanding officers keeping, 97; conscription, 245; control over, 152; of courts martial, 245; creation of, 7, 39-40, 128; and Cruikshank's history, 42; in Currie's lawsuit against *Evening Guide of Port Hope,* 57-60; CWRO and (*see* Canadian War Records Office); destruction of, 53; determination of value, 131; DHH control over, 245-6; disposition of, 245; documentation of, 32; as documentation of actions, 38-9; Edmonds on, 51; and Edmonds's history, 51; essence of battle in, 240; extracts from, for training, 103-4, 105; fifty-year rule, 212, 213; freedom of research in, 150; fullness of, 21; German, 133; of high-level strategic decisions, 132; historians' impact on, 128; historical officers' ensuring creation of, 114; historiography and, 40; importance of, 160; memories vs, 93; and military history, 217; mundane nature of keeping, 128; narratives compared with, 107; neutrality of, 7, 38; official historians and, 5, 254; and official histories, 39-40, 89, 147; opening of, 130, 256-7; as opening old wounds, 142; operational, 16, 96, 114, 153, 245; personal archives, 49, 131, 181, 240; policy, 143, 145-6; postwar survival, 131; power of, 62-3; private soldiers in, 110-11; processing of, 47; RCAF, 118-19, 139, 143, 232; RCN, 121, 122; reconstruction based on, 8, 132; reliance on, 241; repatriation of, 79; securing of, 96; shaping of content, 23, 109-10; in Sicilian campaign, 102; size of, 60; squadron, 114; strategic, 131, 140, 148; survival of, 131; transfer to Canada, 32, 148; "tyranny" of, 49, 90; War Cabinet, 149; and war of reputations, 85; at War Office, 15

Referendum of 1995, 234
Regan, Frank, 57, 58-9
The Regiment (Mowat), 188-9, 198
regimental associations, 64
regimental historians, 63, 65, 67, 70, 81, 90, 172, 218
regimental histories, 33, 63-70, 136, 200, 219, 237
Regina Trench, 28
Reid, Gordon, *Poor Bloody Murder,* 219
Reilly, Henry J., 70-1
Reinke, F.H.C., 118-19
Remarque, Erich, *All Quiet on the Western Front,* 75, 77
repatriation, 131
reports: after-battle, 136; company, 23; extracts from, 103-4, 105, 113; from field historical officers, 107; intelligence, 106-7; Japanese, 185; Naval Service, 120; operational, 21, 179; RCAF, 113; RCN, 126
reputations, 85; battles/wars of, 85, 233, 234, 254, 255; of Canadian soldiers, 10, 11, 88-9, 255; of CEF, 88-9, 91-2, 255; of military historians, 161; of official historians, 6; official historians as defenders of, 63, 162; protection of, 90
revisionism, 227, 228, 230, 233, 250
Reynolds, Quentin, 100
Roberts, Charles G.D., 18, 26-7
Roberts, John Hamilton, 154
Roberts, Leslie, *Canada's War at Sea,* 127, 166
Roberts, Theodore G., 18, 21, 24, 30
Robertson, I.T., 22
Roskill, S.W., 6
Ross rifle, 65, 84, 89
The Roundel, 188, 191
Roy, Reginald, 205, 210, 219
Royal Air Force (RAF): archival holdings, 112, 113; blocking of access to records, 139; Bomber Command, 227 (*see also* Bomber Command); and popular history of RCAF, 115
Royal Canadian Air Force (RCAF), 71, 72, 73; in British histories, 143; command historian, 243; Directorate of Staff Duties, 111; Estates Branch, 117; historical officer, 93; Historical Section, 111-17, 118, 138, 139, 141, 164-5, 188, 200, 201; histories, 190, 191, 196-7, 237; "lessons learned" documents, 141; narratives on, 188; narrators, 139, 141,

143; No. 6 Group, 227; official historians, 138-9, 211; official histories, 113, 114, 138-44, 160, 163-5, 188, 212, 216, 220, 224, 229-30, 232-3; operational files, 113; Overseas Headquarters, 112-13, 114-15; personal accounts, 117; popular histories, 113-14, 115; recording officers, 114; records, 116, 139, 143, 188, 212, 232. See also squadrons
Royal Canadian Army Medical Corps (RCAMC), 44, 55-6, 172-4
Royal Canadian Navy (RCN), 87, 115; Admiralty criticism of, 251; attitude toward history, 145; as Blue Water navy, 144; C.2, 125; chaplains, 125; command historian, 243; Controller of Naval Information (CNI), 120; criticisms in reports, 126; and D-Day landings, 125-6; early history, 121, 122, 126; hierarchy within, 123; historians, 120-1; historical officers, 93, 99, 124; Historical Section, 126, 139, 166, 201, 223; historical vs operational concerns, 125-6; histories, 190-1, 196-7, 223-4, 237-9; narratives, 127; narrators, 144; Naval Service Headquarters, 125; Naval Service reports, 120; official historians, 211, 239; official histories, 142, 144-6, 165-8, 216, 238-9, 246; paymasters, 125; popular history, 127; radar in, 126; records, 119-20, 121, 122, 212; resources for operations vs history, 144; Senior Canadian Naval Officer, 125; signals intelligence, 123
Royal Canadian Regiment, 102
Royal Commission on National Development in the Arts, Letters and Sciences. See Massey Commission
Royal Military College of Canada (RMC), 177, 211, 247, 248
Royal Navy: Historical Section, 123; histories, 119
Rumilly, Robert, 171
Russell, E.C., 201, 212
Rye, S.R., 171

Saguenay, 167
St. Catharines Standard, 87
St. Eloi, Battle of, 25-6, 27, 43, 47
Saints, Devils and Ordinary Seamen (Pugsley), 190
Salty Dips series, 223

Sarty, Roger, 220, 221, 224, 238, 239, 243; *Canada and the Battle of the Atlantic*, 238-9; *Tin-Pots and Pirate Ships*, 238
Saskatoon Star-Phoenix, 164
Saturday Night, 140, 159, 164
Scheldt, battle of the, 110, 235
Schlesinger, Arthur, 159
Schreiber, Shane, *Shock Army of the British Empire*, 240
Schull, Joseph, *Far Distant Ships*, 166-7, 196, 201, 238
Second World War, 93; anniversaries of, 234-5, 247; casualties, 130; hidden history, 153; home front, 251, 253-4; memoirs resulting from, 191, 241; oral histories, 218-19; perceptions of, 253-4; popular history of flyers in, 113-14, 115; regimental histories, 219
Second Ypres, Battle of, 14-15, 42, 49-54, 69, 84, 88
Sesia, A.T., 101, 102
Seven Years War, 178
shellshock, 55
Sherwood, Robert, 181
Shock Army of the British Empire (Schreiber), 240
Shrieks and Crashes (Kerr), 75-6, 77-8
Sicily landing, 101-2
Simonds, Guy, 198, 199, 256; and *Canada's Battle in Normandy*, 136-7; and CGS position, 135, 181; and Crerar, 135, 154, 215-16; and Dieppe raid, 154, 215-16; Foulkes and, 137, 193; on historical officers' coverage, 102; memoirs, 171, 191; and official histories, 96, 134-5, 181-2; and Stacey, 96, 153, 157, 181-2, 184, 185, 193, 194-5, 256; support for Sesia, 101; and Ultra intercepts, 215
Simonds, Peter, *Maple Leaf Up, Maple Leaf Down*, 189
Sims, R.F. Manly. *See* Manly Sims, R.F.
Sir John A. Macdonald prize, 240
Six War Years (Broadfoot), 218-19
Six Years of War: The Army in Canada, Britain and the Pacific (Stacey), 185-7
Slemon, C.R., 115, 188
Snow, T.D'O., 51, 53
Socknat, Thomas, 225
soldiers: enlisted men in regimental histories, 65; generals and, 207; in Great

Index 323

War, 206-7; memoirs of, 67, 240-1; memories of, 51; and War Diarists, 240-1. *See also* Australian soldiers; Canadian soldiers; German soldiers; veterans
Somalia Affair, 243
Somme, Battle of the, 11, 21, 26-7, 28, 43, 69, 205-6
Sorel, W.J., 163-4
South African War, 11, 36, 254
Soviet Union entry into Second World War, 253
Spencer, Robert, 136
Spreckley, R.O., 63-4
Spring, David, 127
Spring operation. *See* Verrières Ridge
Spurr, John, 106
squadrons: 400, 114; 401, 114; 417, 116; 418, 114; diaries, 143; histories, 237; officers, 112-13, 118-19; records, 116, 143; sketches, 188
Stacey, Charles P., 6; and academic historians, 129; and access to records, 131-2, 170-2, 212; achievement of, 93, 197, 216; and administrative flow of records, 96; and Angus Macdonald papers, 215; appointment to CMHQ, 94; and archivist's role, 170; *Arms, Men and Governments*, 197, 213-16, 225; balance in work, 154, 199; blame on regimental vs senior officers, 193-4, 195, 236; on Buckley's *The Raid on Dieppe*, 175; and Burns, 96; and Campney, 184; *Canada and the Age of Conflict*, 216; *Canada and the British Army*, 86, 94; and *Canada's Battle in Normandy*, 136-8; *The Canadian Army, 1939-1945: An Official Historical Summary*, 147-60, 163, 175, 181, 182, 185, 202; on Canadian operations in theatre-wide context, 132; and Canadian soldiers, 156, 195, 198-9; *Canadians in England*, 223; and Claxton, 142-3, 182; and combined Allied records, 149-52, 153; creation of records, 197; and Crerar, 95-6, 99, 105, 106, 108, 153-4, 193, 194-5, 256; critical interpretation of Second World War, 232; criticisms by, 159, 193-5, 198, 237; on cuts to official histories, 142; *A Date with History*, 257; dedication to projects, 153; diaries of, 194; and Dieppe raid, 153-4, 186-7, 215-16; and Directorate of History, 211-12; on disclosure, 96; on distribution of drafts of narratives, 105; and Duguid, 88, 105, 134, 205, 255; early life and career, 94; on editorial control, 152; encouragement of military histories, 172-4; as expert on Second World War, 175; on Falaise, 138; and Feasby, 172-4; and field historical officers, 102-3, 123; and Foulkes, 135, 136, 147-8, 193, 256; *From Pachino to Ortona*, 136; and generals, 96, 105, 106, 132, 152, 194-5, 198; on German soldiers, 180-1, 195-6, 199; and Great War official history series, 201-2; guidelines for narrative writing, 105; *The Half Million*, 223; historical monographs, 142-3; on Hong Kong, 155-6, 185-6; impact on documentation, 97; on importance of records, 160; intellectual honesty of, 135, 152, 256; and interviews with German commanders, 133; on Japanese troops, 155-6; and King's personal diaries, 214; Kippenberger and, 203-4; liaison with British, 98; and Mackenzie King, 214; and McNaughton, 95, 96, 98, 99, 100, 106, 192, 194-5, 256; and Malone's *The Maple Leaf*, 189-90; and Maltby, 156, 174-5; mandate of, 95; meeting with Marshall, 111; as military historian, 82, 218; on military history, 221; *The Military Problems of Canada*, 94; on Mowat's *The Regiment*, 188-9; on narratives of field operations, 102-3; narratives produced by, 96, 97; and narrators, 197; on naval histories, 165, 167; and Nicholson, 179-81, 202, 204-5, 206; on Nile voyageurs, 197; as official historian, 130, 133-4, 197-8, 199; and official histories, 98-9, 100-1, 184-5, 254; *Official History of the Canadian Army in the Second World War*, 136-8, 178-81, 182-5; as official vs academic historian, 194; and other historians, 215; on PJBD, 183; preservation of records, 96, 131, 169-70, 197; as president of CHA, 197; previous publications, 94; production of narratives, 96, 97; professionalism of, 160; qualifications of, 153; *Quebec, 1759*, 197; and Ralston's papers, 215; on RCAF official history series, 212; record gathering by, 96, 97; on records as base

for histories, 132; relations with staff, 106; reliance on narratives, 160; reliance on participants vs records, 154-5; reputation of, 161, 200; and reputations, 172, 233, 255; retirement of, 197, 213; role and responsibilities, 97, 175-6; on Schull's *Far Distant Ships*, 166; and senior commanders, 153-4, 159, 193; and Sesia, 101; and Simonds, 96, 193, 194-5, 256; *Six Years of War*, 185-7; on staffing of AHS, 147-8; and study of military history, 199; summaries produced by, 96; Tucker compared to, 127; and Ultra intercepts, 215; at University of Toronto, 204, 210, 212; use of criticisms vs first-hand accounts, 192-3; and use of extracts, 103-4; on Verrières Ridge battle, 136-7; *The Victory Campaign: The Operations in Northwest Europe*, 192-6, 197, 199; viewed as spy, 95; visits to units, 97; White Paper on Dieppe raid, 99-100, 122, 153; and Wise, 212; writing style, 198, 214

Stanley, George, 6, 106, 129, 175, 210, 219; on access to records, 170, 172; *The Birth of Western Canada*, 86; *Canada's Soldiers*, 178; *The Canadians in Britain*, 136; as military historian, 82; as official historian, 98; on *The RCAF Overseas: The Sixth Year*, 164

Statute of Westminster, 130

Steele, Ian, 257

Steiger, A.G., 250

strategic bombing campaign, 140, 220-1, 227-8, 229, 230, 242

strategic records, 131, 132, 140, 148

The Struggle for Europe (Wilmot), 170, 181

Stuart, Kenneth, 101, 102, 156

Sudbury Star, 87

Sullivan, Alan, 72

A Sunny Subaltern: Billy's Letters from Flanders, 46

Supreme Headquarters Allied Expeditionary Forces (SHAEF), 132, 149, 150, 151, 153

Surviving Trench Warfare (Rawling), 239

Sutherland, Donald, 80

Swettenham, John, 191, 201, 204, 210-11; *To Seize the Victory*, 209

Symons, T.H.B., 216-17

Taylor, A.J.P., 219; *The First World War: An Illustrated History*, 207

Taylor, Ken, 222

television programs, 242, 249

Ten Lost Years (Broadfoot), 218

A Ten-Day Submarine Hunt in 1943, 118

Terraine, John, 203

textbooks, military history in, 241-2

Thacker, H.C., 60-1

The 13th Battalion Royal Highlanders of Canada, 64, 67

Thompson, John. *Harvest of War*, 218

Thompson, V.E., 64

Thompson, Walter, 228

Thompson, W.R., 112-13, 118

A Thousand Shall Fall (Peden), 190

Tin-Pots and Pirate Ships (Hadley, Sarty), 238

To Seize the Victory (Swettenham), 209

Topp, C. Beresford, 65

Toronto *Globe*, 117

Tory, Henry Marshall, 61

Totalize operation, 193

Tovell, Freeman, 124, 126

training: of flyers, 112; historical extracts for, 103-4, 105; military history as, 176

Treasury Board, 204, 213

trench warfare, 75, 77, 206, 239-40

Trotter, R.G., 142

Trudeau, Pierre, 213

Tucker, Gilbert, 4, 144-6, 199; and academic historians, 129; access to records, 145; based in Ottawa during war, 126; and destruction of naval files, 169; early career, 120; and George, 122, 124-5, 126; Great War historical research, 121, 124; on historical writing, 145; isolation of, 133; lack of operational and administrative records, 127-8; lack of personal papers, 128; *The Naval Service of Canada: Its Official History*, 144-5, 160, 165-6, 167-8, 196, 238, 239; on official histories, 246; and overseas historical officers, 93; and RCN attitude toward criticism, 126; as RCN historian, 120-1, 126; recruiting by, 126-7

Turner, G.R., 95

Turner, Sir Richard, 105; Beaverbrook and, 19; death of, 88; and Duguid's history, 84, 85, 91; mishandling by, 17; performance of, 53; at St. Eloi, 26, 27; and Second Ypres, 84, 85, 89; and War Diaries, 52

Tuxford, G.S., 52; *The War as I Saw It*, 74

The U-Boat Killer (Macintyre), 223
U-boats, 87, 116, 119, 121, 127, 144, 166, 224, 238, 251; *U-69*, 127; *U-210*, 121; *U-744*, 125
Ultra intelligence intercepts, 198, 215, 238
Underhill, Frank, 47, 62, 86
United Kingdom: access to records in, 149-52, 213; Admiralty Intelligence, 123; Air Liaison Mission, 112; archives, 149; army's impact on Canada, 86; Canada as strongest ally, 253; collaboration on histories, 148, 149; Committee for Imperial Defence, 36; generals, 251; Great War as seen in, 253; Great War official histories, 4, 202-3; historical officers in field, 123; histories including RCAF, 143; and Normandy campaign, 195; official diplomatic publications, 152; official historians, 112, 230; official histories, 134, 146, 167, 175; reappraisal of Great War, 240; records, 204; resources for historical program, 98. *See also* headings beginning British
United States: access to records by, 150; amphibious landings in Pacific, 186-7; border with, 178; and Canadian North-West Atlantic Command, 165; civilian historians in, 152; collaboration on histories, 148, 149; entry into Second World War, 253; in Great War, 70-1; historical officers, 111; and Normandy campaign, 195; official historians, 151, 233; official histories, 160, 167, 175, 233-4
Université du Québec à Montréal, 244
University of New Brunswick, 247
University of Western Ontario, 247
Unknown Soldier, return of, 247

The Valour and the Horror, 227, 228, 229, 230, 231, 232, 233
Van Paassen, Pierre, 74
Vance, Jonathan, *Death So Noble*, 240
Verrières Ridge, 136-7, 156, 193
veterans, 63-4; Charter, 191; and *Crucible of War*, 230, 231; deaths of, 219; diaries, 64; educational and memorial programs, 231-2; and Great War official histories, 135, 147, 202; and historians, 251; influence of, 235; and interpretation of history, 234; interviews with, 133; journalists vs, 228; memoirs, 241; memories of, 51, 63, 69, 77, 83-4, 233; and Nicholson's history of CEF, 204, 205; in 1990s, 235; and RCAF histories, 233; reactions to films, 227-8, 230, 231, 233; regimental historians as, 67; soldiers' histories for, 210; wait for Duguid's official history, 79, 80
Victoria, University of, 247
Victoria Cross, 33
The Victory Campaign: The Operations in Northwest Europe (Stacey), 192-6, 197, 199
Vietnam War, 208, 209, 210, 211, 218
Vimy Ridge, Battle of, 30, 47, 209, 243, 244, 250
Vincent, Carl, 237
VLB, 244
Vogel, Robert, 235-6, 248
Vokes, Chris, 191, 193

Walker, Sir Edmund, 20
war archives. *See* records
war art, 78, 100, 101, 102, 106, 108
war artifacts, 148
The War as I Saw It (Tuxford), 74
War Diaries: Aitken and, 16; availability of, 170, 171, 212; British historians and, 103; of Crerar, 95; DHH management of, 245; diarists' view of battles, 22; frequency of entries, 59; Historical Section and, 101; incomplete, 62; missing, 52; and Mons lawsuit, 57, 59, 60; narratives vs, 52; Nicholson's use of, 179; 19th Battalion, 63; numbers of, 153; official, 240-1; RCAF, 143; squadron, 113, 114; Stacey and, 95, 96, 97, 103, 170, 171; 3rd Division, 109; use by narrators, 136; weakness of, 4, 21; Willson in charge of, 18-19; in writing of narratives, 107
war historians. *See* historians
war histories. *See* histories; official histories
The War in the Air, 72, 112
War of 1812, 30, 43, 178
War Office (Britain), 50, 104; Canadian war records at, 15
War on Terrorism, 247
war records. *See* records
war trophies, 32-3, 78, 113, 148
war writing: archives and, 200; canon of, 4, 8, 91, 162, 255, 256; in 1960s, 200. *See also* antiwar writing; histories
wars: academic historians and, 81; frequency in twentieth century, 254; gender and, 250; impact on society, 217; necessity of,

249; objective recording of, 96; and shaping of Canadian society, 254. *See also* world wars
The Wars (Findley), 242
Warsaw Pact, 217
Waterloo, University of, 247
Watson, Sir David, 27, 31, 35, 91
Webster, Sir Charles, 230
Western Front, 10, 112, 206; military history of, 177; reputation of Canadian soldiers on, 11
When Your Number's Up (Morton), 239
Whitaker, Denis, 225
Whitby, Michael, 238, 239
Whitelaw, R.G., 104-5
Wilfrid Laurier University, 247, 248
Willson, Henry Beckles, 18-19, 20
Wilmot, Chester, *The Struggle for Europe*, 170, 181
Wilson, Barbara, *The Half Million*, 223
Winged Warfare (Bishop), 46
Wise, S.F., 6, 212, 219-20, 221, 228, 257; *Canada's Airmen*, 226; *Canadian Airmen and the First World War*, 224; *Men at Arms*, 212
Wolff, Leon, *In Flanders Fields*, 206-7
women: enfranchisement of, 41; participation in warfare, 250
Wood, H.F., 201
Wood, William, 32
world wars, 3; impact on individuals, 4; impact on society, 4; interpretation of, 251; reappraisal of, 252; re-evaluation of, 242. *See also* Great War; Second World War; wars
Worthington, Peter, 231
Wrinch, Joe, 106

Yocom, John, 140, 164
Ypres, Second Battle of, 14-15, 42, 49-54, 65, 69, 84, 88

Zimmerman, David, 167, 223-4